CLASSICS OF STRATEGY AND COUNSEL

The Collected Translations of
Thomas Cleary

CLASSICS OF STRATEGY AND COUNSEL

VOLUME ONE

The Art of War
Mastering the Art of War
The Lost Art of War
The Silver Sparrow Art of War

VOLUME TWO

Thunder in the Sky
The Japanese Art of War
The Book of Five Rings
Ways of Warriors, Codes of Kings

VOLUME THREE

The Art of Wealth
Living a Good Life
The Human Element
Back to Beginnings

CLASSICS OF STRATEGY AND COUNSEL

VOLUME TWO

Thunder in the Sky

The Japanese Art of War

The Book of Five Rings

Ways of Warriors, Codes of Kings

SHAMBHALA

Boston & London

2000

SHAMBHALA PUBLICATIONS, INC.
Horticultural Hall
300 Massachusetts Avenue
Boston, Massachusetts 02115
www.shambhala.com

9 8 7 6 5 4 3 2 1

FIRST EDITION
Printed in the United States of America

⊗ This edition is printed on acid-free paper that meets
the American National Standards Institute z39.48 Standard.
Distributed in the United States by Random House, Inc.,
and in Canada by Random House of Canada Ltd

LIBRARY OF CONGRESS CATALOGING-IN-PUBLICATION DATA
Classics of strategy and counsel: the collected translations of
Thomas Cleary.
p. cm.
Includes bibliographical references.
Contents: v. 1. The art of war—Mastering the art of war—The
lost art of war—The silver sparrow art of war—v. 2. Thunder in
the sky—The Japanese art of war—The book of five rings—Ways
of warriors, codes of kings—v. 3. The art of wealth—Living a good
life—The human element—Back to beginnings.
ISBN 1-57062-750-9 (set)—ISBN 1-57062-727-4 (v. 1)—
ISBN 1-57062-728-2 (v. 2)—ISBN 1-57062-729-0 (v. 3)
1. Military art and science. 2. Strategy. 3. Management.
I. Cleary, Thomas F., 1940–
U104.C484 2000
335.02—dc21
00-030765

CONTENTS

Publisher's Note   ix

THUNDER IN THE SKY

Foreword   3
Translator's Introduction   6
The Master of Demon Valley   11
    Opening and Closing   13
    Response   17
    Acceptance and Solidarity   21
    Stopping Gaps   26
    Excitation and Arrest   28
    Opposition and Alliance   31
    Figuring Out Psychological Conditions   34
    Pressuring   37
    Assessment   41
    Strategic Thinking   45
    Decision Making   50
    Talismanic Sayings   52
    Basic Course: Seven Arts of Covert Correspondence   55
    Holding the Pivot   66
    Course from the Center   67
    Notes   72
The Master of the Hidden Storehouse   87
    Preserving the Way Intact   89
    Applying the Way   93
    The Way of Government   96
    The Way of Leadership   105
    The Way of Administrators   108
    The Way of the Wise   111
    The Way of Education   116

The Way of Agriculture   121
The Way of War   125

THE JAPANESE ART OF WAR

Introduction   131
A Martial History of Japan   133
Zen in Japanese History   142
Bushidō and Martial Arts   150
The Way of the Zen Warrior   170
Schemes of the Samurai   200
The Thirty-six Strategies   219
Bushidō and Christianity: Ethical Crossroads   226
A Zen Razor   251
Summary   258

THE BOOK OF FIVE RINGS

Translator's Preface   265
Translator's Introduction   266
The Book of Five Rings   273
    Preface   275
    The Earth Scroll   277
    The Water Scroll   289
    The Fire Scroll   304
    The Wind Scroll   319
    The Scroll of Emptiness   329
    Notes   331
The Book of Family Traditions on the Art of War   333
    The Killing Sword   335
    The Life-Giving Sword   354
    No Sword   368
    Notes   375
Bibliography   378

WAYS OF WARRIORS, CODES OF KINGS

Introduction   383
Lessons in Leadership from the Chinese Classics   387

Sources   469

PUBLISHER'S NOTE

The works contained in The Collected Translations of Thomas Cleary were published over a period of more than twenty years and originated from several publishing houses. As a result, the capitalization and romanization of Chinese words vary occasionally from one text to another within the volumes, due to changes in stylistic preferences from year to year and from house to house. In all cases, terms are rendered consistently within each text.

THUNDER IN THE SKY

Secrets on the Acquisition and Exercise of Power

FOREWORD

In today's demanding business world the fierce game of competition has literally evolved into bloodless warfare. The result is, as the Chinese say, *"Shang chang ru zhan chang,"* or, "The marketplace is a battlefield." Although this militaristic view of business may seem novel, it isn't news to Asians, whose leaders for centuries have drawn from ancient art-of-war treatises to help them achieve and maintain power. The Asian people view success in the business world as tantamount to victory in battle, with both directly affecting the survival and well-being of their nation. Since they perceive that the true nature of business competition is that of war, they act accordingly.

Asians believe that mastering tactics and strategies is essential for success in the marketplace. Asian rulers, from ancient to modern, have always placed great importance on the study of classical Chinese treatises of subtle wisdom and strategy. These scholarly works brought great power to those who were able to apply their principles to the affairs of daily life. One of the most important principles of Asian thought is that all elements of life are interconnected, so there are no real divisions between philosophy, spirituality, the art of war, the art of acquisition, the exercise of power, and political and business affairs. The wisdom that guides the general in battle is the same wisdom by which the politician exercises power and the business person maneuvers financial advantage. Asians don't tend to find anything strange in searching a text devoted to military strategy for principles that apply to situations in the family, the work place, or the world at large.

For thousands of years, the Chinese have been observing and documenting the dynamics of life and nature. In the process they discovered a certain rhythm of universal force that is unfailing and consistent, and applicable to every aspect of life. The philosophers captured this rhythm and later taught princes and scholars how to incorporate these principles into the administration of state affairs. The ultimate goal was to achieve absolute rule over China and its subjects. This was particularly true from 700 through 221 B.C.E., when China was going through a period of weak central government and total division among all the feudal lords. Conquering was the aim, and survival was the game. Because of this chaotic environment, China became a natural incubator for some of the greatest philosophical doctrines and art-of-war treatises. Great thinkers and strategists such as Confucius, Lao-tzu, Chuang-tzu, and Sun-tzu all lived and left their marks during this period.

One of the great masterpieces of the time was called *The Master of Demon Valley* (translated here for the first time by Thomas Cleary as part of *Thunder in the Sky*). *The Master of Demon Valley* was particularly prized by Chinese scholars and power-brokers and has had profound influence on the course of Chinese history. In 221 B.C.E., using theories found in *The Master of Demon Valley*, the great Emperor Chin was able to unite China and end its prolonged five-hundred-year brutal civil war. *The Master of Demon Valley* is a work that continues to enjoy extraordinary stature in Chinese literature because of its subtle and profound wisdom. However, this book was not written for casual reading. Ancient sages and scholars often devoted their entire lives attempting to master this erudite and elusive knowledge.

It is exciting to see this great Chinese treasure (accompanied by another Taoist classic, *The Master of the Hidden Storehouse*) finally presented to Western readers. These two powerful texts have inspired emperors and strategists throughout Chinese history. Now the forces that guided the ancient emperors to victory can also navigate today's business people to profitability.

It is important to understand that the profound wisdom of China is not the property of the Chinese people but belongs to all humankind. The wisdom revealed in this book relates to experiences that all people encounter, enabling us to recognize the universality of the forces that shape our lives. In fact, the true treasure of *Thunder in the Sky* lies in its ability to uncover the mysterious relationship between spiritual insight and physical attainment.

In today's fierce domestic and international economic warfare, it is gratifying to see that American business people will be able to study this profound Eastern wisdom—translating these theories for practical use in the day-to-day quest for a better life.

CHIN-NING CHU
President, Asian Marketing Consultants
author of *Thick Face, Black Heart,*
The Asian Mind Game, and
The Chinese Mind Game

TRANSLATOR'S INTRODUCTION

"Thunder in the sky" is an ancient Chinese symbol for great power, meaning progress and growth, strength going into action. Understanding the development, exercise, and consequences of every kind of power is a traditional element of Chinese thought.

The original Chinese philosophy of power came from participative observation of nature, society, and the inner mind. In early times, this led to the quest for mastery of the powers in plants and metals, in order and organization, and in extraordinary perceptual and cognitive capacities.

As a result of this interest in the attainment, use, and abuse of power, an advanced science of human behavior was developed and employed over the course of centuries. This study of human weakness and strengths was originally carried out in a comprehensive context of moral and psychological training, but the refinement of strategic arts eventually became a specialty among some thinkers because of preoccupations with questions of power and national security.

This book presents the first English translations of two secret classics of the ancient tradition, *The Master of Demon Valley* and *The Master of the Hidden Storehouse*. Each of these texts, from its own perspective and in its own way, provides a practical course in special modes of human development and empowerment.

The first work, *The Master of Demon Valley*, is a highly controversial classic generally attributed to the Warring States period of ancient China, which began around the middle of the first millennium B.C.E. The military classic by Sun-tzu, *The Art of War*, is also from this period, as is the Taoist classic *Chuang-tzu*. Although very closely related to both these martial and Taoist traditions, *The Master of Demon Valley* is ordinarily associated with a relatively obscure school of thought known as *Tsung-heng hsueh* (*Zongheng xue*).

A number of meanings are contained within the name of this controversial school, which is generally concerned with the psychological and strategic aspects of statecraft. The surface reading of the term is "vertical and horizontal learning," which uses the names for specific geographical patterns of alliance in Warring States China to represent the science of strategic diplomacy and statecraft in a rapidly changing world.

Another way to read *tsung-heng hsueh* is as "the learning of freedom of thought and action." This refers to the ability to evade imprisonment by the forces of conventions and pressures of events, while nevertheless retaining the capacity to interact meaningfully and effectively with the world at large. In strategic terms, this aspect of the science is defined as learning to "control others without being controlled by others."

A specialized reading of the name of this school based on the same meanings for the characters *tsung* and *heng* can be best rendered by a colloquialism: *tsung-heng hsueh* means "the science of letting all hell break loose." This is a special sense of the term only in that it represents just one of the techniques of a more comprehensive learning.

Even in this sense, however, it can be construed in two ways. Where there is unrest that would only be exacerbated by direct confrontation, the unrest may be purposely allowed to burn itself out. Where there is complacency and lethargy, unrest may be deliberately triggered to produce reaction and movement.

Many of these techniques are well known through history, not only in China but all over the world. It is easy to see, just from the meanings of *tsung-heng hsueh,* and reflection on the obvious abuses to which these ideas are susceptible, why there has always been ambivalence and controversy surrounding this school of thought.

The contents of *The Master of Demon Valley* would lead us to suspect that *Tsung-heng hsueh* was either a splinter of Taoism or a separate school profoundly influenced by Taoism. A third possibility is that the Taoist element in the text, which is very prominent, represents a later attempt by philosophical Taoists to "encapsulate" the virulent ideas and practices of *Tsung-heng hsueh* in such a way as to mitigate harmful abuses.

In any case, the text of *The Master of Demon Valley* closes with this warning: "Petty people imitating others will use this in a perverse and sinister way, even getting to the point where they can destroy families and usurp countries. Without wisdom and knowledge, you cannot preserve your home with justice and cannot preserve your country with the Way. The reason sages value the subtlety of the Way is truly because it can change peril into safety, rescue the ruined and enable them to survive."

The Master of the Hidden Storehouse follows up on the implications of these statements regarding the science of power analyzed in *The Master of Demon Valley.* It is a classic Taoist text, following on the ancient philosophical tradition but adapted specifically for secular leaders.

The Master of the Hidden Storehouse is attributed to Keng Sang-tzu, who is featured in the Taoist classic *Chuang-tzu* as a disciple of the ancient sage Lao-tzu, traditionally considered the author of the *Tao Te Ching* and a seminal figure in Taoist lore.

Conventional scholars ordinarily consider *The Master of the Hidden Storehouse* an apocryphal text. While there is no actual proof of this assumption, based as it is on the supposition of a rigid division between oral and written traditions, there is every reason to believe, on the basis of classical principles, that the original core of the work was deliberately adapted to conditions of another time.

Nothing concrete is known of the text of *The Master of the Hidden Storehouse* until the T'ang dynasty, more than a thousand years after the time of the reputed author. This text was presented to the imperial court of T'ang China in the eighth century, in response to official efforts to reintegrate Taoist studies into the mainstream of intellectual life and scholastic curriculum. *The Master of the Hidden Storehouse* was so highly valued by the emperor Hsuan-tsung (r. 713–55) that it was given an honorific title, *Tung-ling ching (Dongling jing),* or "Scripture on Open Awareness."

The Master of Demon Valley and *The Master of the Hidden Storehouse* are both included in the vast canon of Taoism. The former text is unusually obscure, even for an ancient Taoist classic, indicating the antiquity of the oral tradition from which it derived as well as the concern of the early transmitters with safeguarding its knowledge from shallow meddlers. The latter text, in contrast, is unusually clear, even in distinguishing between exoteric and esoteric domains of learning, illustrating thereby its characteristic nature as a presentation of practical Taoism for general public purposes.

These two extraordinary texts complement, balance, and enhance one another; being therefore most profitably read together, in this their first rendition into English they are presented in one volume for the safety and convenience of the thoughtful reader.

The Master of
Demon Valley

Opening and Closing

[1]

Let us consider how ancient sages existed between heaven and earth. Being leaders of others, they watched the opening and closing of yin and yang in order to direct people thereby and knew the doorway of survival and destruction. Assessing the ends and beginnings of all types, they arrived at the principles of human psychology and saw the foresigns of change therein; and they kept vigil at the doorway.

[2]

Therefore the Way by which sages live in the world has always been one; while its transformations, which are endless, each has a specific purpose. Sometimes it is yin, sometimes yang; sometimes yielding, sometimes firm; sometimes open, sometimes closed; sometimes relaxed, sometimes tense. For this reason sages consistently keep watch at the doorway and carefully examine what should precede and what follow. They assess strategies, measure capabilities, and compare strengths and weaknesses of technical skills.

[3]

There are differences between the worthy and the unworthy, the intelligent and the foolish, the brave and the cowardly, the humane and the righteous; so it may be appropriate to open up, or to shut down; it may be appropriate to promote, or to demote; it may be appropriate to despise, or to value. Sages govern them without artificial contrivance. They carefully determine what people have and what they lack, in terms of their substantiality or vacuity. They follow what people like and desire, in order to observe their will and aspiration. They subtly brush aside what people say and press it back on them to find out what reality there is to it; and once they get the point, they clam up and put it into effect to find out what benefit there is to it.

[4]

Sages sometimes open up in an evident manner; sometimes they are closed and secretive. They are open to those with whom they sympathize, closed to those with whose truth they differ. As to what will do and what will not, sages examine and clarify people's plans to find out if they are in harmony or at variance.

[5]

Whether they separate or join, there is that which sages maintain; so they first go along with the aims of others: then when they want to open up, they value thoroughness; and when they want to shut down, they value secrecy. Thoroughness and secrecy are best subtle, for then they are on the trail of the Way.

[6]

Opening up is to assess people's feelings; shutting down is to make sure of their sincerity. In each case it is only after seeing people's plans and evaluating their worth that calculations are to be made for them; so sages make the relevant considerations on this basis. If people's plans do not measure up, and do not fit the dimensions and elements of the situation, then sages themselves therefore do the thinking. So opening up may be for the purpose of rejection, or for the purpose of acceptance; shutting down may be for the purpose of taking, or for the purpose of discarding.

[7]

Opening and closing are the Way of heaven and earth: opening and closing are used to transform and activate yin and yang and the four seasons; opening and closing are used to influence the rise and fall of all things. Maneuvers such as reversing to repel, reversing to cover up, and reversing to oppose, all have to come from this. Opening and

closing are the great influences of the Way, changes of persuasion: it
is necessary first to examine their transmutations.

[8]

The mouth is the door of the mind; the mind is the host of the spirit.
Will, intention, joy, desire, thought, worry, knowledge, and planning
all go in and out through the door. Therefore they are governed by
opening and closing, controlled in their exit and entry. Opening
means speech, or yang; closing means silence, or yin. Yin and yang
should be harmonious; end and beginning should be correct.

[9]

Thus to talk of longevity, happiness, wealth, status, honor, fame,
love, fondness, material gain, success, joy, or desire, is yang: this is
called the beginning. And so to talk of death, grief, trouble, poverty,
lowliness, disgrace, rejection, loss, disappointment, injury, punishment, execution, or penalty, is yin: this is called the end.

[10]

All speech in the yang category is called a beginning, meaning that
one speaks of what is good in order to initiate projects. All speech in
the yin category is called an ending, in that one speaks of what is bad
in order to conclude strategic planning.

[11]

The course of opening and closing is proven by yin and yang. When
speaking with those who are in a yang mode, go by the exalted and
the lofty; when speaking with those who are in a yin mode, go by the
humble and the small. Seek the small by lowliness, seek the great by
loftiness. Follow this procedure, and what you say can be expressed
anywhere, will penetrate anywhere, and can suit any situation. It will
thereby be possible to persuade inviduals, to persuade families, to persuade nations, to persuade the world.

[12]

To be small means there is no inside; to be large means there is no outside. The phenomenal expressions of increase and reduction, rejection and acceptance, opposition and reversion, are all controlled by yin and yang. Yang is mobile and active; yin is still and unobtrusive. When yang emerges in activity, yin accordingly goes into concealment. When yang comes to an end, it returns to the beginning; and when yin reaches a climax, it reverts to yang.

[13]

Using yang to act means development of character; using yin to be still means development of the body. Using yang to seek yin means enveloping with virtue; using yin to crystallize yang means exercise of power. The mutual seeking of yin and yang depends on opening and closing.

[14]

This is the Way of yin and yang of heaven and earth; and it is the method of persuading people. Being the forerunner of all undertakings, it is called the door of the round and the square.

Response

[1]

The great civilizing influence of ancient times arose together with the formless. By reflective examination of the past, you can investigate and check on the future; by reflective acquaintance with the ancient you can know the modern; by reflective understanding of others you can gain a clearer understanding of yourself. When principles of action and stillness, or emptiness and fullness, do not fit the present, then turn back to the past to look for them. The idea of the sages was that things have changes and can be reversed: it is imperative to examine closely.

[2]

The speech of others is movement; one's own silence is stillness. You listen to people's statements by means of their speech. When statements are inconsistent, reflect and inquire critically, and the response will surely be forthcoming.

[3]

Words have images, works have categories: observe their order by their images and categories. Images symbolize phenomena, categories group expressions. Use formlessness to inquire critically into that which is voiced. When statements made to draw people out are consistent with actualities, then you find out the reality in people.

[4]

When you set out snares to catch animals, you set many of them where the animals may be expected to run into them, and you watch over them. When your way is in conformity with actuality, others will emerge and come to you of their own accord: this is a net that catches people.

[5]

Always hold that net and motivate people. If there is nothing in your words to which they can relate, then you change for this reason. Use imagery to move them, in a manner responsive to their mentalities; seeing their feelings and states of mind, you can govern them accordingly. If you yourself turn around and go to them, they will turn around and come to you. When speech contains images and analogies, by their means you can establish a foundation. Repeat them over and over, reflect on them over and over, and the appropriate rhetoric and expressions for all affairs will not be lost.

[6]

Those whom sages attract do not doubt, be they ignorant or intelligent. Therefore those who are skilled at reflective listening change ghosts and spirits so as to be able to find out their feelings. When the change is appropriate, they are governed knowledgeably. If they are not governed knowledgeably, their feelings are not clearly apprehended; and if their feelings are not clearly apprehended, then the establishment of the foundation is not done with clear understanding.

[7]

When you change images and analogies, there are bound to be words of opposition; listen to them in silence. When you want to hear others' voices, return to silence; when you want to be expansive, then be withdrawn; when you want to rise, then lower yourself; when you want to take, then give.

[8]

When you want to bring out feelings and states of mind, use symbolism and analogies to muster the appropriate expressions: those with the same voice call to each other, true principles have the same ultimate end. Sometimes the process starts from you, sometimes from another; sometimes it is used to work for superiors, sometimes it is used to govern subordinates.

[9]

This is listening for reality and artifice, to know whether there is commonality or difference, and to find out truth and falsehood. In any case, it is by first making these determinations that it is possible to formulate appropriate guidelines. This procedure is used because you seek to convert others by questioning them and observing what their feelings depend upon.

[10]

You need to be equanimous and calm yourself in order to listen to people's statements, examine their affairs, assess myriad things, and distinguish relative merits. Even if you repudiate specific matters, see their subtleties and know their types. If you are searching into people and live in their midst, you can measure their abilities and see into their intentions, with never a failure to tally.

[11]

Therefore, knowledge begins from knowing yourself; after that you can know others. This interrelated knowledge is likened to a mythological fish that has only one eye and thus must travel in pairs. With this knowledge, perception of form is like the relationship of light and shadow; then you can see into words without missing anything, like a magnet attracting needles. Your dealings with people are subtle, your perception of their feelings and mental states is quick. It is like yin to yang, like yang to yin; it is like round to square, like square to round.

[12]

Before you can see formations, you guide people in a rounded way; once formations have taken shape, you employ people with rectitude.

In matters of promotion and demotion, dismissal or honor, you use this method to oversee them. If you have not made the appropriate determinations yourself beforehand, the way you govern people will not be correct.

[13]

When affairs are handled unskillfully, this is called ignorance of feelings and loss of the Way. When you have thoroughly clarified matters yourself, and have determined measures whereby it is possible to govern others, and yet you reveal no obvious form, so that no one can see into your privacy, this is called genius.

ACCEPTANCE AND SOLIDARITY

[1]

In the relationship between ruler and minister, or between superior or subordinate, there may be those who are on friendly terms in spite of distance, and there may be those who are alienated in spite of closeness.

[2]

Someone who tries to cleave to a ruler may not be employed, while someone who leaves a ruler may on the contrary be sought after.

[3]

There may be those who come forward day after day but are not taken seriously, and there may be those who are heard of from afar yet are given consideration.

[4]

In all affairs there has to be acceptance and solidarity to form the basic bonding at the start. Ties may be made by virtue, by partisanship, by money, or by sex.

[5]

When you go by others' wishes, then get involved when they want to get involved, stay away when they want to stay away, approach when they want to approach, be distant when they want to be distant, join up when they want to join up, depart when they want to depart, seek when they want to seek, think when they want to think.

[6]

This is like a mother ground-spider following the needs of her off-spring: when she leaves her burrow, she leaves no gap; and when she goes back into her burrow, she leaves no trace. She goes out independently and comes back independently, and no one can stop her.

[7]

Acceptance is a matter of presenting convincing statements, solidarity is a matter of holding firmly to what is planned. Those who wish to be convincing strive to make their calculations in secret; those who plan things strive to follow orderly procedures.

[8]

By inwardly considering what is appropriate and what is not, then clearly stating what is advantageous and what is harmful, it is possible to direct another's will.

[9]

When measures are brought forth in response to the time, thus do they accord with appropriate strategy. Think over carefully what to bring up, and when you go forth you respond to the necessities of the time.

[10]

Now, if there is disharmony within them, measures cannot be carried out. Then figure out what is appropriate for the time, and change what you do accordingly, in order to seek a suitable adaptation.

[11]

Seeking acceptance by adaptation is like a lock taking a key. When speaking of the past, first use conventional terms; when speaking of the future, use adaptable words.

[12]

Those who are expert at adaptation examine the lay of the land and understand nature; thereby they transform the four seasons and make ghosts and spirits harmonize with yin and yang. Thus do they govern people: seeing the things they plan, they know their aspirations and intentions.

[13]

When there is disharmony in affairs, that means there is something unknown. When there is collusion but not solidarity, there is overt alliance but covert alienation. When there is disharmony in affairs, sages do not make plans for them.

[14]

Thus when there is intimacy in spite of distance, that means there is hidden virtue. When there is alienation in spite of nearness, that means there is disparity of aims.

[15]

Those who try to cleave to rulers but are not employed are those whose plans are ineffective; those who leave rulers but then are sought after are those who are subsequently proven to be right.

[16]

Those who come forward day after day but are not taken seriously are those whose proposals are inappropriate; those who are heard of from afar yet are given consideration are those who fit in with plans and are counted on to decide matters.

[17]

Therefore it is said that those who speak without seeing what type of person they are talking to will be opposed, and those who speak without finding out the state of mind of the person they are talking to will be denied.

[18]

When you apprehend people's feelings and states of mind, then you can use your arts masterfully. Applying this method you can put people off, and can bring them in; you can form ties with people, and can separate yourself from them.

[19]

Therefore when sages set things up, they use this means to get to know people beforehand and establish solidarity with them. Based on reason, virtue, humanity, justice, courtesy, and culture, they figure out plans.

[20]

First they take up classical poetry and documents, mixing in talk of loss and gain, considering what to abandon and what to take up. Those with whom they wish to collaborate, they deliberately admit; those of whom they want to be rid, they deliberately exclude.

[21]

In order to exclude or admit effectively, it is necessary to understand the logic of the Way, figure out coming events, and settle any doubts that are sensed. Then there will be no miscalculation in the measures taken, which will then be successful and worthwhile.

[22]

To direct a populace in productive work is called solidarity and inner cooperation. If the leadership is ignorant and cannot manage, those below get confused without even realizing it; reverse this by solidarity. If the leadership is self-satisfied and pays no attention to what outsiders have to say, then laud it to the skies. If a summons comes spontaneously, then rise to it and take over command. If you want to leave, then give up on account of danger.

[23]

Adapt fluidly to changes, and no one will know what you are doing; you accomplish great things while remaining in the background.

Stopping Gaps

[1]

Things have natural courses; events have combinations and divisions. There is that which is near but cannot be seen; there is that which is remote and yet can be known. The near at hand is unseen when you do not examine what is said; the remote can be known when you question the past to discern the future.

[2]

A gap is an opening; an opening is a space between barriers; a space between barriers makes for tremendous vulnerability. At the first sign of a gap, it should be shored up, or repelled, or stopped, or hidden, or overwhelmed. These are called the principles of stopping gaps.

[3]

When things are perilous, sages know it, and preserve themselves in solitude. They explain things according to developments, and thoroughly master strategy, whereby they discern the subtle. Starting from the slightest beginnings, they work against tremendous odds. What they provide to the outside world, strategies for nipping problems in the bud, all depend on stopping gaps. Stopping gaps is an application of the arts of the Way.

[4]

When the land is in confusion, there is no enlightened leadership above, and the public officials have no real virtue. Then petty people slander and despoil, wise people are not employed, and sages go into hiding. Greedy connivers go into action, rulers and ministers confuse each other, fall out with each other and attack each other. Parents and children separate, and there is rebellion and antagonism. These are called budding gaps.

[5]

When sages see budding gaps, they plug them up with laws. If society can thereby be ordered, then they stop up the gaps. If it is unruly, they overwhelm them. Sometimes they attack the problem in one way, sometimes another: sometimes they attack in such a way as to effect a restoration, sometimes they attack in such a way as to effect an overthrow.

[6]

Ever since there has been the cyclic process of combination and separation of heaven and earth, there have always been gaps. It is imperative to see into them. The purpose of seeing into them is to be able to open and close them. One who can apply this principle is a sage.

[7]

Sages are servants of heaven and earth: if society is in an irremediable state, they hide deeply and await the right time to act. In a time when something can be done, they plan for it. They can accord with the higher, they can regulate the lower; able to follow, able to conform, they are guardian spirits of heaven and earth.

EXCITATION AND ARREST

[1]

In general, assessing strategy and measuring ability is instrumental in attracting those far away and drawing them near.

[2]

To establish power and control affairs, first it is imperative to discern sameness and difference: to distinguish right and wrong speech, see expressions of what is inside and what is outside, know the logic of what is and what is not, decide which plans are safe and which dangerous, and determine what is nearby and what is far off.

[3]

After that you can weigh and measure: and if there are ways to correct errors, then you can call for them, find them, and employ them.

[4]

By using "hooking and clamping" expressions, you can excite and arrest people. Hooking and clamping talk involves speaking in a manner that is now the same, now different. Considering the thoughts going on in their minds, examine their ideas to know what they like and dislike; then speak of what they value, using exciting and arresting words to hold them fast by hooking onto what they like.

[5]

As for those who cannot be managed well, you may first invite them, then lay a heavy responsibility on them. Or you may first belabor them with a heavy responsibility, and then criticize them afterward. Or you may use a heavy responsibility itself to tear them down, or tear them down in order to lay a heavy responsibility on them.

[6]

If you are going to employ people, you may assess their attitudes toward money, material goods, and sex, in order to position them accordingly. Or you may assess their abilities, empower them, and thereby hook them. Or you may watch them, and clamp down when you see an opening. These practices depend on stopping gaps.

[7]

When you are going to use this on a whole land, it is imperative to assess power and measure abilities, to perceive the waxing and waning of natural timing, to control the lay of the land, to know the difficult and easy terrain, to determine how much or little money and goods the people have, and to know which of the local leaders with whom you associate are friendly and which are distant, which of them like you and which of them dislike you.

[8]

Once you have examined people's mentalities, intentions, and thoughts, and gotten to know what they like and dislike, then you speak of what is important to them, using intoxicating and arresting expressions to hook into their inclinations and thereby hold them and attract them.

[9]

When you use this on individual people, you measure their knowledge and ability, weigh their talents and strengths, calculate their energy and force, and then devise means of regulating and controlling them. You may go out to meet them, then go along with them to bond and harmonize, using their own ideas to get through to them. This is the linkage of intoxication and arrest.

[10]

When you use this on people, it starts out unreal but comes to be real. Link up unerringly, thus finding out the truth of otherwise of what they say, and you can control their obedience and control their freedom: you can lead them in any direction, and can lead them to reverse themselves, or even overturn. And even if they are overturned, you can restore them, without losing appropriate measure.

OPPOSITION AND ALLIANCE

[1]

In matters of rapprochement, alliance, rejection, and revolution, there are suitable strategies. Adapting to changes fluidly, each has a configuration, regulated according to events.

[2]

Therefore sages dwell between heaven and earth, cultivate themselves, govern society, dispense education, elevate the reputable, and clarify terms. In doing so, they always use the opportunities afforded by events and phenomena, observing the timing of Nature. Based on this, they know what to increase and what to decrease. By knowing all this beforehand, they can adapt to changes.

[3]

The world has no fixed values, events have no fixed guide. Sages have no fixed involvements, yet there is nothing they do not affect. They listen to nothing, yet there is nothing they do not hear. If they are successful in what they do and appropriate in their planning, they are made into leaders.

[4]

If plans are suitable for one party but not for another, then they are not faithful to both sides. There must be contrast and opposition. To return to one side, you oppose the other; to oppose one side, you return to the other. This is the technique.

[5]

When you use this technique on a nation, you must evaluate the nation before applying it. When you use it on a state, you must evaluate the state before applying it. When you use it on a household, you must evaluate the household before applying it. When you use it on an individual, you must evaluate the individual's capacity and power before applying it. Whether on a large or small scale, advancing or withdrawing, the function is the same. It is imperative to first think strategically and determine a plan before putting it into action by means of the art of intoxication and arrest.

[6]

In ancient times, those who were skilled in using rejection and acceptance brought about cooperation within the four seas, enveloping the grounds of local leaders' disputes and alliances, and transforming them, after that seeking unity thereby.

[7]

That is why Yi Yin went to King T'ang five times and King Chieh five times without being able to clarify anything; only later did he join with T'ang. Lu Shang went to King Wen three times, entering the palace three times, without being able to clarify anything; only later did he join with King Wen. They knew the clamp of the decree of Heaven, so they accepted it without doubt.

[8]

Only perfect sages of profound understanding can direct society. Without mental effort and intense thought, one cannot get to the bottom of things. Without understanding mentalities and perceiving feelings, one cannot attain success. One with talent but no kindness cannot command an army. One with loyalty but no reality cannot know people.

[9]

Therefore the method of opposition and alliance demands that you gauge your own ability and intelligence, and assess your own strengths and weaknesses, seeing who does not compare among those far and near. Only then can you advance and withdraw freely and independently.

FIGURING OUT
PSYCHOLOGICAL CONDITIONS

[1]

Those in ancient times who skillfully operated countries always measured the powers in the land and figured out the psychological conditions of local leaders. If measurement of powers is not thorough, you do not know the strong and the weak, the light and the heavy. If psychological conditions are not figured out thoroughly, you do not know the activities of hidden changes and developments.

[2]

What does it mean to measure powers? It means to calculate the size of territory, how many or few participate in planning, how much there is in the way of money and goods, how big the population is, how rich or poor the people are, whether they have surpluses or shortages, where the terrain is dangerous and where it is easy, what is advantageous and what is harmful, whose strategy is better, whether the leadership and the administrators are close or distant, who is worthy and who is unworthy, and whose hired counselors are more intelligent.

[3]

Observe whether the seasons bode ill or well, and see whether the alliances of local leaders are useful or not. Observe the minds of the common people, how they behave and how they change, whether they are secure or insecure, who they like and who they hate, and who is in a position to rebel. If you can ascertain all of this, that is called measuring powers.

[4]

As for figuring out psychological conditions, you must go to people when they are in a very good mood, and emphasize what they want; then if they have desires, they will not be able to hide their feelings. And you must go to people when they are in a very fearful mood, and emphasize what they dislike; then if they have aversions, they will not be able to hide their feelings. Feelings and desires inevitably emerge when people go through changes.

[5]

When they are emotionally stirred but you still do not discern how they change, then leave such people alone and do not talk to them. Instead, question their familiars to find out where their feelings and desires lie.

[6]

When psychological conditions change within, physical manifestations appear outwardly. Therefore it is always necessary to discern what is concealed by way of what is visible. This is what is called fathoming the depths and figuring out psychological conditions.

[7]

Therefore, those who would plan national affairs should carefully examine the quantity of power; those who would persuade leaders should carefully figure out psychological conditions. Strategic consideration of psychological conditions and desires must emerge from this. Then it is possible to ennoble and to demean, to esteem and to belittle, to help and to harm, to bring about success and to bring about failure: the formula is one and the same.

[8]

Therefore, even if you have the Way of ancient kings and the strategy of sages, unless you figure out psychological conditions there is no way for you to find out what is hidden. This is the basis of strategy, and also the method of persuasion. You are always one up on other people, and none can precede you. To get there before events arise is most difficult to do.

[9]

So it is said that figuring out psychological conditions is most difficult to master. This means that it is necessary to time strategic thinking appropriately.

[10]

Thus if you observe how everyone and everything, even down to insects, can be beneficial in some way and harmful in some way, then you can produce excellence in undertakings. What gives rise to undertakings is subtle momentum. This is to be discussed after having figured out psychological conditions and framed them in elegant expression.

PRESSURING

[1]

Pressuring is a technique for figuring people out. Inner correspondence is the subject figured out. There is a Way to employ this; that Way is necessarily covert and subtle.

[2]

Pressure people with what they desire in order to sound them out, and the inner correspondence will inevitably respond. What they respond to is what they would surely do.

[3]

Therefore you subtly stand apart from this. That is called shutting off openings, hiding the point, concealing what you like to avoid emotions, so that no one knows what you are doing, and therefore you can accomplish your task without trouble.

[4]

Pressuring is up to you; response is up to others. When you use this accordingly, nothing is impossible.

[5]

Those in ancient times who were skilled at pressuring were as if fishing in a deep body of water, casting in bait and never failing to catch fish therein. In this sense it is said that when you direct affairs you succeed day after day, yet nobody knows; when you direct the military you win day after day, yet nobody fears.

[6]

Sages plan this in secret, so they are called genius; they carry it out in the open, so they are called enlightened.

[7]

Daily success in directing affairs means accumulating virtue, so that the people feel secure yet are not conscious of why they have bene-fited; it means accumulating goodness, so that the people are guided by it without knowing why it is so. Thus everyone compares this to genius and enlightenment.

[8]

Daily victory in directing the military means battling not to fight, not to waste, so the people do not know why they submit and do not know of a reason to fear. So everyone compares this to genius and enlightenment.

[9]

The pressuring may be done by means of placidity, or by means of correctness, or by means of joy, or by means of anger, or by means of reputation, or by means of action, or by means of honesty, or by means of faith, or by means of profit, or by means of abasement.

[10]

Placidity means silence. Correctness means appropriateness. Joy means pleasing. Anger means stirring. Reputation means motivating. Action means accomplishing. Honesty means moral purity. Faith means expectation. Profit means seeking. Abasement means flattery.

[11]

Thus the reason that sages alone employ all this is that while it is available to everyone, yet no one does it successfully, because they use it wrongly.

[12]

So in pressuring there is nothing more difficult than thoroughness. In persuasion there is nothing more difficult than being heard completely. In doing things there is nothing more difficult than ensuring success. These three can be handled only by sages.

[13]

Therefore strategy must arise from thoroughness. It is imperative to choose something in common as a medium of persuasion. This is why it is said that there may be bonding that has no gaps.

[14]

When undertakings succeed, they invariably conform to logic. Therefore it is said that the logic of the Way is partner to the time.

[15]

When persuasion is accepted, it invariably conforms to feelings. Therefore it is said that when feelings meet there is acceptance; people listen to those with compatible feelings.

[16]

So beings return to kind. Of those who run to a bonfire with an armload of kindling, the fastest burn first. When water is poured on level ground, a moist patch will absorb it first. This is natural correspondence between things of a kind; power configurations and momenta are also like this. This means that inner correspondence responding to external pressure is like this.

[17]

Therefore it is said, "Pressure people according to their affinities; if there is no response, then pressure them by what they desire." There are those who do not listen or accept, so it is called a path that is traveled alone. Those who perceive the subtle and see opportunities are not late; they succeed without getting caught up in it, and eventually their civilizing influence fully develops.

Assessment

[1]

Persuasion is a matter of convincing or pleasing others. When you persuade people, you take your material from them. When you embellish words, you are borrowing them; when you borrow them you adjust them.

[2]

Answering responsively is a matter of convenient expression; convenient expression is light discourse. Being meaningful means clarifying; clarification is a matter of tallying with experience.

[3]

Talk may go back and forth, indicating an inclination to mutual rejection. Critical words are opposing argument. Opposing argument fishes out subtleties.

[4]

Crafty talk uses flattery in seeking to appear loyal. Ingratiating talk uses breadth in seeking to appear knowledgeable. Grandiose talk uses determination in seeking to appear brave. Concerned talk uses calculation in seeking to appear trustworthy. Calm talk uses opposition in seeking to appear victorious.

[5]

Anticipating wishes and catering to desires is flattery. Abundant quotation of literature is breadth. Abandon without hesitation is determination. Planning, making choices, and developing tactics is calculating. Discerning insufficiency to stop error is opposition.

[6]

Therefore the mouth is a mechanism, by means of which one can shut up feelings and ideas. Ears and eyes are assistants of the mind, means of seeing through treachery and perversion. Therefore it is said that when these three respond in harmony, they act in a beneficial way.

[7]

So those who say a lot without confusion, who soar to the heights and go back and forth and all around without getting lost, who change without being imperiled, have seen the essential principle.

[8]

Colors and forms cannot be shown to the blind, voices and music cannot be conveyed to the deaf. So those to whom you should not go are those whom you have no means of enlightening, and those who cannot come to you are those to whom you are not receptive. Some people do not understand, so sages do not work for them.

[9]

An ancient said, "The mouth should be used for eating rather than speaking," because there are taboos about what can be said; "the mouths of the masses can melt metal," because words have nuances that can be twisted.

[10]

Human feelings are such that when people speak, they want to be heard; and when they undertake things, they want to succeed. Therefore wise people do not use the weaknesses of the ignorant but their strengths; they do not use the clumsiness of the ignorant, but use their skills: they are not frustrated. That means they follow the strengths of those who can be of help, and avoid the weaknesses of those who can do harm.

[11]

So the defense of insects with shells necessitates thickness and hardness in the shell; the action of poisonous insects necessitates a venomous sting. Thus birds and beasts know how to employ their strengths, while speakers know what is useful and use it.

[12]

So it is said that there are five kinds of verbal expression, conveying affliction, fear, anxiety, anger, and joy. Affliction involves a sense of declining energy and a lack of liveliness. Fear involves such extreme upset that there is no self-control. Anxiety is suffocating, with no outlet. Anger involves arbitrary stirring and unruliness. Joy involves being scattered and lacking concentration. These five you can use if you are an expert; if they are beneficial, then put them into action.

[13]

Thus when talking with the knowledgeable, base it on breadth; when talking with the broadly learned, base it on discernment; when talking with the discerning, base it on quintessential focus. When talking with those of high status, base it on power; when talking with the wealthy, base it on loftiness. When talking with the poor, base it on profit; when talking with the lowly, base it on modesty. When talking with the courageous, base it on bravery; when talking with the ignorant, base it on acuity.

[14]

This is the art; but people usually do the opposite. For this reason, when speaking to people with knowledge, you use this to enlighten them; when speaking to people without knowledge, you use this to educate them, but it is very hard to do.

[15]

So, talk is of many kinds, affairs undergo many changes. Thus if your talk is always of the appropriate kind, your affairs will not be disorderly; if you never change, you do not lose your autonomy.

[16]

Thus when it comes to knowledge, what is important is not to forget; when it comes to listening, what is important is to be clear; when it comes to wisdom, what is important is to understand; and when it comes to rhetoric, what is important is to be exceptional.

Strategic Thinking

[1]

All strategy has a way, which demands that you find the bases to discover the conditions. Having carefully examined and apprehended conditions, then you set up three categories: higher, middling, and lower. These three having been established, you use them to produce unexpected strategies, which will not know any obstacle. This begins with following the perennial.

[2]

Thus people on a treasure hunt use a compass to avoid getting lost: measuring capacities, assessing abilities, and figuring out feelings and psychological conditions are the compass of behavior and political affairs.

[3]

So when two parties who share the same feelings are on friendly terms, that means they are both succeeding; when two parties have the same wishes and yet are estranged, that means one side is getting hurt. When those with the same aversions are friendly, that means they are both getting hurt; when those with the same aversions are estranged, that means only one party is getting hurt.

[4]

Thus when people profit each other they are friendly, and when they cause each other loss they become estranged; it is the operation of natural law. This is a means of perceiving the separation between difference and sameness.

[5]

So a wall crumbles at the seams, wood breaks at a knot: this is the significance of separation.

[6]

Thus changes give rise to tasks, tasks give rise to strategy, strategy gives rise to planning, planning gives rise to discussion, discussion gives rise to persuasion, persuasion gives rise to progress, progress gives rise to withdrawal, withdrawal gives rise to control. By thus controlling affairs, everything can be accomplished in the same way, following the same principles every time.

[7]

Now then, humane people think lightly of wealth, so they cannot be seduced by profit, but they can be induced to make expenditures. Brave people think lightly of difficulty, so they cannot be intimidated by trouble, but they can be gotten to manage perilous situations. Wise people are perfectly logical and reasonable, so they cannot be fooled by untruth, but they can be edified by truth and induced to perform worthy deeds. These are three types of ability.

[8]

Thus it is easy to blind the ignorant, easy to intimidate the unworthy, and easy to seduce the avaricious. This is a matter of dealing with them according to actualities.

[9]

Therefore those who are strong have built it up from weakness; those who are straightforward have built it up from tact; and those who have a surplus have built it up from lack. This is the action of the relevant arts of the Way.

[10]

So if there is outward friendliness but inward estrangement, reconcile the inner relationship. If there is inward friendliness but outward estrangement, reconcile the outward relationship. Thus you change others based on their doubts, affirm them based on their views, make pacts with them based on what they say, reinforce them based on what they do, assess them based on what they dislike, fend them off by what distresses them. Frighten them by pressure, stir them by excitement, prove them by surrounding, confuse them by disturbance—these are called tactical strategies.

[11]

In the use of tactical strategies, it is better to be private than public; and alliance is even better than mere privacy, alliance meaning a partnership that has no gaps. It is better to be unconventional than conventional, the unconventional being that which flows unceasingly. So when persuading leaders, it is imperative to talk to them of the unconventional; when persuading administrators, it is imperative to talk to them privately.

[12]

Those who are themselves on the inside but speak to outsiders are ostracized. Those who are themselves outsiders but whose talk goes too deep are in danger. What people do not like should not be forced on them; what does not concern people should not be taught to them.

[13]

When people have likes, learn them and adapt to them. When people have dislikes, avoid them and do not mention them. Thus you make your way covertly, yet gain the result openly. Therefore when you are going to get rid of people, you indulge them, then get rid of those who do indulge.

[14]

When people's appearances are neither too attractive nor too repulsive, they are wholeheartedly trusted. Those who can be known
can be employed; those who are inscrutable are not employed by
planners.

[15]

So it is said that in professional affairs it is considered important to
control others, not to be controlled by others. Controlling people
means holding power and authority; being controlled by people
means your life and fate are controlled. Therefore the Way of sages is
covert, while the way of the ignorant is obvious.

[16]

It is easy to work for the wise, hard to work for the unwise. From
this perspective, since what makes for destruction cannot produce
survival, and what makes for danger cannot produce safety, there is
nothing to do but value wisdom.

[17]

Wisdom employs what is unknown to most people, and can use what
is invisible to most people. Once wisdom is in use, seeing what can
be chosen and doing it is how one acts on one's own; seeing that
which affords no choice and doing it is how one acts for others.

[18]

Therefore the Way of ancient kings is unseen. A saying has it, "The
evolution of heaven and earth is in the heights and the depths; the
sages' Way of mastery is in concealment and covertness. It is not just

faithfulness, truthfulness, humanity, and justice; it is a matter of balance and accuracy."

[19]

When people's reasoning has arrived at the meaning of this, then they are worth talking to. Through attainment of this, it is possible to bring in the just from far and near.

Decision Making

[1]

All decision making is based on doubt. What enables people to prosper they consider good; what involves trouble they consider bad. The consummation of skill in this matter is to draw others; if there is ultimately no confusion or bias, then there is benefit in it. Eliminate the benefit, and a decision is not accepted. This is the reason for unorthodox tactics.

[2]

When there is benefit for good, but it is concealed and made out to be bad, then a decision is not accepted, and produces alienation. Thus it is possible to cause loss of benefit, or even cause harm; these are slips in business and political affairs.

[3]

The means by which sages can accomplish their tasks are five. They may do it by overt benevolence, or they may do it by covert attack. They may do it by use of honesty, or they may do it by cover-up. They may also use plain simplicity.

[4]

Yang is diligent at one word, Yin is diligent at two words: [1] simplicity; and [2] essential function. Using four things, exercise them subtly. Now assess past events as an indication of future events, compare this with the ordinary, and if appropriate you decide on that.

[5]

In the affairs of rulers, the general public, or important people, if something lofty and noble is possible and appropriate, decision is made in favor of that. If something that does not require expenditure of energy and is easy to accomplish is possible and appropriate, decision is made in favor of that. If something that requires effort and intense exertion but cannot be avoided is possible and appropriate, decision is made in favor of that. Decision is made in favor of that which eliminates trouble, if possible and appropriate; decision is made in favor of that which leads to good fortune, if possible and appropriate.

[6]

So determining conditions and settling doubts are the foundations of all tasks. To bring order to chaos correctly and determine success and failure are difficult to do. That is why ancient kings even used oracles to decide for themselves.

Talismanic Sayings

[1]

Be peaceful, easygoing, upright, and calm; then the measures you impose will be accommodating. If you are good at managing but are not calm, then empty your heart and even your mind, and wait for unease to fall away. This helps master rank.

[2]

Eyes and ears should be clear; the mind should be wise. Those who see through everyone's eyes see everything; those who hear through everyone's ears hear everything; those who think through everyone's minds know everything. When all of these are combined and advanced together, then understanding cannot be blocked. This helps master understanding.

[3]

The art of virtue is this: do not be stiff and forbidding. When you are forgiving, then you are protected; when you are forbidding, then you are shut off. Even a high mountain can be seen all the way to the top, and even a deep body of water can be measured; but the upright calm of the art of virtue practiced by the spiritually enlightened is unfathomable. This helps master virtue.

[4]

A system of rewards should be reliable; a system of punishments should be correct. That the giving of rewards should be reliable means that it is imperative to prove what eyes and ears see and hear. As for those who are not heard of or noticed, none will fail to be unconsciously influenced. Truthfulness is expressed for the world and the spirits, so the treacherous can hardly affect the leader. This helps master reward.

[5]

First consider heaven, second earth, third humanity. In the four directions, the zenith and the nadir, left and right, in front and behind: where does ill omen lie? This helps master inquiry.

[6]

The mind is the government of nine openings, the ruler is the chief of five officials. To those who do good, the ruler gives rewards; to those who do wrong, the ruler metes out penalties. When the ruler gives according to what is sought, then there is no toil or trouble. Sages apply this, and therefore are competent at giving rewards. Following reason based on this, then they are able to last a long time. This helps master logic.

[7]

Leaders should not fail to be comprehensive. If leaders are not comprehensive, the multitudes of administrators will create confusion and business will be erratic. When those on the inside and those on the outside do not communicate, how do they know what to express? When expressiveness and reticence are not skillful, you do not see the source. This helps master comprehensiveness.

[8]

First, extend your vision; second, widen your information; third, stabilize your clarity of mind. When you clearly know what is going on covertly a thousand miles away, this is called spying out all the villains in the world, so none are not unknowingly changed. This helps master respect.

[9]

When actualities do in fact accord with names, there is peace and wholeness. Names and actualities give rise to each other; they turn into conditions of one another. Therefore it is said, "When names are accurate, they give rise to actualities; actualities give rise to principles: principles produce the virtues of names and actualities; virtues produce harmony; harmony gives rise to accuracy." This helps master naming.

Basic Course
Seven Arts of Covert Correspondence

A. INVIGORATING THE SPIRIT: THE METHOD IS MODELED ON THE FIVE DRAGONS

[1]

Within the invigorated spirit are five energies. The spirit is their leader, the mind is their abode, virtue is their chief. The place to develop energy is ultimately the Way.

[2]

The Way is the origin of heaven and earth; the One is their foundation. Whatever is made by things or produced by nature contains a formless developmental energy, which was there before heaven and earth: no one can see its form, and no one knows its name; it is called spiritual and miraculous.

[3]

So the Way is the source of spiritual illumination: unity is the beginning of its evolution. Through this virtue one nurtures the five energies: if the mind can be unified, you will attain the art.

[4]

The art is that whereby the Way of mental energy is housed; the spirit acts as its functionary. The senses are the gateways of energy, under the general control of the mind.

[5]

Our life as received from Nature is called real human being. Real human beings are one with Nature. Those who inwardly cultivate refinement with this knowledge are called sages.

[6]

Sages know things by analogy. People are born with oneness, then develop changes along with things. Discerning types is up to the senses; if there is any doubt or confusion, it is penetrated by mental technique. If the mind lacks appropriate technique, there will inevitably be failure to penetrate. With this penetration, the five energies are nurtured. The task is a matter of sheltering the spirit. This is called development.

[7]

Development involves five energies, including will, thought, spirit, and character. Spirit is the unifying leader. Calmness and harmony nurture energy; when energy attains the right harmony, then will, thought, spirit, and character do not deteriorate, and these four facets of force and power all thereby survive and stay there. This is called spiritual development ending up in the body; this is what we call the real human being.

[8]

Real humans assimilate to Nature and merge with the Way: holding the unity, they nurture and produce myriad things. Embracing the heart of Nature, they disburse blessings and nourishment; while enveloping all with noncontrivance, they act on power only with deliberate reflection and thoughtful intention. When people can master this invigoration of spirit, then they can develop will.

B. DEVELOPING THE WILL: THE METHOD IS MODELED ON THE SPIRIT-TORTOISE

[1]

Development of will is for when the energy of mind does not reach the intended object. When you have some desire, your will dwells on it and intends it. Will is functionary of desire. When you have many desires, then your mind is scattered; when your mind is scattered, then your will deteriorates. When your will deteriorates, then thought does not attain its object.

[2]

Therefore, if the energy of the mind is unified then desires do not roam around. When desires do not roam around then will does not deteriorate. When will does not deteriorate, then thought of true reason reaches its object.

[3]

When true reason is reached, then harmony pervades. When harmony pervades, then unruly energy does not trouble the heart. So inwardly you thereby develop will, while outwardly you thereby get to know people. When you develop will, then your mind is penetrating and perceptive; when you know people, then the division of labor is clear.

[4]

If you are going to use this in dealing with people, it is imperative first to know their development of energy and will. Knowing how robust or deteriorated people's energy is, you nurture their willpower and examine what makes them feel secure in order to know what they are capable of doing.

[5]

If will is not developed, then the energy of mind is not stable. If the energy of mind is not stable, then thought and reflection do not arrive at understanding, when thought and reflection do not arrive at understanding, then intent and will are insubstantial. When intent and will are insubstantial, then response is not powerful. When response is not powerful, then will is lost and the heart is drained. When the heart is drained, then the spirit is lost. When the spirit is lost, that results in vagueness; with vagueness, the combination of mind, spirit, and will is not unified.

[6]

In the beginning of developing will, the thing to do is to make yourself peaceful. Making yourself peaceful is a matter of substantiality and stability of will. When the will is substantial and stable, then your power is not fragmented. When spiritual illumination always keeps you secure, then you can impart this.

C. SOLIDIFYING INTENT: THE METHOD IS MODELED ON A SUPERNATURAL SERPENT

[1]

Solidifying intent refers to the formulation of mental energy into thought. The mind should be calm and quiet, thought should be deep and far-reaching. When the mind is calm and quiet, then brilliant measures are conceived; when thought is deep and far-reaching, then strategic plans are perfected. When brilliant measures are conceived, then the will cannot be disturbed. When strategic plans are perfected, then achievements cannot be blocked.

[2]

When intent and thought are stabilized, then the mind is easygoing and peaceful. When the mind is easygoing and peaceful, then its activities are not mistaken, and the spirit is self-possessed, and being self-possessed is therefore stable.

[3]

Perceptibly manifest energies or moods are acquired; treachery can subdue them and fraud can confuse them, so that what is said does not come from the heart. Therefore the mental art of the trustworthy is to maintain true unity unchanging, awaiting the interaction of people's ideas and thoughts, listening to them and watching them.

[4]

Strategic planning is the pivot of survival and destruction: if thinking is not fitting, then hearing is not clear, and timing is inaccurate, resulting in mistakes in planning. Then intention is unreliable; it is vacuous and insubstantial. Therefore in strategic thinking, the thing to do is solidify intent; and solidification of intent must begin with mental technique.

[5]

Seeking by noncontrivance calms and tunes the internal organs: when the vitality, spirit, celestial soul, and earthly soul are steadfastly kept unmoving, then you can look inward and listen backward, settling will and thought in the cosmic void, helping the going and coming of the spirit.

[6]

Thereby you observe the opening and closing of heaven and earth, discern the creations of myriad things, and see the governance of human affairs. You know the whole world without going out the door, you see the course of heaven without looking through the window, you direct without seeing, arrive without going: this is called the knowledge of the Way, whereby you become attuned to spiritual illumination, respond to the unexpected, and are imbued with spirit.

D. Dividing power: the method is modeled on a crouching bear

[1]

Dividing power is a matter of being enveloped in the spirit: so quiet your mind and stabilize your will so that the spirit returns to its abode; then you will be fully enveloped in power.

[2]

When you are fully enveloped in power, then you are inwardly solid and stable. When you are inwardly solid and stable, then no one can stand up to you. When no one can stand up to you, then you can divide people's power and divert their momentum, as if you were their god.

[3]

Take the empty by solidity, take the lacking by having, like using pounds to weigh against ounces; then movements will surely be followed, initiatives will surely find cooperation. Bending a single finger, you observe the rest in order; setting changes in motion, you see how they take shape. No interloper can get in your way.

[4]

When you are thoroughly versed in how initiatives draw cooperative response and use stealth to spot interlopers, then it is clear how to set changes in motion, and thus power can be divided.

[5]

When you are going to set changes in motion, it is imperative first to nurture the will and conceal intent so as to espy gaps, leaks, and interlopers.

[6]

Those who know to stabilize solidity nurture themselves; those who make themselves deferential nurture other people. So when the spirit is there, armaments disappear. Then you give shape to trends in a constructive and beneficial manner.

E. DISPERSING MOMENTUM: THE METHOD IS MODELED ON A BIRD OF PREY

[1]

Dispersing momentum is an operation of the spirit. To do this, it is necessary to act in pursuit of openings. When your forcefulness is fully developed within, if you figure out gaps and deploy that forcefulness, then momentum can be dispersed.

[2]

Those who can disperse momentum keep their mind empty and open and their will full to overflowing. If intent deteriorates and forcefulness is lost, the vital spirit is not focused, and one's speech is irrelevant and erratic.

[3]

Therefore you observe people's will and intent in order to calculate measures for them: then you use logic to persuade them and plan things, making full use of adaptation and convention, and balancing weaknesses and strengths.

[4]

If there is no gap, then you will not disperse momentum. To disperse momentum, await an opening to move, so that when you go into action the momentum of [opposing] force is split.

[5]

To be skilled at seeking out gaps, it is necessary to inwardly refine the five energies and outwardly observe emptiness and fullness, not losing the solidity to split and disperse [opponents] when going into action. Then movements follow your will, and you know the underlying strategies.

[6]

Momentum is a determining factor of gain or loss, a force in strategic change. Those whose momentum gets dispersed are those who have not been watching with the carefulness of the spirit.

F. TRANSFORMING FREELY: THE METHOD IS MODELED ON A PREDATORY BEAST

[1]

F. Transforming freely means inexhaustible strategy. To be inexhaustible, it is necessary to have the mind of a sage, thereby getting to the source of unfathomable knowledge, and using unfathomable knowledge to master mental arts.

[2]

Thereby the spirit and the Way merge into one: discerning myriad types by changes, you can expound principles inexhaustibly.

[3]

Strategies and plans have individual forms: they may be adaptable or definitive, covert or overt, lucky or unlucky. The types of undertakings involved are not the same. Therefore sages take this to heart and use the capacity of transforming freely to seek what is appropriate.

[4]

Therefore those who participate in creative activity, in performing initiating actions, always embrace the Great Way to observe the realm of spiritual light. Heaven and earth are infinite, human affairs are inexhaustible: in each case you see the appropriate planning in terms of what will successfully complete that type of affair. Then one will know whether it will be auspicious or inauspicious, and whether it will end up in success or failure.

[5]

Those who transform freely may turn to good luck, or they may turn to bad luck: sages use the Way to foresee survival and destruction, and then know to turn freely but follow the right direction.

[6]

Free adaptation is the basis of harmonizing words; right direction is the basis of managing affairs. Transformation is the basis of examining plans. Dealing with people is the basis of examining intentions behind advance and retirement. For all of them you must see what is fitting in order to sum up the essential and communicate coherently.

G. FOCUSING THE MIND'S EYE: THE METHOD IS MODELED ON PSYCHIC DIVINATION

[1]

Focusing the mind's eye is for determining impending perils. Events have natural courses, people have successes and failures: it is imperative to examine movements signaling impending perils.

[2]

Therefore sages await virtuous people without artificial contrivance; they examine the content of their discourse and assign them to appropriate tasks.

[3]

The mind's eye is knowledge, focus is practical action. When sages focus on something and talk about it, if there is something inappropriate, they will not express it in words.

[4]

So wise people do not miss what others say just because they themselves can speak. Therefore their rhetoric is not prolix; and their hearts are not empty, their wills are not deranged, and their intentions are not evil.

[5]

Only when they have confronted the degree of difficulty do they devise strategy for it; they consider it fruitful to follow the natural course.

[6]

When they can stop opponents from adapting and can unsettle their order, this is called great achievement.

[7]

If they add anything or subtract anything, in each case they express it in words.

[8]

Use tactics that divide power and disperse momentum in order to see the mind's eye of others. Threaten their vulnerabilities and you can be sure about them.

[9]

Skillful focus of the mind's eye is like splitting open a ten thousand-foot dam and letting the water gush out, like rolling round boulders into a valley ten thousand feet deep: the ability to carry this out is a matter of formation and momentum making it have to happen thus.

Holding the Pivot

[1]

Holding the pivot refers to production in spring, growth in summer, harvest in autumn, and storage in winter. This is the order of Nature, which is not to be opposed; those who oppose it inevitably fail even if they have some success.

[2]

Therefore human leaders also have a natural pivot, producing, growing, harvesting, and storing, which is also not to be opposed; those who oppose it inevitably decline, even if they flourish. This Way of Nature is the overall guideline for human leaders.

COURSE FROM THE CENTER

[1]

The course from the center means helping those in distress and attending to emergencies. Intelligent and benevolent people are needed to carry this out. Those who are rescued and given support in distress never forget the favor.

[2]

Intelligent people associate with the good, but are benevolent to all. Those who exercise benevolence follow the Way. And those who help out captives develop and employ small people.

[3]

Generally speaking, when intellectuals find that society is abnormal and the time is dangerous, it may somehow be possible to avoid being buried; society may attack and destroy the intelligent, or it may consider immorality to be virile and heroic. They may be suppressed and condemned, they may anxiously preserve themselves, or they may establish themselves after repeated setbacks.

[4]

So the Way values controlling other people, not being controlled by other people. Those who control people hold the handle of power; those who are controlled by people lose their own direction.

[5]

This is how you make a description when you see a form; make an image of an entity to depict it; discern the tone when you hear a voice; dissolve enmity; fight antagonists; create ties with people as they part; reject speech; concentrate attention; and preserve justice.

[6]

To make a description when you see a form and make an image of an entity to depict it means to produce a symbolic representation. This can be grasped by influence, appearance, and image.

[7]

People with a discipline do not look at anything improper and do not listen to anything unorthodox. Their speech is based on classical literature; their behavior is not indecent. They take their Way for their form, and its virtues for their appearance. Their mien is dignified, their expression warm. They cannot be captured by images. Hide your feelings, be guarded, and keep at a distance from them.

[8]

As for discerning the tone when you hear a voice, this means that when the moods of voices are not the same, caring does not connect. Disparate tones do not match; only the middle note, it seems, can be master of all tones.

[9]

When the tone is not harmonious, that means grief. For this reason, when voices scatter injury, disgrace, and destruction, their words inevitably offend the ears. Even if people like that are well known for fine deeds, it will not do to form partnerships with them. This is because their moods are not compatible, and their tones are not harmonious.

[10]

As for dissolving and fighting antagonists, these expressions mean resolving matters with weak enemies and fighting the strong. Having fought strong antagonists, those who attain victory become high in merit and full of power. The weak grieve over their loss and lament their lowliness, vilify their names and disgrace their clans.

[11]

So when the dominant hear of merit and power, they proceed rashly and do not know when to withdraw. When the weak hear grieving over defeat and see the casualities, they fortify themselves to resist to the death. When aggressors have no great power, and defenders have no great power, both can be taken over by threat.

[12]

As for creating ties with people as they part, this refers to statements that bind others to you, causing them to keep thinking of you. Thus when you deal with those who are honest and trustworthy, you praise their conduct, sharpen their will, and speak of what may be done and when you may meet again, such that they are glad. Then call on others near them for witness, to wrap up what has transpired and make your own earnest sincerity clear before letting them go.

[13]

As for rejecting speech, this refers to spying out shortcomings. When words are many, they inevitably contain numerous shortcomings. Perceiving people's shortcomings, test them: shake them up by mention of taboos, and scare them by making reference to the prohibitions of the times, so that people are intimidated. After that, form a bond of trust with them to pacify their minds. Keep what they say confidential, concealing it and warning them not to reveal their own incompetence to people of many devices.

[14]

As for concentrating attention, this means that when you meet people fond of learning technical arts, you praise them far and wide, test them by means of the Way, and startle them with strangeness: then people will have their attention fixed on you. Present them to society, test them against precedent, rectify their past errors, and ally yourself with those who are honest and sincere to you.

[15]

If you meet people addicted to alcohol and sex, have music played to move them, worry them with the prospect of inevitable death and shortening days of life, and amuse them with things they have not seen, so that ultimately they may observe life in a broader context, enabling them to have a reconciliation.

[16]

As for preserving justice, this means keeping intact with humanity and justice, and searching out what lies within hearts, in order to mesh with them.

[17]

Searching hearts means finding out what rules them; by way of the external you control the internal. If matters have complicated twists and turns, you go along with them accordingly.

[18]

That is why petty people imitating others will use this in a perverse and sinister way, even getting to the point where they can destroy families and usurp countries.

[19]

Without wisdom and knowledge, you cannot preserve your home with justice and cannot preserve your country with the Way. The reason sages value the sublety of the Way is truly because it can change peril into safety, rescue the ruined and enable them to survive.

Notes to *The Master of Demon Valley*

Opening and Closing

"Opening and closing" means activation and deactivation, switching on and switching off.

1. The opening and closing of yin and yang refer to the alternation of opposite or complementary trends of events or modes of behavior.

The doorway of survival and destruction refers to the critical pivot of every situation or course of affairs, the crucial point at which success or failure of adaptation spells survival or destruction. To "keep vigil at the doorway" means to watch for these key factors or moments.

The "ends and beginnings of all types" means the aims and motivations of all kinds of people, and the processes of all sorts of events.

2. The unity of the Way and the endless variety of its transformations are simultaneously manifest in the capacity of universal adaptation to any circumstances.

3. The essential point of this passage is that sages do not impose order by external fiat, but achieve order by working responsively with the pattern of actualities. Several strategic actions mentioned illustrate ways in which sages bring people's inner qualities and ideas to light, and put them to the test to see their real worth. Whatever their good and bad characteristics, whatever their strengths and weaknesses, only by accurate assessment of people can leaders manage them effectively.

4. Here opening and closing refer to the activation and deactivation of lines of communication. Again emphasis is placed upon the need for opening and closing to be based on well-considered decisions.

5. Sages can first go along with others because of what they themselves maintain: they have their own principles and their own discipline, so they can go along with others to find out all about them without danger of losing their own purpose or compromising themselves.

When they want to open up lines of communication they value thoroughness, so that there is no confusion or misunderstanding. When they want to shut down and break off contact, they value secrecy, so that nothing leaks out.

In either case, it is best done in a subtle manner, so that confusing emotions are not aroused.

6. Shutting down is used to make sure of people's sincerity when it is necessary to see whether their loyalty or interest is based on truth or principle, or whether it is based on enthusiasm fueled by personality gratifications such as the enjoyment of giving and receiving attention.

7. Opening and closing are natural principles, observed in natural phenomena and imitated by Taoists in their physical, social, and spiritual exercises. Maneuvers characterized by "reversing" refer to strategic acts designed to reverse the mode from open to closed or vice versa: a reversal in either direction might be used to repel an attack, to cover up a weakness, or to oppose an offense.

8. Knowing when to speak and when to remain silent, what to express and what to conceal, is an essential science of "opening and closing."

9. It is instructive to note the tremendous breadth of meaning traditionally associated with yin and yang, as compared to the relative narrowness of popular Western usage, which largely follows the misapprehensions of Carl Jung on this point.

10. One speaks of good to initiate projects because it is necessary to articulate a positive purpose; one speaks of bad in order to conclude strategic planning because it is necessary to take problems into account in order to develop a comprehensive approach to undertakings.

11. To get people to accept what you say, speak to them in accord with their state of mind.

12. In the context of strategy, to be so small as to have no inside means to be so selfless and inconspicuous as to be unnoticed and unreadable, while to be so large as to have no outside means to embrace all in your field of awareness so as to apprehend the total situation and take everything into account.

Yin and yang modes are used to achieve strategic adjustments such as those mentioned here, switched on or off according to what is needed and what can be accomplished at a given time.

13. Development of the body through stillness refers to Taoist "quiet sitting," which is used for a number of purposes, including healing and tuning the internal organs.

Using yang to seek yin means enveloping with virtue in the sense of using the safety of virtue as a basis for attaining sublime rest. Using yin to crystallize yang means exercise of power in the sense of using serenity and selflessness to control and stabilize energy.

14. The round and the square refer to adaptation and regulation, two

primary approaches to accomplishing undertakings. The door of the round and the square means that upon which the appropriate use of adaptation and regulation hinges. It could be called the sum total of the key elements of the situation, or it could be called the knowledge of what will work.

Response

1. The "formless," the Tao, or Way, is the metaphysical ground of being, the matrix of natural law. The "great civilizing influence of ancient times" refers to the Way of government and leadership, which according to Taoist belief developed from emulation of natural law. The idea that adaptation and change are inevitable and necessary in government and law was a logical consequence of this way of thinking, but it was resisted by conservative Confucians.

2. Both inward and outward stillness are techniques for listening to others without influencing what they say by your reactions. Because Asian businessmen and politicians employ these techniques as a matter of course, Westerners who do not understand what is happening tend to think they are being typical "inscrutable Orientals." One of the techniques of mind control, of course, is to make use of stereotypes to trap attention within narrow limits; by knowing how to do this, stereotypees can even take advantage of stereotypers by manipulating the resulting blindness for their own purposes.

3. To use formlessness to inquire critically into that which is voiced means to exercise the ability to look at matters from all angles by virtue of entertaining no mental fixations or attachments, which would automatically affect one's perception and understanding.

4. People may be drawn to organizations by prospects of success and reward, or they may be drawn by a sense of affinity of aims and ideals, or they may be drawn by admiration and faith. It is essential to understand the nature of the attraction in order to understand the character of those attracted.

5. To work effectively with others, particularly in a supervisory or leadership capacity, it is important to understand their mentalities so as to be able to predict their patterns of response. Skillful use of language to establish a basis of communication also demands perceptive attention to the effects of specific words and images on each individual and each group in order to evolve a workable attunement of minds and ideas.

6. Sages of all the great spiritual traditions have been known for uncanny psychic influence over other beings, including plants, animals, ghosts, and spirits, as well as fellow humans. They also developed less invis-

ible ways of influencing the less sensitive and the more recalcitrant; these were imitated by enterprising and ambitious people, but without the inner knowledge of sages, the desired harmony could not be achieved, and so tyranny was adopted to take the place of the charisma that was lacking.

7. Listen before speaking, coil before springing, start at the beginning, sow before reaping. More of the seemingly paradoxical but actually logical Taoist tactics like those represented in this passage of *The Master of Demon Valley* are found in the *Tao Te Ching* (chap. 36), which calls this kind of strategy "subtle illumination" and explains its effectiveness by saying that "flexibility and yielding overcome adamant coerciveness."

8. The techniques taught by the Master of Demon Valley have applications for both leaders (or potential leaders) and those who are working (or may be considering working) with or for them.

9. This passage sums up the importance of discerning observation in managing people. The classic *Book of Change* says, "Overseeing by knowledge is appropriate for a great leader." It also says, "Attentive overseeing is auspicious and impeccable."

10. Equanimity and calm are needed for objectivity in assessing people, lest perceptions be distorted by temporary emotions. Even if you reject some things, it is important to understand them, because your rejection does not mean you will not have to deal with them or their consequences. Serenity and detachment are needed to gain objective understanding, not only of that which touches off obvious aversion or attraction, but also of that which seems relatively neutral and therefore does not set off such a clear signal of the need to examine one's opinions.

11. If you do not know yourself you cannot really know others, because you have no way to gauge the effect of unconscious subjective bias on your thought and perception. This is why Ch'an Buddhists, for example, used to insist on the absolute necessity of self-enlightenment before attempting to teach others. *The Art of War* says, "If you know others and know yourself, you will not be imperiled in a hundred battles" (chap. 3, "Planning a Siege").

12. To guide in a "round" or "rounded" way means to be flexible and ready to adapt; this is necessary "before you can see formations," when things are indefinite. To employ people "squarely" or "with rectitude" means to employ them in a just and reasonable manner, according to mutually recognized principles and standards; this is possible "once formations have taken shape" and it becomes clear just who is who and what is what.

13. The *Tao Te Ching* says, "Very great leaders are only known to exist" (chap. 17). The purposes of revealing no obvious form and maintaining privacy are to thwart interlopers, baffle would-be flatterers, and prevent mechanical routine from usurping the throne of real knowledge and compromising the ability to adapt to changing actualities in a sensitive and creative way.

Acceptance and Solidarity

1. Those who are on friendly terms in spite of distance are those who may have different histories and be in different situations yet spontaneously share similar outlooks and ideals, or people whose relationship is not essentially based on outward personality but on inner character. Those who are alienated in spite of closeness are personal or professional associates whose natures are not in psychological or spiritual harmony in spite of existing social and/or political alliances.

2. Someone who shows every sign of willingness to cooperate and be of service may be rejected, if the leader can see that this individual is really serving personal ambition and will therefore eventually betray the greater good. Someone who is willing to work for a government or organization, in contrast, may by this very act of conscience open the eyes of would-be employers to dysfunction in the working environment that would thwart the best intentions and efforts of even the most intelligent and able individuals.

It is related that one of the Sufi saints of thirteenth-century Spain who had the habit of denouncing tyrants regardless of possible consequences to himself was on one occasion imprisoned at the command of the grand vizier and sentenced to death. Brought up before the ruler for review, as was customary with cases involving capital punishment, the Sufi was asked if he had retained his belief in the unity of God. The Sufi recited some verses of sacred Recital and expounded their meanings to the sultan, who was so impressed that he asked the Sufi to join his court. At this the saint began to laugh at the ruler, telling him to go to hell, denying his right to rule, and venting his wrath upon the corrupt and decadent nobles and aristocrats of his court. Seeing that he couldn't hire the Sufi, the ruler presented him with gifts and a pardon. The saint accepted the pardon, returned the gifts, and went on his way. The grand vizier, meanwhile, who had been trying to get rid of the Sufi for a long time because he exposed the faults and evils of the powerful people of the time, was himself removed for his villainy and put to death.

3. Taoist manuals of leadership place particular emphasis on looking for talent in unknown places, in consideration of the fact that most of the self-seeking pretenders to knowledge are easily visible as they crowd around potential employers. The great strategist, general, and statesman Zhuge Liang of second-century China wrote, "For strong pillars you need straight trees; for wise public servants you need upright people. Straight trees are found in remote forests; upright people come from the humble masses. Therefore when rulers are going to make appointments they need to look

in obscure places" (*Mastering the Art of War*, "The Way of the General: Pillars of State").

4. Virtue can be interpreted to mean worthy and laudable qualities, or charismatic power, or even character in general, whatever it may be. Ties made by virtue may thus refer to bonds cemented by such feelings as admiration, trust, or the fascination of charisma; or to the general feeling of commonality and familarity sensed among people of similar character. Ties made by partisanship are commonplace bonds of mutual association involving sharing of agreements and conventions identifying that association. Ties made by money are also commonplace and may take many forms, from business arrangements to gifts and bribes. Ties made by sex range from political, social, and/or economic ties formed by marriage and concubinage to circles of personal and political influence cemented by gifts and bribes using sexual favors as a medium of exchange.

5. In the context of strategic arts, "going by others' wishes" is an application of the principle enunciated in the *Tao Te Ching*, "If you want to take, first you must give" (chap. 36). The idea is that in order to see what people have to offer in the way of ideas and abilities, and in order to discover what people really want and need, the best method is to go along with them for a while, becoming an emptiness to their fullness in order to elicit expression of what is within them, without distorting or deflecting anything by your own projections or reactions, like becoming silent to listen.

6. This passage depicts the hidden mastery of the sage going along with others selflessly in order to find out what they can do and what they need for the fulfillment of their lives. No one can see what the sage is doing at the time, like the spider leaving no traces. Therefore the sage is left to operate freely and see things as they are in themselves, without the interference of others' contrived opinions and devices, such as are always forthcoming "once formations are evident."

7. "Those who wish to be convincing strive to make their calculations in secret" because strategy without freedom to maneuver unexpectedly can hardly be effective. *The Art of War* says, "The formation and procedure used by the military should not be divulged beforehand" (chap. 1, "Strategic Assessments").

8. Threats and promises from a human source of authority are not as powerful as informed understanding of perils and possibilties. The skill of leadership in this case is to present principles and facts in a manner consistent with the interests of those in their charge.

9. Taoist teachings emphasize the importance of timing in all affairs, be they political, professional, or spiritual. The *Book of Change*, when read in a Taoist manner, is all about times and timing, showing how to meet each situation with an appropriate manner of response.

10. Internal contradictions can thwart measures even if they seem right for the external time. Therefore it is important to examine the structure of undertakings and establishments in themselves, as well as in terms of their coherence within the overall context in which they are expected to operate.

11. When speaking of the past, conventional terms are used at first (before the "bonding" of parties has been effected) in order to avoid creating useless emotional upset by contravening customarily accepted views of history. Adaptable words, such as abstract principles or general patterns, are used to speak of the future, so that they can accommodate the broadest possible range of contingencies and still retain useful and meaningful coherence.

12. This is a typically Taoist description of how sages are said to govern: not by trying to impose their own personal wills upon the national polity and the masses of the people, but by determining what is already there and skillfully arranging existing facts and forces such as they are in working relations designed to bring out the optimum efficiency and advantage possible under any circumstances. Thus in order to govern people, sages need to guide and direct them; to guide and direct people, sages need to know their aims and hopes; to know their aims and aspirations, sages need to watch what people undertake of their own accord.

13. Disharmony means something is unknown, because it is more the lack of knowledge, rather than the possibly sinister nature of the "something" itself, that makes constructive adaptation impossible. "Better the devil you know . . ." is one reflection of this principle.

"When there is collusion but not solidarity, there is overt alliance but covert alienation." The ability to discern this in opponents is half of victory.

14–15. These passages resume the idea of different combinations of intimacy and alienation introduced in the first paragraph of this chapter. The intervening passages have been dealing with specific principles of relationships; the concluding passages first summarize the extreme poles of working relationships, then turn to the use and purpose of this understanding.

16. This paragraph resumes the ideas introduced in paragraph 3.

17. A Ch'an Buddhist classic says, "When you meet a swordsman, draw your sword; do not recite poetry to one who is not a poet."

18. When you understand the mechanisms of formation and dissolution of relationships, you can employ them at will. In this context, relationships include those between or among individuals, and those between individuals or groups and the total context of events. Thus your actions can be successful if you can predict the reactions they will evoke; you can also use this knowledge to avoid or prevent action. The key point emphasized is to get the critical mechanism: the often unannounced "trial" testing the inner character of the individual is how this knowledge is used or unused.

19. Note that tyrants also have their versions of reason, virtue, humanity, justice, courtesy, and culture. Thus the Taoist sage Chuang-tzu said, "Nothing compares to using clarity."

20. Classical poetry and documents (such as would be included in the Bible, for example) provide a common ground for impersonal yet mutually meaningful discourse; thus such literature is especially useful as a matrix of conversation, in order to underline certain things without making it seem like insistence on subjective views. This device can be used to draw out others, and also to veil oneself if necessary; it can be used to clarify things to those with whom you wish to work, and also to muddle things for those who you wish would leave you alone.

21–22. Paragraph 21 is addressed to rulers and leaders; paragraph 22 is addressed to administrators and advisors.

"If the leadership is self-satisfied and pays no attention to what outsiders have to say, then laud it to the skies." People in positions of authority who are self-satisfied cannot hear anything but praise: so crafty advisors first get their attention by praise, then gradually sneak in advice on the "praise channel," making it seem to the otherwise heedless rulers like they thought of it themselves.

23. The *Tao Te Ching* says, "The great image has no form, the Way hides in namelessness; only the Way can lend and perfect" (chap. 41). It also says, "It produces but does not possess; it acts without presumption, it fosters growth without ruling: this is called hidden Virtue" (chap. 51).

Stopping Gaps

1. The near at hand is unseen when you only regard superficial appearances or strategic projections, and do not examine the underlying premises and intentions of what is said. The remote can be known when you heed the lessons of past events in order to predict the course of future events. The best-known and least effective version of the practice of "questioning the past to discern the future" is looking for someone or something to blame. The least-known and most effective version is seeking to find out what actually happened, how, and why, in order to obtain an intelligent understanding of causes and effects.

2. Different ways of closing a gap are used according to the nature of the opening. There may be countless variations, but some essential defensive or remedial tactics might be defined in general terms. A gap caused by a defect or deficiency is "shored up." A gap caused by the intrusion of alien elements is "repelled." A gap caused by inefficient or counterproductive activity is "stopped." A gap caused by an accidental or inherent weakness

is "hidden." A gap caused by a temporary breakdown in defense mechanisms is "overwhelmed." The expression "stopping gaps" can in some cases also be read, "striking gaps," in which case it represents offensive strategy (in contrast to preventative and defensive strategy).

3. Here the essentially preventative and defensive nature of the art is made clear. Offensive maneuvering (striking gaps), from this point of view, is legitimate only in the sense that surgery is a legitimate way to remove a malignant growth in order to restore the balance and harmony of the whole system. The *Book of Change* devotes particular attention to advice on these seven skills of personal success and leadership: preserving oneself in times of peril, clarifying things as they happen, mastering strategy, discerning the subtle, starting from slight beginnings, working against long odds, and nipping problems in the bud.

4. Early Taoist texts such as *Huainan-tzu* (see *The Book of Leadership and Strategy*) and *Wen-tzu* contain many diagnostic descriptions of malignant social and political behavior that is actually aberrant yet in fact the norm under certain conditions of ignorance and alienation.

5. The methods of "plugging gaps" noted here were expounded by followers of other philosophies, but the Taoists held the view that no particular method could be regarded as a fixed standard or unconditional imperative. The criterion of political orthodoxy, therefore, was seen by Taoists as a matter of effect rather than an issue of dogma.

6. Closing gaps is a means of "effecting a restoration." Opening gaps is a means of "effecting an overthrow."

7. "Sages are servants of heaven and earth," not of their own personal ambitions or their own party's agenda. This is not a moral injunction; it is simply a working definition of a "sage."

Excitation and Arrest

1. People of intelligence and ability will more likely be attracted to those who can in fact fairly judge them, because that is the most efficient way for both parties to make positive use of their perception and their talents. Charlatans and adventurers with private agendas are drawn to rich and powerful idiots, not to those who can see what is what.

2. To discern sameness and difference means to gain a thorough and detailed understanding of whatever is of concern, to see through superficial similarities and differences in order to determine what harmonizes with what, who is in tune, and who is on a separate line.

3. The idea is to get to know what kind of brains and abilities are around, and what kinds of problems need to be addressed; then it is possible

to go into effective action, after a truthful assessment of the relevant human and material factors.

4. "Hooking and clamping" means grabbing attention (or emotion) and fixating it on something. Excitation makes the brain more sensitized and susceptible to being "grabbed," and the experience of unconscious association causes one thus "grabbed" to be "arrested" (fixated) on the source of the excitement, or on something or someone perceived to be associated with or representative of that source. Professional advertising, including that branch of this industry specifically involved in political campaigning, has recognized and practiced this principle with enormous effect.

5–10. These and other strategies are also discussed in *Huainan-tzu* and *Mastering the Art of War*.

Opposition and Alliance

2. The point of "clarifying terms" is to establish an open, public standard by which public affairs can be measured and discussed. Specifically, the purpose is to make it impossible for pedagogues and politicians to distort public perceptions by habitual abuse of language (such as speaking exclusively in emotionally charged but otherwise vacuous clichés).

3. "The world has no fixed values." This statement, which is an observation anyone who lives more than a few decades can confirm in some sense, also has no fixed value. Here it means that sages do not arbitrarily impose on the world; as servants of heaven and earth, they "do nothing" for personal profit, yet "there is nothing they do not effect" when it is necessary to do so in order to maintain or restore the balance and harmony of the world.

4. The first sentence of this paragraph is a statement of the criterion for fairness and equitable justice in social policy. When fairness is lacking, then it is necessary to restore balance. The rest of this paragraph outlines the abstract principle of herding factions onto an open ground of objectivity and equal justice, discouraging bias and encouraging fairness.

5. If accurate evaluation is key to success in promoting fairness and justice, then fairness and justice are key to accuracy in evaluation.

7. Yi Yin was a Taoist man of knowledge who helped King T'ang found the Shang dynasty in the eighteenth century B.C.E. King Chieh was the last king of the Hsia dynasty preceding the Shang. Lu Shang was a Taoist man of knowledge who helped King Wen found the Chou (Zhou) dynasty in the late twelfth century B.C.E.

Figuring out Psychological Conditions

1. For material on Taoist character analysis, see *Mastering the Art of War*, "The Way of the General," and *Vitality, Energy, Spirit*, "On Human Characters."

2–3. See also Sun Tzu, *The Art of War*, "Strategic Assessments."

4. This paragraph cites another critical piece of psychological knowledge that is put to use today with tremendous effect.

5. The classical strategic device of inscrutability is like a two-edged sword; it can cut both ways.

Pressuring

Most of the content of this chapter bears a close affinity to the teachings of the Taoist sages Lao-tzu and Chuang-tzu. See *The Essential Tao* and *Wentzu*.

Assessment

1. "When you persuade people, you take your material from them," in that persuasion is accomplished by suiting, or appearing to suit, the ideas and feelings of others.

8. See Chuang-tzu, "The Human World."

12. Coercive agencies may use what appears to be reason or logic to induce emotional states, rendering the people thus influenced the more susceptible to specific types of suggestions and directions.

16. "When it comes to rhetoric, what is important is to be exceptional," insofar as the purpose of rhetoric is to capture attention and focus it on a specific point. The repetition of familiar slogans and clichés reinforces previously accepted conventions and convictions, but it also tends to lull the brain into a semiautomatic quasi trance that ultimately undermines the efficacy of the individual and group. The use of exceptional rhetoric is important when it is essential to boost perception to a new point of view.

Strategic Thinking

1. "Unexpected strategies" are unobstructed by reason of their very unexpectedness. This is the value of inscrutability.

"The perennial" is the Tao, or Way, which refers to the natural laws inherent in things. Following the Tao is the beginning of all strategy, because any effective measure needs to harmonize with the way things actually work.

3–4. These are directions illustrating how to analyze, formulate, or realign alliances according to the needs and potentials of the situation.

6. "Withdrawal gives rise to control" according to the Taoist theory of success, which states that a continued and unrelenting push for "progress" actually leads to breakdown and regression when it reaches a certain point. Those who know when to move forward and when to withdraw are the successful who master their options. Here, withdrawal does not mean regression, but a special kind of relaxation and removal, somewhat like the adjustment of a cooking soup from a preliminary boil to a maturing simmer.

10. "Prove them by surrounding" means to see how people handle pressures like the experience of being hemmed in on all sides.

15. "The Way of sages is covert" in not presenting an obvious target to interlopers.

Decision Making

4. The "four things" are yin, yang, yin within yang, and yang within yin. See "Opening and Closing," para. 1 of this same text. For fuller descriptions of pragmatic functions and combinations of yin and yang, see *The Taoist I Ching* and *Awakening to the Tao*.

6. In ancient times, court oracles were customarily read by a committee of scholars, not by individual soothsayers or fortune-tellers.

Talismanic Sayings

These sayings are mostly traditional Taoist teachings on the qualities of leadership. See the Huainan-tzu *for further context and detail.*

Basic Course: Seven Arts of Covert Correspondence

These materials are also Taoist teachings. See Wen-tzu *for further lessons in this vein.*

A. Invigorating the Spirit

1. For the "five energies" see "Invigorating the spirit," paragraph 7, and "Solidifying intent," paragraph 5. Also see *Understanding Reality*, II.17, and *The Inner Teachings of Taoism*, "On the Firing Process."

7. The "five energies" in this context are will, thought, spirit, and character, as named here, plus the basic energy of mind.

C. Solidifying Intent

3. Here again the defensive or preventative function of inscrutability is stressed. "Acquired" means artificial or unnatural; acquired moods or energies disturb the original equilibrium of the mind, thus causing an overflow or spilloff of feelings that is perceptible, subject to manipulation, and therefore hazardous to the one so affected.

5–6. See *Tao Te Ching*, chaps. 10, 47.

D. Dividing Power

1. Dividing power refers to defensive diversion and dilution of enemy powers.

2. The total concentration and unity of "being enveloped in the spirit" is needed insofar as "dividing power" is like driving a wedge into a gap; the wedge has to be solid and "pointed." The next section, entitled "Dispersing Momentum," pursues the same general type of maneuver, but from the angle of offensive tactics.

F. Transforming Freely

2. "Discerning myriad types by changes" is the purpose of the *I Ching* or "Book of Change," which analyzes the proportions and balances of forces that produce and guide changes in relationships, activities, and events.

6. "Transformation is the basis of examining plans" because plans cannot be judged as if they were applied to static situations, but must be seen as also being themselves participating factors in the evolution of ongoing situations. Their function and value have to be considered in the context of the processes in which they participate.

G. Focusing the Mind's Eye

2. There is a saying that virtuous people can be awaited but not sought. See *The Master of the Hidden Storehouse* for a fuller explanation.

4. "Wise people do not miss what others say just because they themselves can speak." This bit of wisdom applies to every department of life, not just matters of leadership.

9. At the conclusion of the chapter "Force," in *The Art of War*, Sun Tzu says,

> Letting the force of momentum work is like rolling logs and rocks. Logs and rocks are still when in a secure place, but roll on an incline; they remain stationary if square, they roll if round. Therefore, when people are skillfully led into battle, the momentum is like that of round rocks rolling down a high mountain—this is force.

Holding the Pivot

See *Tao Te Ching*, chap. 32.

Course from the Center

This chapter might be described as a Taoist course on uses of the mainstreams of current thought, including Confucian idealism, Legalist pragmatism, and Taoist psychology and strategic arts.

The Master of the
Hidden Storehouse

Preserving the Way Intact

The Master of the Hidden Storehouse lived for three years on the south face of Feather Mountain, during which time there was no sickness among the local folk, and the grain crops ripened regularly. The people privately said to one another, "When the Master of the Hidden Storehouse first came, we were surprised and thought him strange. Now we find our yearly income to be more than enough even though our daily income seems insufficient: could it be that he is a sage? Why don't we pray to him, and make a shrine to propitiate him?"

When the Master of the Hidden Storehouse heard about this, he appeared uneasy. A disciple tried to induce him to go along, but the Master said, "I have heard that people of ultimate attainment live independently in humble cottages, while ordinary people, in frantic madness, do not know where to go. Now the people of Feather Mountain are talking among themselves about propitiating me by ceremony—am I the man to be their target? This is why I am uneasy, considering the words of Lao-tzu."

The disciple said, "I disagree. A small pond has no room for a huge fish to swim around in, but a mud puppy can sport freely in it; a small hill has no place for enormous beasts to hide, but it is good for little foxes. Moreover, since the time of the ancient kings Yao and Shun it has been an established practice to honor the wise and employ the able, to invite the good and take to the beneficial; so why should the folk of Feather Mountain not do likewise? You should listen to them and let them do what they propose."

The Master said, "Oh, come now! Were Yao and Shun in the know? When a huge beast strays far from the mountains, nets and snares trap it; when a giant fish is beached, insects torment it. Therefore the abodes of birds and beasts should be in high places, and the abodes of fish and turtles should be in deep places. Now, when people who would keep their bodies and lives intact conceal themselves, they cannot be too deeply hidden or too remote.

"I tell you, the basis of great disorder has its roots in the time of Yao and Shun; and its aftermath will remain even after a thousand generations. After a thousand generations there will surely be people eating each other."

Now before the Master had even finished speaking, a certain earl in his audience became obviously uneasy; kneeling at his seat, he said, "I am getting old; how can I put aside my business to put what you say into practice?"

The Master of the Hidden Storehouse said, "Keep your physical body intact, embrace your life, don't let your thought and rumination work frantically: if you live out your years in this way, you may thereby be able to reach what I'm talking about.

"But even so, my ability is slight, insufficient to teach you. Why don't you go south and call on my teacher Lao-tzu?"

Once the Master of the Hidden Storehouse had sent the earl away, without making an explanations to the folk of Feather Mountain he made himself like a dragon in the world.

The nature of water is inclined to clarity, but when soil muddies it, water cannot be clear. It is in the nature of human beings to want longevity, but when things confuse human nature, people cannot live long.

Things are means of nurturing life, but many deluded people today use their lives to nurture things. Thus they do not know their relative importance.

Therefore, in matters of sound, color, and flavor, sages take what is beneficial for life and reject what is harmful to life. This is the way to preserve life intact.

If ten thousand people shoot in concert at a single target, no target will not be hit; when the disturbances of ten thousand things erode a single life, no life will not be injured.

Therefore the way sages govern myriad things is to keep their own nature intact. When nature is intact, then the spirit is intact. People in whom the spirit is intact can succeed without cogitation and hit the mark without planning. Their spiritual illumination is all-encompassing; their will stabilizes the universe; their virtue is as if heaven-sent. They may rise to become emperors, but that does not make them haughty; they may be lowly commoners, but that does not make them ignorant. These are people who keep the Way intact.

When the mind is even and straightforward, and not seduced by external things, that is called purity. If purity can be sustained for a long time, it becomes clarity. If clarity can be sustained for a long time, it becomes openness. When the mind is open, the Way abides there intact.

When one of the associates of Lao-tzu passed away, the Master of the Hidden Storehouse mourned him. His apprentice said, "Everyone in the world dies—why do you mourn him?"

The Master replied, "Everyone in the world mourns; how can I not mourn?"

The apprentice said, "But mourners grieve, whereas you have never sorrowed; what about that?"

The master responded, "I have no pleasure or happiness with anyone in the world—what would bring on sorrow?"

"Remove the solid, and there is liquid; remove liquid, and there is gas. Remove gas, and there is emptiness; remove emptiness, and there is the Way.

"Emptiness is the storehouse of the Way; tranquillity is the ground of the Way. Reason is the net of the Way; consciousness is the eye of the Way.

"The Way is the means of preserving the spirit. Virtue is the means of broadening capacity. Etiquette is the means of equalizing manners. Things are the means of supporting the body.

"In something that should be white, blackness is considered pollution; in something that should be black, whiteness is considered pollution. So how do we know what in the world is truly pure or polluted? For this reason, I do not focus solely on the purity or pollution of things.

"Those whose vision is dim mistake yellow for red and blue for gray. Now how do we know that what we call black and white would not be considered red and yellow by the perceptive? And how do we know what in the world are true colors? For this reason, I do not get lost in the colors of things.

"Those whose fondness for money is extreme do not see anything else as likable; those whose fondness for horses is extreme do not see anything else as likable; those whose fondness for books is extreme do not see anything else as likable. so how do we know what in the world is actually likable or detestable? For this reason I do not see anything to be attached to. Nothing can mix me up!"

The ruler of the state of Ch'en sent one of his grandees on an official visit to the state of Lu. One of the aristocrats of Lu said to him privately, "We have a sage in our state—do you know him?"

The grandee of Ch'en inquired, "What actually shows that he is a sage?"

The aristocrat of Lu replied, "He is able to still his mind and yet use his body."

The grandee of Ch'en said, "Although my humble state is small, we also have a sage; but he is different from the one you mention."

The aristocrat of Lu asked, "Who is that sage?"

The grandee of Ch'en answered, "Someone named the Master of the Hidden Storehouse, who is foremost of those who have attained the Way of Lao-tzu. He can see with his ears and hear with his eyes."

When Lord Ting of Lu heard about this, he considered the Master unusual. He had the aforementioned aristocrat return the visit to Ch'en and invite the Master of the Hidden Storehouse to the state of Lu, where he would be treated with the highest honor.

When the Master arrived at the court of Lu, he was received in the Lord's private quarters. The Lord of Lu questioned him in a humble manner, and the Master explained, "I can see and hear without using my eyes and ears; I cannot exchange the functions of eye and ear. Your informant was exaggerating."

The Lord of Lu exclaimed, "Who is like you? I am even more amazed. What is your Way? I really want to hear about it."

The Master of the Hidden Storehouse said, "My body is merged with mind, my mind is merged with energy, my energy is merged with spirit, my spirit is merged with nothingness. If there is the smallest object or the slightest sound, no matter how far away they are, they are as close as the space between my eyebrows and eyelashes. Whatever comes to me, I know it completely. And yet I do not know if this is sensed by my senses or limbs, or if it is known by my internal organs or conscious thought—apparently it is just spontaneous knowing."

Applying the Way

Heaven cannot be trusted, earth cannot be trusted; humanity cannot be trusted, mind cannot be trusted: only the Way can be trusted. How can intelligent rulers and outstanding scholars know this?

In ancient times, Chieh believed that Heaven had given him authority over the land; but since he did not apply himself to the Way, Heaven took his country away from him and gave it to the Yin dynasty. Chau also believed that Heaven had given him authority over the land; but he did not apply himself to the Way, so Heaven took his country away from him and gave it to the Chou dynasty.

Nowadays, lazy farmers believe the fruitfulness of the earth produces all grains, and they do not work on their Way: so earth deprives them of their crops and devastates them.

The Lord of Ch'i believed in human nature: he was courteous and deferential, but did not understand the Way clearly; he entrusted his whole realm to others, and they were in fact so greedy and rapacious that they took possession of his domain.

Whenever people fail to practice the Way and instead follow their minds obediently, calculations and desires proliferate, so troubles and afflictions act collectively to damage the body and reduce the life span. It is the mind that has injured them.

This is why it is said that only the Way can be trusted. Heaven and earth could not endure but for the Way. The common people cannot be orderly without the wise; government cannot be reasonable without the capable.

People who apply the Way do not reveal their function, but the blessings enrich all beings; they make nothing of their achievements, but secretly help others with unobtrusive efforts: and the common people think it happens to them naturally. Spiritually effective, work flourishing, ethereal joy endures forever.

To know this discursively is called perception; to know this non-discursively is called the Way. Perception is used to govern people; the Way is used to stabilize people.

Going to work at dawn, toiling under the sun, sweat dripping on the ground—this is the Way of farmers.

Picking up from below, taking from above, sharpening the mind, thinking diligently, concentrating thoroughly, seeking beneficial profit—this is the Way of merchants.

Absorbing energy to nurture the spirit, detaching from thought and rumination, transcending the world, rising lightly above it, taking in the vitality of the sun, and cultivating spiritual immortality—this is the Way of the highest intellectuals.

Detaching from emotions in order to think straight, devoting full attention to the principles of order for which they work, tirelessly planning so as to successfully manage their positions—this is the Way of public servants.

Purifying the mind, eliminating subjective thoughts, examining and testing close associates, diligently seeking the talented and the worthy to bring peace and security to all people—this is the Way of leaders.

When you class them in this manner, each follows its order: if they do their work steadily without a change of heart, then it is said that the land is imbued with the Way.

Exercise the physique, and the body will remain intact; pare away emotional desires, and the spirit will remain intact; be careful of your speech, and blessings will remain intact. Keeping these three things intact is called purity and goodness.

When you are full of the Way and virtue, then ghosts and spirits will help you. When your truthfulness and justice are rich, then cultivated people will cooperate with you. When your courtesy and righteousness are complete, then ordinary people will embrace you.

Those who are perceptive affirm themselves; those who are not perceptive also affirm themselves. Those who are imbued with the Way are calm and quiet; those who are ignorant and dull are also calm and quiet. There are certainly things that seem to be right but are wrong, and things that seem to be wrong but are right.

Those who lament at first may laugh later on; what starts out auspiciously may end up unfortunately. A person may be approachable, yet have talents that cannot be approached; one may have respectable talents, yet be unworthy of respect as a person.

When respect is extreme, then there is no familiarity; when familiarity is extreme, then there is no respect. People may distance themselves from you when you approach them, and they may approach you when you distance yourself from them. When favor is extreme, then resentment arises; when there is too much love, then hatred comes about.

In some cases, speed is valuable; in some cases, slowness is valuable. In some cases, directness is valuable; in some cases, indirectness is valuable. In all affairs, the reasons for what is appropriate are very subtle, but it is imperative to know them. This is why the wise consider it difficult.

When calm, the spirit is effective. When in straits, the will is effective. When one's rank is high, one's words are effective. When one is wealthy, one's person is effective. It is the course of nature that makes this so.

Those on the same path care about each other, while those with the same skill envy each other. Those who give the same things care about each other, while those who take the same things envy each other. Those who suffer the same illness care about each other, while those who are similarly robust envy each other. This is how human feelings naturally are.

Those who are very talented yet cleave to modesty, those who are poor and lowly yet do not flatter anyone, those who labor yet do not consider that disgrace, and those who are noble and rich yet all the more respectful and diligent—such people may be said to be imbued with virtue.

The Way of Government

People have no way to know how cold or hot the four seasons will be, or the courses of the sun, moon, stars, and planets. If they knew precisely how cold or hot the seasons were going to be, and how the celestial bodies would course, then all living beings would find their proper places and be secure in their productive activities.

Public servants also have no way to know how the rulers will distribute rewards and punishments, entitlements and emoluments. If they knew just how the rulers will distribute rewards and punishments, entitlements and emoluments, then everyone near and far, worthy and unworthy, would employ their talents and powers to the fullest in order to serve usefully.

When trust is complete, the world is secure. When trust is lost, the world is dangerous. When the common people labor diligently and yet their money and goods run out, then contentious and antagonistic attitudes arise, and people do not trust each other.

When people do not trust each other, this is due to unfairness in government practices. When there is unfairness in government practices, this is the fault of officials. When officials are at fault, penalties and rewards are unequal. When penalties and rewards are unequal, this means the leadership is not conscientious.

Now, when the leadership is conscientious, then penalties and rewards are uniform. When penalties and rewards are uniform, then officials obey the law. When officials obey the law, then order reigns. When order reigns, the common folk find their places and interact trustingly.

So we know that when the people do not trust each other, it is because the leadership is not conscientious.

The Master of the Hidden Storehouse lived in the state of Chou for five years. The king of Chou sent one of his nobles to him with a gift of silk and jewels, extending an invitation to the court of Chou.

The king said to the Master, "I am an insignificant person, lacking in virtue, a disgrace to the throne. The weather here has become irregular, with wet and dry spells at the wrong times, causing the people to suffer. How can I clear up this problem?"

The Master of the Hidden Storehouse said to the king of Chou, "Flooding is a yin disturbance. In government, yin typifies punishment; in social matters, yin typifies personal bias. Drought is an excess of yang. In government, yang typifies reward; in social matters, yang typifies plenitude.

"It seems to me that whenever there is a flood or a drought, the rulership should rectify punishments and rewards, the officials should eliminate personal biases and beware of excess. Then corresponding problems will disappear, and a hundred blessings will arrive day by day."

Among the treasures of the state of Cheng were a magnificent gem and a mighty bow from foreign lands. When at some point Cheng had lost political party with the state of Hsing, the latter demanded the gem and bow from the former, on pain of armed attack.

The ruler of Cheng, disturbed by this, went to see the Master of the Hidden Storehouse. The ruler said to the Taoist sage, "The gem and the bow were obtained from foreign lands by a past ruler of Cheng and have been passed on through generations as hereditary emblems of achievement.

"Now Hsing is taking advantage of its size to demand them, threatening my state with armed aggression otherwise. What I want to do at this point is take them another gem and bow; how would that be?"

The Master of the Hidden Storehouse said, "Please calm down a bit, sir. As a matter of fact, I also have treasures here, but to display my treasures and thereby occur the blame of a ruler is something I cannot do.

"You should hand over the real things. Hsing is now using a small mistake as an excuse for putting on airs of authority and behaving in an arbitrary and dishonest manner, ravaging its allies. It will lose the loyalty of the lords.

"At this point, it is a matter of the lords hearing about this, so that they can be alerted and urged to take precautions. Let them cooperate as equals, with diligence and intelligence, and higher justice will be preserved intact. Cheng will be a leader; just wait a while. Will that not be felicitous?"

So the ruler of Cheng took the foreign gem and bow to Hsing. Before he reached the capital, however, the people of Hsing had already heard about what had transpired. They said, "The ruler of Cheng is employing the advice of a sage. How can we take these treasures and thus expose our iniquity to the world, and cause the lords concern? Let's return the goods right away and treat Cheng better."

The human condition is to want to live and hate to die; to want security and dislike insecurity; to want glory and despise disgrace. When people get what they want, then they are happy; and when they are happy, then they are at peace. When people do not get what they want, then they are miserable; and when people are miserable, then they are insecure.

If leaders indulge their own desires, then officials and functionaries all extend their desires. If officials and functionaries all extend their desires, then everyone is affected: the poor are drained of their labor, the rich are drained of their wealth, and society loses its order; all people fail to obtain what they want.

When people fail to obtain what they want, then they band together for protection and flee into concealment and vagrancy, gathering wild fruits to live on. The police also pursue and arrest them. Thus the insecurity and misery of the people is unbearable; so mobs gather and rebelliousness grows. If there is mobbing and rebellion, then the state is no more.

Do not be greedy for population, or the common people will run from you. Do not build huge castles and moats, or the common people will tire of you. When taxes are unfair, the poor grow poorer day by day. When punishments and awards are arbitrary and discriminatory, the rich grow richer day by day. When regulations and prohibitions are not observed in practice, then the state crumbles.

If officials and functionaries lack ability, they lose the proper measure of leniency and sternness. They may even struggle with the common people for their own profit and advantage. Because of this, craft and deceit arise, which make people treacherous and unpredictable.

Now then, when the ruled are unpredictable, the rulers are suspicious; and when the rulers are suspicious, the ruled increase in confusion. Once the ruled are confused, the officials weary of their tasks.

When officials weary of their tasks, then awards are not adequate for motivation, and punishments are not adequate for deterrence. It is easy to cause a stir, hard to bring calm. This state of affairs is due to failure to find the right people for office.

The most essential thing in the art of government is to screen personnel. If people have the talent and conduct to harmonize a village, let them govern a village. If people have the talent and conduct to harmonize a county, let them govern a county. If people have the talent and conduct to harmonize a province, let them govern a province. If people have the talent and conduct to harmonize a state, let them govern a state. Only then is it possible to eliminate disaffection among the educated class.

When people do wrong in their villages, then they are to be admonished by their villages. If they do not reform, and deliberately do wrong, then they are to be beaten by county authorities. If they still do not reform, and deliberately do wrong, then they are to be exiled by the provincial authorities. If they do not reform, and deliberately do wrong, then they are to be executed by state authorities. Only thus is it possible to eliminate disruptive behavior.

When things are really done in this way, then no one in the world harbors sprouts of rebelliousness and contempt at heart. This is called bringing peace to people.

Of all the tasks of government, none is as great as finding people for public service. To prepare people for public service, nothing is as good as mastery of political science; and the best political science of all is bringing peace to people.

As far as ability to bring peace to people is concerned, generally speaking you will scarcely find 4 or 5 percent of those who have it if you test them by writing. If you test them by verbal discourse, you may find 10 or 20 percent. If you test them by psychology, behavior, and attitude, you will find a full 80 to 90 percent. This all refers, of course, to a felicitous age with a wise rulership having the clear perception and discriminating choice to make it possible.

By contrast, if it is a perilous age under an inferior rulership, if they choose people for public service by written tests, then those who indulge in artificial rhetoric show up more and more, while the upright and genuine increasingly disappear. If they choose people for public service on the basis of verbal discourse, those who are glib and superficially ornate show up more and more, while those who speak honestly and straightforwardly increasingly go into concealment. If they choose people for public service by psychological, behavioral, and attitudinal testing, then those who are outwardly upright but inwardly crooked are increasingly honored, while those who are pure, disciplined, enlightened, and genuine are increasingly obscure. In such cases, the more intellectuals get involved, the more biased government becomes; the more insistent commands become, the more disorderly people become.

A country is an enormous instrument; rulership is a serious position. If good people are found for public service, there is peace; if good people are left out, there is disorder. Leaders work hard to seek the wise and the good, and are lackadaisical about appointing ambassadors. How can those who would preserve Nature and unite humanity fail to treat good people seriously?

It is a profound disgrace for leaders when they lose the goodwill of their people. There is no more painful way to major loss of goodwill than punishment and imprisonment. When those with the power of clear understanding hear lawsuits, they may draw out the facts by pretense, or scare them out by threat, or bring them out by frankness: but even though the strategies they set up may differ, they are obliged to be impartial and fair. Thus they make it so that those who live do not feel gratitude to them, and those who die do not feel resentment toward them.

If the operation of national government, with the establishment of functionaries and maintenance of law, is done in this manner, that can be called perfect management. In an age of perfect management, the minds of the masses are harmonious and upright, all products are wholesome, and people communicate deeply with love and respect. The solidarity of upper and lower classes is unshakable, all beings are one family: even if there is some disorderly conduct or criminal misbehavior, how can that cause disturbance?

When King P'ing of the Chou dynasty restored order, once he had taken up residence in the capital he went to work looking for talented people. If he got to hear of even one example of goodness, he would be happy for days on end. The courtiers kept on telling him that there were intelligent and exceptional people among the great ministers.

Thus a year passed. The king said, "I am not enlightened in matters of virtue. While I strive to seek the wise and the exceptional, all the more it seems they run away to the wilds and will not take up public office. Why should I shut myself up listening eagerly to tales of goodness? These flattering courtiers keep on praising the great ministers to the skies; they must think I am weak and stupid, unable to determine facts clearly. They just band together, relying on each other, eventually ruining virtue by self-aggrandizement. And this is nothing yet—if I don't stop them in time, they will solidify their faction."

So the king had his three closest cabinet members executed in public, and banished five of the great ministers. He declared, "Let not those in the service of a government band with subordinates to destroy their leaders or hold onto their salaries by servile flattery."

When this was heard of throughout the land, King P'ing was lauded for impartiality and enlightenment; and seven states declared their allegiance to him.

In an age of perfect order, vehicles and clothing are plain, laws are accommodating and simple, the web of prohibitions is coarse. When vehicles and clothing are plain, then people do not struggle for the sake of envy and desire. When the laws are accommodating and simple, then the common people are not inhibited. When the web of prohibitions is coarse, then it is easy to avoid what is forbidden, and hard to transgress.

If people do not struggle for the sake of envy and desire, then their desires are few and they work at their jobs with zest. When the common people are not inhibited, then suppression is relaxed and they take pleasure in social relations. When what is forbidden is easily avoided and hard to get into, then good and bad are clearly distinct, and there is respect for virtue and a sense of conscience.

Working at your job with zest means accord. Taking pleasure in social relations means harmony. Respect for virtue and a sense of conscience means rectitude. Unstable people are incapable of accord, immoral people are incapable of harmony, dishonest people are incapable of rectitude. Accord, harmony, and rectitude constitute the basis of governing a state.

In a decadent era, vehicles and clothing are adorned elaborately, laws are many and complicated, and prohibitions are unfairly biased. When vehicles and clothing are adorned elaborately, then fashions fan the flames of desire. When laws are many and complicated, then the common people have many inhibitions. When prohibitions are biased and unfair, then no one knows how to avoid them.

When fashions fan the flames of desire, the people are not faithful and pure: they are ashamed of simplicity and value ostentation. When the common people have many inhibitions, then feelings and aspirations are not communicated, so the relationship between the rulers and the ruled is twisted. When no one knows how to avoid the forbidden, then intrigues will repeatedly occur, and the masses will not fear death.

To be ashamed of simplicity and value ostentation is called superficiality. When the relationship between rulers and ruled is twisted, this is called obstruction. When the masses do not fear death, this is called recklessness. Truly upright people have nothing to do with superficiality, fair and honest people have nothing to do with obstruction, and capable and talented people have nothing to do with recklessness. Superficiality, obstruction, and recklessness are steps to throwing a state into chaos.

The Lord of Hsing asked about flood and drought, order and disorder. The Master of the Hidden Storehouse said, "Flood and drought come from Nature; order and disorder come from humankind. If human affairs are harmonious and orderly, even if there are floods or droughts they cannot cause harm. That is why an ancient document says, 'When people are strong, they overcome Nature.' If human affairs are spoiled and confused, then even if there are no floods or droughts, there is daily dissolution. Do you think the downfall of ancient tyrants was only due to flood or drought?"

The Lord of Hsing bowed to the Master of the Hidden Storehouse and said, "Heaven has not abandoned me—that is why I have gotten to hear these words." Then he gave the Taoist sage ten pairs of large jewels and appointed him to an administrative post, saying, "I hope my state will be cured."

The Master of the Hidden Storehouse had no choice; camping out along the way, clad in light clothing, he fled to another land.

In an age of perfect order, there are no false hermits in the mountains, no dishonest profit in the markets, and no salaries for flattery at court.

One of the grandees of Cheng asked the Master of the Hidden Storehouse, "How can we get people's way of life to be pure and simple?"

The Master said, "When government is complicated and cruel,

then people are unruly and deceitful. When government is sparing and unified, then people are pure and simple.

"People's mores go along with the quality of the government, like insects that take on the colors of the leaves they eat."

The grandee asked, "How can the people be enriched?"

The Master of the Hidden Storehouse said, "Tax them according to the season, have officials be pure and frugal, and the people will prosper. If taxes are levied immoderately, and officials are extravagant and indulgent, then the people will be impoverished.

"The arrows of the southeast are tipped with pure gold and fletched with eagle feathers. If used for beating, they are no different from plain sticks; but when they are shot by powerful bows in war, no one can stand up to them within a range of three hundred yards.

"There is a marvelous sword with a brilliance outshining the sun and energy greater than a violet rainbow. If used for cutting grain, it is no different from a sickle; but when it is wielded against evil, viciousness, and unrest, nothing can stop it for a thousand miles.

"There are distinctions in capacities, and there are appropriate applications. What is important is skillful accord with the time.

"When there were enlightened leaders and sage rulers in ancient times, the land was at peace, all beings flourished, and all natures attained their peak development. They skillfully adapted to the times, and were disturbed by nothing.

"More recently, the dishonest are many and the honest are few; superficial profiteers abound, while conscientious and modest people are rare. Connivers speak out, without faith or truth. This has caused people everywhere to be suspicious and malicious toward each other. How sad it is!

"In the creation of laws, it is important to make them easy to abide by and difficult to transgress. When rectifying corruption, it is important to minimize projects and unify directives. Get rid of irresponsible behavior, and officials will be at ease. Make sure penalties are enforced, and officials will not dare to work for private personal profit. When officials dare not work for personal profit, then the common people prosper.

"The classical penal code says, 'Crimes committed by mistake are to be pardoned.' Pardon should not be repeated, for if pardon is repeated, then evil people will succeed in their schemes and ordinary people will get ideas, while the wise and the good are obstructed.

"People sometimes commit major crimes, for which they are arrested, but then they falsely implicate upright and good people, getting so many involved that they are ultimately pardoned in the interests of maintaining social order. Those who have been injured, in contrast, ultimately get no relief; all they have is their own bitterness and resentment.

"Because of this, ordinary people come to produce cunning schemes; officials are under stress, the government is cruel, and no one can put a stop to it all. This is due to the mistake of repeatedly granting pardons.

"The reason people do not like to do what is unethical or unjust is that there are penalties. The reason they strive to do what is right and just is that there are rewards. Now if the unethical and unjust are pardoned, while the ethical and just are envied and not rewarded, will it not be hard to induce people to take to goodness? If there are any intelligent leaders in the world, let them examine this thesis.

"When people are resentful, that does not mean you have nothing to do with them. When the gods are angry, that does not mean you do not worship them. When craftiness is extreme, people grow increasingly resentful; when obscene rites flourish, the gods grow increasingly angry."

THE WAY OF LEADERSHIP

What originates and produces is Nature; what develops and completes is humanity. One who is able to nurture what Nature has produced, such that people follow along, is called a true leader.

The action of a true leader is for the purpose of keeping the energy of Nature intact; this is why officialdom is established. The establishment of officials is for the purpose of keeping life intact. Under the deluded leaders of the present age, there are so many officials as to be, on the contrary, detrimental to life, thus losing the fundamental reason for the establishment of officials.

When grass is choked, it rots; when trees are choked, they are worm-eaten; when people are choked, they become ill; when a country is choked, a hundred troubles occur at once, and danger and chaos cannot be stopped.

What it means to say that a country is choked is that the favors of the leadership do not extent to the common people, while the wishes of the common people do not come to the attention of the leadership.

Therefore, sage rulers esteem loyal ministers and upright officers for having the courage to speak straightforwardly and cut through choking obstructions.

When rulers master themselves and return to order, then the wise and the good naturally come to them. When the king himself tills the soil and the queen herself makes cloth, the common people are spontaneously civilized.

From this point of view, the wise and the good are properly to be awaited, not to be sought. Those who are found by seeking are not sages. The common people are properly to be civilized, not to be tortured or killed; the practice of torture and execution is not true reason.

The ancient kings Yao and Shun had the diligence to be leaders, but not the desire to be leaders; thus all in the land were able to fulfill their wishes. Yao and Shun had the position of leadership, but not the ambition of leadership, so all in the land could relax.

Among the educated are those whom everyone in the land likes but the ruler dislikes; and there are those whom the ruler alone likes and everyone else dislikes. If those liked by everyone are employed, then the land is peaceful and secure; if those liked only by the ruler are employed, then the land is in peril. How can leaders indulge their personal likes and dislikes? To value those loved by the whole land, therefore, one should control one's own feelings.

The whole land includes all the beings therein; it is called a country in reference to its human population. Countries are based on people: if its people are secure, a country is secure. Therefore leaders who are concerned for their countries strive to find those who have the ability to manage people.

The reason jade is hard to distinguish is because there is another kind of stone that looks like it; the reason gold is hard to distinguish is that there is another kind of metal that looks like it. Now, if falcon feathers are pasted onto a quail, those who cannot see clearly will take it for a falcon, while those with clear vision will see it is a quail. These days there are many petty people who recite classics and esoteric writings, or study unusual arts or rhetoric: putting on elegant suits, they cause the ignorant who hear and see them to believe they are actually cultivated people. Those with understanding, however, see that they are really petty people.

Therefore, if the leadership is truly enlightened, it is reasonable to choose people based on what they say, it is reasonable to choose people based on their talents, and it is reasonable to choose people based on their actions. If the leadership is not enlightened, it is arbitrary to choose people by what they say, it is arbitrary to choose people by their talents, and it is arbitrary to choose people by their actions.

When sages employ people, they value the ability to not hear, the ability to not see, the ability to realize what cannot be said. Thus the common people are easygoing yet spontaneously orderly.

If leaders value the ability to hear, then everyone in the land will use their money and pursue profit in order to buy and sell fame and repute. If leaders value the ability to see, then everyone will seek advancement by exaggerated physical appearances and unusual arts. If leaders value the ability to speak, then everyone will adorn their words and speak glibly. Have everyone buy and sell fame and repute, compete for advancement, decorate speech, and seek distinction, and government is ruined.

Leaders all know that mirrors show what they look like, yet dislike it when educated people show what the leaders look like. The effectiveness of a mirror in showing a leader himself is small compared to the effectiveness of educated people showing a leader himself. To know the small but miss the great is ignorance.

If leaders would purify their hearts and minimize their affairs, and administrators would be respectful and frugal and mind their duties, then peace would arrive at once. And yet society seems to consider this difficult. I do not know. If the hearts of leaders are not clear and decisive, then all creatures lose the Way.

When people are picked by the ears and eyes, offices proliferate and government is confused. When people are picked by mind and thought, offices are minimized and government is pure. This is how we know that in an orderly and reasonable society effort is made to find people with abilities that cannot be seen or heard, while in a corrupt society effort is made to get people with abilities that can be seen or heard.

Do leaders know this? If people are picked by the ears and eyes, then everyone will take whatever they can get in order to buy a reputation. If people are picked by mind and thought, then everyone will strive for virtue calmly and correctly. When officials strive for virtue calmly and correctly, then people become civilized even if not told to do so. When officials take whatever they can get in order to buy a reputation, then people are not intimidated even by punishment. Do world leaders know this?

THE WAY OF ADMINISTRATORS

When a country is going to rise and flourish, the officials at court have weaknesses and strengths; some are repulsive, some are attractive, some are genial, some are stern, some are right, and some are wrong. When you listen to their words and observe their appearances, they seem to be dissimilar, but when you look into their aspirations and examine their hearts, you find them thoroughly dedicated to service of the nation. Therefore they are not resentful when strongly attacked, and they are not disturbed when dismissed from office. Knowing the mean, they do not deviate from reason; therefore Heaven does not confuse their timing, Earth does not diminish their gains, people do not disrupt their affairs. Ghosts and spirits sing praises, and foreign nations harmonize. Great peace being kept together, all beings develop and grow.

When a country is going to perish, the officials at court are splendidly attired, their countenances are harmonious, their speech is flowery and genteel, their movements are careful and elegant. Although the administration of a moribund country may outwardly appear to be harmonious and obedient, inwardly the officials harbor suspicions and aversions, each pursuing his own personal aims, secretly plotting each other harm. When you observe their appearance and listen to their words, they seem to be happy and harmonious, but when you look into their aspirations and examine their hearts, you will find them competing for rank. That is why they are suspicious when they hear of something unusual and startled when they see something different. Envious of each other, keeping each other in ignorance, ultimately they lose the right Way. Therefore Heaven declares disasters and Earth produces weird things. People act evilly, and ghosts and spirits cause calamities. Foreign peoples repeatedly invade, loss and chaos run rampant, and nothing develops.

When work is accomplished and government is established without ruining finances, overstraining workers, or interfering with officials, such that those below are treated well and the appreciation of the leadership is won, those who do this are loyal and wise administrators.

If they waste money, overburden people, endanger officials, take pride in temporary successes in hopes of rewards from the rulers, pay no heed to their mistakes, and leave a disastrous legacy to the nation, these are treacherous administrators.

In an age of perfect order, people are found for offices. In an age of order, offices are found for people.

The Master of the Hidden Storehouse was asked how to work for a leader. The Master said, "Once you become an administrator, your mind should be impartial, your demeanor should be harmonious, and your speech should be correct. Impartiality should not be overbearing, harmonization should not be random, and correctness should not be offensive.

"What was pure diligence in perfecting government for service of the nation in ancient times has now become pure diligence in cultivating repute in service of the self. When those who work on perfecting government for the sake of the country handle matters and clarify their reasons, their actions are appropriately suited to the totality. When those who cultivate a reputation for their own sakes handle matters and clarify their reasons, they do not understand the long run and get stuck in small measures.

"So we know that when the mind is directed by the Way, then when one encounters affairs one finds the appropriate placement. When mind is directed by affairs, then when one encounters things one misses the appropriate placement.

"If ministers in high positions do not criticize the leadership constructively, or if ministers of lesser rank are not fair, they should not be given their salaries. If the leader is not dignified and serious, and the great ministers do not show trust, then lesser ministers should not work for that court.

"The talented are not necessarily loyal, the loyal are not necessarily talented. Ministers do not worry about not being loyal; they only fear being totally loyal yet still not being trusted by the leadership. Leaders do not worry about not trusting; they only fear trusting those who cannot handle business.

"When people of higher caliber can be themselves, the world is orderly. When people of mediocre caliber can be themselves, the world is disorderly. When enlightened leaders employ people of higher caliber, they should entrust them with the authority to adapt to changes, not interfering with their actions. When they employ people of mediocre caliber, they should regulate their activities and direct them by means of rewards and punishments."

THE WAY OF THE WISE

The reason why the wise and the good do not go even where they are repeatedly invited, hardly advance and easily withdraw, is not that they are so concerned about themselves that they will not die for the public good; it is just that they fear exercising utmost loyalty yet not being trusted by leaders.

Those who know themselves to have talent and perception are outwardly respectful and conscientious; thus inwardly they have no anxieties. Their relationship to the masses is correct and not contemptuous. Treated familiarly, they are all the more dignified; alienate them and they leave, yet without resentment. In desperation and danger, they ease their minds by accepting it as fate; in glory and success, they correct themselves by means of the Way.

There are those who appear to be wise, and sound as if they are wise, but on examination of their spirit and perception, they may disappoint expectation.

As for people who actually are wise, when they are in office they criticize and commend, and when out of office they maintain silence. At work, they are diligent and competent; at home, they are frugal and reserved. When they are not employed in public service, they conceal themselves among the masses, conceal their perception in their eyes, conceal their words in their mouths. Eating to their fill, they walk in peace, taking care of themselves as best they can in private, upright and unembittered.

The wise do not have doubts about events; the perceptive do not have doubts about people. People with perception are strict in their behavior, yet their demeanor is not distant; their speech is conciliatory, yet they cannot be dissuaded from reason.

Those who are worthy of the name "wise" do not call themselves wise. The test of their efficacy is in civil administration; the merit of their achievement is in managing affairs.

In a time of great peace, the best people use their perception and knowledge, mediocre people put forth all they can, and lesser people contribute their strength.

There was a man of Ch'i named P'ou-tzu, "The Exactor," who had the talent to manage a country, and had the discipline to be independent. He took care of his parents and was respectful to his neighbors. Considering that he was poor and had no material resources, for a long time he went around giving out truthfulness and justness. Wherever he went, few sympathized; sometimes he was ridiculed and tricked by opportunists.

Because of this, he went to the Master of the Hidden Storehouse and asked, "I have heard that perfect people forget feelings, while ordinary people cannot employ feelings constructively. Those who retain feelings strive to educate them, honoring truthfulness and justice.

"Now I consider not minding to be a skill, and regard not being trusted as being truthful. Being truthful yet not being trusted is truthfulness. Deliberate diligence aspiring to justice is considered justness, but I consider justness being just without expecting justice.

"Therefore troubles recede from the truthful and the just as long as they are always alone; how can they gain honor in their time and teach what reason places foremost?"

The Master of the Hidden Storehouse looked down, his chin to his chest, then he looked up and sighed. Serenely aloof, he began to sing:

> When the time is positive,
> truth and justice shine.
> When the time is silenced,
> truth and justice hide.
> Positivity or silence, shining or hiding,
> I have no personal standpoint at all,
> I do not know what to say.

"If you operate true nature in such a way as to conform to what is appropriate," the Master continued, "and yet no one responds, that means truth is not current. When truth is not current, furthermore, that is called loss of the Way.

"In times when the Way is lost, superior people hide. The reason concealment is just is that nothing can be done."

,

Lord Chi asked the Master of the Hidden Storehouse, "In what way can the wise and talented be attracted?"

The Master said, "The wise should properly be awaited, not sought. Talent is there if you take care of it; if you seek it without care, it is not there.

"If the ruler is peaceful and the ministers are enlightened, if the upper clases are not exempt from punishments and the lower classes are not excluded from benefits, then wise people will come on their own to seek employment.

"When wise people are employed, all within the four seas hear with clear ears and see with clear eyes; they are even minded and have no depression. The weather naturally fulfills its cycle, the earth is naturally peaceful, myriad beings evolve, and ghosts and spirits cannot affect anything.

"That is why it is said that the wise should properly be awaited, not sought. If personnel are sought by a ruler who is diligent and enlightened and by great ministers who are harmonious and orderly, then this will attract those who are broad-minded, magnanimous, impartial, honest, and able to bring peace and stability to the people.

"If personnel are sought by a ruler who is cruel and demanding and by great ministers who are impulsive and hasty, this will attract people who are evil-minded, opportunistic, destructive, and immoral.

"If personnel are sought by a ruler who is suspicious and by great ministers who are crafty and servile, this will attract strange people who show off weird arts.

"If personnel are sought by a ruler who considers himself wise and by great ministers fixed in their positions, this will attract superficial people who seek praise, are polluted by greed, and are ostentatious in outward display.

"If personnel are sought by a ruler who is capricious and whimsical and by great ministers who are devious and dishonest, this will attract people who are outwardly loyal but inwardly crooked, whose feelings are poison but whose words are conciliatory.

"This is why it is said that talent is there if you are careful, but not if you seek it without care.

"When ancient kings found wise ministers, it was through a scientific and logical process. When a ruler embodies the Way, exhalts humaneness, spreads enlightenment, is both wise and valiant, thoughtful and congenial, brilliantly luminous, magnanimous and considerate, correct and upright, then the wise will spontaneously gather, seeking employment in public service. They are not found by selection."

Lord Chi asked, "You say that the wise will come spontaneously, without being sought. Will unwise people also come on their own, without being sought?"

The Master of the Hidden Storehouse replied, "The unwise who come of their own without being sought are sure to be numerous! When the land has the Way, then wise people spontaneously come without being sought; when the land lacks the Way, unwise people come on their own without being sought. Human leaders who have the Way are rare; human leaders without the Way are plentiful. There are few good and wise people in the world, and many unworthy people. Obviously the unwise who come on their own without being sought will be numerous."

Lord Chi asked, "The wise can certainly manage the land, and the talented can also manage the land. How do the wise and the talented differ?"

The Master of the Hidden Storehouse said, "That is a very pointed question! Those who do not pursue entitlement and honor when their work is done and their task accomplished, but are gracious and retiring, simple and frugal, are those who are called wise. Those who glory in remuneration and honor when their work is done and their task accomplished, who glorify their fulfillment of aspiration, are those who are called talented.

"The wise can keep a nation secure, the talented can keep a nation orderly. Keeping a nation secure is harmonious, peaceful, and uncontrived, so people are not aware of that power. Keeping order involves diligently taking a leading role in affairs, so people know where to attribute the credit.

"One wise person is more than able to direct many talented people, but even a multitude of talented people cannot take the measure of a single wise person.

"Such are the different domains of the wise and the talented.

"There are those who live in mountain forests yet are still clamorous; there are those who live in ordinary society yet are calm. There are those who are clamorous but upright, and there are those who are quiet but devious. People who appear to be base and vulgar yet can be sagacious are so rare as to be hardly one in ten thousand. People who are proper and elegant in appearance yet are really petty people are so common as to be fully nine out of ten.

"Those who understand writings without working on the wording, who assess measure without fussing about individual manners, who know the good regardless of whether people praise them, and who stop the bad regardless of criticism, these can be called the perceptive."

THE WAY OF EDUCATION

Min Tzu-ch'ien [son of a disciple of Confucius] asked Confucius, "How far apart are the Way and filial piety?"

Confucius replied, "The Way is a sublime function of Nature; filial piety is a supreme virtue in the course of human life. What envelops and operates the universe, produces and develops all beings, perfects the forms of all species, disburses nature and life, is most real in effect and is not ruled by beings, not governed by things, not controlled by effort, not accessible to the senses, and yet is there—this is called the Way.

"When this is used in the human context, it is called filial piety. Filial piety means serving your parents well. Serving your parents well is based on respect and obedience. When you are consciously receptive to them, the outward manifestation of obedience reaches everywhere. Whatever you say, whatever you think, you dare not forget your parents; with each action, each step, you dare not forget your parents. In government service, you dare not be disloyal; in association with friends, you dare not be unfaithful. In dealing with subordinates, you dare not be disrespectful. In promoting good, you dare not be lax. Even when you are alone indoors, you still dare not relax your sincerity. This is called complete filial piety.

"So filial piety is the consummation of sincerity. It reaches the spirits and illumines the land. When something is sensed, there is unfailing response; this is a result of serving your parents well.

"In ancient times, the great filial piety of the sage King Shun was such that even though his father's concubine fooled his father into attacking him repeatedly, Shun was ever more respectful and deferential, harboring no resentment. His father had him go down into a well to dig it deeper, and then had it filled in with earth. At this time, Heaven quaked its approval of Shun, and the spirits raced to light up a way for him to get out through a hole. After that he supported his father even more circumspectly. Due to this, his mysterious virtue flourished, and he became the ruler of the land. This was a result of serving his parents well.

"When King Wen was crown prince, his great filial piety was such that every morning and evening he would go to the threshold of the royal chambers and ask the attendants how his parents were. When he was told they were fine, the crown prince would smile warmly. If they were a bit out of sorts, the face of the crown prince would be filled with anxiety. At mealtimes, the crown prince would unfailingly see that the food was neither cold nor too hot; in the course of meals he would unfailingly supervise the portions and then withdraw.

"If the attendants announced an illness, the crown prince would formally fast. The crown prince would respectfully examine their food and personally taste their drink. If the food tasted good to the king, the prince would also be able to eat; if the king tasted little of the food, the prince would not be able to eat to satiety. When the king recovered from illness, only then would the prince also revert to normal. If the queen mother made a mistake, the crown prince would admonish her in a pleasant tone of voice; he would always be respectful toward anyone or anything the queen liked, even her pets.

"Thus, filial piety perfected in himself, his Way spread through the land. A classic song says, 'The ascent and descent of King Wen was assisted by Nature in both calm and action, both advancement and retirement.' This is why the tyrant Chau was not able to assassinate him. He was informed by a dream how long he would live, and he divined a thirty-generation and seven-century reign for the dynasty he established, as decreed by Nature. This was a result of serving his parents well."

Min Tzu-ch'ien said, "Now that I have had the fortune of hearing about the logic of serving our parents well, may I ask about the principles of educating children?"

Confucius responded, "When the Three Kings educated their children, they always taught them etiquette and music. Music is a means of cultivating the interior, etiquette a means of cultivating the exterior. When etiquette and music are cultivated together, then the countenance of virtue shines in one's appearance, so one can be warm yet reverential, cultured and civilized.

"The vassal of another will even kill himself if it would benefit his lord; how much the more will he do what profits himself if it is good for his lord. Therefore, the kings selected people who were true and upright to establish as royal tutors for their children, wishing their children to know the ways proper to parents and children, rulers and subjects, the old and the young.

"Only after you know how to be a son can you become a father. Only after you know how to work for someone else can you become the director of others. Only after you know how to serve others can you employ others. These are the Three Kings' principles of educating children."

Min Tzu-ch'ien withdrew and put this into practice at home. After three years, no words were said causing division among members of the family. His associates praised his trustworthiness, his neighbors praised his humaneness, his clan praised his brotherliness; the fame of his virtuous behavior flooded the land. This was a result of serving his parents well.

The crown prince of Ch'i was sitting in an observatory tower. Chuang T'a, Lord of Yen, showed up in a tall hat, with a dignified appearance, wearing a jade-hilted sword in his belt at his left side, with a jade ornament hanging from his belt at his right side, so lustrous that the shine of the left lit up the right, and the shine of the right lit up the left.

The crown prince, reading a book, paid no attention to him.

The Lord of Yen asked, "Does the state of Ch'i have a treasure?"

The crown prince said, "The ruler is trustworthy, the ministers are loyal, and the farmers support the government. This is the treasure of Ch'i."

Hearing this, the Lord of Yen took off his sword and left.

Ah, well! If people have biases and blind spots, they never get to know themselves. The wise view them with magnanimity and forgiveness, and do not criticize. Petty people talk too much out of contempt and attraction. Parents and relatives disagree in their sympathies and jealousies. When people have biases and blind spots, how do they not know themselves?

This is why cultured people examine themselves at all times to see if they have any faults. Wearing the appropriate clothing, eating the appropriate food, if they realize when they are at fault and are unable to correct it, cultured people consider this shameful.

When they want to say something but know it cannot be put into practice, cultured people seldom speak. When they are to criticize the evils of the hoi polloi, they look to see if they themselves are good. When they are to criticize the perversity of the hoi polloi, they look to see whether they themselves are upright. This is called introspective clarification.

The son of Mr. Ti Hsi was very dutiful and diligent. Ti Hsi cared for his son, but liked to fool him. Ti Hsi went out one morning and returned home at night to announce that so-and-so had died. His son believed him, even though that person was still alive. Another night, he announced that a certain individual had done him harm. His son went to get revenge, but found that no wrong had been done. Another night, he declared that such-and-such a person was ailing. His son went to see the patient, only to find that there was nothing wrong with him. It was like this every time.

As the years went on, Ti Hsi's son was certainly dutiful and diligent, but when it came to what his father told him, the son felt less and less confidence in what he heard from his father.

Eventually the people of the locality got sick and tired of Ti Hsi's misleading talk, and they plotted to kill him. Ti Hsi heard about this and ran home in fear to tell his son. His son did not really believe him, and so Ti Hsi got killed.

People who talk a lot are called indiscreet, but there are also people of few words who do not keep secrets. Compulsive people are called unstable, but there are also those who are physically relaxed yet mentally excitable. Promiscuous people are called base, but there are also those who are outwardly pure while inwardly polluted. No end of similar examples could be cited: if not for penetrating perception, how can you find out the whole truth?

At times when there are things to which one cannot but respond, even if inwardly still, one is outwardly active; it is easy to act and hard to be still. At times when there are things that one cannot but seek, one is inwardly pensive while outwardly expectant; after what is anticipated arrives, one is happy.

Therefore, those who are outwardly calm but inwardly astir damage their nature by activating thought. Those who race after profit injure their reputations by exerting efforts.

There may be things in human life that do not succeed as one wishes; in such circumstances, to announce that the time is not right is no different from accepting the death sentence and waiting to be executed. Is that not dangerous?

People of tremendous talent and comprehensive knowledge who have been employed should properly say it is not that the age is impure, but that destiny has not yet given the command; would that not be so?

Those who are skilled at criticism strive to preserve the essential nature of the persons they are addressing, while trimming and regulating that from which their feelings arise. Because of this, both sides make progress; they are friendly and respectful, earnest and serious.

Those who are not skilled at criticism strive to attack the essential nature of the persons they are addressing, yet are ignorant of the source of their feelings. Because of this, enmity and suspicion build up day after day.

What children choose is rejected by the elderly; what the ears and eyes enjoy is disliked by the intellect. Those who fiercely blame the ignorant of the world are themselves as yet unwise; those who fiercely blame the confused of the world are themselves as yet unenlightened. When the unwise criticize the ignorant masses, the unwise perish because of it. When the unenlightened criticize the confused masses, the unenlightened suffer because of it.

THE WAY OF AGRICULTURE

If people abandon the fundamental for the secondary, then there is disunity. Without unity, defense is impossible, and war is not feasible.

If people abandon the fundamental for the secondary, then their productivity will be limited. When productivity is limited, people easily drift into vagrancy. When people easily drift into vagrancy, the country suffers disasters from time to time, and everyone wants to emigrate, no longer wishing to live there.

When people abandon the fundamental for the secondary, then they crave knowledge; and when they crave knowledge, there is a lot of deceit. When there is a lot of deceit, then laws are artificially elaborated. When laws are artificially elaborated, then what is right is considered wrong, and what is wrong is considered right.

The means by which ancient sage kings governed people was by first striving to get people to farm. Getting people to farm is not just for the sake of amassing profits; what is valued is carrying out their aims.

When people farm, they are uncomplicated; when people are uncomplicated, they are easy to employ. When people are easy to employ, the land is secure; when there is security, the leadership is respected.

When people farm, they are innocent; when they are innocent, they have few personal prejudices. When people have few personal prejudices, then fair common law is established, with deep and far-reaching power.

When people farm, their produce is abundant. When their produce is abundant, they do not drift into vagrancy. When they do not drift into vagrancy, they live out their lives where they are, without second thoughts, and the whole land is of one mind. Even the social order of ancient sage kings was not beyond unifying the hearts of all in the land.

The reason ancient sage leaders worked at plowing and spinning was to make these basic education. That is why emperors personally led the lords in plowing the sacred fields of the ancestral shrines, and the grandees had ranks according to their work; it was to encourage people to honor productivity. The empress and the concubines would lead the palace ladies in raising silkworms in the suburban mulberry groves and public fields as an instructive example for housewives.

Males do not weave, yet they wear clothes; females do not plow, yet they eat. Men and women exchange the fruits of their labor, helping each other do their work. This is the system of the sage kings.

Therefore they respected the seasons and loved the days; they measured their fruits to determine accomplishments. They did not stop working unless they were old, and did not take time off unless they were sick. One person working thus could feed ten people.

When they were engaged in seasonal work, they did not undertake major construction projects and did not equip armies. The men did not take wives from elsewhere, and the women did not go elsewhere to marry. The men did not go out riding, and the women did not take trips, because that would interfere with agriculture.

The Yellow Emperor said, "The four seasons cannot be corrected. We only correct the five grains." The one who sows and cultivates them is humanity; the one who creates them is Heaven; the one who nurtures them is Earth. Therefore the sowing requires feet, raking soil over newly sown grain requires a harrow, weeding requires hands. This is called the Way of tilling.

Agriculture takes care of food, crafts take care of utensils, commerce takes care of money and goods. If the seasonal work is not respected and is usurped by construction projects, this is called a great ill. When the sowing is too early, it is ahead of the season; if too late, it is behind the season. If cold and heat are irregular, the crops suffer many blights.

The earth produces growth fifty-seven days after the winter solstice; this is when the first plowing is done. The Way of agriculture is to sow the living when seeing life, and to reap the dead when seeing death.

Heaven creates the seasons and produces wealth without making promises to humankind. In years of abundance, honor the earth; in fruitless years, honor the earth. Do not miss human timing; act when the time is right, desist when the time has passed. Then the old and young can be fully aroused.

Those who do not know the timing of the seasons violate them before they have even arrived and long for them after they have gone; and right at the precise timing of the season, they slight it. This is the lowest way of going about the work.

Plowing should be done in dry weather, making the soil fertile and the earth warm. Crops like to germinate in soft soil and grow in firm earth. Be careful not to sow seed too thickly or too sparsely, and do not spread too little or too much soil over it. Irrigation channels should be deep and straight, and fields should be moistened evenly.

When there is yin (water) below and yang (sunlight) above, only then does everything grow. When seedlings are set out in rows, they grow quickly; because the strong and the weak do not encroach upon each other, they enlarge rapidly. Keep the rows straight, with space in between to let the air circulate. Then there will be a harvest, at a highly efficient rate of return on labor.

If crops look abundant from a distance but turn out to be sparse when you get up close, this means the soil is depleted. When ground grows wild when not weeded, but nothing grows after it has been weeded, that means the soil has been damaged by the way it has been treated.

When sprouts are young, they should be separate; when grown, they should be together; when ripe, they should support each other. Set them in groups of three, and the plants will produce much fruit.

Seedlings are affected negatively when they do not grow in unison and die in unison. This is what makes the first to grow produce fine grain, while that which grows later makes only empty husks. Therefore when you thin them out, you let the earlier ones grow and remove the later ones.

When planting on fertile ground, do not crowd seedlings; when planting in poor soil, do not isolate them. If you plant too thickly on fertile ground, there will be a lot of empty husks; if you plant too thinly on poor soil, many of the plants will die. Those who do not know how to cultivate will get rid of the earlier ones and nurture the later ones, with the result that they reap husk instead of grain.

When conditions above and below are unstable, much of the crop dies. Grain in good season has long stems, big stalks, round kernels, and thin husks. The grain is sweet and fragrant, easy to polish, and nutritious. Mistimed grain has long beards, small stalks, slender kernels, a lot of bran, and the fruits tend to fall off while still green.

Millet in good season has ears without long tassels; the grain can be removed by hand, and there is little bran. Mistimed millet has big roots, flowering stalks, big leaves, and short ears.

Rice in good season has large stalks with long joints and ears like horsetails. Mistimed rice has slender stalks and is not thick; it is poor and dies in the fields.

Hemp in good season has sparse nodes and is light in color; it has strong fibers and small roots. Mistimed hemp has many branches, short stems, enlarged nodes, and worm-eaten leaves.

Beans in good season have long stalks with short feet; their pods are clustered in double sevens; they have many branches, sparse nodes, luxuriant foliage and plenty of fruit, which weighs in heavy and is filling when eaten. Mistimed beans stretch out like creepers, with insubstantial foliage and weak roots, few nodes and small pods.

Wheat in good season has long stalks in clusters, with heads of double rows of seven, thin husks and tawny color; it is rich in calories and nutrition. Mistimed wheat is tubercular and sickly, with weak seedlings and excessive beards.

Therefore crops in good season are abundant, while mistimed crops are limited. The cereals are all good to eat accordingly; they strengthen people's limbs and make the ears and eyes clear and bright, so injurious energies do not get in, and the body suffers no cruel disasters.

Excellent indeed are the words of Confucius: "Eat enough in winter, and the body is warm; eat enough in summer, and the body is cool." When warmth and coolness are appropriate to the season, then people have no sickness or fever. When people have no sickness or fever, then epidemics do not go around. When epidemics do not go around, all can live out the years given by Heaven.

Therefore it is said that grain is the heaven of the people. This is why kings who prosper work at agriculture. If kings do not work at agriculture, they are abandoning the people. If kings abandon their people, what constitutes their countries?

THE WAY OF WAR

When King Ching of Ch'in was going to show his military strength to the world, he sent an emissary to fetch the Master of the Hidden Storehouse, to whom he offered fifteen conquered towns as an inducement.

When the Master of the Hidden Storehouse arrived, he was given lodging in the quarters reserved for important guests. King Ching was unable to ask him any questions for three days.

Taking a lower seat and humbly according fullest respect to the Master, the king said, "Has Heaven no intention of pitying me?"

The Master of the Hidden Storehouse serenely looked to the side and said, "I thought the king would ask something different. Why are you so distressed? Because of killing. Being pressed, I will go along with your wishes, so that you can find out how to do it correctly; but that does not mean it is right."

The king made a full prostration, rose and straightened his robe, then sat formally with bowed head and said, "Whatever Heaven commands."

The Master of the Hidden Storehouse looked up at the eaves and sighed, then lowered his face. With a somber mien, he said, "War has existed ever since humankind has existed. All wars come from human force. Forcefulness in humans is received from Heaven. Therefore war comes from above, and there is never a time when it is not in operation. The upper and lower classes, the old and the young, the wise and the foolish, are the same in this.

"When you look into the signs of war, they are in the mind. When there is anger at heart but it has not yet been expressed, this is war! Hateful looks and angry faces are war. Boastful words and shoving matches are war. Exaggerated contention and aggressive combat are war. These four are conflict, large and small.

"Even before Pao Kou [who opposed the Yellow Emperor in the

twenty-fourth century B.C.E.], people actually took up pieces of wood and fought. The Yellow Emperor used water and fire. Kung Kung fomented disorder. The Five Emperors struggled with each other; one was deposed as another arose, with the victor taking charge of affairs.

"There are those who have died from ingesting drugs, but it is wrong to wish to ban all medicines because of that. There are those who have died sailing in boats, but it is wrong to forbid the use of boats because of that. There are those who have lost countries by waging war, but it is wrong to wish to ban all warfare because of that.

"Warfare cannot be dispensed with, any more than water and fire. Properly used, it produces good fortune; improperly used, it produces calamity. For this reason, anger and punishment cannot be done away with in the home, criminal and civil penalties cannot be done away with in the nation, and punitive expeditions cannot be done away with in the world.

"Ancient sage kings had militias of justice; they did not do away with warfare. When warfare is truly just, it is used to eliminate brutal rulers and rescue those in misery. People's joy is as that of devoted children seeing their kind parents, like starving prisoners getting delicious food—they run to it with a cry, like a powerful catapult shooting into a deep canyon.

"What determines victory or defeat should not be sought elsewhere; it is imperative to go back to people's feelings. Human feelings are such that they want to live and hate to die; they want glory and hate disgrace. When there is but one way to determine death or life, disgrace or glory, then the soldiers of the military forces can be made to be of one mind.

"Generally speaking, it is desirable to have many troops, and it is desirable that their hearts be united. When all the military forces are of one mind, then order can be made unopposed.

"The best militias of ancient times esteemed order. To those whose order was strong, adversaries are weak; in the presence of those whose order was trustworthy, adversaries were humbled. First master the one, and you master the other.

"If you can really achieve this, then how could opponents even be worth beating? Whenever opponents approach, it is in search of profit; if all they will get by approaching is death, then they will consider it profitable to run away. Then there is no need to cross words. This is what is called the best militia.

"Extravagance, cruelty, treachery, and deceit are opposites of just principles. These forces cannot both win; they are incompatible. Therefore when a just militia enters enemy territory, the people know they are being protected. When the militia come to the outskirts of cities, it does not trample the crops, does not loot the tombs, does not plunder the treasures, and does not burn the houses. Prisoners are treated with consideration and returned. People are given reliable promises. Thus the support of adversaries is taken away, good and bad are illustrated, and disharmony and harmony are demonstrated.

"If you are like this, and there are still those who are obstinately vicious, who are contemptuous, self-indulgent, and heedless, then you may even take military action against them. First you make the announcement that the coming of the militia is to get rid of the enemies of the people, to follow the Way of Heaven; therefore it conquers the country without slaughtering the people, only executing those who deserve to be executed.

"Then you nominate and select outstanding people, the wise and the good, to honor them with entitlements. Seeking out the orphaned and widowed, the sick and the elderly, you rescue them and come to their assistance. Opening up the treasuries and granaries, you do not keep the goods to yourself, but share them respectfully.

"Now if there is someone who is able to safeguard the life or to cause the death of a single human being, everyone in the world would strive to serve that person; since a just militia safeguards the lives of individual human beings many times over, why would people not like it?

"Therefore, when a just militia arrives, people of the neighboring countries join it like flowing water; the people of an oppressed country look to it in hope as if it were their parents. The further it travels, the more people it wins."

Before the speech was even ended, King Ching rose and bowed, saying, "Now that I have gotten to hear your teaching, my energy has filled the universe, my will knows where to go, and yet my mind is ever more reverential."

THE JAPANESE ART OF WAR

*Understanding
the Culture of Strategy*

INTRODUCTION

Use anger to throw them into disarray, use humility to make
them haughty.
Tire them by flight, cause division among them.
Attack when they are unprepared, make your move when
they do not expect it.
Be extremely subtle, even to the point of formlessness;
Be extremely mysterious, even to the point of soundlessness;
Thereby you can be the director of the opponent's fate.

SUN TZU, *The Art of War*

During one of the recent flareups of trade friction between the United
States and Japan, a prominent critic was complaining to a member of
the Diet about the Japanese attitude toward international relations.
The critic contended that even as Japan claims it is misunderstood, it
does not try to make itself understood. The dietman smiled ironically. "*That*," he said, "is Japanese!"

Perhaps everyone has heard of the mysterious East or the inscrutable Orient. It may be assumed that the Japanese are inscrutable, for
example, because Oriental cultures are inherently difficult for outsiders to understand. Less frequently suspected is the originally deliberate and later subconscious use of bafflement and mystification, as
part of the ancient art of war.

All sorts of Western attempts to take advantage of Japanese resources, from their economic power to their Zen Buddhism, have
been thwarted or distorted by bafflement and mystification, in cases
where the ulterior logic and method of bafflement and mystification
are unknown. The impression of mystery may appear to veil a secret,
but the main secret may turn out to be that mystery itself is a
weapon, an art of war.

The veil of mystery is just one of the arts of war that permeate

Japanese political, cultural, and social life. For those trying to understand the Japanese mind and civilization—and that may include anyone involved in the modern world—there is no practical way to overlook the military rule and martial culture that have dominated Japan for many centuries, virtually up to the present day. So steeped in the way of the warrior has Japanese civilization been that some of the manners and mentality of this outlook remain embedded in the deepest strata of the individual and collective unconscious of that nation.

The sword is one of the three basic symbols of Shintō, the ancient Japanese religion, and so of the imperial heritage, which emerged after centuries of racial and tribal ward in ancient Japan. The sword became the soul of the samurai, who gradually extended their control from the frontiers and provinces to become the dominant power in Japan for nearly eight hundred years.

Even in the social and cultural spheres, Japan today still retains indelible impressions of the samurai Bushidō, the way of the warrior. This is true not only in education and the fine arts, but also in characteristic attitudes and conduct marking the course of political, professional, and personal relations. Well-known attributes such as the reserve and the mystery of formal Japanese behavior, as well as the humility and the hauteur, are deeply rooted in the ancient strategies of the traditional art of war. To understand Japan and the Japanese in depth, therefore, it is essential to understand the culture of strategy crafted by the Japanese art of war.

A Martial History of Japan

The legend of the imperial house of Japan emerged from two stages of armed conquest. The first stage involved the Japanese domination and destruction of other races of people inhabiting the islands that were to become Japan. The second stage, which was partially concurrent with the first, was marked by the ascendancy of some Japanese clans over others.

As the early Japanese grew in numbers and expanded their territories, they subjugated or annihilated the minority races, and also fought among themselves. There were evidently several waves of migration from North Asia resulting in the rise of the people now known as the Japanese. The earliest migrations from the continent through and from the Korean peninsula long predate history. Chinese and Korean culture and technology supported the development of the early Japanese in prehistoric ages, and renewed waves of migration in historical times stimulated by wars, conquests, and empire building continued to enrich and empower dominant Japanese clans.

By the fourth century of the common era, there were dozens of tribal Japanese nations centered around powerful clans of shamanic leaders, hunters and warriors, artisans, and agriculturists. As the Japanese nations grew, increasing competition and renewed immigration from the continent led to the rise of a powerful alliance of clans who sought an end to hostilities through the establishment of a unified state on the Chinese model. After subduing direct challenges to the central state, the alliance established its priestly clan as the imperial house and organized hierarchies of tribal nobility to accommodate the traditional leaders of the independent nation states within the structure of the proposed unified rule. The mythology of the ancient tribes was then collected and arranged to reflect the political hierarchy of the clans under the imperial rule.

The new central government was not able to exert absolute authority over all the clans in Japan, however, especially not those in more remote areas. An official document issued more than a century after the founding of the imperial state notes the limited extent of central authority and the persistence of territorial competition and conflict. As a customary part of the training of traditional tribal warrior elites, military power was not monopolized by the imperial government, and powerful clans were able to retain considerable independence.

The gradual separation of a cultural aristocracy from a martial aristocracy advanced in pace after the capital of Japan was established in Heian, the ancient city of Kyoto, at the end of the eighth century. Leading families of powerful clans with extensive land holdings gathered in the capital and patronized the development of a colorful and romantic urban culture. In the meanwhile, frontier warrior families continued to expand territories, while provincial warrior families administered and policed the extensive holdings of the court nobles.

After the other inhabitants of the islands had been vanquished and an imperial state with a central bureaucracy had been established, the Japanese warrior elites retained their importance in society through positions as governors of territories and administrators of lands and serfs held by absentee landlords. They also continued to provide the military underpinning of the entire aristocracy, as well as of the various territories and clans.

Armed conflict reemerged along complex lines after the establishment of the social and cultural hierarchy by the impartial clan and its powerful allies. Clan warfare was particularly exacerbated by territorial pressures resulting from the practice of polygamy among the upper classes and the social inequalities built into their customary inheritance practices.

Ultimately the imperial family was dominated by the wealthy Fujiwara clan, which provided all the principal wives of the emperors. The imperial family was also divided within itself across generational lines, with retired emperors often exercising more power from their Buddhist retreats than enthroned emperors did from their courts. Through their extensive connections with the nobility of all ranks, certain Buddhist monasteries also became powerful landholders, complete with their own estates, serfs, industries, banks, governments, and armed forces.

Internal division of power and the lack of strong central direction fostered competition among regional interests, which intensified through the tenth and eleventh centuries. The warrior elites in the provinces gradually increased their demands upon the revenue of the land, wresting more of the power and wealth from the hands of the court aristocrats holding legal title to the land. This political movement also encouraged the warriors to compete among themselves.

By 1100, most of Japan outside of the immediate Heian/Kyoto area was under local military control, and the twelfth century saw virtually constant civil war. In 1185 the most powerful of the warrior clans established a centralized military government, the first of three such regimes to dominate Japanese society, politics, and culture for centuries to come.

The strong military presence marking internal Japanese history has imprinted certain elements of the warrior ethos onto important areas of Japanese thought and society, well beyond the context of the original art of war. For hundreds of years the samurai not only were masters of the political fate of the nation, but were considered the leaders of the popular conscience. The morale and spirit of the warrior was as important to their influence on society as was their material power.

For a few centuries after the importation of T'ang-dynasty Chinese culture to bolster their own national ambitions, the Japanese imperial house and the noble families of its court had maintained extensive land holdings throughout Japan while living a life of luxury in the imperial capital and its environs. The upper-class warriors who administered and policed the estates of the aristocrats gradually increased their own demands for compensation for services rendered, and over the centuries massive blocks of land and land rights came under the control of the samurai. By the end of the twelfth century, a central domestic office of Shōgun, or Generalissimo, was officially recognized and a military paragovernment was established with its own capital in eastern Japan.

During the thirteenth century, the new samurai leaders of Japan again looked to China for inspiration. Now Zen Buddhism and Neo-Confucianism, by this time well established in China as dominant ways of thinking, drew the attention of the Japanese. Both central and local military authorities patronized Zen masters from China, including Japanese pilgrims who had studied Zen in China and Chinese immigrants who were fleeing the invading Mongol conquerors. This patronage ushered in a new epoch in Japanese civilization, in which the warriors superseded the old aristocracy in both political and cultural leadership. Over the following centuries, certain aspects of Zen and Neo-Confucianism were espoused by the samurai, influencing the development of Bushidō and Japanese ethics.

Near the end of the thirteenth century, the Mongol rulers of China launched two attempts to invade Japan. Momentarily forgetting persistent rivalries among their own military baronies, Japanese warriors fought off one invasion fleet. The other fleet was destroyed by storm winds, said to be a *kamikaze*, or "divine wind," believed to protect the sacred land of Japan. These events left a deep impression on the minds of the samurai, but they also disrupted the military order. As in ancient tribal Japan, in feudal Japan the traditional reward for victory in war was the land conquered; but the defeat of the Mongols did not produce any new territory with which to reward the deeds of the Japanese warriors.

The resulting disgruntlement exacerbated the frictions inherent in the military feudal system, ultimately resulting in the toppling of the reigning dynasty of Shōguns in the fourteenth century. It was replaced by a new Shogunate, established in the imperial capital of Kyoto by another samurai clan and its allies. Never as politically or militarily powerful as the first Shogunate had been in its heyday, the new Kyoto Shogunate went further than its predecessors in patronage of Zen Buddhism and the arts associated with Zen. At the urging of one of the leading Zen masters, the Kyoto Shōgun also renewed contacts with China.

The politial fragmentation of the era, however, continued to breed conflict among the baronies. The weaknesses of the feudal lords and the ambitions of the vassals fueled generations of warfare among the various ranks of samurai. The last third of the fifteenth century and most of the sixteenth century saw virtually continuous civil war. Japanese historians describe the life of warriors in those times with the phrase *ge koku jō,* "Those below overcome those above," as long established houses and alliances of warrior chieftains were attacked and overthrown by hungrier samurai from the lower ranks of the military classes.

In spite of the turbulence of this period, known as the era of the Warring States, foreign trade continued according to the enterprise of the various baronies able to participate. In the course of prolonged warfare and military rule, the Japanese had developed what was considered the best swordcraft in Asia and exported enormous quantities of fine steel blades to Ming-dynasty China, itself embroiled in civil war. Japanese freebooters and pirates *(wakō)* were infamous along the coast of China and Southeast Asia, and Japanese colonies were established in the countries along the major trade routes there.

It was near the end of the era of Warring States that Europeans first came to Japan, when both they and the Japanese were at new thresholds in their histories. The powerful warlord Oda Nobunaga soon saw the political and military advantages in welcoming Christianity and Western technology. Waging relentless wars against his rivals, including the wealthy and powerful Tendai, Nichiren, and Shinshū Buddhist sects, Oda reunified nearly all of politically fragmented Japan in the sixteenth century.

After Oda was assassinated by an associate, his former ally Toyotomi Hideyoshi took over Oda's territories and attempted to expand his own control even further. Now somewhat in command of Western weaponry, Hideyoshi distanced himself from the Europeans and began his own imperial ventures. After having consolidated his power in Japan to a degree he deemed sufficient for his purposes, Hideyoshi tried to take Korea and the Philippines. He was completely unsuccessful in these adventures, and his military-political successor Tokugawa Ieyasu ultimately rejected colonialism along with the rest of Western culture, virtually excluding the whole range of Western religious, social, technological, political, and economic ideas and practices.

The isolationist policy initiated by Tokugawa Ieyasu was to last for two and a half centuries, with profound implications for Japan's development on every level from its internal social structure to its international relations. Centuries of free intercourse with the West from the sixteenth century onward would undoubtedly have resulted in not only a different Japan, but a different East Asia. In the context of martial history, had Hideyoshi actively collaborated with European colonialists or recruited European mercenaries, that would have boosted the power of his forays into greater Asia. The main thing that had prevented Japan from becoming a major colonial power in Asia over the two centuries preceding Europe's arrival seems to have been its own internal disunity.

A Japan allied with one or more European powers at the time of its reunification under Oda Nobunaga, Toyotomi Hideyoshi, and Ieyasu four centuries ago would have been able to interact with Asia (and

Europe) on terms very different from those of an isolated and technologically backward nation. This in turn would have affected the development of the Muscovite empire in the fifteenth and sixteenth centuries, changing the face of Eurasia.

Japan's retreat into isolationism in the early seventeenth century does not seem to have been motivated simply by insularity, lack of foresight, or the failure of adventures in greater Asia. The Japanese were not sure they could contain the aggressiveness of the Western powers, who were believed to also want Japanese territory and wealth. In its view, the Japanese government seems to have been facing the possibility of direct conflict with the West, and also the possibility of having Western powers fighting for spoils among themselves on Japanese territory.

From a strategic point of view, the Japanese warriors might have tried to safeguard Japan by keeping European allies preoccupied in China and the rest of Asia, but the Western powers seemed intent on reaching everywhere and must have appeared uncontainable to Tokugawa Ieyasu.

Japan finally came out of isolation after two hundred and fifty years of introversion, at the adamant insistence of the Americans, who wanted to trade and seemed prepared to shoot their way in if necessary. After a brief honeymoon with Western civilization, a time of misery for some Japanese and of opportunity for others as the social structure realigned itself to a new environment, the military reasserted control and began to imitate Western imperialism again, just as Hideyoshi had done three centuries earlier.

In 1894–1895, Japan fought a war against China, usurping Taiwan, the Pescadores, and the Liaodong peninsula of Manchuria. This raised some eyebrows, and a consensus of Western powers forced Japan to give back the Liaodong concession. Decades later, in the years before the beginning of World War II, Japanese political writers and speakers were still fuming about this insult. They felt that Japan was arbitrarily being excluded from the modern way of life that the Westerners themselves had urged upon them, a way of life which at that time evidently included, on the level of international politics, the race for power over old Asia.

In 1902, Japan formed an alliance with Great Britain, which enhanced its prestige in the West. This prestige increased dramatically when Japan fought and defeated Russia at war in 1904–1905. Western

Europe had been concerned about Russia for some time, as competitors for influence and concessions in Central, South, and West Asia, from Turkey and Armenia to Afghanistan, India, and Tibet.

Although pleased to see Russia take a trouncing, the West could not help wondering whether Japan might not be an even more redoubtable rival if its military capabilities continued to develop at such a rapid pace. The American president Theodore Roosevelt stepped in to negotiate a speedy end to the Russo-Japanese War, and Japan was now recognized as a world power. By 1910, Japan had even been able to annex Korea.

In 1914, Japan officially declared war on Germany and invaded a German leasehold in northeastern China. The following year Japan presented a list of twenty-one demands to the Chinese government, providing that Japan take over Germany's leasehold; that Manchuria and Mongolia be reserved for Japanese colonization and exploitation of resources; that the principal coal mines in China be placed under Japanese control; that no more territory be ceded to other world powers; and that Japan direct China's military, commercial, and financial affairs.

The boldness of these demands is in itself a telling statement of the conditions of those times. The other world powers thwarted Japan's attempt to control China's policy, but China accepted the rest of the Japanese demands. Japan further reinforced its claims in 1917 and extracted a second agreement in 1918. Japan was also awarded the German possessions in northeastern China at the conclusion of World War I, through a secret agreement with the Allies.

After the war, Japanese expansionism turned for a time from military to economic and diplomatic channels. In 1922 Japanese occupation troops were withdrawn from Siberia, where they had been since 1918. In 1923, an enormously destructive earthquake in the capital area wrought havoc on the economy, already seriously weakened by the diversion of easy money from domestic production into foreign imports. The growth of city life around this early burst of consumerism was further exaggerated by the influx of massive numbers of disenfranchised peasants no longer able to pay exorbitant land rents.

The panic of 1929 and the ensuing Great Depression came down on an unstable Japan with devastating force. Cities teemed with unemployed refugees from rural poverty, while the minds of the people were torn by the rift between their traditional frugal ideals and the emphasis on consumption and competition inherent in the influence of Westernization; now certain elements of Japanese political and military thought turned again to expansionism, nationalism, and disciplinarianism.

Expansionism was envisioned as a means of releasing social and economic pressures caused by the rising numbers of unemployed Japanese. Nationalism was seen as a remedy for addictive fascination with things Western, something that had already proved to cause economic problems within the framework of the existing system. An intensified, pseudo-Shintoistic form of nationalism was also used as a justification for Japanese colonial expansion. Disciplinarianism, basically a civil form of militarism sometimes disguised as Zen or Zen martial arts, served as a method of countering the influence of Western democratic libertinism, which was also perceived by reactionary thinkers as a direct threat to the social and economic structure of Japanese society.

In 1931, a desperate Japanese military faction provoked an incident in Manchuria, and Japan quickly occupied that territory as a "response" to the incident. Splitting Manchuria off from China, Japan set up the puppet state Manchukuo. This became a major outpost in Japan's long-term vision of an Asia united under Japanese leadership. Continuing its penetration of northern China through the mid-1930s, Japan turned into a police state at home and an aggressive colonial power abroad.

Finally, cornered by British and American attempts to restrict its acquisition of essential industrial materials for the war effort, Japan proceeded to make the fatal blunder of taking on all its adversaries at once. This same misstep, directly contrary to the classical principles of the art of war, also proved fatal to Japan's ally Germany, which at that time had the most advanced armaments in the world and might have been able to devour the bulk of Europe had it not invaded the Soviet Union so hastily.

After its unconditional surrender to the Allies in 1945, Japan was induced to turn over the results of its grisly Manchurian experiments in modern chemical and germ warfare, and forced to renounce war forever by constitutional decree. At the same time, the emperor of Japan was made to deny his divinity, and the structure of state Shintō was dismantled. In spite of these developments, however, Japan retained a martial force and rebuilt its armament-related industrial capabilities during the Korean War through the patronage of its former enemies.

Even though the Japanese empire was thus dismembered and the threat of Japanese imperialism seemed to have been eliminated by the crushing defeat of 1945, the racial feelings that underlay the fanaticism of Japanese militarism were by no means obliterated. As late as 1960, a book purporting to be about Zen and Shintō was saying that Japan has a divine mission to lead the world; and the Japanese popular press of the 1980s has from time to time revived controversy over whether or not Japan actually surrendered, and whether or not the emperor actually renounced his divinity.

At present, Japan is rapidly approaching global superiority in technology with military applications. Assuming for some reason that Japan will forever identify its own interests with that of its present allies, in recent years the United States has stepped up its pressure on Japan to mitigate the power of its economy by investing more heavily in armaments. Considering the ill will toward the United States that this and related pressures are fostering in the Japanese consciousness, the prudence of this policy is in doubt today when the United States may be in danger of becoming dependent on Japanese technology even in its own national defense.

Other Asian nations, which bore the brunt of Japanese militarism earlier in this century, are certainly conscious of the dangers of military revival in Japan and have expressed their alarm at signs of Japanese ultranationalism perceived in diplomatic, economic, educational, and military spheres of activity. In this respect the Western nations, the United States in particular, are seen as either too arrogant or too naive to fully realize that the attempt to resolve economic problems by expanding the armament industry carries with it dangers that history has already shown to be ultimately beyond the control of diplomacy alone.

Zen in Japanese History

Politics and religion have been intimately connected throughout most of Japanese history. Zen is one of several schools of Japanese Buddhism to arise in concert with the decline of the court aristocracy and the establishment of a centralized power structure by the military elite. It is the only one of these schools to have been freshly imported from China, lending it even greater prestige in the eyes of its samurai adherents.

Zen was patronized by the early Shōguns partly as a ploy to foster a sort of cultural revolution to enhance the prestige and legitimacy of warriors as secular leaders. Therefore, it has come to be associated with the military class, and even called the religion of the samurai.

Zen was not the only sect of Buddhism that attracted adherents from among the warriors, however, and professional warriors were by no means any more successful in mastering Zen than were members of any other class. There remain, nevertheless, seemingly indelible traces of militaristic influence on Japanese Zen as well as Zen influence on the Japanese military. Eventually it became difficult to separate the two directions of influence, even as both affected the political and cultural life of the nation.

The newly introduced Chinese Zen brought Neo-Confucianism into Japan along with its own special teachings. A combination of ancient Confucian social idealism and Buddhist mysticism, Neo-Confucianism was used by the early Zen masters in their attempt to instill humanistic values in the minds of the new warrior elite.

At first Zen also produced a vigorous inspiration toward pure spirituality, and the movement of warriors to bend Zen to their own ends does not seem to have taken over until several generations later. From the time of the second Shogunate, however, there is a clear distinction to be made between the Zen of spirit and the Zen of power. The gap between politicized church Zen and spiritual Zen grew throughout the Middle Ages, until there was almost nothing left of the latter by the time of the founding of the third Shogunate in the early seventeenth century.

Zen and the other new schools of Japanese Buddhism arising around the late twelfth and early thirteenth centuries were facilitated by the decline of the court aristocracy that had patronized the established churches and by the deterioration of the upper-class Buddhist priesthood. The early Zen masters were learned monks of the classical schools who had become revolted by the materialism and politicization of church Buddhism and who had been unable to find practical solutions within the current curricula.

Some of these monks went to China in search of answers, and found Chan (Zen), a form of Buddhism unlike what was generally known in Japan at that time. Although Chan had been flourishing centuries earlier when groups of Japanese pilgrims went to China in search of knowledge for the development of Japanese civilization, at that time almost all of the Chan schools went unnoticed by the pilgrims. By the thirteenth century, however, Chan Buddhism had penetrated the fabric of Chinese civilization so deeply and its teachers and schools had attained such prestige over hundreds of years of continuous work, that it was by then the preeminent form of Buddhism in China.

Chinese Chan Buddhism was, however, already considered by its own leading masters to be in a moribund state when the Japanese began to import it in earnest. Already six hundred years old, Chan Buddhism suffered from the ordinary ailments of institutionalization that arise from the arousal of proprietary sentiments in regard to a religion or an organization. Chan also suffered from a parallel involution in its method, with increasing intricacy and formalization vitiating its efficiency.

The early Japanese Zen pilgrims were already learned in classical Buddhist theory and had personally witnessed institutional decadence in even more extreme forms in their own churches. These factors undoubtedly helped them in their Zen studies in China, and most of them returned to Japan within five or six years. Since China was itself in a state of ferment, the Japanese pilgrims were generally not able to travel extensively and therefore did not meet many of the Chinese Zen masters. On the other hand, the Japanese Zen movement was also fertilized by Chinese monks seeking political refuge from the regime of the Mongol Yuan dynasty.

According to historians, as many as twenty-seven or more schools of Zen were set up in medieval Japan, most of which were affiliated with the sect of Rinzai (Chinese Lin-chi or Linji). Zen students were not bound to any school and commonly studied in more than one of them. This diluted their identities as separate schools, and only a few of the original Zen lineages continued to exist for more than three or four generations after being imported into Japan.

The second Shogunate, which replaced the first one in the fourteenth century, patrionized Zen Buddhism in the Kyoto area, using its facilities not only for religious purposes but as a foundation of learning and culture in general. Zen arts of scholarship, poetry, painting, ritual, and environmental design were developed and elaborated throughout this period. The Kyoto Shogunate also reopened communications with China at the suggestion of the leading Zen master of its early days.

Interest in Chinese culture during this period reached the point where groups of as many as fifty Japanese Zen pilgrims were going on tours of Chinese monasteries. The manifest influence of Zen on Japanese culture had reached its zenith. The government established a twin hierarchy of elite Zen monasteries headed by establishments around the seats of the first and second Shogunates in Kamakura and Kyoto. The liberal education of upper-class samurai was entrusted largely to the learned Zen monks of the capital.

These schools are especially famous for their poetry, art, and secular scholarship, but the elite monastic society in the service of the upper classes came to be considered decadent and spiritually bankrupt in terms of the original Zen enlightenment. Followers of spiritual Zen tended to avoid the prestigious monasteries, preferring to look for unobtrusive masters in the provinces. In later generations, practitioners of Zen had little use for the poetry of the elite Zen institutions known as the Gozan, or "Five Mountains." The tradition of secular Five Mountain poetry and scholarship was continued by Neo-Confucian specialists who eventually broke away from Zen churches, while the tradition of Zen poetry for practical rather than ornamental use was renewed in a later Zen revival movement.

Because of the corruption in its institutions, by the end of the fifteenth century Zen was virtually extinct spiritually, if not socially and politically. An exceptional Zen monk of the fifteenth century, the beloved folk figure Ikkyū, wrote that the Zen schools had all lost their transmission and were names without realities. Considered one of the very greatest Japanese Zen masters in history, Ikkyū was an incisive critic with an irrepressible sense of humor. His vernacular writings forged a unique link with popular culture, and he was eventually turned into a folkloric figure, the subject of countless tales of wit and wisdom.

Ikkyū is famous for carrying around a wooden sword, saying that the Zen of the time did not even have the "killing sword" of penetrating insight, let alone the "life-giving sword" of objective compassion. He is also said to have destroyed his *inka shōmei,* a traditional testament of approval given him by his Zen teacher. According to one story, Ikkyū destroyed such a document twice, saying that it had lost its meaning in the contemporary milieu, with the disappearance of Zen enlightenment and the proliferation of corrupt Zen priests. He also wrote that people had formerly gone to monasteries to seek enlightenment, but now they were leaving monasteries to seek enlightenment.

It is difficult to find many records of the works of authentic Zen masters in the sixteenth century; only a few fragments and anecdotes remain of them. Intellectual Zen monks in the capital were involved in art, literature, education, and politics, but Zen practice had become so formalized that few of them attained enlightenment. Except for the activities of a relatively small number of practitioners outside the major urban establishments, Zen Buddhism had largely become a cultural movement.

The state of Zen Buddhism changed radically in the seventeenth century, with the rejection of the cultural and intellectual Zen of the Middle Ages and the establishment of vigorous new schools of Zen teaching. Civil wars ended and the Tokugawa Peace was established throughout Japan, making it easier for students to go on pilgrimage to recollect the scattered lore of medieval Zen practice. There was also a movement to revive study of the Chinese Chan classics, in parallel with a movement to abstract the essence of Zen practice for popular use. In many cases the same Zen masters were active in both movements. These Zen masters, most of whom still avoided the long-corrupted elite monastic establishments, succeeded in bringing about a great revival in Zen Buddhism.

This revival reached its apogee around the middle of the eighteenth century, and stagnated thereafter. One obstacle to the further development of Zen was government policy, under which a number of measures were instituted to rigorously circumscribe the activities and influence of Buddhism. All monasteries, nunneries, and temples, even in the most remote provinces, were incorporated into a hierarchy under the authority of one of the elite central monasteries, which were in turn under the authority of the military government.

Provincial temples were also incorporated directly into the government machinery, serving as the equivalent of today's city halls and registry offices. Many local temples also ran primary schools, but the curriculum was limited to the version of Neo-Confucianism sanctioned by the government. Lay people were forbidden to teach Buddhism, even if they were recognized as competent by Zen authorities themselves. Each sect of Buddhism was required to submit a list of doctrines, and these were then declared dogma by the state; innovation was now officially forbidden.

Buddhism had always been considered something of a threat to the state when it was not part of the state's own mechanism of authority. The Tokugawa attempt to prematurely fossilize Buddhism and reduce its power was initiated in the seventeenth century, with the resurgence of Zen itself. This external threat to the spiritual life of Zen was then compounded in the eighteenth century by attachment to the forms of religion.

According to Zen technical literature, characteristic symptoms of attachment to forms include fascination with secondary phenomena and an inability to gain access to the source of creativity. This is viewed as a habit of mind that is ordinarily enacted on both individual and collective levels of human history and must be newly transcended in every generation. Involution set in again as Zen became intricate, arcane, and forced, in repeated attempts to wring generation after generation of inspiration out of limited systems and doctrines. The official curriculum became a caricature of the originally flexible Zen teachings that had initiated the seventeenth-century revival.

In the middle of the nineteenth century, with the replacement of the third Shogunate by direct imperial rule and the end of late feudal Japan's radical isolationism, Zen Buddhism was subjected to new pressures. From within Japan, Buddhism was attacked as a foreign religion by the establishment of state Shintō under the leadership of the emperor. This antiforeign and anti-Buddhist trend was ideologically backed by extremists of a xenophobic academic movement called Patriotic Studies (Kokugaku), which had arisen in the previous century and now commanded great prestige. Many Buddhist temples were confiscated and converted to Shintō shrines.

From abroad, Buddhism was threatened by aggressive Christian missions attempting to link the Western technical knowledge now avidly sought by the Japanese with Christianity as understood in the West. Since part of the Christian missionary method was to criticize and rebuke the local religions it hoped to supplant, much of early Western scholarship on Buddhism began from this effort and was shaped by its purpose.

Japanese Buddhists reacted to European polemics in different ways. Some of them plunged more deeply into Buddhist scriptures and classics to defend their faith against Western slander. Others became fanatical yogis, disciplinarians, or marital artists. Yet others imitated the methods of Western scholastics and tried to use them to analyze their own classics and histories, becoming professional academics and intellectuals in conformity with European models.

Traces of all of these trends still exist in Japan today, but the yogic, disciplinarian, and martialized forms of Zen and Buddhism tend to attract more general interest than either traditional or Westernized academics. After the fall of the last Shogunate and the end of state patronage of Buddhism, increasing attention was given to winning popular enthusiasm and support. One of the outstanding pioneers of this movement was an unusual Zen monk named Nantembō (1839–1925), who had grown up in feudal Japan and later attracted many followers among the aristocracy and the military elite.

Nantembō rocked the Rinzai Zen world with his blasting attacks on its hereditary priesthood and campaigned for a universal qualifying system for Rinzai Zen masters. Failing to persuade the authorities to institute such a system, Nantembō eventually gave up hope of reforming monastic Zen. Considering established monastic Zen politically and morally corrupt, he devoted his time to developing lay Zen. He generated a wave of enthusiasm by introducing a special technique for rapid attainment of concentration and ecstasy. His intensive meditation retreats became popular among the social elite, whose families were traditionally patrons of Rinzai Zen or were involved in the classical arts anciently associated with Rinzai Zen.

Although only a few disciples of this Zen master learned his complete teaching, he had thousands of lay followers, and his influence was widely diffused through extensive correspondence, personal interviews, and Zen revival meetings in which people would gather for intensive concentration exercises punctuated by rough-and-tumble encounters with the master. Nantembō himself claimed that six hundred people had attained experience of an elementary stage of Zen under his guidance, including some of the most prominent people in civil and military society.

Since Namtembō's intensive technique as employed in his crash programs was therefore spread without the context of the whole teaching, the dangers inherent in such a method often went unchecked among Zen enthusiasts of subsequent generations. The militant ferocity of the style of training used by Nantembō and other old Zen monks brought up in feudal times was absorbed not only by the military and police forces through the schools of hard marital arts they pursued, but also by the civilian world thought the *jigoku* ("hell") methods used to train students and corporate employees.

Nantembō's methods spread further through one of his erstwhile disciples, a layman whom he acknowledged to have passed through the whole system but who eventually left the master, saying he "had no eyes." Although this expression normally refers to blindness or ignorance, it can have several meanings. Sometimes it refers to naive ignorance in the sense of lack of awareness. It can also be used to refer to cultivated ignorance, such as comes about through fixation on totems.

The term is also a classic description of a kind of "Zen illness" caused by overindulgence in excessive concentration on meditation of the type that stops the mind. On the most refined level, the expression means that the Zen master in question is absorbed in nirvana. In this last connection it is interesting to note that Nantembō was one of the rare latter-day Zen masters to have his funeral held before he died, an ancient ceremony performed for certain warriors, priests, and human sacrifices.

The meaning of the graduate disciple leaving Nantembō and going to another teacher depends on the intention of the statement that Namtembō had no eyes. However this matter may be interpreted, it is clear that the former disciple brought at least part of the intensive technique of Nantembō to his new school, through which it spread even further, particularly among lay Zen practitioners.

Some Zennists have also used this kind of method in attempts to popularize Zen in the West, on the premise that the rapidity and drama of its initial effects would be able to interest and inspire Westerners as yet unaccustomed to more subtle impressions. Certain imitations of this sort of technique have also developed elsewhere in modern Western culture through interaction with a dilute yet discernible input from Japanese Zen culture.

The blinding side effects of overestimating and overusing hyperintensive methods showed up again in later generations and remain among the issues faced by modern Zen schools and the training systems of the movements they have influenced. Parallel and derivative techniques have already appeared in the West, sponsored by both Japanese and Western organizations and employed in both religious and secular contexts. These relics of feudalistic martial styles of Zen are so intimately connected with the *jigoku* "hell" style of Japanese soldier-citizen training that their background in Bushidō stands out for objective examination in any pragmatic study of the interface between Japanese and Western cultures, whether in the realm of religion, education, or industry.

BUSHIDŌ AND MARTIAL ARTS

In his famous *Book of Five Spheres,* the swordsman Miyamoto Musashi introduces the subject of the art of war as one among the various traditional Ways of Japanese culture, to be studied and practiced by political leaders as well as by professional warriors.

> The arts of warfare are the science of military experts. Leaders in particular practice these arts, and soldiers should also know this science. In the present day there are no warriors with accurate understanding of the science of martial arts.

Shortly before Musashi's birth, Japan had been more or less reunified after a century of civil wars. His era was still highly militarized, and marked by armed conflict at home and abroad. He died shortly after the final destruction of opposition to the new Shogunate established during his lifetime. Writing his classic of strategy near the end of his life, Musashi claims that no warriors of his day really understood the martial arts; it is not clear whether he regarded this lapse of tradition to be rooted in the conditions of war or the conditions of peace.

It is evident, nevertheless, that Musashi regarded the way of the warrior as a special calling. As with any other Way, mastery depended in great measure on the affinity of the practitioner with the path. Musashi compares the art of war with other arts as a specialization demanding its own characteristic inclination.

> People practice the ways to which they are inclined, developing individual preferences. Buddhism is a way of helping people, Confucianism is a way of civilization, healing is a way of curing illnesses. Poets teach the way of poetry, others take to the ways of fortune telling, archery, and various other arts and crafts. Few people like the art of war.

Musashi's assertion that few people like the martial arts contrasts sharply with their modern popularity, both in Asia and in the West. In Musashi's time, however, the way of the warrior was not a hobby but a total lifestyle. Such a life involved rigors and perils that were soon to disappear, even from the world of the Japanese samurai.

One characteristic Musashi's way had in common with classical Chinese philosophical concepts of warriorhood was his emphasis on a balanced combination of practical learning in both cultural and martial arts: "First of all," he wrote, "the way of warriors means familiarity with both cultural and martial arts." In ancient China, when wars were still fought exclusively by men of the aristocratic houses, the single word *shi*, or "knight," meant both scholar and warrior. The training of this class of men was considered to be one of the most important tasks of the culture.

In later times, scholars were still schooled in martial arts, while warriors were also taught cultural arts. This practice was taken up by the upper-class samurai in Japan, where the identification of the civil and military elites was more complete and longer lasting than in China. While he followed the tradition of the cultured warrior in both theory and practice, however, because of his background Musashi inevitably laid greater stress on martial arts.

> Even if they are clumsy at this, individual warriors should strengthen their own martial arts as much as practical under the circumstances. . . . In China and Japan, practitioners of this science have been legendary as masters of martial arts. Warriors should not fail to learn this science.

One of the characteristics of the warrior's way that seems to distinguish it from the way of culture is the ever-presence of death. It is commonly said that one reason warriors liked Zen Buddhism was because it taught them to face death with equanimity. Musashi, himself deeply interested in Zen, rejects this reasoning.

> People usually assume that all warriors think about is getting used to the imminent possibility of death. As far as the process of death is concerned, warriors are not the only ones who die. All classes of people know their duty, are ashamed to neglect it, and realize that death is inevitable. There is no difference among social groups in this respect.

From the point of view of cultural transmission, or transcultural communication, it is noteworthy that this passage from Musashi's *Book of Five Spheres* has been rendered differently by some translators, in such a way as to draw a distinction between the way of the warrior and the ways of other walks of life. Considering the central importance of death in both Buddhism and Bushidō, this is worth examination.

Two translators construe Musashi as saying that people other than warriors only resign themselves to death when duty or disgrace commands them to do so. Grammatically, this is within the realm of possibility, but Musashi does not overtly say this—something he could easily have done with but a single particle. One translator even replaces the last line with its opposite, saying that the way of warriors and the ways of the other walks of life are completely different. These readings seem to be strongly influenced by the very preconceptions Musashi is dismissing. This phenomenon is also common in translations of certain Zen writings.

In the literal meaning of the original, Musashi's statement specifically includes monks and nuns, women, farmers, and "even those below them," which would mean artisans, merchants, outcastes, and untouchables. In Musashi's own lifetime the ancient Japanese class system underwent its most extreme phase of ossification, hardened by government fiat into a caste system. Most people were simply born into a way of life that they had no choice but to accept; that became their duty and their reason for being. Death was the only alternative.

But there were different grades of death in Musashi's world. There was social death, and there was physical death. Some people chose physical death when they experienced social death, and this choice was always honored if properly executed. On the other hand, people who had failed in their own walks of life could possibly run away and join despised professions frequently pursued by untouchables, becoming tinkers, peddlers, undertakers, shoemakers, and so on. They could also join the world of the outcastes, becoming prostitutes, panders, gamblers, and entertainers. Another possibility was to become a monk or a nun, although as monks and nuns in those times people still might wind up in one of the untouchable or outcaste demimondes.

The outstanding fact of seventeenth-century Japanese society, however, was that people in all walks of life realized the inevitability of death without having to connect that with duty or conscience at all. Ordinary peasants were just as close to death as any warriors, let alone the bureaucratic warriors for whom the martial arts were a pastime. The policy of the Shogunate was to keep people uncertain of their fate, and they did not need Buddhism to remind them of the evanescence of life.

Farmers, who comprised four-fifths of the population at that time, were taxed so intensively that they were constantly dogged by starvation. They were also subject to the threat of *burei-uchi* ("being killed for insolence") whenever they were in the presence of samurai. So whether they were warriors or peasants, it was not that the traditional culture of Buddhism reminded people of death so much as that the real nearness of death provoked interest in Buddhism.

Therefore Musashi denied the usual idea that awareness of imminent death is the prime distinguishing mood of the warrior's way. Instead, he said it is the overriding need to win. Even granting the relatively limited role of competition in Musashi's times, he is perhaps naive in regarding this need to win as particular to warriors, as naive as he deemed others in their opinions. The narrowness of his thinking in this respect, on the other hand, is not his own but a by-product of the caste system in which he lived.

Reflecting his point of view as a samurai in feudal Japan, Musashi describes the way of the warrior in the following terms:

> The way of carrying out the martial arts of warriors is in all events based on excelling others. Whether in winning an individual duel, or winning a fight with several people, one thinks of serving the interests of one's employer, of serving one's own interests, of becoming well known and socially established. This is all possible by martial arts.

This was already true of other professions in Musashi's time, and it is even more so in the present day. The popularity of writings by Musashi and other warriors today attests to their relevance to other walks of life. Musashi himself amends his view elsewhere in the book. As for the martial arts themselves, the formal stylization and abstraction that characterize them today were already beginning when Musashi wrote his famous treatise, years after the last of the dynastic wars. Because of this, Musashi warns against dilettantism in the warrior's way, stressing the need for ability to apply it. The way must not only be useful in combat, he writes, but in every aspect of life as well.

There are no doubt people who think that even to be practicing martial arts will not prove useful when a real need arises. As far as that is concerned, the true way of martial arts is to practice them in such a way that they will be useful at any time, and to teach them in such a way that they will be useful in all things.

In this connection, Musashi laments the commercialization of martial arts, resulting in fragmentation of the science, with impractical elaborations and movements based on showmanship rather than on efficiency in warfare.

In recent times, people who make their living as martial artists are swordmasters only. It is only in latter days that Shintō priests from certain regions travel the provinces teaching people various styles of swordplay that the priests developed and passed on as having been transmitted from the spirits.

The practice of attributing arts and sciences to ancient or even divine precedents is not uncommon in the East. The martial art known as T'ai Chi Ch'uan or Taijiquan ("absolute boxing"), for example, is sometimes said to have been first revealed to its originator by a spirit in a dream. Note here how Musashi associates popular schools of martial arts with Shintō, not Zen Buddhism. He goes on to speak of the "art of the advantage," the abstract core of the art of war.

Since ancient times "the art of the advantage" has been added to traditional arts and crafts, but once we are talking about the art of the advantage, this shouldn't be limited to swordsmanship alone. What is more, swordsmanship itself can hardly be known by considering only how to win by use of the sword.

"The art of the advantage" is a more inclusive term than "martial arts," in that it refers to the science of strategy in general. Here the practical meaning of martial arts deviates somewhat from their function in Zen training, insofar as it is focused on personal advantage rather than on resourcefulness itself. Musashi goes on to speak of the alienation of all the arts from their educational applications through commercialization.

As I see society, people make the arts into commercial products. They even think of themselves as commodities, and also make implements for their commercial value. This attitude is like flowers compared with seeds: the flowers are more numerous than the seeds; there is more decoration than reality.

In martial arts particularly there is a lot of showmanship and commercial popularization. The result of this must be, as someone said, "Amateuristic martial arts are a source of serious wounds."

Musashi therefore insisted on technical expertise in the fundamentals of the warrior's craft, much as would be required in any profession. For warriors this means knowledge of weaponry, but Musashi's admonitions on this point have the power of unlimited metaphor:

> The science of martial arts for warriors requires construction of various weapons and understanding the properties of the weapons. A member of a warrior familly who does not learn to use weapons and understand the specific advantages of each weapon would seem to be somewhat uncultivated.

Extending this general principle further in his simile of the master carpenter, Musashi stresses the wisdom of learning all aspects and all skills of a profession or business. This underlay the ancient institution of apprenticeship, through which people might master a trade in every respect through a natural process of development. The principle has also been applied by the Japanese in the corporate world of the latter half of the twentieth century, and is one of the major factors supporting well-known technical and sociological successes seen in Japanese business and industry. Musashi writes:

> I will use the way of carpentry to talk about the martial arts. The simile of the carpenter refers to the master carpenter who builds houses. Aristocrats, military families, and schools of art and culture are all spoken in terms of tradition, style, and "house," so since we are using the expression "house" I have used the mastery of carpentry as a symbol.

Use of the image of a master carpenter to represent leadership goes back to ancient Taoist classics, and is particularly marked in the political treatises of *Huainanzi*, one of the major books of philosophical

Taoism. Although it was not commonly studied in Japan, Musashi may have come in contact with this book through his association with Zen Buddhism. Taoist scholarship is known to have been one of the many accomplishments of the famous Zen master Takuan, an elder contemporary of Musashi and teacher of the Shōgun and of the master swordsman Yagyū Munenori.

In any case, the organizational ideas Musashi used had become traditional because of the prestige of their source, especially in a cultural milieu under the influence of Zen. In *Book of Five Spheres* [also known as *The Book of Five Rings*], Musashi explains his own craft in the classic metaphor, thus leaving its own symbolic potential unbounded:

> The word for carpenter is written with the characters for "great skill." Since the science of the art of war is a great skill, it is symbolized by the carpenter. If you want to learn the science of the art of war, meditate on this book; let the teacher be the needle and the student be the thread, and practice it always.
>
> As the master carpenter is the overall organizer and director of the journeymen, it is the duty of the master carpenter to understand the system of measurement, keep local measurements accurate, and attend to the measurements of the master carpenter's own establishment.
>
> The master carpenter, knowing how to build all sorts of structures, employs people to erect houses. In this respect the master carpenter is the same as the master warrior.
>
> When sorting out timber for building a house, if logs that look good, logs that are straight and without knots, are used for front pillars; logs with some knots but still straight and strong are used for back pillars; logs that may be somewhat weak but have no knots and look good are used for framing; and logs that may be gnarled and crooked but nevertheless strong are used thoughtfully in consideration of the various members of the house, then the house will last a long time. Even gnarled, crooked, and weak logs can be used for scaffolding, and can be made into firewood later.
>
> As the master carpenter directs the journeymen, he knows their various levels of skill and gives them appropriate tasks. Even the unskilled and the clumsy can be given chores suiting

their abilities. If the master carpenter exercises discernment in assignment of jobs, work progresses smoothly. Efficiency and smooth progress, prudence in all matters, knowing the total dynamic, knowing different levels of energy and temperament, instilling confidence, knowing what is not possible—such are the matters on the mind of the master carpenter. This is the way it is with the martial arts.

The Taoist classic *Huainanzi* talks about social equality in terms of full employment according to individual abilities. Under the direction of sages, according to the ancient book of statecraft, "there are no wasted people and no wasted things." This is the art of a master politician as well as the art of a master warrior. Now Musashi turns his attention to the position of the apprentice.

As journeymen, warriors sharpen their own tools, they make various useful implements and keep them in their carpentry boxes. Following the instructions of the master carpenter, they do all the necessary tasks, making sure the measurements are correct and seeing that all the work is done properly. This is the rule for journeymen.

When they have developed practical knowledge of all the skills of the craft, eventually they may become master carpenters themselves.

An essential habit for carpenters is to have sharp tools and keep them whetted. It is up to the carpenter to use those tools to fashion a whole range of articles. This is the way it is for warriors.

As Musashi himself suggests, this is not only the way things are for warriors, but also the way things are for everyone else in a changing world where skills and fluidity are essential tools of survival. While the outer framework of the warrior's learning is based on the interdependence of many factors, the inner dimension of it is based on the relationship between the learner and the learning. The precise balancing of outer and inner elements was always considered one of the highest skills of mastery, and was an art studied with particular attention by ancient Zen schools.

The swordsman Yagyū Munenori, an older contemporary of Musashi who also took an intense interest in Zen, wrote extensively on the Zen attitude toward learning in his *Book of Family Traditions on the Art of War*, where he based his argument on what he had heard from Zen master Takuan.

> Masters of the arts cannot be called adepts as long as they have not left behind attachments to their various skills.
> A mendicant asked an ancient saint, "What is the Way?"
> The saint said, "*The normal mind is the Way.*"
> The principle of this story applies to all arts. This is the stage where sicknesses of the mind are all gone, when you have become normal in mind and have no sicknesses even while in the midst of sicknesses.

As Yagyū explains later, "sickness" here means fixation or lingering of the attention. This is considered an abnormality or deviation from the Zen ideal in that it results in inhibition of spontaneous responsiveness and free function. Therefore Yagyū extols the level of expertise at which one reaches "normalcy" in the Zen sense of natural, unself-conscious mastery in one's occupation.

> To apply this to worldly matters, suppose you are shooting and you think you're shooting while you're shooting: then the aim of your bow will be inconsistent and unsteady. When you wield a sword, if you are conscious of wielding a sword, your offense will be unstable. When you are writing, if you are conscious of writing, your pen will be unsteady. Even when you play the harp, if you are conscious of playing, the tune will be off.
> When an archer forgets consciousness of shooting, and shoots in a normal frame of mind, as if unoccupied, the bow will be steady. When using a sword or riding a horse as well, you don't "wield a sword" or "ride a horse." And you don't "write," you don't "play music." When you do everything in the normal state of mind, as it is when totally unoccupied, then everything goes smoothly and easily.
> Whatever you do is your Way. If you are obsessed with it, or think that this alone is of importance to you, then it is not the Way. It is when you have nothing in your chest that you are on the Way. Whatever you do, if you do it with nothing in your chest, it works out easily.

There is a Zen proverb that says, "This is it, but if you fixate on it, then it isn't anymore." This means that immediate reality is itself enlightenment, as Zen teaching so often states, unless the conceptual recognition that "this is it" replaces the direct experience, triggering the mechanism of fixation all over again. Therefore the symbol of the mirror, reflecting spontaneously without subjectivity and without retaining any images, came to be used as a popular simile for the basic Zen mind. Yagyū continues:

> This is like the way everything reflects clearly in a mirror precisely because of the formless clarity of the mirror's reflectiveness. The heart of those on the Way is like a mirror, empty and clear, being mindless yet not failing to accomplish anything.
>
> This is the "normal mind." Someone who does everything with this normal mind is called an adept.
>
> Whatever you do, if you keep the idea of doing it before you and do it with singleminded concentration, you will be uncoordinated. You'll do it well once, and then, when you think that's fine, now you'll do it badly. Or you may do it well twice, then do it badly again. If you're glad you did it well twice and badly only once, then you'll do it badly again. There is no consistency at all, because of doing it with the thought of doing it well.
>
> When effective work builds up unawares and practice accumulates, thoughts of quickly developing skill quietly disappear, and whatever you do you spontaneously become free from conscious thoughts. At this time you don't even know yourself; when your body, feet, and hands act without you doing anything in your mind, you make no misses, ten times out of ten. Even then, if it gets on your mind at all, you'll miss. When you are not consciously mindful, you'll succeed every time.
>
> However, not being consciously mindful does not mean total mindlessness; it just means a normal mind.

Zen master Takuan explained the paradoxical relationship between training and spontaneity to Yagyū Munenori in terms that the swordsman would later incorporate into his own family tradition of martial arts. The Zen master wrote to the warrior:

> You need to realize that when you practice from the state of the beginner all the way to the stage of immutable wisdom, then you must go back to the status of the beginner again.

Let me explain in terms of your martial arts. As a beginner you know nothing of stance or sword position, so you have nothing in yourself to dwell on mentally. If someone strikes at you, you just fight, without thinking of anything.

Then when you learn various things like stance, how to wield a sword, where to place the attention, and so on, your mind lingers on various points, so you find yourself all tangled up when you try to strike.

But if you practice day after day and month after month, eventually stance and swordplay don't hang on your mind anymore, and you are like a beginner who knows nothing.

This is the sense in which it is said that the beginning and the end are the same, just as one and ten become neighbors when you have counted from one to ten. It is also like the highest and lowest notes of a musical scale becoming neighbors below and above a cycle of the scale.

Just as the highest and lowest notes resemble each other, since buddhas are the highest human development they appear to be like people who know nothing of Buddha or Buddhism, having none of the external trappings that people envision of buddhas.

Therefore the afflictions of unaware lingering in the beginning and the immutable wisdom in the end become one. The cogitating side of your brain will vanish, and you will come to rest in a state where there is no concern.

Completely ignorant people don't show their wits, it seems, because they haven't got any. Highly developed intelligence doesn't show because it has already gone into hiding. It is because of pseudo-erudition that intelligence goes to one's head, a ludicrous sight.

A Taoist proverb says, "A clever merchant hides his goods and pretends to have nothing." Taoist and Zen classics also speak of "softening the light to harmonize with the world." Self-conscious display is considered not only unbecoming but counterproductive. A Sung-dynasty Chinese Zen master said, "Those who have no real virtue within but outwardly rely on flowery cleverness are like leaky boats brightly painted—if you put manikins in them and set them on dry ground they look all right, but once they go into the rivers and lakes, into the wind and waves, are they not in danger?"

The practice of "hiding one's light" so as to appear ordinary to others was carried on deliberately by ancient Buddhist and Taoist mystics after they had attained enlightenment, believing that they could thereby reach higher levels of refinement than if they allowed themselves to be admired for their knowledge. This was a higher form of modesty than that prescribed for students, for whom the compulsion to show off was considered fatally destructive to their chances for enlightenment. Fushan, one of the great Chinese Zen masters, said, "Those who flash their learning and run off at the mouth without having ever learned to actually attain the Way, using eloquence and sharpness of tongue to gain victories, are like outhouses painted vermilion. The vermilion only increases the odor."

In his own book of family traditions, Yagyū both concentrates and expands upon the teaching of Zen master Takuan.

> It becomes easier to do everything when you come to have nothing on your mind. For this reason, study of all the Zen arts is for the purpose of clearing away what is on your mind. In the beginning you don't know anything; you hardly even have any questions on your mind. Then when you enter into study, there is something on your mind, and you are blocked by it. This makes everything difficult to do.
>
> When what you have studied leaves your mind entirely, and practice also disappears, then when you perform whatever art you are engaged in, you accomplish the techniques easily, without being concerned over what you have practiced, and yet without deviating from what you have practiced. This is spontaneously conforming without being aware that you are doing so.

In virtually all domains of traditional Japanese arts, it was customary to begin with strict adherence to standard forms and rites. This was supposed to induce the student to get the "feel" of the art intuitively, without stopping to rationalize and project subjective ideas onto the action itself. The purpose of this rigid discipline, however, was not to automatize the learner but to provide a dependable framework of support for an extra faculty of perception that could be exercised once conscious attention to the formal foundation was no longer necessary.

The ultimate goal of freedom and spontaneity was thus not pursued arbitrarily, but in accord with a gradual process that had already been tested. Adepts who had passed beyond formal systems were known to discover techniques and movements naturally, without having learned them from a teacher.

Zen master Takuan summed up his discussion of independent spontaneity and factual practice in terms of principle and action.

> There is the practice of principle and the practice of action. Principle is as mentioned before: When you have arrived at mastery, you don't struggle with anything. It is all in the way you give up minding at all.
>
> However, if you don't do practice of action, you will only have principle in mind and won't be able to do anything about it.

In Buddhist terminology, "principle" is often used synonymously with "emptiness" or "noumenon," which means subjective mental freedom in Zen psychology. The need to practice "action" refers to the externalization of inner freedom, a more advanced level of Zen mastery. Principle also means theory, which is ineffective without applicable practice.

The warrior Musashi also followed the Zen teaching on clarity and fluidity of mind as the basis of the art of learning itself, as applicable to the martial arts and the way of the warrior as to any other art or way. In the "Water Scroll" of Musashi's *Book of Five Spheres*, the warrior writes in a vein similar to that of Yagyū and Takuan, with more technical elaboration.

> According to the science of martial arts, the state of mind should remain the same as normal. Center your mind so that there is no imbalance, no difference between your ordinary mind and your mind when practicing martial arts. Let your mind be broad and direct, neither tense nor lax. Calmly relax your mind, and savor this moment of ease thoroughly, so that the relaxation does not stop its relaxation even for an instant.
>
> Even when you are still, you mind is not still; even when hurried, your mind is not hurried. The mind is not dragged by the body, the body is not dragged by the mind. Pay attention to the mind, not the body. Let there be neither insufficiency nor excess in your mind. Even if superficially weakhearted, be inwardly stronghearted, and don't let others see into your mind.

Let your inner mind be unclouded and open, placing your intellect on a broad plane. It is essential to polish the intellect and mind diligently. Once you have sharpened your intellect to the point where you can see whatever is reasonable and what is not, where you can tell whatever is good or bad, and when you are experienced in various fields and are incapable of being fooled at all by people of the world, then your mind becomes imbued with the knowledge of the art of war.

There is something special about knowledge of the art of war: it is imperative to master the principles of the art of war and to learn to be unmoved in mind even in the heat of battle.

As the testaments of Yagyū and Musashi illustrate, warriors followed the Zen teaching of emptying the mind for several purposes: one was to learn the secret of learning itself; another was to learn to act with spontaneous efficiency, free from doubt, hesitation, and fear, in whatever circumstances they might find themselves; they wanted to see realities independently, without extraneous influences; and they wanted to learn to see things before they happened, to make themselves invulnerable to enemies and become masters of their own fate.

This last function of the Zen technique depends on sharpening discernment of the fine web of subtle causal relations by removing the veil of mental preoccupations. Zen teachers use it for predicting how their students will react to the ideas and exercises they are given to work with. Strategists and warriors use it for predicting how their opponents will respond to the perceived possibilities of a given time. The sword master Yagyū wrote on this subject in these terms:

Removing afflictions is for the purpose of perceiving intentions. If afflictions are not removed, you will be distracted by them and fail to see. Fail to see and you've lost.

"Afflictions" are illnesses of mind, meaning that the mind is dwelling on one point or another. The mind should be made not to dwell anywhere for so long as it takes to strike a blow. This is abandoning the mind without abandoning it.

Seeing with the heart and mind is fundamental. It is only when you see from the heart and mind that your eyes catch on. So seeing with the eyes comes after seeing with the heart and mind. Seeing with the eyes, after that you should see with the body, hands, and feet.

Affliction, or sickness, means to think obsessively about something. It is also sick to think obsessively about using the art of war. It is sick to think obsessively of showing what you have learned. It is sick to think only of attacking, and it is sick to think only of waiting. It is also sick to think obsessively about getting rid of sickness. When the mind dwells on anything exclusively, this is called sickness.

Since all of these sicknesses are in the mind, the thing is to remove sickness and tune the mind.

Again, in his book of family traditions here Yagyū echoes the teaching of Zen master Takuan, who used Buddhist iconography to drive his point home. Citing the image of the Monarch of Immovable Light, traditionally portrayed as a warrior defending the Buddhist teaching. Takuan explains the meaning of the imperturbable Zen mind in action. He also uses the image of the Thousand-Handed Seeress, a personification of compassion whose "thousand hands" represent practical skills employed in the service of humanity and in liberating people from bondage to illusion. Takuan interprets this symbol in terms of the flexibility and versatility of the individual with an unfettered mind. In a letter to the swordsman Yagyū, the Zen master shows how these familiar icons illustrate practical exercises and attitudes applicable to the warrior's way:

> The Buddhist image of the Monarch of Immovable Light represents the state where one's unified mind does not move, which means not changing or upsetting oneself. Not changing or upsetting yourself means not dwelling on anything.
>
> Seeing things at a glance and not fixing the mind on them is called being unmoving. The reason for this is that when your mind lingers on things, various analytic thoughts take place in your heart, moving in various ways within your mind. When that stops, even if the lingering mind moves, you are nevertheless unmoved.
>
> For example, suppose ten people strike at you in succession. Parrying the first blow, if you do not let your mind linger on the impression, but take on one after another, leaving each behind as you go along, you will not be at a loss to deal with all ten

opponents. Although your mind works ten times with ten adversaries, if you don't let your mind linger on anyone, taking them on in turn, you won't be at a loss in action.

Then again, if your mind lingers in front of one adversary, you might parry that one person's blow, but when the second opponent strikes you will fumble.

There is another Buddhist image called the Thousand-Handed Seeress. If her mind stayed on one hand holding one particular tool, the other nine hundred and ninety-nine hands wouldn't work. It is because she doesn't keep her mind on one point that all of her hands are useful.

Why would the Seeress have a thousand hands on just one body? This is a representation to show people that even if you have a thousand hands they are all useful once immovable wisdom is opened.

If you gaze at a single leaf on a single tree, you do not see the other leaves. If you face the tree with no intention and don't fix your eyes on a single leaf, then you see all the many leaves. If your mind is preoccupied with one leaf, you don't see the others; if you don't set your attention on one, you see hundreds and thousands of leaves. Someone who has understood this is actually the Seeress of a Thousand Hands and a Thousand Eyes.

A famous story illustrating this in practice is told of another Zen master of the late seventeenth century, popularly known as Shōjū Rōjin, the Old Man with Right Perception, an important yet little-known Zen master of premodern Japan.

According to his biographers, Shōjū Rōjin had been one of the bastard sons of a samurai family. As a youth at the age of thirteen he had become intensely introspective after an encounter with an old Zen monk. Several years later, he experienced what Zennists refer to as death and revitalization after an accident in which he temporarily lost consciousness. Subsequently he spent years looking for Buddhist teachers who could confirm his realization.

Eventually he met the Zen master Bunan and studied with him for eighteen years, until the master's death. Even with this experience, however, Shōjū Rōjin said that he did not achieve continuity in "right perception" until the age of fifty-five. Because of his emphasis on continuity of right perception, the clear seeing of a clear mind, the old man called his hermitage "The Hut of Right Perception" and was himself popularly known by the same name.

Very few professional Zennists ever found their way to the door of this old man, now one of the greatest masters in Japan, direct heir of an ancient lineage. Sometimes certain warriors, however, used to call on him for advice on clarification of mind. One day such a group was practicing Zen concentration by fencing in the master's view. When they paused, one of the warriors remarked to the Zen master, who was then a hermit, "As far as the principle is concerned, your understanding is superior to ours, but when it comes to actual fact, we are superior to you."

Seizing the opportunity to make a point, the old Zen master challenged the samurai swordsmen to hit him.

The warrior who had boasted of their skill handed the old man a wooden sword, but the Zen master refused, saying that as a Buddhist monk he would not handle any weapon, even an imitation. Instead, he said, he would use his fan, which had metal backings and could serve the purpose of defense. "Try to hit me," the old Zen man repeated, urging the samurai to strike.

The warriors could not refuse the challenge. Taking up their practice swords, they attacked the old man from every angle. Their wonderment grew and their stamina dwindled as they saw the old man give a virtuoso display of the special art of opposing a long sword with a dagger. Each and every blow the warriors struck was deftly parried by the Zen master's fan, which seemed to fly to the path of the swords like iron drawn to a magnet.

Finally exhausted, the warriors were forced to concede that the old man was fully able to turn his abstract knowledge into concrete action at will. One of them asked him how he did it. "Simple," the old Zen master replied; "when your objective perception is clear, you don't miss one out of ten thousand."

According to the understanding of the warrior Yagyū, there are two levels in the practice of removing sickness in the mind in order to attain the clarity that would enable one to act this accurately and effectively in the midst of events. In his book of family traditions, he describes the first level in these terms:

> The first level is where you get into thought yet have no thoughts, get into attachments yet have no attachments: this

means that thinking of removing of sickness is thought. To think of getting rid of sicknesses in the mind is to get involved in thought.

Sickness means obsessive thought. To think of getting rid of sickness is also thought. Therefore you use thought to get rid of thoughts. When you get rid of thoughts, that is called having no thoughts. This is why we speak of getting into thought having no thoughts.

When you take thought to get rid of the sickness that remains in thought, after that the thought of removal and the thoughts to be removed all become nothing together. This is what is known as using a wedge to remove a wedge.

When you can't get the wedge out, if you drive another one in so as to ease the tightness the first wedge comes out. Once the stuck wedge comes out, the wedge driven in afterwards no longer remains there.

When sickness is gone, the thought of getting rid of sickness no longer remains, so this is called getting into thought to have no thought.

To think of getting rid of sickness is to be attached to sickness, but if you use that attachment to get rid of sickness, the attachment won't remain; so this is called getting into attachment to have no attachment.

According to the classical Chinese Zen master Baizhang, as long as there is deliberate practice and realization in Zen, the teaching is still incomplete. It is only after having transcended the steps of practice and attainment that the complete teaching is realized. Wansong, a later Chinese master, summarized this in a proverb: "It is easy to advance with every step; it is hard to let go of each state of mind." Following the Zen teaching, the Japanese swordsman Yagyū defines the advanced level of his art in terms of spontaneity and natural freedom.

In the advanced level, getting rid of sickness means having no thought whatsoever of getting rid of sickness. To think of riddance is itself sickness. To let sickness be while living in the midst of sickness is to be rid of sickness.

Thinking of getting rid of sickness happens because sickness is still in the mind. Therefore sickness doesn't leave at all, and whatever you do and think is done with attachment, so there can be no higher value in it.

Masters of the arts cannot be called adepts as long as they have not left behind attachment to their various skills.

The *Tao Te Ching*, a Taoist classic studied in Zen master Takuan's school, says that "the great adept seems as if inept." While this may outwardly resemble humility as ordinarily understood, in esoteric tradition it is at once a protective device and a means of keeping the mind clear of exaggerated self-importance, which is in Buddhist terms a "sickness" that screens consciousness from objective perception.

A common conception of the detachment of the Zen outlook is that it constitutes the goal of practice and is itself the liberation proposed by Buddhism. Classical masters openly deny this, teaching that detachment is properly speaking an avenue of extra perception and extra opportunity. Original Zen literature abounds with criticisms of practitioners who rest in detachment for their own comfort and do not employ it for constructive development.

In the work of the warrior Musashi, it becomes clear that the clarification of mind for which elementary Zen practice is designed becomes as it were a door to enhanced performance. In his *Book of Five Spheres*, Musashi stresses the importance of perceptive discernment not only in the warrior's way but in all walks of life, to gain an objective understanding of the mechanisms of timing and success.

> There is rhythm in everything, but the rhythms of the art of war are especially difficult to master without practice. . . . There are also rhythms in the ups and downs of all careers. . . . Carefully distinguish the rhythm of rise and decline in all things. . . . In battle, the way to win is to know opponents' rhythms while using unexpected rhythms yourself, producing formless rhythms from the rhythms of wisdom.

The necessary practicality of the warrior's way tended to prevent followers of the martial arts from becoming mere Zen cultists, even if it did not stop similar involuntary trends from taking place within their own speciality. Musashi's obsession with martial arts seems to have been mainly responsible for the relative shallowness of his Zen realization; or it may be the other way about, based on something in Musashi's early personality development.

Musashi did nevertheless attempt to establish a theoretical and practical basis for rounding out the personality of the warrior, in a manner characteristic of the later Neo-Confucian schools under the influence of Zen Buddhism. This effort can be seen in his own cultural pursuits, and above all in the introduction to his own famous treatise on strategy and the martial arts, where he outlines a general program for the overall mental development of the individual warrior.

1. Think of what is right and true.
2. Put the science into practice.
3. Become acquainted with the arts.
4. Become acquainted with the crafts.
5. Understand the negative and positive qualities in everything.
6. Learn to see everything accurately.
7. Become aware of what is not obvious.
8. Be careful even in small matters.
9. Don't do anything useless.

THE WAY OF THE ZEN WARRIOR

Throughout the strife-torn Middle Ages of feudal Japan, people in all walks of life were experimenting with Zen, learning to master the essence of their own way. Some of the Zen masters were themselves warriors; others were intellectuals, farmers, artisans, merchants, physicians, soothsayers, vagrants, and outcastes. Some might be all of these things in the course of a lifetime.

When the prolonged Warring States era ended around the year 1600, a movement began to recollect and systematize the scattered arts and sciences of that turbulent yet strangely brilliant era. Modern knowledge of the traditional arts and sciences, including Zen and the way of the warrior, is largely based on elaborations of those reconstructed and systematized versions of ancient knowledge.

Yagyū Munenori and Miyamoto Musashi were extraordinary warriors who lived through a historical watershed in Japanese civilization. In their works they employed an ancient core of educational techniques and learning methods to play their part in the adaptation of the culture to a new historical climate. The peculiarity of their particular role as warriors was that war no longer existed for them, for all that were left were administrative and police functions.

Under those conditions, the need for danger to use the warrior's way as a means of self-perfection could easily become a menace to society. For warriors like Musashi, this need became an obsession with dueling itself, which eventually seemed to prevent him from fully realizing Zen. It is not easy to tell whether in the end Musashi himself knew whether he had studied Zen to master the art of war, or whether he had studied the art of war to master Zen. They say that he died of an ulcer, aggravated beyond measure by years of fanatic austerities.

This solitary struggle was undoubtedly a major factor in the formation of Musashi's thought and writing on warriorhood, with its particular attention to strategic detail and methodical approach. His injunctions on learning typify this characteristic, simple yet inclusive, summarizing both Buddhist and Confucian principles of learning in a manner that is easy to remember and that, like the classics themselves, yields more with time and reflection.

One reason for Musashi's interest in basic education was, as he himself wrote, that "particularly in this science one can fall into perversions through even a little bit of misperception of the way, or confusion about the way." Yagyū also considered learning important but at the same time stressed two points: that its function within the total design of the way is preparatory; and that it is to be distinguished from mere intellectualism.

> Learning is the gate, not the house. When you see the gate, don't think it is the house. You have to go through the gate to get to the house, which is behind it.
>
> Since learning is a gate, when you read books don't think this is the Way. This misconception has made many people remain ignorant of the Way no matter how much they study and how many words they know.

This is characteristic of the Zen attitude toward learning, which is judged by function and utility, not by appearance. The original Buddhist teaching applies this to all kinds of learning, both conventional and sacred. One of the main thrusts of Zen teaching is to dethrone intellectual knowledge from its status as a personal appurtenance. According to *The Flower Ornament Scripture,* one of the all-time favorite texts of Zen teachers, "Like someone counting others' treasures without half a coin of his own: so is the one who is learned but does not apply the teaching. Like someone on a corner saying all kinds of fine things, but with no real virtue inside: so are those who do not practice."

Eventually this outlook was carried over into other schools of thought, which tended to become more universal and more pragmatic under the influence of Zen, which had originally developed in China out of a distillation of the essences of all the Buddhist teachings. This naturally included the "outside" teachings belonging to host cultures as they were absorbed and employed by Buddhists in their missionary activity. This is illustrated by the Japanese Zen master Takuan, who identifies several schools of learning in terms of a common underlying aim rather than distinguishing them in terms of external cultural differences. This aim, in turn, he identifies with the essence of Zen.

Although Shintō, poetics, and Confucianism are various in their ways, all of them speak of the clarification of the universal mind.

It is to be expected that there are people in this world who don't know the mind. Those who do understand it are rarely seen. And even if someone does clearly know, it is still hard to put into practice. Even if you can talk about the universal mind, that doesn't mean you understand mind.

Even though Buddhism and Confucianism both talk about mind, the mind without the personal conduct implied is something that is not clearly known—if you do not practice the teaching, you do not really know it. As long as people don't seriously investigate the origin of mind and come to realize it, they do not understand, it is not clear to them.

It is important to realize here that the schools of Shintō, poetics, and Confucianism to which Zen master Takuan refers as having a common theme are not their original forms, but are special developments that took place under the impact of Zen. Takuan is therefore referring not simply to his own subjective appreciation of these various ways, but also to historical facts in the history of their development.

Confucianism had already been assimilated to Zen in China five hundred years earlier, while certain types of Shintō and Japanese poetics (which were already closely related disciples from their very origin) were strongly influenced by Zen Buddhism in medieval Japan. During the seventeenth century, in the time of Takuan, Yagyū, and Musashi, it was customary for Zen masters to speak as if Buddhism, Confucianism, and Shintō were basically identical in spirit.

In both theory and practice there are, of course, many counterexamples to this generalization, but the Zen swordsman Yagyū pursued the unitarian theme even further than his teacher Takuan had in their correspondence. In defining adepthood, Yagyū found the ultimate unity to be in the combination of essence and totality, and in this he follows the root teaching of The Flower Ornament Scripture rather than a sectarian Zen line such as would be formulated in the following century. Because this is not an undefined or undifferentiated unity, while on the one hand Yagyū regarded the boundaries between fields of thought and action as real only in appearance and not in essence, on the other hand he acknowledged general distinctions of universality versus hyperspecialization or sectarianism, and genuineness versus imitation. In his book on family tradition he wrote:

Those who master one skill or one art are called expert in their particular ways, but that is not to be called complete adepthood.

There is also imitation Zen. A lot of people say similar things that are not really the right path. So people who are supposedly Zennists are not all the same.

There are people who preach that mind is empty, but people who realize this clearly are rare.

The emptiness of mind is not visible to the eye, but do not think that it is nothing: once this mind-emptiness moves it does all kinds of things. The action of the hands and feet, however varied and skilled, all are accomplished from the movement of this emptiness, this mind.

It is hard to really understand this mind by reading books or listening to talks. People who have written and spoken about it since olden times have just written and spoken in standard terms; rare are they who have attained the way mind-to-mind.

The mood of total detachment means to detach from all sorts of afflictions at once. Afflictions are afflictions of mind. This means that you make all the various afflictions in your mind into one, and lightheartedly detach from the whole bunch.

Generally speaking, affliction means fixation of the mind. In Buddhism this is called attachment, and it is considered extremely undesirable. If the mind sticks to one place and dwells on it, you fail to see what there is to see and unexpectedly lose.

The challenge for the student of Zen and Zen arts, therefore, was to distinguish the levels of practitioners: there were the complete adepts, who were masters of both Zen and art; the experts, who knew enough Zen to master an art, or who knew one art to the threshold of Zen; the dilettantes, who tried to imitate the externals of the experts for their own amusement; and the charlatans, who imitated experts for their own profit. Generally speaking, they could be distinguished by the specific spheres or fixations of attention governing their lives, but only if people trying to assess them had no personal prejudices of their own. For this reason the Zen interest in objective knowledge was reflected in a Zen interest in the educational process itself.

Suzuki Shōsan, a contemporary warrior turned Zennist who went even further than Musashi and Yagyū in educational work, was not just an individual dueling artist like those two warriors, but earlier in life had actually fought in war. Like many victorious warriors, Shōsan had given up arms when peacetime came, and even in his most chilling Zen writings does not display the murderous fanaticism or give off the scent of blood that marks the work of Musashi, the perpetual competitor.

Shōsan's work is still no less cutting than Musashi's, even on the level of mundane realities; and the ex-commander Shōsan also demonstrates a purer and more articulate understanding of Zen and the other spiritual ways than does the idiosyncratic dueler Musashi. Like many other disarmed warriors, Shōsan also later worked as a healer, even successfully reviving an ancient method of spiritual curing. In spite of its lofty idealism, his approach to education is therefore extremely perceptive and sympathetic to the particular needs of the individual as well as to the needs engendered by the general currents of behaviors and events.

Shōsan deflated the sort of thinking that conceived of Zen awakening as a magical cure-all, and that thought of Zen practice as a sort of training applied *to* the person. In this he followed classical Zen teaching, which maintained that the evolutionary transformation of the individual had to come from within to permeate the whole mind and behavior. Unless inner change is effective, according to ancient teachers, external disciplines can have a reverse influence on the self and promote such dangerous qualities as arrogance and insensitivity.

One of the first Zen principles of learning is summed up in the proverb, "Gazing at the moon in the sky, you lose the pearl in your hands." A Chinese proverb also says, "Hurry, and you won't arrive." The early Japanese Zen master Dōgen, a long-neglected pioneer of native Zen literature in Japan and one of Suzuki Shōsan's major inspirations, expressed this in a poem:

> Dig the pond
> Without waiting for the moon.
> When the pond is finished,
> the moon will come by itself.

Shōsan followed many of Dōgen's teachings, and also spoke of Buddhism as something that could be practiced at any given moment without being inhibited by remote aspirations.

People today think that Buddhism is useless if you don't become enlightened. This is not right. Buddhism means using your present mind well, so it is of immediate usefulness. Buddhist practice is using your mind as strongly as possible. As your mind becomes stronger, it gradually becomes more useful.

Shōsan further stressed the negative effects of exaggeration and impatience in both ordinary and spiritual pursuits; he observed, "Those who have gone to hell because of the world can be saved by Buddhism, but what can save those who have gone to hell because of Buddhism?" Therefore he emphasized the importance of right orientation in the practice of a discipline.

Beginners undertaking a discipline should see to it that they themselves are genuinely sincere. People should not force themselves to do any discipline without being really genuine. If you exert yourself unreasonably or undergo austerities, you will exhaust yourself and diminish your potential, all to no avail.

When your psychological state is bad, disciplines will just make it worse. Discipline is a matter of fortifying potential, so it is imperative to avoid depletion.

Nowadays countless people have depleted their potential and become ill or insane by practicing discipline wrongly or doing imitation Zen meditation. One should just develop one's will and become truly genuine.

These warnings strike a note different from that of popularizers who portray meditation as something that is good for everyone, at any time. There is no lack of contemporary examples of psychological and physical ailments such as those Shōsan mentions occurring in practitioners of meditation, fostered or exacerbated by the grafting of "spiritual" techniques onto an unsuitable basis.

In the West this has often been attributed to cultural differences, but the same problem exists in the East, as Shōsan's own remarks bear witness, and madness also occurs in native Japanese Zen schools, particularly those in which certain practices are routinely performed under intensive pressure without regard to traditional caveats such as those mentioned here by Suzuki Shōsan. Mental disturbance of some kind seems to be particularly common in stories of Japanese Zen monks of the last hundred years, an especially trying time for traditionalized Zen as a whole. This was also exacerbated by the fragmentation of Buddhist sects, which preserved fixed forms of practice in isolation from the total context of Buddhism.

In a typically Buddhist fashion, Suzuki Shōsan's teachings were cast in different styles to address the specific problems and mentalities of the various stations of life in his society. Although increasing numbers of children from among the farmers, artisans, and merchants were soon to learn reading and writing through the work of local Buddhist grammar schools, in Shōsan's time and for centuries thereafter the warriors were the most educated class in Japan. Therefore those of his talks and writings directed specifically to warriors contain the most advice on the subject of education and character development. Again characteristically Buddhist in this sense, these works of Zen master Suzuki Shōsan are a mine of quotations that are useful even in their most obvious meanings, and yield more as experience and understanding deepen:

> Stand up and be responsible for yourself. Even people who are prudent in everything will hide their secret faults when they are only concerned about public opinion and outward appearances. So even very conventional and conservative people will have faults in their inner minds. Beware of your mind, and take responsibility for yourself.

This contrasts sharply with the image of Japanese morality as fundamentally other-directed. Ordinarily shame is considered the operative element in ruling Japanese social behaviors; but here Shōsan illustrates the shortcomings of shame in comparison with conscience, with which it was originally linked in Buddhist psychotherapeutics. Western Christian moral feeling and Japanese moral feeling are commonly compared in terms of a distinction between guilt and shame. By pairing shame and conscience, in contrast, traditional Buddhist psychology includes both social and personal moral feelings in a continuum of consciousness. Shōsan also shows how the inward personal experience of being directly affects the outward interpersonal experience. The kind of Zen introspection and self-knowledge Shōsan teaches is therefore not a form of self-involvement to distract one from external realities, but is in evident fact a way to survey the foundation of ordinary social psychology and the roots of social behavior.

Be aware of yourself and know yourself. No matter how much you have learned and how much you know, if you don't know yourself you don't know anything. Indeed, if you don't know yourself you cannot know anything else.

People who don't know themselves criticize others from the point of view of their own ignorant selves. They consider whatever agrees with them to be good, and hate whatever doesn't go their way. They become irritated about everything, causing themselves to suffer by themselves, bothering themselves solely because of their own prejudices.

If you know that not everyone will be agreeable to you, know that you won't be agreeable to everyone either. Those who have no prejudices in themselves do not reject people, and therefore people do not reject them.

Buddhist philosophy and psychology are based on logical and experiential relativity of subject and object. Therefore objectivity is approached through analytic criticism combined with inner exercises to minimize the influence of subjectivity, in order to develop the ability to outmaneuver self-deceptive biases. According to Zen master Dōgen, "Studying Buddhism is studying self. To study the self is to forget self. To forget self is to be enlightened by all things."

In this Zen context, self-study not only means investigation into the real self, it also means learning about the subjective biases of false selves. Forgetting self means penetrating the barrier of self-deception by a false self. Being enlightened by all things is direct learning through the experiences of life as it is, without the mythology of false selves imposing their judgments and preconceptions on what it means to be.

Shōsan goes on to describe the attitude of detached yet intentional self-monitoring. This is used in Buddhist practice to overcome unnecessary limitations imposed on the capacity and function of mind by unchecked wandering:

Developmental exercise is a matter of being as strongminded as possible. Our conditioned senses and ideas are like bandits that can steal our original mind. These bandits arise from weakness in our minds. Therefore you should use your energy strongly to watch intently over your own mind. People misunderstand the Zen term "no thought" and use it to become absentminded dolts. This is a big mistake. You should keep a strong mind.

The misunderstanding of "no thought" to which Shōsan refers would appear to have plagued Zen movements over the centuries, from earliest times to the present day. Sometimes there is no one like Shōsan around to point out that this is not Zen, and the aberration has been mistaken for the real thing. This polarizes the uninformed public exposed to such a movement, in a manner that is not entirely useful either to those who accept Zen or those who reject Zen on this basis.

Misunderstanding has at times reached the point where irrationality has come to be considered the measure of Zen, not only by opponents but even by proponents. Many of the incoherent utterances of modern popularizes such as D. T. Suzuki and C. G. Jung testify to the existence of this phenomenon in the present day.

Somewhat less flamboyant than the irrationalists are the quietists, who also have appeared from time to time and who have earned for Zen a reputation of social irrelevance at best and parasitism at worst. Shōsan was among the foremost of those to counter these negative images with the assertion and demonstration that Zen mind is not blank, otherworldly, or irrational, but in fact eminently practical in ordinary life.

> Buddhist practice means eliminating obstacles caused by historical events, thus getting rid of all misery. This mind is a treasure that brings physical and mental peace and happiness to all classes and occupations when used in their lives.
>
> Buddhist practice is eliminating foul, polluted attitudes, becoming pure and unblocked in mind, turning misery to happiness, turning evil to good. This mind is a treasure useful in all undertakings and all good works.
>
> Buddhist practice is eliminating confused and ignorant attitudes, so as to be beyond greed, hatred, and delusion. This mind is a treasure of mental health that ends psychological afflictions.

Far from being irrational, Zen teaching points out the irrationality of a life dominated by instincts and emotions. One of the first steps of Buddhist practice is to take stock of the effect that compulsions have on the individual, and how this makes one internally and externally vulnerable to control by unmanageable forces.

Fools disregard their lives for the sake of desires. Even though they trouble themselves mentally and physically by their cravings, they are never satisfied; and yet they never give up.

Buddhism teaches ways of transcending compulsion and attaining freedom through "forgetting the self," in Zen master Dōgen's words. This does not mean that there is no awareness of self, only that awareness is not enclosed in any self. The enlightenment attributed to buddhas includes awareness of all selves, including actual and possible selves as well as the "self of selves." This naturally includes what are ordinarily thought of as the selves of others, which means that the individual aware of the selves of others is also aware of the selves of self. Shōsan therefore distinguishes among practical qualities and scales of remembrance and forgetfulness of self.

Shōsan makes it clear that to forget the self does not mean to act impulsively or irrationally, or to live with heedless abandon. In the same way that he warns people against exaggerated misunderstanding of the technique of "no thought," Shōsan is careful to balance a reasonable practice of self-forgetting with a conscientious practice of self-awareness. In this way the individual is centered between extremes, neither too involved with self nor too careless of self.

Forget yourself, yet don't forget yourself. When people are ambitious and greedy, they are concerned exclusively with themselves, forgetting even their own relatives. On the other hand, when in pursuit of what they like they forget themselves and lose their conscience, so they do not understand the implications of what they do and are unconcerned about even the direst of consequences. Much unworthy behavior derives from this, so don't forget yourself.

Following traditional Zen Buddhist teaching, Shōsan explains further that self-indulgence is not confined to what is ordinarily thought of as selfish or immoral behavior, but also infects activity that is conventionally considered good or virtuous.

There is contaminated goodness, and there is uncontaminated goodness. What is done without self-consciousness is called uncontaminated goodness. What is done for your own sake, in hopes of reward, is called contaminated goodness.

Ancient Zen masters have in fact said that self-centered virtue can be even worse than self-centered vice. Piety does not call down on itself the opprobrium of conventional society, because it is clothed in acceptable appearances; therefore the unreflective individual is not put under any pressure to reexamine personal behavior and its subjective interpretations. Under these conditions it is much easier to become set in one's ways, fortified by a self-perpetuating circle of rationalizations and justifications.

For these reasons, fluidity and nonattachment are considered essential prerequisites for attainment of a perspective comprehensive enough to assess the purpose and effect of behaviors, whether secular or sacred, in the objective light of its total context. The martial artists preach detachment for the purpose of mastering their special skills, and in a sense the warrior who has suffered a mortal defeat in battle may have nothing else but detachment as an ultimate resort, a final personal victory. As a Buddhist wayfarer, Shōsan also faces the reality of death, but he extends the principle of fluidity to an art of progressive living.

> There is virtue in not stagnating. People get fixated at one point or another, with the result that they are unaware of what went before or what comes after. Thus they lack virtue. In their livelihood as well as in their perceptions of others, they often lose much for a little gain. They are, however, unaware of this in themselves. So if you want to leave the small for the great, notice your fixations and detach from them.

Even apart from the awareness of death obligatory for professional warriors, remembrance of impermanence and the inevitability of personal death has been used by Buddhists in all walks of life as one of the most accessible and efficient methods of freeing the mind from compulsive attachment to things. This is one of the basic exercises of elementary Buddhist practice, found throughout the broad spectrum of Buddhist schools and scriptures.

Early Western investigators who became fixated on this particular type of practice and treated it in isolation from the greater tradition of unitarian Buddhism were naturally horrified by this consciousness of death and consequently portrayed Buddhism as a pessimistic religion. Far from being morbid, as emotional Western critics have claimed, this aspect of Buddhism actually enables practitioners to appreciate life more fully, to be freer and more efficient in whatever they do. It also teaches them to meet sickness and death serene and unafraid.

This is in any case just one part of a much larger teaching, and the emphasis given to death by professional soldiers over centuries of warfare in medieval Japan should not be considered the measure of Buddhist consciousness. There is something very positive in the immediate awareness of evanescence, something that is neither in the grim stoicism of the warrior in the field nor in the wistful pining of the poet in a garden. Shōsan explains how the tendency to forget or ignore transitoriness affects the whole mood and conduct of life.

> When people forget that they are going to die, and act as if they think they are going to live forever, they do not fully appreciate and utilize the passing months and years. As long as they are like this, they only act on greed, anger, and falsehood, turning away from social and family duties, not understanding human kindness and obligation, employing flattery and cajolery, neglecting home and work for useless hobbies and amusements.

Shōsan's Zen is rooted in the practicalities of earthly life. He had no time for airy-fairy "spirituality" divorced from the needs of everyday existence. Even the extraordinary phenomena of enhanced intellect and psychic powers were made by Shōsan to serve common needs such as education and healing. His intellectual and practical amalgamation of social and Buddhist teachings is summarized in an essay "On the Daily Life of Warriors," which is not meant for professional samurai alone, but is intended as a model for responsible people in all walks of life.

> A samurai asked, "They say Buddhist principles and social principles are like the two wheels of a chariot. But even if there is no Buddhism, that does not imply any lack in the world. Why are the two sets of principles likened to the twin wheels of a chariot?"
>
> Shōsan answered, "Buddhist principles and social principles are not two separate things. According to a Buddhist saying, 'If

you can enter the world successfully, you are totally beyond the world.' "

To say that ability to enter the world successfully means ability to transcend the world means that efficiency reduces confusion, thus freeing mental energy from preoccupation with matters pending. In contrast to this, premature attempts to get "beyond the world" solely by supposedly "spiritual" exercises can result in slovenly management of daily and long-term affairs, which then increases ordinary anxieties. This in turn has the effect of hindering freedom of mind, closing the open end of life and thus adding spiritual anxiety to preexisting worries about things of the world. The result of this is that neither side of human life, the mundane or the spiritual, receives its due attention, as that due to the one is given to the other and vice versa.

Part of the problem connected with images of irrationality in Zen comes from the definition of rationality with which the interpreter starts. If the modern alliance of warfare and science is considered rational, or the product of rational thinking, it would not be any wonder that someone from modern Japan like D. T. Suzuki would want to throw a monkey-wrench into that machine and at least try to slow it down by touting irrationality to its intellectuals, writing extensively on Zen stories hand-picked for their apparently puzzling character.

Even a scholar and psychologist of the status of C. G. Jung admits to an inability to discern the symbolic meanings of the Zen stories related by D. T. Suzuki in a book to which Jung himself wrote an introduction in 1939. This image of inscrutability was to become one of the hallmarks of the popular Western image of Zen. It was hardly suspected that this might not be an altogether veridical image. Even less considered was the possibility that this mysteriousness was of a strategic rather than essential nature.

Now that these dimensions of behavior have become of concern in the arenas of commercial and political activities, and because Zen has also become commercialized and politicized, there has developed more academic interest in corresponding aspects of Zen. Although there are many outlines and discussions, however, nothing really like a comprehensive study of the subject is yet available.

What the ordinary person in search of information may be most likely to find are books representing particular teachings, sects, or schools; books on the personal experiences of individuals practicing some kind of Zen exercise; or academic tomes on some relic of the past. Many treatments of Zen do in fact contain irrational elements, largely based on personal attachments to what Zen Buddhists themselves call the "traces."

In contrast to irrational or superficial Zennists envisioned through commercialized or propagandistic versions of the teaching, who in view of their mention in Zen literature obviously are not unique anywhere and must exist in all times and places side by side with truth, Shōsan teaches Buddhism in a way that clearly shows its foundation of reason, starting from the premise that "both Buddhist and social principles are nothing but the application of genuine honesty, making reasoning accurate and action just."

This formulation is a typical example of a concrete reflection of the "nonduality" principle as it is understood in Buddhist philosophy. Shōsan can sincerely say that social virtues and Buddhist virtues are one, yet can still distinguish differences in how the same virtues are understood and practiced on different levels of consciousness.

> There are different levels of depth in honesty. Honesty in the social context means not twisting reason, being dutiful and just, giving all social relations their proper attention, harmonizing with others, and being unselfish and fair. This is a way to enter from a relatively shallow dimension into a deeper dimension.

It is a commonplace of Buddhism that social ethics serve as a preparation for the higher psychological development fostered by spiritual practices. This does not diminish the dignity or importance of social ethics, but places them in a broader context than religious dogmatics. One of the great advantages of the wider view of Buddhism is that it reduces the human tendency to stagnate morally through self-righteousness or cynicism. Shōsan exemplifies this as he describes the deeper meaning of honesty in typical Buddhist metaphysical terms.

> Honesty in the context of Buddhism is to realize that all fabricated things are ultimately unreal deceptions, and thus to use the original spiritual body in oneself in its natural spontaneous state.

Here the difficulty of Zen for the pedestrian mind becomes evident. The prospect of being able to utilize a "spiritual body in oneself" may appeal to the ordinary interest in advantage of any kind; but there is still a socially ingrained resistance to the idea that conventionally structured experiences and institutions are ultimately unreal. To ordinary conception, this notion would seem destructive, but Shōsan illustrates how it works in the total context of Buddhism, as a doorway to liberation of creative potential.

In Buddhist terms, the ultimate unreality of mundane things does not mean that they are insignificant or negligible, but rather that they are malleable, which means that they are workable. Realization of emptiness therefore does not mean withdrawal from the world, but rather the capacity for change, the potential for progress. Shōsan goes on to describe the kind of change and progress for which Zen Buddhism aims as it heals the "mental illness" that keeps humans immersed in animalistic behaviors. Here the intimate connection between individual liberation and collective liberation is made obvious.

> Ordinary people are morally ill; buddhas are master physicians. Ordinary people should first of all get rid of their illnesses. In the fluctuating and unenlightened mind, there are the illnesses of delusion and confusion; there are the illnesses of greed and misperception; there are the illnesses of cowardice and injustice. Based on the mind full of the poisons of greed, hatred, and delusion, these poisons produce eighty-four thousand mental illnesses. Getting rid of this mind is called Buddhism. Is this any different from the principle of society?

The Buddhist teaching on the objective unreality or emptiness of conditioned phenomena was typically made a prime target of anti-Buddhist invective both East and West, by those who misconstrued the doctrine as a form of nihilism or quietism. While it is true that some neurotic Zennists with escapist tendencies were greatly attracted to a nihilistic view of emptiness, orthodox Buddhist tradition has always repudiated such exaggerations as perversions. According to Nāgārjuna, a spiritual ancestor of Zen in India and one of the greatest writers on the metaphysics of emptiness, "The enlightened have said that emptiness is departure from all views, but they have also said that those who make emptiness a view cannot be saved."

Shōsan makes it clear that realization of emptiness is not the goal of Zen, but the means by which to eliminate biased views and undesirable psychological complexes rooted in deceptions about the nature of reality. He contrasts the freedom gained through practical use of emptiness with the bondage resulting from fixation on appearances.

Knowing the principle of original emptiness, those who have mastered the Way use reason and justice as a forge to temper the mind daily, getting rid of impurities to turn it into a pure, clear, unopposed mind-sword, which cuts through the thought-root of selfish greed and conquers all thoughts, so that the Way-farers ride on top of everything, untroubled by anything, beginningless and endless.

But ordinary people take deceptions for realities, creating attitudes biased by fixation on appearances, thus starting up thoughts of craving, anger, and misunderstanding. Having produced all sorts of psychological afflictions and lost the original mind, they find that their minds are distracted and unfocused, giving in to whatever thoughts arise. As a result of this, they suffer from handicapped mentalities that make them hurt. They have no psychological buoyancy; they are gloomy and depressed, living aimlessly and without self-understanding, fixating their attention on things. This is called the mentality of the common man.

The distinction made in Zen between ordinary people and enlightened people is not based on formal accomplishments but on the level of mind in which their everyday lives are grounded. Shōsan describes the mentality of the common man as chronically superficial, fixated on appearances and attached to things. This is thought of as a loss, or alienation from the autonomy of the "original mind," which Zen teaching identifies with "buddha nature."

The primary desideratum of Zen is to recover the experience of original mind through itself. From this standpoint it is possible to see through the deception of attachment to superficialities. Shōsan explains the practical qualities of original mind as experienced in Zen, with emphasis on the psychological freedom and security attained through its penetrating insight and autonomy.

We should know different names for the original mind. It is called the indestructible true substance, or the stable spiritual body. This mind is not caught up in things, is not fearful or alarmed, does not worry or withdraw. Imperturbable and unchanging, it becomes the master of everything. Those who have penetrated this and can actually use it are called great sturdy folk, people with hearts and guts of steel, or people who have attained the Way. People like this, unimpeded by all thoughts, can freely employ all things, events, and situations.

Because of the persistent tendency of the superficial mentality to cling to externals, the discipline needed to free the energy of mind from entanglements cannot really be imposed on the individual from without, but must come from within. In the absence of corresponding inner strength, outward discipline itself becomes an attachment, an appurtenance of the ego, leading to the kind of cultism and sentimental religiosity so often encountered in self-proclaimed spiritual coteries. Shōsan's own background made no allowance for make-believe discipline; he was therefore adamant in his insistence on the necessity of inner strength and independent will power.

So people who practice the way of buddhas first need to have courage and intensity of purpose; otherwise it is hard to succeed. It is impossible to enter the way of buddhas with a timid heart. If you do not protect yourself surely and cultivate yourself strongly, you will suffer from whatever mental afflictions occur.
Those who use a firm heart and a stable mind to overcome all things are called people of the Way. Those whose thoughts stick to appearances and who thus suffer miserably, at the mercy of events, are called ordinary people.

Shōsan's attitude would seem to be characteristic of a warrior, and he did bring his experience in military training and combat to bear on the issues of Zen psychology in dealing with the general problems of life and death. Yet he was careful to distinguish the "courage" required of the independent Zen mind from the "courage" of warriors associated with force and violence.

So people who stir up the courage of bloodlust with afflicted minds may at some point have the force to break through iron walls, but there is inevitably a time when bloodlust is exhausted and moods change. A sturdy heart, in contrast, is immovable and does not change. If warriors cultivate it, why wouldn't they develop such a sturdy heart?

If they have afflicted minds, even people of tremendous martial valor will find that when they face the end of their lives and the killer ghost of impermanence comes after them, their usual forcefulness will run out, their courageous ferocity will be gone, and they will be unable to muster any strength.

The distinction between the animal ferocity of the armed warrior killing opponents and the spiritual ferocity of the Zen warrior cutting through illusions was not always remembered and observed by Zennists following the practices of schools influenced by or oriented toward the life of the Japanese samurai. Even today one can hear and read seemingly endless tales of physical and mental violence in certain Rinzai Zen monasteries, as if this sort of fierceness were a measure of the quality of their discipline.

All too often this brand of samurai machismo is tied to the same superficial mechanism of self-importance that deludes the ordinary mentality. As a result of this the ego is not transcended but aggrandized and hardened by the discipline to which it is trained. Shōsan therefore made it clear that the cultivation of moral fiber in the Buddhist sense centers on dispelling the illusions created by self-importance.

The root source of misery is the thought, "Me, me." To know this is so is reason. Acting on knowledge of this reason with a mind of true courage, only justice can extirpate that thought.

People without reason do not understand the source of misery and happiness; people without justice cannot cut the halter of life and death. This calls for close attention.

As in his interpretation of "honesty," here again Shōsan uses Buddhistic understanding of "reason" and "justice" that penetrate more deeply than the commonplace Confucian definitions of these terms. In Shōsan's time, an academic form of Neo-Confucianism was officially adopted as state orthodoxy, but this doctrine typically suffered from a tendency to lapse into sterile intellectualism without practical means of empowering its principles. Therefore most Confucian scholars without political ambitions were more inclined toward the unorthodox versions of Neo-Confucianism that contained more of the pragmatic elements of Buddhism.

Drawing on both Zen and Neo-Confucian teachings, Shōsan concludes his essay on the daily life of warriors with a discussion on ways of developing the strength of character he deemed so important for both social and spiritual life. He contrasts attitudes or moods of what he calls a buoyant mind that rises above mundane conditions with depressive states of mind that are overcome by mundane conditions.

In the mind of the ordinary person there are buoyant moods when they overcome things, and there are depressed moods when they are overcome by things. Use of buoyant moods is a way into the world of enlightenment; use of depressed moods is a way into prison. Concentrating the power of aspiration for liberation, one should keep a buoyant mood day and night.

Here are buoyant moods that overcome things by means of a courageous mind: mindfulness of life and death; gratitude for blessings; indomitability in making progress; awareness of causality; insight into unreality and impermanence; respect for the value of time; watchfulness over oneself; self-abandon; self-criticism; respectfulness; humanitarian justice; attention to the sayings of the enlightened; kindness, compassion, uprightness, and honesty; reflection on what is most important.

Such states of mind come from a courageous and firm mind, so they leave off all sorts of attachments and rise above things. Therefore when you maintain a buoyant state of mind you will suffer but little even if you suddenly go to your death.

When this courageous attitude is continuous, the citadel of the heart is secure, with virtuous power that is unhindered and independent. Even if all sorts of bewilderments should arise, they cannot face up to this firm heart; they will lose their force and disappear when their energy is gone. Should warriors not have such a firm heart?

If you are weakminded and your thoughts are fixed on appearances, bewilderments get power over you with increasing force, invading your nature, confusing your mind, and making you lose control of yourself.

There are also depressive moods that are overcome by things: negligence, tourism, incivility; indifference to consequences; disregard for the facts of impermanence and unreality; desire for fame and fortune; luxury; doubt and distrust; stickiness; timid-ity; merciless stinginess and greed; jealousy and envy; ingratitude; obsequiousness; heedlessness of life and death.

In contrast to Suzuki Shōsan's detailed explanation of Zen in the warrior's way, Zen master Takuan's instructions to the martial artist Yagyū Munenori all hinge upon the central principle of fluidity. It is also possible to interpret many of Suzuki's sayings as elaborations of this principle in practice, and even Takuan's tightly centered writings draw a great deal of practical wisdom from this simple premise. The characteristic beauty of Takuan's writings is their insistent return to fundamentals, one of the hallmarks of Zen.

The first of Takuan's letters to Yagyū recorded in the collection entitled *Writings on the Wonders of Immovable Knowledge* is entitled "The Affliction of Unaware Fixation." Here he introduces the topic of Zen perception in the context of dueling, symbolic of human confrontation, contention, and conflict.

> In terms of the art of war, when you see an opponent's sword slashing at you, if you think to parry it then and there, your mind fixes on the sword. Then your action falters and you get cut by your adversary. This is called fixation, or lingering.
>
> If you don't set your mind on the striking sword even as you see it, and don't keep any thoughts in mind, and meet the oncoming sword directly as soon as you see it, without fixing your mind on it at all, you can take away the sword intended to kill you, and have it turn into a sword to kill your opponent.
>
> In Zen this is called taking the head of the lance and turning it around to stab the other. This means the same thing as taking away the adversary's sword to kill him with what you call "no sword."
>
> Whether the opponent strikes first or you strike first, if you fix your mind on the person at all, or on the sword, the distance, or the timing, your actions will falter. The result will be that you can be killed.
>
> Since your mind is taken up with your opponent when you put yourself in an adversarial position, you shouldn't keep your mind on yourself either.
>
> Reining in your mind to keep it on your body is something to be practiced only as a beginner.
>
> If you set your mind on the sword, your mind is taken up

with the sword. If you set your mind on timing, your mind is taken up with timing. If you set your mind on your own sword, your mind is taken up with your own sword. In any case, your mind lingers and your action falters.

Although this was written for a martial artist and therefore uses the appropriate idiom, in the customary Zen manner it naturally extends analogically beyond its overt context. According to Buddhist understanding, the nature of ordinary reality is interactive, not static; so the image of the duel symbolizes the dynamic relationship of the individual to the constantly changing situation presented by the surroundings, especially by the conditions and milieu of one's professional occupation. The "no sword" maneuver, in which an unarmed warrior makes use of an opponent's weapon to snatch victory from defeat, symbolizes the ultimate resourcefulness of the independent Zen adept; it is also a good metaphor for the process of Japan's modernization over the last century.

In his shorter essays "No Gap" and "Mind Like a Spark," Takuan uses Zen terms to explain the way of fluidity in action. He explains spontaneous responsiveness in terms of immediacy, but he does not identify this with speed. It is not quickness of action but immediacy of attention that makes this possible, the Zen master writes, emphasizing freedom of mind.

When you clap your hands a sound comes out immediately, without any interval. The sound does not deliberately come out a while after you clap, it comes right out as you clap.

If your mind stops on the sword your opponent is swinging at you, a gap opens up; and in that gap your action falters.

If there is no gap between your opponent's striking sword and your action, the sword of the adversary will become your sword.

A mind like a spark means the state of mind where there is no gap. When a flint is struck, sparks fly at once. This also means there is no interval for the mind to stop and linger.

It is wrong to understand this only in terms of speed. It means you shouldn't let the mind linger on things, that you shouldn't set the mind on anything, even speed.

If attention lingers, your mind is taken over by others. If you act quickly counting on speed, your mind is also taken over by this attitude.

For centuries there has been a marked tendency in Zen circles to identify speed with spontaneity, due to the use of the former as an imitation or substitute for the latter. It is to this illusion that Zen master Takuan alludes here. The same idea still exists in Zen schools where ritual dialogue is highly prized. It was also fostered in the West by the popular writer D. T. Suzuki, who often gave the impression that Zen depends on quickness of wit, to the degree that any sort of nonsensical statement or action will do as long as it is so rapid as to appear spontaneous.

As a result of this, the distinction is blurred between automatic reactions (such as saying or doing whatever springs to mind at the moment) and the precise awakened response of fluid awareness as originally developed in authentic Zen. D. T. Suzuki's professed belief that Zen enlightenment is irrational also helped to shield this sort of misperception from critical examination within the context of Zen itself as it was known though his writings in the West.

Zen master Takuan, in contrast, points out that the very idea of speed as spontaneity becomes a point of fixation itself. This is amply borne out by Western literature on Zen following the doctrines of D. T. Suzuki. Fascination with quickwitted repartee had already been repudiated by the great Chinese Zen master Dahui five centuries before Takuan, but samurai-oriented Japanese Zen schools seem to have reinstated the cult of speed because of their own concern with the practice of martial arts.

Nevertheless, genuine spontaneity emerging from the immediacy of centered open awareness (rather than from conditioned reflex) is prized not only by Zen warriors, but by all who seek to apply Zen consciousness to actual life situations. In his essay "Where to Set the Mind," Takuan thus proceeds to enumerate the points at which the warrior's mind is unwittingly trained to stop and linger. Finally he shows how the Zen mind transcends these fixations, even the most abstract. This includes a common fixation of Zennists, concentration on one yogic technique that warriors and cultists pursued to great lengths.

Where to set the mind?

If you set your mind on an opponent's actions, you have your mind taken up by the opponent's actions.

If you set your mind on an opponent's sword, you have your mind taken up by the opponent's sword.

If you set your mind on the thought of killing an opponent, you have your mind taken up by the thought of killing the opponent.

If you set your mind on your own sword, you have your mind taken up by your own sword.

If you set your mind on your determination not to be killed, you have your mind taken up by the determination not to be killed.

If you set your mind on people's postures, you have your mind taken up by people's postures.

The point is that there is nowhere at all to set the mind.

Some people say, "If we have the mind go anywhere at all, the mind will be fixated by where it goes, putting us at a disadvantage to adversaries. So put the mind in your gut and keep it there, while adapting to what adversaries do."

Of course, this could be, but from the point of view of an advanced stage of Buddhism, to keep the mind in the lower abdomen is a low stage. It is the stage of practice, the stage of remembrance of seriousness, the stage referred to as "seeking the free mind." It is not the higher transcendental stage, it is the mood of seriousness.

If you force your mind into your gut below your navel and determine to keep it there, your mind is taken up by the determination to keep it there, so your forward action is deficient and you become extraordinarily unfree.

The now popular practice of settling attention in the lower abdomen *(hara)* was apparently introduced to Japan around the year 800 C.E. It was part of the meditation lore of the Tendai school of Buddhism, which was established in Japan about that time. In the context of Tendai Buddhism, this exercise is presented as an ancient healing technique. Its immediate efficacy in promoting the power of mental stability *(jōriki)*, however, seems to have been its main source of attraction to martial artists. Although it is now commonly associated with Zen Buddhism (which originally was closely related to the Tendai school) as a means of cultivating concentration *(zenjō)*, there is hardly any notice of it at all in the meditation instructions of the classical Japanese Zen masters.

The practice of concentration in the *hara* was attributed to Taoist health lore by an eighteenth-century Japanese Zen reviver. He used it to cure some acute nervous and physical problems that he suffered as a result of pondering Zen koans too intensely; among the followers of his school, however, it seems to have become a general method of concentration. The practitioners of this form of Zen will say that they work on koans, or Zen stories, in their gut. Over the last century and a half, this school of Zen acquired great influence among the upper classes in Japan, and the deceptively easy belly-concentration technique passed readily into Western versions of Zen, with virtually no questions asked.

Nevertheless, it was probably through Bushidō rather than pure Zen that this practice spread among the common people of Japan to the degree that expressions such as *Hara ga dekite iru* ("The gut is accomplished") and *Hara ga suwatte iru* ("The gut is set") are colloquially used to refer to a calm, collected, imperturbable personality. It can be an image of maturity in general, but it can also apply to serenity and sobriety in face of a particular life-and-death challenge. In either case, the manner of usage is very typical of Bushidō over the last two centuries.

According to the *Tao Te Ching,* "A way that can be articulated is not a permanent way." In this gut meditation exercise, Zen adopted only a small portion of the more complete tradition of Taoism. Later Zennists and followers of Bushidō in Japan seem inclined to make it into a permanent mind-body posture. Some Chinese Taoists do the same thing, but unlike modern Japanese Zen literature, Chinese Taoist writings abound with warnings about dangers in this practice, especially for women.

Most of these caveats are based on the harm on overdoing things. The premodern reviver of the culturally dominant Rinzai school of Zen took up Taoist techniques to cure some very serious symptoms admittedly caused by overdoing meditation on Zen koans. Taoists also say that their own traditional practices are harmful when overdone. And yet ever since the time of the Rinzai revival there have been Zennists who overdo both koan meditation and belly-attention.

This is not only irrational in itself in Buddhist and Taoist terms, it also makes a person who does it for a long time become irrational. D. T. Suzuki's image of illogical Zen may not have been merely his own understanding of the classics, or his own attempt at the art of the advantage, but also a genuine belief based upon personal observations and experiences of a highly involuted meditation system in early modern Japan.

One of the dangers of focusing attention in the lower abdomen, according to classical and modern Taoist sources, is that the practice produces results easily in the realm of calmness and concentration, but it cannot lead to higher enlightenment. The lure of its ease and comfort seems to be a major reason for the prevalence of fixation on it in popular Zen and Taoist cults.

Concentration without wisdom is one of the endemic ills of Japanese Zen, particularly the forms of Zen under the influence of Confucianism and Bushidō. Takuan is one of the rare Japanese Zen masters to point out the negative potential in this simplistic mind-body posture. Referring to focus in the *hara* as an elementary practice not to be kept up permanently, Takuan said that the more advanced Zen posture of nondwelling not only liberates the mind but likewise the body.

If you don't put your mind anywhere, it will pervade your whole body fully, spreading through your whole being, so that when you need hands it works your hands, when you need feet it works your feet, when you need eyes it works your eyes. Since it is present wherever you need it, it makes the functions you need possible. If you fix the mind in one place, it will be taken up by that place and thus deficient in function.

If you ruminate, you are taken up by rumination, so you should let go of the mind in the whole body, without leaving any rumination or judgment there, and fulfill the function of each place accurately without stopping and lingering anywhere.

If you put the mind in one place, you become warped. To be warped is to be onesided; to be straight is to reach everywhere. The straight mind, or right mind, means the mind extended throughout the whole body, not sticking to one area or direction.

When the mind is put away in one place, with the result that it is deficient elsewhere, this is called a warped mind. It is the warp that we disdain. Fixation on things is called becoming warped, and is disdained on the Zen Way.

If you don't think of where to put it, the mind pervades the whole being. Placing the mind nowhere, employ your attention to each situation as it happens, according to what opponents do.

Takuan further elaborates on mental freedom and bondage in terms of the traditional ideas of practical Zen psychology. The free fluid mind he is trying to convey to the warrior is now described as the *basic mind* or the *unminding mind*. The fixated mind he tells the warrior to abandon is now called the *errant mind* or the *minding mind*. The Zen master Takuan resumes his previous discussion of physical freedom emerging from mental freedom, to explain specific practical details:

> The basic mind is the mind that does not stay in one place but pervades the whole body and whole being. The errant mind is the mind fixed on one spot, brooding over some thing.
>
> When the basic mind congeals and focuses on one point, it becomes the errant mind. Once the basic mind is lost, its various functions become deficient. So the fundamental idea is to try not to lose it.
>
> The basic mind is like water, not remaining anywhere; the errant mind is like ice, with which you cannot wash your hands or head.
>
> If you melt the ice into water, so that it will flow anywhere, then you can wash your hands and feet.
>
> If your mind fixes on one spot and lingers on one thing, it freezes. As a result it cannot be used freely, just as ice cannot be used for washing.
>
> If you melt your mind and use it like a flood throughout the whole body, you send it where you want to and put it to use as you will. This is called the basic mind.

It is not too much to say that recovering the basic mind is given primary importance in Zen. The natural poise of the basic mind was also sought by warriors as a center of balance, from which spontaneous action could emerge without inhibition caused by self-consciousness. In his book on martial arts, the warrior Yagyū Munenori also includes a discussion of the basic mind and the errant mind, following this teaching of Zen master Takuan into more concrete avenues:

> The false mind is passion and selfishness. When the false mind arises, the basic mind is hidden and becomes false consciousness; so nothing but bad things come out.
>
> When we make up falsehoods while saying that there is no

falsehood, this is itself the false mind, so its falsehood has already become evident. If the heart is true, people will eventually
know, without explanations. The basic mind needs no explanations or excuses.

The false mind is sickness in the basic mind. To get rid of the
false mind is called getting rid of sickness. When you get rid of
this sickness, you have a healthy mind. This healthy mind is
called the basic mind, or the original mind.

If you are in accord with the basic mind, you can become a
master of the art of war. This principle also applies to anything
you may do.

Zen masters and the martial artists who tried to follow the Zen
way typically considered the core mental attitudes of their particular
ways to be useful in all activities and all walks of life, as they never
tired of repeating. They did not believe that they were ultimately
training the mind to conform to arbitrary patterns imposed upon the
practitioner, but rather to have available the ability to unfold natural
potential for fluid response to the situation at hand. Zen master Takuan also elaborates in terms of the Buddhist definitions of "minding" and "unminding," contrasting attitudes that characterize the
so-called "errant" and "basic" minds. He illustrates the difference between "minding" as excess thought and "unminding" as unburdened
awareness. Like Suzuki Shōsan in his warning about misunderstanding "no thought," Takuan also explains the distinction between
"unminding" in a positive sense as fluidity and freedom, and "mindlessness" in a negative sense as blankness or oblivion.

The minding mind is the same thing as the errant mind. Minding means to mull over one thing, whatever it may be. When
you think about something in your mind, judgments and rumi-
nations arise, so this is called the minding mind.

The unminding mind is the same as the basic mind, the mind
as it is when not frozen or fixated, without judgments or rumi-
nations. The mind that pervades the whole body and permeates
the whole being is called the unminding mind. It is the mind
not set anywhere. It is not like stone or wood; unminding mind
means the mind that does not stay anywhere.

If you linger, there is something on the mind; if you don't

linger, there is nothing on the mind. When you have nothing on your mind, that is called unminding mind.

When this unminding becomes your mind, you do not dwell on anything and do not miss anything. In your body it comes out when a need faces it, to fulfill that need.

The mind that stays fixed in one place doesn't work freely. A wheel turns precisely because it isn't fixed. If it is stuck in one place, it won't turn. The mind won't work either when it is fixed in one place.

If you're thinking about something in your mind, you don't hear what people are saying even as you listen. This is because the mind is staying on what you're thinking about.

When your mind is on the thing you're thinking about, it is onesided. When it is onesided, it does not hear when you listen or see when you look. This is because there is something on your mind, meaning something you are thinking about.

When you have removed whatever that is, you mind is unminding and only works when needed, as needed.

The mind that wishes to get rid of what is on the mind also becomes something on the mind. If you don't think of it, it goes away by itself, and you become unminding spontaneously.

If you always act thus, you will eventually reach that state by yourself some day. If you try to do it right away, you don't get there.

An ancient poem says:

To think you will not think
Is also thinking of something;
Will you resolve not to think
Even of not thinking?

Takuan extends this principle to all the arts in his explanation of a famous passage from Buddhist scripture, "We should enliven the mind without dwelling on anything." One of the most popular Zen legends tells of the enlightenment of an illiterate woodcutter on hearing this passage. That woodcutter later became the supreme master of Zen in China, his story enshrined as an emblem of the capacities hidden in the ordinary mind. Both the scriptural quotation and the traditional Zen associations are perfect settings for the point that Takuan tries to convey to the warrior.

"We should enliven the mind without dwelling on anything."

In any kind of occupation, when the thought of doing your work arises, your mind lingers on what you are doing. So this passage means that we should enliven the mind without lingering anywhere.

If the mind is not alive where it is to come alive, your hands don't work; if you're walking, you stop right there. Those who enliven the mind to do specific things yet do not stop and linger in the process are called the experts of the various arts.

From the lingering mind there arises the clinging mind, and repetitious routine existence also begins from here. This lingering mind becomes the bond of life and death.

The point is not to stop there with the consciousness that you are seeing the flowers and foliage even as you see the flowers and foliage.

The ultimate point is not to park the mind in one place, even as you see and hear.

Finally, Takuan clarifies the distinction between "seriousness," mentioned earlier as an elementary practice, and the Zen practice of "not dwelling anywhere." This is a point that often confuses Westerners, because the Japanese generally practice "seriousness" more than they do "nondwelling," and the outsider may easily miss the distinction. Takuan explains:

When you take seriousness as concentration on oneness or unity of attention, not drifting off, you are still fixing the mind in one place. The essential thing is not to let the mind go to the one you are going to kill, even if that means you are not the first to draw your sword.

The (Neo-Confucian) expression "concentration on oneness, not drifting off" and the (Pure Land Buddhist) expression "single-minded, undisturbed" mean the same thing. However, the mind of "seriousness" is not the ultimate in the context of Buddhism. It is a method of training and practice in controlling the mind and keeping it orderly. When this practice has been built up over the years, your mind goes freely wherever you send it.

The stage of "not dwelling on anything" is the higher, final rank. The mind of "seriousness" is the stage at which you deliberately stop the mind from going elsewhere, thinking that it will become disorderly if you let it go, keeping the mind in check with constant vigilance. This is just a temporary measure, to avoid scattering the mind for the time being. If you are this way all the time, you are inhibited.

From this point of view, followers of Zen or Zen arts who impress others with lifelong dedication to "practice" may actually be the most diligent failures. The signs that the warrior Miyamoto Musashi did not succeed in attaining the deepest level of Zen mostly revolve around this very point. His consuming anguish may have been a ruse, on the other hand, in which case Musashi the educator would appear to have been as master of strategy in the Buddhist way as well as in the way of the warrior.

SCHEMES OF THE SAMURAI

In their study of strategy the Japanese warriors used some of the Zen models, but much of the elaboration of the martial arts went beyond the domain of pure Zen. This is particularly true of many of Musashi's tactics, which are undoubtedly powerful when practiced effectively. His devices often seem to have the gut of Zen without the eye of Zen; but this is not at all unusual even among professional Zennists in Japan.

While Musashi's foremost concern is winning, which he has called the root of the warrior's way, Yagyū Munenori focuses more heavily on the ethical underpinnings of warfare, and goes further to extend practical applications of the strategic thinking of warriors into the domain of political and civil affairs. In his book on family traditions, Yagyū writes:

> When a country is pacified, the consideration given to the selection of officials and the security of the nation is also an art of war. When officials pursue personal interest and thus oppress the common people, this above all is the beginning of the end for a nation. To observe this situation carefully, planning in such a way as to avoid letting the state perish through the self-seeking of officials, is like watching an opponent in a duel to see his move before he makes it.

Whereas Musashi wrote of martial arts in terms of a career in society, and pursued them as a science and a way of life, Yagyū's approach is more ethically oriented. In this the Zen and Taoist influences can be seen. This distinction is not made clearly enough when Bushidō, or the unwritten samurai code, is loosely associated with Zen Buddhism, or when a dueler like Musashi is taken to represent the Zen spirit. In contrast to Musashi's militaristic need to win, Yagyū's sense of moral necessity is more Buddhistic:

It is bias to think that the art of war is just for killing people. It is not to kill people, it is to kill evil. It is a stratagem to give life to many people by killing the evil of one person.

There is an old saying, "Weapons are instruments of ill omen, despised by the Way of Heaven. To use them only when unavoidable is the Way of Heaven."

The reason weapons are instruments of ill omen is that the Way of Heaven is the Way that gives life to beings, so something used for killing is truly an instrument of ill omen. So it means that what contradicts the Way of Heaven is despised.

Nevertheless, it also say that to use arms when unavoidable is also the Way of Heaven. What does this mean? Although flowers blossom and greenery increases in the spring breeze, when the autumn frost comes leaves always drop and trees wither. This is the judgment of nature.

This is because there is logic in striking down something when it is completed. People may take advantage of events to do evil, but when the evil is complete, it is attacked. That is why it is said that using weapons to kill people when unavoidable is also the Way of Heaven.

It may happen that myriad people suffer because of the evil of one man. In such a case, myriad people are saved by killing one man. Would this not be a true example of (the Zen saying) "The sword that kills is the sword that gives life"?

The doctrine of killing one tyrant to save many people from oppression is found in the works of the Confucian philosopher Mencius, in the Buddhist "Scripture of the Great Decease," and in Chinese antecedents of the Tendai school of Buddhism. There is not, however, much emphasis placed on this concept in Japanese thought, even by the samurai who could have used it to rationalize their own profession and historical rise to power over the old aristocracy.

In this Japanese Buddhist political thought differs from that of China, where there are many more Buddhist-inspired uprisings than in Japan. This was probably not so much due to differences between Chinese and Japanese Buddhism as to differences in the political philosophies of the two nations. Whereas in China the legitimacy of revolution against tyranny was clearly defined in native classical philosophy, in Japan the Shintō bias of political thought represented the ruling classes as racially superior to the peasantry, and therefore inviolable in respect to socio-political privileges vis-à-vis the common people.

In this respect, the writing of Yagyū Munenori is distinguished by the dominance of Buddhistic morality over the authoritarian concepts of personal loyalty that Bushidō derived from a combination of Shintō and state Confucianism. Although Yagyū Munenori was a teacher of the Shōgun, his Zen teacher Takuan did not spare him criticism, or admonitions on the perils of his situation. Yagyū in turn showed his Zen spirit in his critical attitude toward the structure and practice of government. His moral basis of military action was not obedience to temporal authority, as was so often the case with samurai warriors. In spite of its setting in the context of hierarchical personal relations characteristic of Japanese governments, or perhaps because of that setting, Yagyū's ethical manifesto is directed toward objective ideas.

There are treacherous people surrounding rulers, who pretend to be righteous when in the presence of superiors yet have a glare in their eyes when they look at subordinates. Unless these people are bribed, they present the good as bad, so the innocent suffer and the guilty gloat. To see the potential for this happening is even more urgent that to notice a concealed scheme.

The country is the ruler's country, the people are the ruler's people. Those who serve the ruler personally are subjects of the ruler just as are those who serve at a remove. How far apart is their distance? They are like hands and feet in the service of the ruler. Are the feet any different from the hands because they are further away? Since they both feel pain and itch the same, which can be called nearer, which further away?

Therefore people would resent even an honest ruler if those close to the ruler bleed those far away and cause the innocent to suffer.

There are only a few people close to a ruler, perhaps five or ten. The majority of people are remote from the ruler. When many people resent the ruler, they will express their feelings. Now when those close to the ruler have all along been after their own interests and not acting in consideration of the ruler, and therefore serve in such a way that the people resent the ruler, when the time comes those close to the ruler will be the first to set upon him.

This is the doing of those close to him, not the fault of the ruler himself. It is desirable that the potential for such situations be clearly perceived, and that those distant from the rulership are not excluded from its benefits.

Here Yagyū uses a tactic well known in circumstances where there is no reliable mechanism for questioning rulers effectively. Instead of directing criticism at the ruler, he blames the ruler's advisors for the flaws in government policy and administration. In Japan, the power of the position of rulership is traditionally such that weak individuals may occupy it without their personal weakness actually compromising the authority of the rank itself; it is then that courtiers surrounding the ruler may become the determining force of government while avoiding personal liability by working within the framework of peer consensus in the shadow of an unquestioned authority figure.

So Yagyū indirectly recognizes the limitations on the real power of the ruler as an individual person, but this only intensifies his consciousness of a ruler's need to perceive what is actually happening within and without the circle of his cabinet of advisors. Therefore he stresses the need for enhanced perception not only in strategic combat but even more fundamentally in the strategy of statehood.

To see potential situations accurately is the art of war.

Not forgetting about disturbance when times are peaceful is the art of war. Seeing the situation of states, knowing when there will be disruption, and healing disturbance before it happens, is also the art of war.

The ideal of seeing events before they happen is pursued so as to be able to deal with them before much effort is needed. This concept comes from ancient Taoism by way of Zen, and is applied to all the individual martial arts as well as all sorts of other things. Because the central concern is perceptive fluidity, one of the classical Zen masters even said, "I don't talk about what you do from day to day, my only concern is that your vision is accurate." Yagyū places similar emphasis on keen perception, and shows how it applies to human interactions, in both war and peace.

The vanguard of the moment is before an opponent has begun to make a move. This first impulse of movement is the energy, or feeling, held back in the chest. The dynamic of the movement is energy, feeling, or mood. To accurately see an opponent's energy, feeling, and mood, and to act accordingly in its presence, is called the vanguard of the moment.

The hinge is inside the door. To see the invisible workings hidden inside, and to act upon that, is called the art of war at the vanguard of the moment.

In social and professional relationships, since you are acting as you see situations develop, the attitude is the same as that of the warrior, even when there is no discord. The mindfulness to observe the dynamic of situations even in a group is the art of war.

If you do not see the dynamic of a situation, you may remain too long in company where you don't belong and get into trouble for no reason. When people say things without seeing the states of others, get into arguments, and even forfeit their lives as a result, this is all a matter of the difference between seeing or not seeing the dynamic of a situation and the states of the people involved.

Even to furnish a room so that everything is in the right place is to see the dynamic of a situation, and thus involves something of the mindfulness of the warrior's art.

Yagyū's work is generally more abstract and theoretical than that of Musashi, including his treatment of strategy. Musashi outlines a comparatively large number of specific maneuvers, Yagyū delves more deeply into the philosophy and psychology of strategy. In his discussion of "appearance and intention," a compound word for strategy that literally means "outside and inside" or "surface and interior," Yagyū summarizes what is now considered a hallmark of Japanese transactional behavior:

> Appearance and intention are fundamental to the art of war. Appearance and intention mean the strategic use of ploys, the use of falsehood to gain what is real.
>
> Appearance and intention inevitably ensnare people when artfully used, even if people sense that there is an ulterior intention behind the overt appearance. When you set up your ploys

and opponents fall for them, then you win by letting them act on your ruse.

As for those who do not fall for a ploy, when you see they won't fall into one trap, you have another set. Then even if opponents haven't fallen for your original ploy, in effect they actually have.

In Buddhism this is called expedient means. Even though the real truth is hidden inside when strategy is employed outwardly, when you are finally led into the real truth, the pretenses now all become real truth.

Yagyū's statement about the relationship between expedients and truth in Buddhism is not really in accord with the scriptural teachings, but it is characteristic of much formal Japanese church Buddhism. The apparent ultimate identification of means and end reflected here underlay the formation of all sorts of cults that carried on ritual observances long after their original meaning had been forgotten.

The monumental *Zongjinglu*, a pan-Buddhist encyclopedia used by early Zen founders in Japan three centuries before Yagyū, explains the classical Buddhist position: "You may follow expedient explanations to the extent that you cling to the provisional, to the detriment of the real. But if you attain the complete immediate teaching, then you understand the real and open up the provisional. If you cling to the provisional, then teaching and perception are divided." From this point of view it is hard to avoid the impression that even warriors who studied Zen like Musashi and Yagyū never got over their attachment to the particular way they followed in ordinary life.

This is not to say that there was necessarily anything sinister in Yagyū's simplistic understanding of Zen Buddhism. The Japanese say *Uso mo hōben* ("Even a lie is an expedient"), but this can be used to refer to any sort of aim or goal, a personal matter without any necessary connection at all to the Buddhist origin or meaning of the idea of expedient means of liberation. Yagyū himself illustrates falsehood becoming true in psychological and ethical terms, using the image of Shintō mystery religion in parallel with the way of the warrior.

In the spirit religion there is what is called the mystery of the spirits. The mystery is kept secret to foster religious faith. When people have faith, they and others benefit from it.

In the warrior's way this is called strategy. Although strategy is falsehood, when the falsehood is used in order to win without hurting people, the falsehood finally becomes true.

The first step of Yagyū's strategy for the warrior is to practice the Zen teaching of nondwelling. It is an ancient observation that fixation of mind makes people vulnerable; the Chinese classic *The Art of War* says, "Attack what they will surely defend." The Zen warrior therefore practices the art of not clinging to anything, so as to avoid being caught by anything, as Yagyū explains, following the teaching of Zen master Takuan.

Spirit is the master of mind. Spirit is within, and employs mind outwardly. The mind also directs energy. Employing energy, mind goes outside in service of spirit. When the mind lingers in one place, efficiency is lost. Therefore it is essential to make sure not to keep the mind on one point.

When a householder sends his servant somewhere on an errand, if the servant stays there and doesn't come back, then he's no longer useful. If your mind lingers on something and doesn't come back to its basic position, then your ability in the art of war slips.

So the practice of not letting the mind stay in one place applies to all endeavors, not only to the art of war.

Yagyū's instructions on balance and spontaneity, interweaving the physical and the psychological, are also influenced by Taoism through Zen. As a result, he subtly achieves the extended metaphorical possibilities characteristic of writings in those traditions.

Steps should not be taken too quickly or too slowly. Steps should be taken in an unruffled, casual manner.

It is bad to go too far or not far enough; take the mean. When you go too quickly, it means you are scared and flustered; when you go too slowly, it means you are timid and frightened.

The desired state is one in which you are not upset at all.

Usually people will blink when something brushes by right in front of their eyes. This is normal, and the fact that you blink your eyes does not mean that you are upset. Also, if something is swung at your eyes two or three more times to startle you, not to blink your eyes at all would actually mean you were upset.

To deliberately hold back spontaneous blinking indicates a much more disturbed mind than blinking does.

The immovable or imperturbable mind is normal. If something comes at your eyes, you blink. This is the state of not being upset. The essential point is just not losing the normal state of mind. To try not to move is to have moved. To move is an immovable principle.

It is good to take steps in a normal manner, and in a normal frame of mind. This is the stage where neither your appearance nor your mind is upset.

Overtly the warrior seems to be talking about a duel, but the expression "to take steps" also means to embark upon any purposeful action. In this sense, the frame of mind in which steps are taken is critical to the whole enterprise. Yagyū goes on to describe the extreme limits of attention demanded by the warrior's strategy by explaining two fundamental code words of his craft: "the first principle" and "the first sword" as used in his art. The ulterior meanings of these terms convey both the mood and the practice of the warrior's way.

"The first principle" is a code word in the art of war. In the general art of war, it means to be independent in every possible way. The important thing is what happens when you are hard-pressed. "The first principle" means that you keep that clearly in mind, pay close attention, and make sure you don't get caught out in a pinch.

"The first sword" is a code word for seeing incipient movement on the part of opponents. The expression "the critical first sword" means that seeing what opponents are trying to do is the "first sword" of supreme ultimate meaning.

Understanding the perception of incipient actions of adversaries as the first sword, understand the weapon that strikes according to what they do as the second sword.

Yagyū also emphasizes the particular point that the enhanced seeing of the "first sword" is not developed by the power of the ordinary eye but by the direct vision of Zen mind as it sees into the heart of things.

To see with the eyes is called perception; to see with the heart and mind is called observation, in the sense of contemplation in the mind.

Conversely, the first line of Yagyū's offensive strategy is also defensive, aimed at canceling out opponents' ability to read his own mind as he would read theirs. As in any sleight of hand, distraction becomes a key to both defensive offense and offensive defense. Again Yagyū turns to Zen terminology for an appropriate metaphor.

> In Zen there is something called "beating the grass to scare the snakes." To startle or surprise people a little is a device, like hitting at the snakes in the grass to startle them.
>
> To do something unexpected as a ploy to startle an opponent is also an appearance concealing an ulterior intention, an art of war.
>
> When an opponent is startled and the feeling of opposition is distracted, the opponent will experience a gap in reaction time.
>
> Even simple ordinary gestures are used to distract an opponent's attention.
>
> Throwing down your sword is also an art of war. If you have attained mastery of swordlessness, you will never be without a sword. The opponent's sword is your sword. This is acting at the vanguard of the moment.

This sort of strategy is commonly employed in all sorts of interactions in Japan, and elsewhere in the Orient. It was originally grounded in ancient Taoist and Buddhist teachings as an educational device, and adapted to *the art of the advantage* in the classic book of strategy known as *The Art of War.* Now it is widely diffused, and may occur in any sort of transaction.

Westerners unfamiliar with this strategy often have difficulty discerning the interior from the surface, even mistaking the appearance for the intention. Western seekers of Zen have double trouble in this respect, since they also need to distinguish what are in fact Japanese social devices from what are in effect real Zen devices.

Yagyū's last-mentioned strategy, the mastery of "swordlessness," is perhaps the crowning achievement of the warrior's way, which enables one to apply Zen to ordinary life. In theory, "swordlessness" means the ability to defend oneself without a weapon, implying that one uses an opponent's weapon against him. This is not only a technique of swordsmanship but of debate, negotiation, and other forms of competition as well; here Yagyū is faithful to Zen ideals, distinguishing the technical aspects of the art from the original purpose, in order to establish a reasonable way of differentiating unavoidable necessity from selfish aggression in both attitude and action.

"Swordlessness" doesn't necessarily mean that you have to take the opponent's sword. It also doesn't mean that you make a show of sword-snatching for your reputation. It is the swordless art of not getting killed when you have no sword.

The basic intention is nothing like deliberately setting out to snatch a sword.

It is not a matter of insistently trying to wrest away what is being deliberately kept from your grasp. Not to grasp (the opponent's) attempt to keep hold (of the sword) is also "swordlessness." Someone who is intent on not having (his sword) taken away forgets what he's opposed to and just tries to avoid having (his sword) taken away, so he can't manage to kill anyone.

Swordlessness is not the art of taking another's sword. Its purpose is to use all tools freely. If you are even able to take away another's sword when you are unarmed, and make it your own, then what will not be useful in your hands?

This "swordless" art is what modern Japan used in order to become a major industrial power in one century in spite of its small territory and lack of industrially exploitable resources other than human labor and ingenuity. Whether it is in the personal realm of the individual warrior, or in the public domain of an entire nation or culture, the essence of the swordless art is to make resourcefulness your resource. In his *Book of Five Spheres*, Miyamoto Musashi also makes this transition of outlook from the warrior's way to the universal struggle for survival and excellence:

In the science of the arts of war, it is particularly hard to become a master without being on a straight path and commanding a broad view.

If this science is learned successfully, it won't let you down even if you face twenty or thirty opponents alone.

First, if you work diligently on a straight path, keeping the art of war in mind, you can overcome people with your hands and outsee them as well.

When you practice to the degree that you have become completely adept at using the whole science freely, you can overcome people physically; and when your mind is imbued with this science, you can also overcome people mentally.

When you get to this point, how could there be any way for you to lose to others?

Also, in terms of the art of war on a large scale, you win at finding good people, you win at employing large numbers of people, you win at conducting yourself correctly, you win at governing nations, you win at developing people, you win at performance of social custom.

In any walk of life, what helps you know how to avoid losing to others, how to save yourself and your honor, is the science of the art of war.

While he recognized the universal applications of the warrior's art, as a warrior and strategist himself Musashi focused primarily on the most intense and acute forms of contention and resolution. His fundamental principles derive more from *The Art of War* than they do from Zen Buddhism. In the "Water Scroll" of Musashi's *Book of Five Spheres*, he describes classical warrior's postures of balance that are also rules for maneuvering armies.

Even when you are still, your mind is not still, even when hurried, your mind is not hurried. The mind is not dragged by the body, the body is not dragged by the mind. Pay attention to the mind, not the body. Let there be neither insufficiency nor excess in your mind. Even if superficially weakhearted, be inwardly stronghearted, and don't let others see into your mind.

Following *The Art of War*, the original classic of his field, Musashi emphasizes the importance of knowing opponents and learning how to respond adaptively.

To assess the intelligence and strategy of each individual opponent, to know the opponent's strong and weak tactics, to use the knowledge and virtue of the art of war of find out how to overcome all others, is called mastery of this science.

In the context of the large-scale art of war, to see conditions means to know opponents' ups and downs, to know the hearts of adversaries' followers, to size up the situation, discern the enemy's condition, take in the crucial point that will enable you to use your forces effectively enough to win by the principles of the art of war, and fight with knowledge of your aim.

When you are facing a single opponent, it is also necessary to discern how the adversary operates, perceive the opponent's character, see the person's strengths and weaknesses, do what the enemy doesn't expect, and know the enemy's ups and downs, becoming familiar with their rhythms, thus to preempt them.

If your knowledge is powerful, individual conditions will be evident to you. When you master the art of war, you will find many ways to overcome opponents by accurately assessing their minds. This demands deliberate work.

One of the fundamental means of knowing adversaries is to deliberately put them to the test. Japanese people do this to strangers all the time. If the strangers are Westerners, they may not realize that they are being tested, and may mistake the superficial content of the interaction for the underlying meaning. In actual situations of struggle, it is possible to carry on a testing procedure, wage a battle of attrition, and practice the technique of "swordlessness" all at once. Musashi writes:

> As far as attacks made on you are concerned, let opponents go ahead and do anything useless, while stopping them from doing anything useful. This is essential to the art of war.
>
> Here, if you consciously try to thwart opponents, you're already late. First, while doing whatever you do scientifically, thwart the opponent's very first impulse to try something, thus foiling everything. To manipulate opponents in this way is mastery of the art of war, which comes from practice.

At some point, when the Japanese warrior feels that he has stored enough energy and that his opponent has presented a suitable gap, there may be a sudden conclusion to an interaction. Although obvious in performances of traditional martial arts, when this phenomenon occurs in the context of more complex events it can bewilder or mystify an uninformed onlooker. It would probably be safe to say that all Japanese warriors conscious of their art tried to cultivate this exercise of power, which Musashi describes in characteristically simple terms.

It is possible to attain certain victory by means of the mood of total absorption of purpose in a single telling blow. The art of war cannot be understood without proper learning. If you can cultivate this sense of the mood of total absorption in a single telling blow, you can master the art of war as a way to win at will.

The power of total concentration has also traditionally been cultivated by Japanese people in other walks of life, often very successfuly. In Musashi's case, a consuming personal absorption in the warrior's way and the martial arts clearly led to his unusual elaboration of the science of strategy in conflict.

Musashi's obsession seems to have adversely affected his other relationships—with women, the world, and Zen—but his *Book of Five Spheres* is in any case ordinarily not read primarily for moral or intellectual values. Whatever Musashi's own intention might have been, the Zen view of this book, as of any other, would be that of the objective observer.

Knowledge of tactics can have defensive as well as aggressive uses. This knowledge can resolve conflict by diffusing it and avoiding it as well as by winning it. From the Zen point of view, one of the arts of this science, as again of any order, is to know when to use it and when not to use it.

This is true of all knowledge, according to the Buddhist concept of *skill in means,* by which is meant the active adaptation of wisdom to situations at hand. It is particularly true of those branches of knowledge dealing with extraordinary powers, such as the art of war.

Miyamoto Musashi's classic of strategy and martial arts may present the greatest need for such caveats, to the extent of its excellence in explaining certain forms of power. His treatment of specific maneuvers is very clear-cut, awaiting only the reader's engagement to translate the abstract principles into understanding of current events.

The following essays from the notorious "Fire Scroll" of Musashi's neo-classic *Book of Five Spheres* are prime examples of the philosophy of winning or "art of the advantage" that distinguishes the warrior's way from Zen Buddhism. These strategies are in themselves amoral from the point of view of the art of war, but to a Buddhist view they are immoral in the service of any cult of win and lose. Perhaps this is why no Zen scholar ever made them more accessible than did Musashi himself.

DISINTEGRATION

Disintegration happens to everything. When a house crumbles, a person crumbles, or an adversary crumbles, they fall apart by getting out of rhythm with the times.

In the art of war on a large scale, it is also essential to find the rhythm of opponents as they come apart, and pursue them so as not to let openings slip by. If you miss the timing of vulnerable moments, there is the likelihood of counterattack.

In the individual art of war it also happens that an adversary will get out of rhythm in combat and start to fall apart. If you let such a chance get by you, the adversary will recover and thwart you. It is essential to follow up firmly on any loss of poise on the part of an adversary, to prevent the opponent from recovering.

MOVING SHADOWS

"Moving shadows" is something you do when you can't discern what adversaries are thinking.

When you can't see your opponent's state, you pretend to make a powerful attack to see what the enemy will do.

ARRESTING SHADOWS

"Arresting shadows" is something you do when adversaries' aggressive intentions toward you are perceptible.

In the art of war on a large scale, this means to arrest the enemy's action at the point of the very impulse to act. If you show the adversaries strongly how you control the advantage, they will change their minds, inhibited by this strength.

You too change your attitude to an empty mind, from which you take the initiative; this is where you win.

In the individual art of war as well, you use an advantageous rhythm to arrest the powerful determination of the adversary's motivation; then you find the winning advantage in the moment of pause, and now take the initiative.

This requires a lot of work.

INFECTION

There is infection in everything. Even sleepiness can be infectious, and yawning can be infectious. There is even the infection of a time.

In the art of war on a large scale, when adversaries are excited and evidently are in a hurry to act, you behave as though you are completely unfazed, giving the appearance of being thoroughly relaxed and at ease. Do this, and adversaries themselves are influenced by this mood, becoming less enthusiastic.

When you think the opponents have "caught" that mood, you empty your own mind and act quickly and firmly, thus to gain the winning advantage.

In the individual art of war as well, it is essential to be relaxed in body and mind, notice the moment an opponent slackens, and quickly take the initiative to win.

ENTRANCING

There is also something called "entrancing" that is similar to "infection." One entrancing mood is boredom. Another is restlessness. Another is faintheartedness. This all takes work to accomplish.

UPSET

"Upset" happens in all sorts of things. One way it happens is through a feeling of being under acute pressure. Another is through a feeling of unreasonable strain. A third is through a feeling of surprise at the unexpected.

In large-scale warfare, it is essential to cause upset. It is critical to attack resolutely where enemies are not expecting it; then while their minds are unsettled, use this to your advantage to take the initiative and win.

In individual combat, you appear relaxed at first, then suddenly charge powerfully; as the opponent's mind changes pitch, it is essential that you follow what he does, not letting him relax for a moment, perceiving the advantage of the moment and discerning right then and there how to win.

FRIGHT

There is fright in all sorts of situations. This is the mind frightened by the unexpected.

If you can seize the moment of fright, you can take advantage of it to win.

STICKING TIGHT

"Sticking tight" means when you are fighting at close range and see that it isn't going well, you then stick tight to the opponent. The essential point is to take advantage of opportunities to win even as you wrestle together.

COMING UP AGAINST CORNERS

"Coming up against corners" means that when you push anything strong, it hardly gives way just like that.

In the art of mass warfare, observe the opposing troops; where they have surged ahead, hit the corner of this strong front, and you should get the advantage.

As the corner collapses, everyone gets the feeling of collapse. Even as they are collapsing, it is essential to realize when each corner is ready to go, and sense when to overcome it.

In the individual art of war also, when you inflict pain on part of his body each time the opponent makes an aggressive move, his body will weaken by degrees until he is ready to collapse and it is easy to beat him.

It is essential to study this carefully to discern where you can win.

FLUSTERING

To fluster opponents means to act in such a way as to prevent them from having a steady mind.

In the mass art of war, it means you assess adversaries' minds on the battlefield, and use the power of your knowledge of the art of war to manipulate their attention, making them think confusing thoughts about what you are going to do; it means finding a rhythm that will fluster adversaries, accurately discerning where you can win.

In the individual art of war also, you try various maneuvers according to the opportunity of the moment, making the opponent think that you are going to do now this, now that, now something else, until you find the opponent starting to get flustered, and thus win at will. This is the essence of battle.

CRUSHING

"Crushing" requires a crushing mood, as when you view an adversary as weak and become strong yourself, thus overwhelming the opponent.

In the art of mass war, this means you look down upon an enemy whose numbers are small; or even if there are many of them, when opponents are demoralized and weakening, you concentrate your force on crushing them, thus mowing them down.

If your "crushing" is weak, it can backfire. You have to carefully distinguish the state of mind in which you are fully in control as you crush.

In the individual art of war also, when your opponent is not as skilled as you are, or when his rhythm is fouled up, or when he starts to back off, it is essential not to let him catch his breath, don't even give him time to blink his eyes; mow him right down.

The most important thing is not to let him recover. This should be studied very carefully.

MOUNTAIN AND SEA CHANGING

"Mountain and sea" means that it is bad to do the same thing over and over again. You may have to repeat something once, but it shouldn't be done a third time.

When you try something on an adversary, if it doesn't work the first time, you won't get any benefit out of rushing to do it again. Change your tactics abruptly, doing something completely different. If that still doesn't work, then try something else.

Thus the science of the art of war involves the presence of mind to "act as the sea when the enemy is like a sea."

This requires careful reflection.

KNOCKING THE HEART OUT

When you fight with an enemy and appear to win by your skill in this science, the opponent may still have ideas, and while appearing to be beaten still inwardly refuse to acknowledge defeat. "Knocking the heart out" is for such cases.

This means that you suddenly change your attitude to stop the enemy from entertaining any such ideas, so the main thing is to see enemies feel defeated from the bottom of their hearts.

You can knock the heart ouf of people with weapons, or with your body, or with your mind. It is not to be understood in just one way.

When your enemies have completely lost heart, you don't have to pay attention to them anymore. Otherwise, you remain mindful. If enemies still have ambitions, they will hardly collapse.

BECOMING NEW

When fighting with enemies, if you get to feeling snarled up and are making no progress, you toss your mood away and think in your heart that you are starting everything anew. As you get the rhythm, you discern how to win. This is "becoming new."

Any time you feel tension and friction building between yourself and others, if you change your mind that very moment, you can prevail by a distinctly different advantage. This is "becoming new."

In the art of war on a large scale it is essential to understand "becoming new." It is something that suddenly appears through the power in knowledge of the art of war.

This must be well considered.

SMALL AND LARGE

When you are fighting enemies and get to feel snarled up in petty maneuvers, remember this rule of the art of war: while in the midst of minutiae, suddenly you shift to a large perspective.

Changing to great or small is an intentional part of the science of the art of war. It is essential for warriors to seek this even in the ordinary consciousness of human life.

A COMMANDER KNOWING SOLDIERS

"A commander knowing soldiers" is a method always practiced in times of conflict after having reached the mastery to which one aspires: having attained the power in the knowledge of the art of war, you think of your adversaries as your own soldiers, understanding that you should do with them as you wish, intending to manipulate them freely. You are the commander, the opponents are the troops. This takes work.

BEING LIKE A ROCK WALL

"Being like a rock wall" is when a master of the art of war suddenly becomes like a rock wall, inaccessible to anything at all, immovable.

THE THIRTY-SIX STRATEGIES

Although the works of such Japanese martial artists as Miyamoto Musashi and Yagyū Munenori are readily available in modern Japan, even there the original Chinese tradition of *the art of the advantage* remains unrivaled. One of the ironies of Japanese history is that this art has always been used most successfully in just about every domain besides armed conflict. One might say that the original science itself would predict such an outcome, but it does appear to be paradoxical or ironic when viewed exclusively within the context of Japanese history.

While the Japanese warriors themselves may have been influenced by Zen Buddhism, most of their strategy comes from the Chinese art of war.

The body of this book began with a look at the way of the Japanese warrior as understood by two of its most famous practitioners. Their primary emphasis at the outset is on learning, not as a hobby or intellectual pursuit, but as a way of learning how to live.

For the warrior, above all this means learning how to live well under duress, how to survive chaos. Therefore this book turns to Zen Buddhism, a wellspring of the unassailable inner equanimity that the warrior seeks. Although there is no such distinction in absolute Zen, there are specific teachings for different human types and personalities. Since the warriors were held up to the people of all classes during the centuries of military rule in Japan, certain aspects of the culture of the samurai, including the art of advantage as well as the Zen teachings specifically directed at warriors, came to exert a pervasive influence in Japanese society.

Because of the extremely long duration of military rule in Japan, the balance in Bushidō between Zen and the art of the advantage seems to have tilted decidedly toward the latter. This would appear to be so much so, in fact, as to have even influenced Zen Buddhism itself into peculiarly Japanese forms heavily marked by elements of the art of war. This book therefore turns from Zen for warriors to the topic of pure strategy.

Whether through traditions of political and military psychology and strategy, or through warrior Zen and the arts it fostered, there is no doubt that the ancient Chinese philosophy and science of war are very much present in the culture and manners of contemporary Japan. One of the most popular classic and still current outlines of the traditional art of the advantage is contained in the famous *Thirty-six Strategies.*

In the manner of a master warrior in the classic tradition of *The Art of War,* the author of the *Thirty-six Strategies* is unknown in spite of the renown of his work. The strategies are encapsulated in mnemonic phrases, many of which passed into proverb and are very widely known and used in the Chinese cultural sphere. Here the strategies are translated and decoded, with brief explanations of their meaning.

1. Sneak across the ocean in broad daylight.

This means to create a front that eventually becomes imbued with an atmosphere or impression of familiarity, within which the strategist may maneuver unseen while all eyes are trained to see obvious familiarities.

2. Surround one state to save another.

When a strong group is about to take over a weaker group, a third part can "have its cake and eat it too," gaining a good reputation by attacking the aggressor in apparent behalf of the defender, and also eventually absorb the weakened defender to boot, without incurring the same opprobrium that would be leveled at outright aggression.

3. Borrow a sword to kill another.

When one side in a conflict is weakening, it may draw its own friends into battle, thus delivering a blow to its enemy while conserving its own strength.

4. Face the weary in a condition of ease.

You force others to expend energy while you preserve yours. You tire opponents out by sending them on wild goose chases, or by making them come to you from far away while you stand your ground.

5. Plunge into a fire to pull off a robbery.

You use others' troubles as opportunities to gain something for yourself.

6. Feint east, strike west.

You spread misleading information about your intentions, or make false suggestions, in order to induce the opponent to concentrate his defenses on one front and thereby leave another front vulnerable to attack.

7. Make something from nothing.

You create a false idea in the mind of the opponent, and fix it in his mind as a reality. In particular, this means that you convey the impression that you have what you do not, to the end that you may appear formidable and thus actually obtain a security that you had not enjoyed before.

8. Cross the pass in the dark.

You set up a false front, then penetrate the opponent's territory on other fronts while they are distracted by your false front.

9. Watch the fire from the opposite bank of the river.

You calmly look on when adversaries experience internal troubles, waiting for them to destroy themselves.

10. Hide a sword in a smile.

You ingratiate yourself with enemies, inducing them to trust you. When you have their confidence, you can move against them in secret.

11. One tree falls for another.

Individual sacrifices may have to be made to achieve a greater goal.

12. Take the sheep in hand as you go along.

You take advantage of any opportunity, however small, and avail yourself of any profit, however slight. This comes from the story of a destitute traveler walking on a road. As he went along, he came across a flock of sheep; making his way through them, when he emerged from their midst he had a sheep with him. He behaved so calmly and naturally, as if he had been leading his own sheep to market all along, that the shepherd never noticed him.

13. Beat the grass to startle the snakes.

When opponents are reserved and unfathomable, you create some sort of stir to see how they will react. Yagyū mentions this, and also notes that it is used in Zen. Certain Zen sayings and stories are used primarily to test people and find out what they are like.

14. Borrow a corpse to bring back a spirit.

You don't use what everyone else is using, but use what others aren't using. This can mean reviving something that has dropped out of use through neglect, or finding uses for things that had hitherto been ignored or considered useless.

15. Train a tiger to leave the mountains.

You don't go into the fastness of powerful opponents' territory, but induce them to come out of their stronghold.

16. When you want to take captives, leave them on the loose for a while.

Fleeing enemies may turn again and strike desperately if pursued too hotly. If they are given room to run, on the other hand, they scatter and lose their energy. Then they can be taken captive without further violence.

17. Toss out a glazed tile to draw a jade.

You present something of superficial or apparent worth to induce another party to produce something of real worth.

18. To capture the brigands, capture their king.

When confronted with a massive opposition, you take aim at its central leadership.

19. Take the firewood out from under the pot.

When you cannot handle an adversary in a head-on confrontation, you can still win by undermining the enemy's resources and morale.

20. Stir up the waters to catch fish.

You use confusion to your advantage, to take what you want. It may specifically mean taking advantage of a general or particular loss of direction in order to gather followers from among the uncommitted or disenfranchised.

21. The gold cicada molts its shell.

This means leaving behind false appearances created for strategic purposes. Like the cicada shell, the facade remains intact, but the real action is now elsewhere.

22. Lock the gates to catch the bandits.

You catch invading predators by not letting them get away. You don't let them get back to their homelands with what they can get from you. If they escape, you don't chase them, because you will thereby fall prey to the enemy's plot to wear you down.

23. Make allies at a distance, attack nearby.

When you are more vulnerable to those close by than you are to those far away, you can defend yourself by keeping those around you off balance, in the meantime cutting off their field of maneuver by securing a broader ring of alliances surrounding them.

24. Borrow the right of way to attack the neighbor.

You secure the temporary use of another party's facilities in order to move against a mutual enemy. After having used these facilities to prevail over the enemy, you then turn and use them against the party from whom you borrowed them.

25. Steal a beam to replace a pillar.

You try to recruit top talent from among allies, inducing them to join your concern.

26. Point at one to scold another.

You criticize indirectly, getting your point across without confrontation.

27. Feign ignorance without going crazy.

You pretend to be stupid and ignorant, but avoid talking loosely.

28. Let them climb the roof, then take away the ladder.

You maneuver enemies into a point of no return by baiting them with what look like advantages and opportunities.

29. Make flowers bloom on a tree.

You dazzle and deceive the eyes of opponents by showy displays.

30. Turn the guest into the host.

This is when a business is taken over by one of its own clients or consultants.

31. Scheme with beauties.

This refers to using the charms of women to influence key figures in an adversary organization.

32. Scheme with an empty castle.

You appear weaker than you really are, so that opponents may defeat themselves by one of three reactions to your supposed weakness: they may become conceited and complacent, leading to their downfall; they may become arrogant and aggressive, leading to their destruction; or they may assume you are setting up an ambush, leading them to flee of their own accord.

33. Scheme with double agents.

You compromise insiders of other organizations to get them to work for you.

34. Scheme with self-inflicted wounds.

This is a technique particularly for undercover agents: you make yourself look like a victim of your own people, in order to win the sympathy and confidence of enemies.

35. Scheme in continuous circles.

When facing a more powerful enemy, you don't oppose by force, and don't concentrate all your resources on only one avenue of strategy; you keep different plans operating simultaneously in an overall scheme.

36. It is best to run.

When overwhelmed, you don't fight; you surrender, compromise, or flee. Surrender is complete defeat, compromise is half defeat, flight is not defeat. As long as you are not defeated, you have another chance to win.

BUSHIDŌ AND CHRISTIANITY
Ethical Crossroads

Two aspects of Japanese culture that have traditionally drawn the unfavorable comment of Westerners in virtually all fields are matters of reason and ethics. A great deal of emotional writing on this subject seems to boil down to the fact that the Japanese have their own reason and morality in addition to what have been borrowed from other cultures.

Those who are unlike the Japanese in their patterns of thinking, believing, and behaving, and who have also been unable to understand the Japanese in these respects, have often written that the Japanese are not reasonable or ethical. Since almost everyone says this about almost everyone else when there are disagreements, this is not in itself a unique phenomenon.

In the case of Japan, what is probably most nearly unique in recent times is the fervor of such denunciations. Writers in this vein, whether in missionary, commercial, or political spheres of operation, will often be found to have a history of unsuccessful attempts to win Japanese people over to what they themselves believe to be reasonable and ethical. As a result, some Japanese have also learned to tell Westerners, when it suits their purposes to do so, that they are by nature not reasonable or ethical people.

It would seem odd that this tactic apparently works like a charm, but it is not so strange when understood in the context of the "art of the advantage," which properly takes place *after* the moral of the situation is determined, and therefore has no ethical content itself beyond the aim of winning for what has been judged right for that time.

There is a great deal of literature touching on this subject, in both Japanese and Western languages. Much of the latter is very recent and quite accessible to the average person. All that can be profitably added here is a summary of the religious roots of Japanese Bushidō and a sampling of the material that is available to the average Japanese today wishing to cultivate those roots. They are not necessarily descriptions of "Japanese culture" in general, but as it may be manifested in particular individuals, organizations, policies, and behaviors.

The Taoist classic *Tao Te Ching* says, "Knowers don't generalize, generalizers don't know." To say that certain ideas or practices are commonly available does not mean that they are actively used in any uniform proportion by the Japanese in general. There are already enormous ranges of quantitative and qualitative differences within each of the root traditions; the same is true of Bushidō and its emanations through Japanese culture. There are many points of contradiction among the root teachings themselves, as well as between religious principles and customary usage.

Then again, philosophical ideas are notoriously subject to varying interpretations and applications, further increasing the breadth of the spectrum of influence that religions can have on societies, far beyond their original purpose. To take generalizations and clichés about Japanese culture at face value, or to take them for their powers of attraction or repulsion, would therefore seem above all to be inviting defeat in the art of the advantage at a very simplistic level indeed.

To be sure, the myths of the difficulty of the Japanese language and the impenetrability of Japanese thinking have contributed most of all to their own authentication. Were even the simplest facts about the language and culture generally known, however, it would be common knowledge not only that these myths can be scientifically disproven, but that their creation and maintenance are among the thirty-six classical strategies outlined in this book.

One might wonder why the West has been so slow to grasp the realities of Japanese thought, in comparison with the well-known alacrity with which the Japanese learned Western ways. It would appear that there were always people who could see both ways, but the mass perceptions of both sides have always been fragmented and exaggerated. The camouflage of mystery and caricature are also part of the art of the advantage, included in the thirty-six strategies; *and it is not only the Japanese who are using them.*

The original roots of Japanese morality are in Shintō, the general term for native religion. Common derivations from Shintō sources are such elements of Japanese culture as cleanliness and other home rituals; belief in spirits, blessings, and curses; sword and other object fetishes; authoritarianism, tribalism, racism, and nationalism. Shintō is not, as commonly claimed, essentially a form of nature worship, although it involves in part the Shintoist's relationship with certain aspects of nature. Some elements of Shintō are very powerful in the modern Japanese subconscious, but no Shintō nature worship has stopped modern Japan from ravaging, pillaging, and polluting nature at home and abroad in the same way that industrialized Christian nations have done.

One of the characteristics of Shintō practice that is commonly noted is its emphasis on benefit in this world. People pray to avert disaster and beckon fortune, whether natural, human, or divine. It is ordinarily said that the Japanese aristocracy took to Tantric Buddhism so readily because its accommodation of this element allowed it to assimilate Shintō easily. The early Zen masters tried to break away from this materialistic orientation in Japanese religion, but an outstanding Zen teacher of the fourteenth century was still complaining that Zen was being ruined by demands that the monks say prayers for the success and welfare of their samurai patrons.

The first Zen master in Japan to write extensively on good and evil was Dōgen Zenji (1200–1253), a prolific author and one of the Zen teachers consulted by Hōjō Tokiyori, distinguished regent of the first central Shogunate. Dōgen was one of the most adamant of those who rejected the widespread use of Buddhism for social, political, and material power; and he was driven out of the capital area for his trouble. In his essay "Don't Do Any Evil," one of the ninety-five chapters of his magnum opus *Shōbōgenzō*, Dōgen wrote on the relativity of conventional morality:

> There are sameness and differences between evils in this realm and evils in other realms; there are sameness and differences between prior times and later times.

Christian thinking tends to absolutize particular frameworks of good and evil as laws of God; Buddhist thinking deals with the relativity of good and evil. This is believed to be one reason for the flexibility of Japanese morality as it is applied in life situations, as compared with Western conceptions of ethics rooted in Christian dogma.

As a Buddhist, Dōgen writes that good and evil are a matter of conditions, including the time, place, and people concerned. According to this philosophy, good and evil depend on context as a whole, their existence and specific characteristics relative to the individual differences in subjective and objective experiences therein. Therefore while Zen master Dōgen wrote extensively on ethics for his time, the central principle of relativity stands out in his metaphysical work on the roots of morality. His greatest philosophical achievement in this domain was undoubtedly in his representation of the total context of human behavior in the light of Flower Ornament Buddhism. One of the most poignant examples of this is found in the *Shōbōgenzō* essay entitled "The Whole Works":

> Life is like when you ride in a boat: although in this boat you work the sail, the rudder, and the pole, still the boat carries you, and you are nothing without the boat. Riding in the boat, you even cause the boat to be a boat.
>
> You should contemplate this precise point. At this very moment, the boat is the world. Even the sky, the water, and the shore have all become circumstances of the boat, unlike circumstances that are not the boat.
>
> For this reason, life is our causing to live; it is life's causing us to be ourselves.
>
> When riding in a boat, the mind and body, object and subject, are all workings of the boat. The whole earth and all of space are both workings of the boat. We that are life, life that is we, are the same way.

While it has historically been at least as difficult for the Japanese to sustain this perspective on a global scale as it has been for other highly self-conscious civilizations, still parallel if less profound and universal concepts of ethical relativity, restraint, and communal interdependence are part of everyday life in Japan. One of the avowed aims for education in post-industrial Japan is to produce the "international person," applying the original Buddhist concept to the needs of the contemporary world.

A sourcebook of Japanese thought more popular than any Zen text may be found in the work known as *Tsurezuregusa*, in which the familiar roots of ordinary Japanese feelings are clearly exposed. Full of Buddhist, Confucian, and Taoist ideas as well as native Japanese ideas, this book is part of a normal Japanese language curriculum and therefore has far wider currency today than any classic scripture or sectarian religious work. Sometimes it directly reflects Japanese ideas and practices that are presently very familiar throughout the modern world; sometimes in voicing Taoist, Buddhist, or Confucian beliefs it is highly critical of customary usage. Because of the literary and exoteric nature of the work, the writer's viewpoint is more easily observed than is the case in classic Zen writings.

As is well known, the family is a traditional seat of civilization and its institutions in the Orient. It is within the family that the individual is originally schooled in the feelings that are to be the individual's bond to society, and that have become the cement of the society itself. Whereas the Christian recites the precept "Honor your father and mother" as a commandment of the supreme God, the Japanese understands familial feelings as a rational duty inherent in the nature of society. The author of *Tsurezuregusa* illustrates this sense of intimate connection between family life and the condition of society as a whole:

> Even people who seem to be ignorant do sometimes say good things. Once a fearsome warrior from the borderlands asked one of his companions, "Do you have any children?" The other man replied that he had none. The first warrior said, "Then you don't understand life. You must be awfully cold. Only when you have children do you fully understand life."
>
> This is certainly true. If not for human love, how could there be compassion in the heart of anyone like this warrior? Even people without any sense of duty towards their parents will come to know how their parents felt once they themselves have children.
>
> People who retire from society to become hermits free from mundane cares are wrong to look down on people with worldly ties and desires who cultivate social relations. If you consider the matter from the point of view of people with worldly ties, it is truly pitiful—for the sake of their parents, spouses, and children, they even forget about shame, and may even have to steal.
>
> So rather than arresting thieves and just punishing crimes, it would be preferable to run society in such a way that people do not go hungry and cold.

When people lack a constant means of livelihood, they lack psychological stability. When they are desperate, people steal. When society is not functioning properly and people are cold and hungry, there can be no end to crime.

Many of the moral teachings whose traces remain imprinted on Japanese feelings in various proportions deal with relationships and attitudes rather than with isolated acts in themselves. The author of *Tsurezuregusa* highlights the emotional source of moral sense, concluding that the recognition of human feeling needs to be incorporated into the logical structure of an argument for rational social organization.

In contemporary Japan a great deal of thought is given to extenuating circumstances in criminal cases. When judgment is impaired by alcohol consumption, for example, or by extreme despair, this is taken into consideration as a real factor in the course of events. Therefore in spite of strict laws and measures, the Japanese criminal justice system does display a certain degree of the human understanding reflected in classic writings.

Some of the social criticism in *Tsurezuregusa* also rings as true today as it did when it was written centuries ago. One of the apparent paradoxes of Japanese society is that whereas almost all the Japanese say that they think of themselves as belonging to the middle class, there is nevertheless a pervasive and compulsive status consciousness. This can become so intense as to become almost unbearably stifling even to those who willingly uphold it. Although this may be considered a relic of former times, its existence and consequences are very real. *Tsurezuregusa* approaches this problem by illustrating the superficiality of the concern for social status as compared with the original values on which it is grafted.

It is desirable to leave an undying reputation to posterity, but even if people have high rank and status, that doesn't necessarily mean they are superior people. Even fools and incompetents can rise to high office and live luxuriously if they are born in the right families and have good luck. There have been many fine people with virtue and wisdom who were of lowly status and never had much of a chance in life.

Obsessive concern for high office is nearly as stupid as obsessive desire for material wealth. While it is desirable to leave behind a distinguished reputation for wisdom and heart, yet on careful examination one will find that a liking for good repute is enjoyment of fame. But neither those who praise nor those who criticize remain in the world, and those who will hear such reports also soon pass away. So whose opinions of you should you be concerned about?

Praise, furthermore, is at the root of criticism. There is no benefit in leaving a name after death. So to wish for fame is nearly as stupid as wishing for high status.

In contrast to the pretensions of ambitious Japanese aristocrats and warriors (which were generally much like those of aristocrats and warriors everywhere), one of the virtues for which the common Japanese people are often praised is the quality of modesty. This has its roots in mystical Shintō, where the simple and honest heart becomes the sacred lodging of the spirit. It is more intellectually refined in Buddhism, where it is a psychological device, a means of streamlining the individual's passage through life. Certain passages of *Tsurezuregusa* underline the foundations of modesty from a point of view that combines feeling and reason, including the simplicity of the Taoist and the sophistication of the Buddhist.

It is best not to pretend to know all about everything. Even if they do know something, cultivated people do not advertise the fact. It is the bumpkin who talks as though he knows everything. Even if one is outstanding in some way, to think of oneself as impressive is unbecoming. It is better not to talk much about what one knows, not to speak of it unless asked.

When ignorant people make assessments of others and think that they know what others know, they cannot be right. For example, when someone who lacks intelligence but is good at chess sees intelligent people who are not good at chess, he thinks they are not as smart as he is. And when he sees people who are skilled at all sorts of arts but don't know how to play chess, he thinks he is better than they are. This is a big mistake.

Earlier, in the discussion of the way of the Zen warrior, it was noted that the attitude of seriousness is one of the psychological exercises of Neo-Confucianism, an educational system that exerted tremendous influence on the Japanese mind over centuries of orthodoxy under samurai rule. This mental set has come to form one of the bases of a certain Japanese moral feeling, according to which a person is judged less by the content of the undertaking than by the mood of seriousness, the depth of devotion and concentration brought to bear on the action. Again *Tsurezuregusa* reflects on the rationale underpinning the absorption in this mood of which the Japanese are so remarkably capable.

> In any field of endeavor, specialists are superior to dilettantes, even if the specialists are not as talented as the dilettantes. This is because specialists always take their art seriously, while dilettantes are mere hobbyists.
>
> This does not apply only to arts. In all actions and attitudes, success is based on singleminded seriousness, while failure is based on whimsicality.

A logical extension of this attitude applied in practical situations spawned what is now referred to as TQC, or Total Quality Control, one of the distinguishing features of excellence in Japanese manufacturing. *Tsurezuregusa* illustrates the reasoning behind TQC through a representative scenario in learning to perfect the performance of an art:

> Once someone learning archery faced the target holding two arrows. The teacher said, "Beginners shouldn't hold two arrows, because counting on the second arrow results in carelessness with the first. Each time, determine that you will settle the matter with this one arrow, without worry about whether or not you will succeed."
>
> With only two arrows, and in the presence of the teacher, would one really be careless with an arrow? You may not be aware of any slackening in your own mind, but a teacher will know.
>
> This admonition should be applied to everything. When people practice an art, they always think they will have another chance to try again, so they are not aware of slackness in their minds at the moment. It is very difficult to work in the immediacy of the present moment.

Although there are many individual aspects of Japanese civilization whose classical roots and historical development are relatively clear and straightforward, as a whole the actual conditions of contemporary Japanese psychology and culture are very complex motleys, since each element therein has its own history of usage; usually quite long and already complicated by centuries of changes in relevance and application to the life of the society and its individual members.

One of the touchiest ethical issues in the context of the encounter between Japanese Bushidō and Western Christianity is the subject of killing. It is well known that taking life is expressly forbidden in Buddhism, just as in Christianity, with the only difference that Buddhism extends its sanction further into the neighboring realms of life than does the more anthropocentric religion of Christianity.

There is, nevertheless, scripturally based rationale for killing in Buddhism, Taoism, and Confucianism, as when a malicious tyrant is assassinated to save the lives of multitudes. Christianity also has its own version of holy war, although the details of its reasoning may not be quite the same in view of its particular theological background. In Tantric Buddhism there are even spells specifically designed for doing away with evil despots; some translators cut them out of the Chinese versions during the Tang dynasty, but the Japanese Tantrists got hold of them anyway, and they are seldom associated with justice. Although the only Buddhist-led wars in old Japan were popular uprisings and self-defense operations, to this day it is the image of wicked barons with devilish Tantric assassins in their employ that is in the popular mind's eye through television drama.

In the twelfth and thirteenth centuries there were a number of major reform movements among Japanese Buddhists. This was when such well-known schools as Zen, Shinshū, and Nichiren arose. One of the outstanding characteristics of early Zen and Shinshū was their rejection of the materialistic inclination that Buddhism had gotten from Shintō. The fourteenth-century National Teacher Musō Soseki, one of the most celebrated Zen Buddhists of all time, was perhaps the most forthcoming in his criticism of prayer for profit. Advisor to one of the co-founders of the second Shogunate, Musō also disallowed the use of justification as a substitute for justice in applying the principle of righteous war; in his famous *Muchū Mondō*, still one of the most accessible classics of Zen, Musō tells the Shōgun's brother:

> The fact that you are now looked up to by a multitude as a military leader is entirely the result of past virtues. Nevertheless,

there are still people who oppose you, and few of your vassals follow your direction selflessly. When I see this, it seems to me that there was still some lack in the good causes in your past. So how can it be said that you are doing too many good deeds now?

If you compare your criminal deeds with your virtues, which do you think are more? And how many people have you destroyed as enemies? Where are their surviving families and dependents to go? And not only the deaths of enemies, but also the deaths of your allies in war are all your sins too.

If nothing else, one has to admire Musō's courage in speaking to a warrior in this manner, let alone the brother of the Shōgun himself. National Teacher or not, he had no guarantee whatsoever that the displeasure of the Shogunate would not result directly or indirectly in his death or banishment. According to the Buddhist *Flower Ornament Scripture,* one of the main classical sources of Zen, this is a characteristic type of courage that emerges in the stage of enlightenment known as Intense Joy.

Evidently there were military and political advisors who were unhappy with the new government's pious and charitable works. This is not an unusual theme in Asian politics. Other famous warriors and empire builders in India and China are well known for becoming zealous Buddhists to atone for their sins after bloody wars of conquest, with mixed results.

A similar phenomenon still occurs in the domain of corporate warfare and other forms of competition and conflict. In the realm of international politics and economics as well, recent increases in Japanese foreign aid are publicly interpreted in parallel ethical terms.

Perhaps no phenomenon more distinctly marks the ideological gap between Japan and the West than does the fact that an extremely small number of Japanese have been converted to Christianity in spite of more then a century of missionary work. Had the Shōguns not turned against Christianity and suppressed it in the late sixteenth and early seventeenth centuries, the story might have been very different.

Once they realized that European political and economic ambitions came with the Christian missions, however, the Shōguns seemed to feel that they had no choice at that point but to reject

Western overtures. Among the most unusual and informative documents of this process is a tract written by Suzuki Shōsan at the behest of the Shōgun to refute Christian doctrine in the wake of a violently crushed insurrection by Japanese Christians.

This remarkable treatise, which is actually a good deal more intelligent than many anti-Western writings, is not mere polemic, and is no more severe than Suzuki's critique of the decadent Buddhism of his time. It reflects astonishment at the slightness of Christian doctrine in comparison with the vastness of Buddhist thought, reflects wonder at the impudence and bigotry of the missionaries, and decries what is perceived as both mental and material imperialism. As one of the earliest writings on premodern Japanese foreign relations, it is of inestimable value as a political document as well as religious tract; several of the essays are translated below, being of particularly great interest for what they reflect of how the Portuguese and the Japanese perceived one another, as well as for their illustration of a Japanese response to foreign pressure.

1. According to what I hear of the Christian teaching, there is a great Buddha called Deus, who is the one sole Buddha, master of the universe and lord over all. This is the creator of the universe and all beings. This Buddha came into the world in some foreign land to save people sixteen hundred years ago. His name was Jesus Christ. Ignorant of this, they say, other countries honor the worthless Amida Buddha and Gautama Buddha, the height of folly.

Refutation: If Deus, as the master of the universe, created all lands and all beings, why has that Deus hitherto neglected countless nations, not appearing among them?

Ever since heaven and earth were opened, the buddhas of past, present, and future have emerged over and over again to liberate beings. How many hundred of millions of years would you say this has been going on? What basis of proof is there for saying that Deus never appeared in other countries all that time, and only recently appeared in such-and-such a country?

If Deus is the master of the universe, he is sure doing a slipshod job of it if he lets a multitude of the nations he has created be taken over by subsidiary buddhas, suffering them to spread their teachings to liberate beings, ever since the opening of heaven and earth. This Deus is indeed a foolish buddha.

Furthermore, they say that Jesus Christ came into the world and was crucified by ordinary men of the lower world. This is the master of the universe? How could anything be so illogical?

The Christians do not know the unified enlightened state of the true likeness of original awareness. In their ignorance they have taken over one buddha to worship. Their fault in coming to this country to spread devilish teachings and false principles cannot avoid the punishment of Heaven.

There are many ignorant people who cannot understand such simple logic, and throw their lives away out of reverence for that teaching. Is this not a national disgrace? One hardly dare mention what this does to our international reputation.

Although Buddhism is now sometimes referred to as a Japanese religion, it is really transnational at heart. A notable difference between Japanese Buddhism and European Christianity is that the former does not have the same emotional tie to the life of the historical Buddha that the latter has to the birth of Christ. In Mahayana Buddhism, the appearance of a living buddha is not considered a unique historical event as the appearance of Christ was by Church Christians; but rather an infinite, omnipresent possibility that is acted out according to conditions. A buddha was regarded as a reflection, or a reflector, of eternal truths to which all could aspire. The attitude of Zen Buddhism in particular was summarized in a classical statement by a Chinese master to the effect that he studied from the same source as the buddhas.

One point of historical resemblance between Buddhism and Christianity was their break with the tribalism of their original host cultures, Hinduism and Judaism. No longer tied to family and nation, Buddhism and Christianity did anciently share a universal outlook that transcended racial, national, and cultural identity. This having been said, however, it must be added that the habit of self-making is so strong everywhere that new forms of pseudo-tribalism did in fact emerge in both Japanese Buddhism and European Christianity, centered around their various patriarchs, evangels, churches, schools, and sects.

At the time when Suzuki Shōsan wrote his anti-Christian tract, the pseudo-tribal elements in both Buddhism and Christianity were especially strong because of their connection with political, economic, and territorial facts of life. The Christian missionaries were suspected of fronting for European colonial interests; and even those who were only involved in spreading the Gospel were not interested in learning anything about Buddhism that did not serve their own purpose. The Japanese military government did not want a lot of foreign influences or agencies to operate on Japanese soil, certainly not on their own and at their own pace.

The Buddhists, for their part, generally enjoyed cordial relations among a wide variety of sects, including those affiliated with Shintō. Some of these churches used doctrines and practices as diverse in respect to externals as the most dissimilar varieties of even Buddhism and Christianity; yet the Buddhist concept of expediency was sufficient rationale to accommodate them all. They were therefore aghast at the aggressiveness and dogmatism of the European Christian missionaries, especially considering the fact that what appeared to be their doctrine—one local god claiming to rule the world—seemed very slight indeed to the Mahayana Buddhists.

That is not to say that the Jesuits did not have bigger intellectual guns than those they used to convert outcastes, peasants, and merchants. They generally seemed to regard the Japanese as heathens still in the Middle Ages at the beginning of the seventeenth century, however, with whom there would be no point in discussing the Summa Theologica. Their own knowledge of Buddhism would not in any case have sufficed for the purpose of "matching meanings" with Japanese Zen masters. Over all, the intellectual and political aspects of the relationship between the cultures paralleled each other closely in the subjective and objective experience of both sides.

For the Japanese leadership, it was enough to sense that here were people no better than anyone else coming around with some story about how the Japanese should let Europe take over in the name of Deus, their god who was also no better than anyone else's god. The umbrage felt by the Japanese side was similar to that felt by other nations later when the Japanese Shintō militarists told them they should let Japan oversee their affairs, and also to that felt by yet others when the militaristic Shintoists declared the Japanese destiny of world leadership received by direct inheritance from the Sun Goddess, who was now elevated to the status of a supreme deity.

In the transcultural Buddhist view, this is no way to get along. Although his patriotic duty is to refute the Christian doctrine, Shōsan consistently uses this assignment as an opportunity to teach something about Buddhism as well. From his comparison of the supranational grandeur of Buddhist salvationism with the globally politicized missionary front of Christianity, Shōsan turns to the inconceivable subtlety of the unspoken teaching of Zen in contrast to the doctrinaire line of the Christians. First the cosmic concepts of Mahayana Buddhism and Christianity were compared; now the very psychology of dogmatism itself is exposed to the Zen razor.

2. The fundamental intention of past, present, and future buddhas' appearance in the world is to guide beings directly to enlightenment. Therefore it is said they "point directly to people's mind, so they see its essence and attain awakening."

When Gautama Buddha came into the world, after the accumulated effects of twelve years of difficult and painful practices had built up, on the eighth day of the last month of the year he realized the design of the true characteristics of all things on seeing the morning star. After that he left the mountains.

Later, when Buddha had finished the discourses on which the scriptures are based, Buddha held up a flower to show to those who had assembled. Now everyone was silent. Only the saint Kasyapa smiled. The Buddha said, "I have a treasury of eyes of truth, and the subtle mind of nirvana. Real characteristics are indefinable; subtle teachings do not stand on words, but are separately transmitted outside of doctrine. This I entrust to Kasyapa."

This was transmitted from Kasyapa to successor after successor, finally coming to Japan, where the principle of communicating mind by mind is still preserved.

What the Christians teach, on the other hand, is focused solely on a view of the reality of existence, which increases thoughts, worries, and conscious emotions, leading them to make up a "creator of the universe," thus reinforcing the hab-

its that make them revolve in mundane routines, while believing this to be the way of enlightenment.

For them to come to this country and try to oppose authentic teachings with such stupid ideas and interpretations
is like a sparrow challenging a roc on wingspread, or a firefly
telling the moon about light.

This essay begins with the traditional Zen myth of the founding of
the extradimensional communication of Zen by Buddha and one of
his chief disciples, the saint Kasyapa the Elder. The tale illustrates
the Buddhist teaching that formulations of doctrine are provisional
expedients designed to provoke special perceptions, not to be elevated
to the status of absolute truths. Everyone is aware that purely subjective impressions and feelings cannot be exactly conveyed in words;
Zen teaching takes this to the limit by insisting that the experience
of the clarified mind cannot be understood just by descriptions of procedures or results, but must be verified in direct experience.

While this is most strongly emphasized in Zen as represented by
the unspoken teaching, it is not really peculiar to Zen but is part of
Buddhist scriptural tradition. The reason it was stressed by Zen
teachers was to counter psychological and political attachments to
the externals of dogma and belief, fixations that veiled their victims
from the underlying meaning of forms and recreated feelings that ran
directly counter to the original purpose of Buddhism. Religion became politicized through these feelings, since sectarian strife could
not exist without the connection of proprietary and territorial interests with items of dogma, belief, and ritual.

In contrast to formal transmission of doctrine, Zen emphasized
"mind-to-mind" communication of the ineffable. This does not mean
something like mental telepathy, however, as it is ordinarily imagined. In early Chinese Zen lore the mind-to-mind acknowledgment is
likened to two mirrors reflecting each other with no image inter-
posed. There is also a classical Zen device known as the meeting of
minds in a specific realm, which could be abstract or concrete and
was often represented overtly only by a symbol, but this practice
eventually drifted into the same involutionary pattern as doctrinaire
approaches.

The term "transmission of mind by mind" (i shin den shin) eventually passed into popular usage in Japan through the spread of Zen, and

came to be used in the various arts to refer to an extra element outside the formal structures that only comes to awareness and life
through conscious experience. It may also at times be used more vul-
garly to describe coincidences of perception or thought that appear to
be more precise than what common habit might predict. The original
Zen meaning, however, is something very precise and clear, the communication of Zen mind-to-mind by objective experience.

The Christian attitude to which the Zen master objects here is the
fixation on assumptions about the reality of existence, not only as
the content of dogma but as the motive force of dogmatic thinking.
Buddhist metaphysics is more complicated than a simple distinction
between existence and nonexistence, or between reality and unreality, so it is not that Shōsan just opposes Christian realism on philosophical grounds alone. Buddhism deals with the psychological
consequences of metaphysical concepts as life attitudes, and the critique of the naive realism of the materialistic mind in Europe presented here by Shōsan is not only peculiarly anti-Christian but also
traditionally directed at other Asian philosophies, such as Confucianism.

Ironically, Shōsan's explanation of the impulse to "create a Creator" as a means of managing the worries engendered by this bent of
mind is fundamentally much the same as that used by one of the
most eminent promoters of Christianity in the twentieth century, the
Swiss psychoanalyst Carl Jung. Although he proclaimed his opposition to presumptuous authoritarianism in religion, however, Jung did
not draw from his psychological argument the conclusion that metaphysical assumptions could be changed as readily as could the psychic facts habitually associated with them.

Zen master Shōsan, in contrast, draws attention to the disparity in
depth between the open mind of Buddhist illuminism and the closed
mind of missionary Christian dogmatism. The metaphors of the sparrow and the roc, and of the firefly and the moon, are ancient Taoist
images used to criticize the mundane, materialistic Confucian political philosophers with their fixed system of rationalizations. The Taoists had much broader perspectives on life than the more rigid and
self-righteous Confucians. Metaphysically as well as psychologically,
the Taoists believed that being comes from nonbeing, while the Confucians believed in preexisting being. Thus the Zen Buddhists, who
were heirs of Taoist thought, could easily see the same patterns in

their intellectual and spiritual relationship to doctrinaire missionary Christianity.

The next essay also uses traditional Buddhist rationales, but this time it is in defense of native Japanese religion.

3. I hear they say it is wrong to honor the spirits *(kami)*, and that we only do it because we don't know Deus.

Refutation: Japan is spirit country. Having been born in spirit country, not to honor the spirit luminescences would be the ultimate impropriety.

It is said that the harmonization of spirit with matter begins the formation of affinity, while the complete attainment of enlightenment in all respects consummates the salvation of beings. Therefore the earlier appearance (of buddhas) as spirits, thus making an impact on this country, was an expedient to soften people's hearts and introduce them to the real Way.

The only difference between spirits and Buddha is that between waves and water. The unified enlightened state of the true likeness of fundamental awakeness appears temporally according to people's minds to liberate them. Therefore the attitude of respect for the spirits is also a gesture of gratitude toward that unified enlightened state.

For example, when you respect the ruler of a nation, it is an established principle that you respect everyone in the whole hierarchy of government and society. This is all out of respect for the one person on top. Do not the Christians in effect teach that it is right for those who respect the top man to have no use for anyone below him?

The early Japanese Buddhist giant and culture hero Kūkai had fostered the idea that the native deities were local reflections of more cosmic truths that were now represented by buddhas. The deities were absorbed into Buddhism as helpers, guardians, or even enlightening beings, manifestations of cosmic principles in action. This idea is well developed in the Flower Ornament *(Kegon)* scripture that Kūkai brought to Japan from China. The same syncretic device was also used by Buddhism in other cultures throughout old Asia.

Here Shōsan gives the psychological interpretation, as Zennists usually did, explaining the significance of the deities in terms of the effect their belief exerted in the minds of believers. The essay is then brought to a sudden close on the abrupt note of the immediate crisis, in which a metaphor nearly assumes the status of the main topic.

In Shōsan's essay, the central experience of Buddhist enlightenment and the attitude of reverent attention to a higher thought are symbolized in Shintō-Confucian garb, as was customary for political encounters, and represented as a social order and its seat of power. This point may be incomprehensible to Christians thinking in theological rather than political terms, but Shōsan suggests that logical extension of the monotheism preached by the missionaries would subvert the Japanese social order, because it absolutizes one source of authority without recognizing any intermediary. This spelled chaos to the mind accustomed to hierarchy; Shōsan was undoubtedly not aware that the Christians had their own cults of saints and evangels, with their own corresponding ideas and institutions of kings and aristocracies claiming divine rights.

The next essay is also Shintoistic, extending the idea of deity into the natural world. The influence of Taoism through Neo-Confucianism and Zen is also evident. The Shintō relationship of humanity to the environment is through a feeling of gratitude *to* the world of energy and matter as much as *for* it; the Western Christian relationship is based more completely on a kind of gratitude *for* the material world, not *to* it.

In consequence of the onesidedness of the Christian mode of gratitude, the Westerner suffered no problem of conscience with the idea of maximum exploitation of nature until the damage done thereby had become so great as to be threatening and thus reactivate the primary instinct of life, the very sense upon which the abstract spiritual essence of Shintō is originally based. Although he encountered the vanguard of Western technological advance in a relatively primitive form, Shōsan already sensed a contradiction in the rationale of its moral feeling.

4. I hear they say that the Japanese reverence for the sun and moon is wrong; that these are lamps for the world, and that our reverence is also because of not knowing Deus.

Refutation: The human body is composed of a combination of elements based on passive and active energy. The sun is the embodiment of active energy, the moon is the embodiment of passive energy. How can the body be maintained without the passive and active energies? Since they are our roots, we cannot honor them enough. If you think passive and active energies are worthless, then don't use water or fire.

The blessings of the sun and moon in the sky lighting up the world can hardly be requited. People have two eyes that shed light on them; are they not imbued with the virtues of the sun and moon? Since they say it is meaningless to honor the sun and moon, will the Christians then keep their eyes closed? Such is their ignorance of correct reasoning. This is truly idiotic.

Under the pressure of Western materialism, Japanese industry also became damaging and destructive to the local and global environment, thus to this extent losing the meaning of Shintō as expressed in this essay. For that very reason, the rationalized Shintō of the Zen master Shōsan, simple and naive as it seems, has no less profound a meaning for the future of world culture today than it did when this tract was written in the seventeenth century, when Western Europe was just opening up the Pandora's box of advanced industrial technology placed in the hands of men who no longer believed that the natural world was imbued with spirits to be respected and thanked. The ancient pagan world was now inhabited only by inanimate matter and force, to be processed and sold in the most lucrative manner available.

Rationalism and technological advance were popularly associated with Christianity in Westernizing nineteenth-century Japan when political relations and missionary activity resumed after the dissolution of the feudal Shogunate, but the Christianity presented to the Japanese public of the seventeenth century made more liberal use of supernatural rather than mechanical miracle stories.

It may have been that the Jesuits imagined that the Shintoistic side of the Japanese psyche would be interested in this sort of thing, but at least in Shōsan's hands the presence of many similar stories in native Japanese traditions redounds against this missionary Christianity. Buddhism had long before relegated the supernatural to the status of relative truth, and did not attribute to it the imagined connection to absolute truth projected by the mind of the naive realist confronted with the inexplicable but undeniable. In response to Christian tales of miracles, Shōsan writes:

5. I have heard that Christians generally honor marvelous things and attribute them to the glory of Deus. They fabricate all kinds of ruses to fool people.

If marvels were valuable, then the king of deceivers should be revered. Foxes and badgers in this country also work marvels.

It is said that when the god Indra fought with the king of the titans, the titan was defeated and led his 84,000 followers into the hole of a lotus fiber to hide. Do you also honor this kind of marvel?

The six psychic powers are clairvoyance, clairaudience, communication with other minds, awareness of past lives, psychic flight, and knowledge of the end of psychological leakage. The first five of these powers are also found in masters of mesmerism and unliberated religions. The power of knowledge of the end of psychological leakage, however, is beyond mesmerism and unliberated religion; it is the awakened knowledge where all psychological afflictions have been ended.

Therefore there is nothing marvelous about the six powers of a buddha. That is why it is said that there are no marvels in Buddhism. Those who do not know this principle can be fooled by mesmerism and unliberated religion.

The six powers of an enlightened one are the power to see forms without being blocked, to hear sounds without being blocked, to smell odors without being blocked, to taste flavors without being blocked, to feel things without being blocked, to be in the realm of phenomena without touching anything, like a reflection in a mirror.

When the mind is one with space, one is called an unobstructed wayfarer with the six powers. A scripture says, "It is even better to give to a single unminding wayfarer than to all the buddhas of past, present, and future." People who practice the Buddha Way study this path. They have no further use for wonders.

Although it is true that some Zen masters were known to have super-normal powers such as foresight and mind reading, nevertheless the general policy was to conceal these things because of the exaggerated reactions of greed and fear that they easily arouse. Shōsan's description of the "six powers of an enlightened one" is taken directly from the *Record of Rinzai*, a Chinese Zen classic influential among the Japanese Rinzai Zen schools. The Rinzai schools were those most favored by samurai interested in Zen, so this book on the Chinese founder has great prestige in Japanese Zen tradition.

This approach to "supernatural powers" undermines the very question of any argument about whether or not they exist, for two reasons. First, its underlying premise is that consciousness is itself an inconceivable miracle; in the final analysis we do not really know how we are aware, yet we are. Second, the Zen attitude towards the supernatural begins by addressing a more primary issue, the mental clarity and objectivity that would be needed to make sober sense of the whole question and its practical implications for human life.

One aspect of Shintō and Buddhist thought that has until recently seemed to Western eyes to stand on the border of the natural and supernatural, or the rational and irrational, is the sense of human kinship with animals and plants. This often reminds Christians of paganism and sorcery, to which the Church long stood opposed in all of its European territories and New World colonies.

To Buddhists of the Far East, on the other hand, it seemed unreasonably subjective and arbitrary to believe, as Christians apparently did, that humans had the only real souls among living beings. This was a logical step from saying that there was no living spirit in the natural world, but it was unconvincing to those who did not see the sense of the original premise to begin with. Recently the growing perception of ecological crisis in the West has given a new respectability to these Shintō-Buddhist sentiments of continuity, at least in terms of their psychological implications for the relationship of human technologies to life in general.

Zen master Shōsan brings up the contrast between Japanese and European concepts in terms of the distinction between animal and human souls posited by Christian belief, but it is not that he dwells on this specific point. Instead the issue leads to questioning the Christian doctrine of the eternal human soul, the reasoning behind the creation of immoral souls that could be evil and therefore damned to eternal suffering. The idea of compassion is so fundamental to Buddhism that the Christian judgment seemed cruel and merciless. Shosan compares the Christian idea of soul with that of a Hindu system, which he considers superior to Christianity but inferior to Buddhism.

6. According to what I hear, the Christians say that animals have no real soul, so their souls die when their bodies die. Human beings, on the other hand, have added to them a true soul created by Deus, so even when their bodies die their souls do not die: depending on their good and bad deeds in this life, their souls experience pain and pleasure. For those who have done good deeds, he made a world of unending pleasure called Paradise, and sends their souls there. For those who have done bad deeds, he made a world of pain called Inferno, and sends their souls there to torture them.

If he created distinct souls in animals and humans, why did he also create evil minds in the souls of humans and cast them into hell? If this is true, it means that human damnation is entirely the work of Deus.

When Gautama Buddha appeared in the world, unliberated religion and philosophy were flourishing in India. They had immense knowledge and proposed all sorts of views. Some of their logic resembled Buddha's, but as long as their own eyes were not clear it was only talk.

The Sankhya philosophy set up twenty-five realities, with which they defined everything in the world. The first reality was called the unknown reality. Although it is before the division of heaven and earth, not in the province of good and bad, inaccessible to sensation, perception, or cognition, and therefore impossible to really name, it is nevertheless called the unknown. This unknown reality is eternal, unaffected by birth, subsistence, change, and extinction.

The twenty-fifth reality is called the reality of the spiritual self. This is named the mind of mortal man, what has been called the spirit or soul. This is also said to be eternal.

In between these two eternal realities are twenty-three other realities, which are the appearances of the world's changes, such as good and bad, fortune and calamity. These are called compounded phenomena.

When the spiritual self produces differentiated appearances, the unknown reality transmutes to manifest their forms; therefore the changes in the composition of the world are due to the arising of feelings in the spiritual self. When the spiritual self does not give rise to any feelings and returns to the unknown reality, the transformation of composite phenomena ceases forever, and the bliss of the uncreate is spontaneously realized. They say that even though the physical body decays and dies, the spiritual self does not perish, just as the master of a house leaves when the house burns down.

Philosophers with views like this expounded various systems of reasoning, but when they eventually faced the Buddha they understood their own essence directly and all became Buddha's disciples. Now these Christians do not even come close to reaching the level of the unliberated Hindus, and yet they think their doctrine is the truth. They are truly frogs in a well [who do not know how wide the sky really is].

The idea of rewards and punishments in an afterlife was not at all foreign to Japanese Buddhists. What was alien to them was the ultimate finality of the reward or punishment. The linear model of Christian time, in which a soul had one chance on earth for eternal salvation or eternal damnation, contrasted sharply with the circular model of Buddhist time, which allowed for a transpersonal and transgenerational vision of human destiny.

In the Buddhist view there was a broader range of opportunities for salvation from the fate of the soul astray than the dogmatic threat-and-promise religion the Portuguese missionaries seemed to offer. Therefore Shōsan again concludes by accusing the Christians of narrowminded bigotry, using the familiar Taoist image of the frog at the bottom of a well who believes that the opening at the mouth of the well is the whole extent of the sky.

In the final essay, Shōsan gets down to the political roots of the whole battle of polemic between the European Christians and the Shintō-Buddhist Japanese. He portrays the missionary front as destructive and deceptive, but he also fully blames the Japanese followers for empowering them. Shōsan condemns the Japanese Christian martyrs much as the modern Japanese do in saying *Damasareta hō ga warui* ("The deceived were wrong") when people have been swindled—that is, when people have been persuaded to pursue vainly high hopes, and then have not only lost out themselves but have in their haste also caused a lot of trouble to others *(meiwaku o kaketa)* on account of their own desires.

7. The Padres and their ilk who have been coming here in recent years have no fear of the Way of Heaven: making up their own Creator of the Universe, they have destroyed Shintō shrines and Buddhist temples, fooling people with all kinds of vain talk, as part of a scheme whereby Portugal will take over Japan.

Thieving bonzes in this country cooperated, calling themselves Irmao-Padre, dragging in numerous others. They said that the buddhas of this country are not buddhas, that the sun and moon are base matter without spiritual luminescence. Their crimes were very serious, and could not avoid the punishment of Heaven, the punishment of buddhas, the punishment of spirits, and the punishment of humanity. They have all been strung up and killed.

The fault for this fills the chests of those who followed them. I don't know how many thousands have died. This was brought about by magic, and is not a political sanction by our government. They usurped the Way of Heaven, constructed fabrications, and led countless people to hell; the fact is evident that they ultimately brought on their own destruction by their evil, perverse, and unprincipled deeds.

If those Padres became true illuminists, to kill even one of them would mean being cursed by the Way of Heaven. Countless Christians have been executed in this country, but what curse has there been? No matter how many times they come here, as long as the Way of Heaven exists, they will undoubtedly destroy themselves. You should know the logic of this.

Although Shōsan winds up on a decidedly Shintoistic note in spite of his main Buddhist interest, this is nevertheless represented as a reaction to foreign aggression, not simply automatic native xenophobia. So great was the Western threat to Japan, in fact, as perceived by the

Shogunate, that Europe was almost completely shut out of Japan—
intellectually, commercially, and politically—for some two hundred
years after Shōsan wrote this anti-Christian tract in the seventeenth
century. The Japanese feeling of being put upon by aggressive Western
powers was not changed by the manner in which relations were reopened in the nineteenth century at the insistence of the United
States, which threatened to use force if the doors of Japan were not
opened to trade.

In spite of vast differences in scale, there are some ways in which
relations between Japan and the West are not much more advanced
than they were one hundred years ago, or even three hundred years
ago. This is exemplified by the persistent vision of "sides" that think
they are opposed to one another, and the structures of interaction
that emerge from this vision. From a Buddhist point of view, it makes
little sense to think along the conventional lines of international
competition and conflict when it is not a people or a system as such
but the alliance of ignorance, greed, and aggression that is the same
problem everywhere. This perspective may prove to be the only viable avenue beyond the emotionally destabilizing influence of current
anti-Japanese feelings in the West and parallel anti-Western feelings
in Japan.

A ZEN RAZOR

While historical connections undoubtedly exist between Zen Buddhism and Japanese martial arts, their spiritual link has quite obviously never been complete. The attempt to use the historical association to imbue martial arts themselves with the dignity of Buddhism may very well be a prime example of the classical art of strategic misdirection. It may seem odd, therefore, that in spite of the widely acknowledged influence of Zen on Japanese culture and personality, virtually no critical study of Zen in modern Japan has ever been made.

A review of academic and sectarian work on Zen Buddhism quickly brings to light one central fact: that the stock of direct information on this subject is extremely limited and fragmentary. This information gap, furthermore, does not exist only in the realm of the classics, but even in what can be learned about modern Japanese Zen from easily accessible sources where the language barrier is considerably less than that presented by the classics. Some reasons for this are not far to seek, being visible in the narrow scope of sectarian and academic specializations.

Political or social reasons for selective study may also strike roots at various levels, from special interest groups to unconscious policies in public education. The barriers of knowledge and understanding do not exist, in any case, because the average Westerner is not intelligent enough to understand Zen, Japan, or the Japanese language; or because the average Japanese is not intelligent enough to understand Christianity, the West, or Western languages.

By now it has at least become a fashionable courtesy to give all humanity credit for a certain degree of basic intelligence, but it would seem imperative to examine the question of whether that courtesy is going to be used to avoid or to confront the whole issue of ignorance, its existence and operation. From a Buddhist perspective, this is a problem that is universal and exists on every side of cultural, racial, and even personal boundaries of identity. Therefore it is by attacking the central cause of the problem, and not the particular parties caught up in it, that the original Zen method of social criticism evolved outside of politics as ordinarily understood.

Zen in the classical sense involved reaching beyond the limits of insular habits so rigidly held that people can no longer use the brains they were born with. In this sense it makes little difference, in the final analysis, whether the culture is Japanese or German, English or American, or whatever it may be. The Zen question is why we feel a need to cling automatically to these presumed limitations of thinking. This was always the Zen question, and it cannot be less so today when the necessity of seeing things globally has never been more openly evident.

The transmission of knowledge about Zen and Japanese culture to the West is a topic whose importance reaches far beyond the realms of intellectual history and religious adventurism, because of needs created by political and economic relations in the modern world. This subject has been studied to some extent, but without data needed for critical analysis, which would have to consider what has not been transmitted as well as what has, and what has been accurately transmitted as compared with what has been distorted in the process.

The undeniable connection between Zen and Bushidō has come to be so taken for granted that it has been attributed to their natures as well as their histories. The distinctions between them are often not clearly defined in books on Oriental martial arts, which like their counterparts on Oriental cultural arts tend to emphasize their connection with Buddhist principles rather than the historical and ideological idiosyncrasies of their development. An examination of relevant primary literature makes it clear, however, that Bushidō is spiritually and pragmatically different from Buddhism, even if some of its practitioners did learn something about Buddhism and apply it to their arts.

The participation of warriors and strategists in shaping the format of Zen in Japan is one way to explain the cloud of mystery surrounding Zen, as the appearance of a ruse, part of the *art of the advantage,* one that has historically been used to dress certain alien and un-Buddhist elements of Bushidō in the dignity of Buddhism. Many Japanese themselves have unknowingly been deceived by this maneuver, to say nothing of Westerners.

The aspects of Japanese culture with which it is most difficult for the average Westerner to sympathize generally are derived not from Buddhism but from Shintō; and it is these very elements that also tend to alienate the Japanese from non-Japanese in their own thoughts. Therefore if one were to look critically at the subject of Zen influence on Japanese culture and Western civilization, one would have to examine with particular care those items that mark Shintō thinking, are thoroughly out of character with Buddhist Zen, yet nevertheless are perceived as part of Japanese Zen.

The Shintoistic elements that have infected Zen over the centuries may be briefly stated as follows: fetishism, including ritualism and attachment to paraphernalia; devotion to persons living or dead; fondness for rice wine, a sacramental libation in Shintō worship; hierarchy and authoritarianism; a tendency to regard the physical body as real; racism; and local sectarianism.

Another feature found in modern Japanese Zen that is neither Buddhistic nor Shintoistic is misogyny, which has been noted in Japanese culture in general, where it might be expected as a consequence of eight centuries of military rule. This quirk is clearly derived from state Confucianism and militarism, not Buddhism or Shintō, but it is so commonly associated with Zen that it needs to be singled out for analysis before any appreciation of authentic Zen in the classical spiritual sense can be realized.

In this connection, it can also be observed that militarism has left its effects on the emotional and sexual life of the Japanese as well, subsurface tensions that are also sometimes associated with the rigors of Zen, but really derive from the attitudes of the samurai soldiers who bent Zen to their own purposes. Even today, in the highly erotic mass media of Japan, sexual intercourse can be portrayed as something inherently very much like rape; and love is ordinarily depicted as inevitably clashing with duty.

These attitudes, which are among those that generally tend to disturb Westerners and affect their views of Japanese psychology, are leftovers of eight centuries of martial rule and have nothing to do with the spirit of Buddhism. Classical Japanese literature suggests that the Japanese were far more comfortable with their tender emotions and erotic feelings before the soldiers took over in the twelfth century. One of the first things the military government did at that time was to suppress left-hand Tantra, a form of Buddhism in which sensual media such as art, song, and erotic ceremony were used as means of awakening hidden powers in the mind.

Several symptoms of alienation of the sexes, all commonly noted by observers of Japan, are linked to this militaristic suppression that began in earnest eight centuries ago: simultaneously stimulated and repressed sexuality, a resulting undercurrent of violence, and acute manifestations of these phenomena in the form of sadomasochism, are quite evidently products of extended military domination. Similar phenomena can be seen in all societies when they are in militaristic phases of their development.

It is no coincidence that the *I Ching,* China's classic *Book of Change,* for thousands of years one of the most prestigious guides to statecraft in the Orient, contains warnings against assumption of civil rule by military men. The negative effects of eight hundred years of samurai rule in Japan would seem to bear witness to the soundness of this ancient caveat.

Militarism has distorted Zen along with the rest of Japanese culture, producing aberrations in which various forms of Japanese machismo or masochism are regarded as not only having some relation to Zen, but even as being products or manifestations of Zen "practice" or "realization." Furthermore, Japanese people today are just as susceptible to being deceived by deviant Zen as are Westerners, with the result that the various conflicting elements in modern Zen are generally not analyzed for what they really are. Perhaps the burden of ignoring these conflicts is the reason why contemporary Zen in Japan generally does not reflect robustness or optimism, and why it does not seem to influence the culture any longer in a fundamental way.

Institutional Zen Buddhism in contemporary Japan is often accused of being moribund even by its own monastic inmates and literary exponents, to say nothing of outside critics. Various facets of this sluggishness are widely acknowledged in Japanese Zen literature, but their fundamental causes are seldom rooted out, nor are they discussed very frankly in Zen for export. The commercialization of Zen in the West, plus the exploitation of Western interest in Zen or Zen-derived cultural forms in efforts to enhance Japan's image, have militated against unbiased information and objective appraisal.

Therefore the philia-phobia polarity in Western thinking about

Japan has not been reduced as much as it could have been by the undoubtedly active interest in Zen and Japanese culture existing in the West today, had the transcendental and cultural aspects of this interest been clearly distinguished and funded with adequate exposure to information about the essential meaning of Zen and about historical institutions established at various times in Japan for the overt purpose of studying or otherwise upholding Zen.

One of the forms of Japanese culture that appears to be strongly influenced by certain aspects of Bushidō-Zen and that calls for critical examination in the contemporary West is the *jigoku* ("hell") style of training used in Japanese education and personnel development. Since Westerners have to deal with the results of this kind of training, and attempts are also underway to import it to the West, there is a distinct need for critical examination of its reality.

Several years ago, something of a stir was created by the suicide of one of the most respected Zen masters in Japan, who was at that time both abbot and spiritual director of a monastery traditionally ranked in the very highest echelon of Rinzai Zen. Various opinions as to the reasons for his suicide were put forth, including ill health, but his own book, *Takuan ishi no satori,* "The Enlightenment of a Pickle-Pressing Stone," contains some very negative observations of Zen and contemporary Japanese life.

Among them are the abbot's views on the use of Zen training to make people stronger and tougher for getting along in the business world, a practice he calls *fuzaketa,* a word meaning ludicrous, or, in a relational context, having the characteristic of mere dalliance or sport. In the West there is also a strong undercurrent of shortsightedness in both academic and popular interest in Zen, which has been relegated to cult status even within their own spheres of interest, and thus treated in a fragmentary and idiosyncratic manner in Western culture as a whole.

Whenever anti-Japanese feeling among Western nations reaches a certain pitch, there is a renewal of the popular Japanese myth that Westerners would feel more kindly disposed to Japan if they understood Japanese culture. The West cannot afford to be mystified by the mystery of Japan, or to allow information to be used as a weapon in what Musashi calls the *art of the advantage.* There are those who glamorize Japan and seem to feel that the West should try to imitate its ways; there are others who vilify Japan and apparently regard it as a menace. Both extremes are casualties of *the art of war*, who in turn victimize others to the extent of their own influence.

One of the main problems faced by both Japan and the West is the intimate connection between special interests and the dissemination of information and knowledge. This is a two-way street, because racist misperceptions and political projections always work together to the detriment of public understanding. The real enemy on either side is ignorance, whether it be natural or contrived.

One of the characteristic marks of ignorance is blind prejudice, and it is useful to watch out for it when assessing subjective reactions to perceptions of attitudes. In the matter of martial arts, militarism, and their influence on human society, the question of function is paramount in the formation of classical philosophy. The Japanese martial arts were more or less transformed into therapeutic and performing arts during the long Pax Tokugawa, which began in the early seventeenth century and lasted some two hundred and fifty years, until the American *Black Ships* threatened to "huff, puff, and blow their house down" if the Japanese didn't let them into Japan in the mid-nineteenth century.

In the first century of the long peace, the development of various competing schools of martial arts formed a relatively harmless channel for male aggression and ambition left over from the bloody *Sengoku jidai*, Era of the Warring States, a hundred years of constant strife. Furthermore, while this remaining violence was thereby largely vented away from government and society into private groups, the ancient Zen connections of Bushidō also exposed the martially inclined to the Buddhist philosophy of self-mastery, and occasionally to Buddhist ethics as well. In the Tantric Buddhist idiom, such use of "instruments of ill omen" to achieve a worthy purpose is called "using a thorn to extract a thorn."

Oriental martial arts are to some extent performing a similar function in urban American society today. This is undoubtedly one of their most rational adaptations, as it was in Japan of the seventeenth century. Over the next hundred years in Japan, however, the growing number and discontent of disenfranchised samurai rekindled some deadly flames. Martial prowess could (as ever) be used for wantonly criminal purposes; and the line between chivalrous competition and political violence was easily overstepped in the name of Bushidō.

In the nineteenth century, the breaking of Japanese isolation fostered diametrically opposed movements in Bushidō, just as they did in Zen Buddhism. On the one hand, through renewed contact with China, certain modern Japanese pioneers took an interest in Taoist martial arts and developed more peaceful, unarmed Japanese martial arts. On the other hand, through confrontation with the aggressive, well-armed West, militaristic factions of Bushidō turned to Spartan training designed to make the entire being, mind and body, into a weapon.

The "soft" martial arts are generally favored by people interested in the spiritual tradition of Zen, while the "hard" martial arts are favored by the police, armed forces, and *jigoku* ("hell") training systems in education, business, and industry. There are also any number of shades in between these extremes, but it is in most concentrated form that their peculiar characteristics, including their specific functions and side effects, can be most clearly seen.

Therefore a stark examination of primitive elements can be construed as prejudicial by the already prejudiced, but it is as impossible to understand a composite without understanding its parts as it is impossible to understand the parts without understanding them as parts of a whole.

SUMMARY

Crucial to understanding Japanese psychology and behavior is an assessment of the influence of centuries of military rule. The development of economic, political, social, and educational structures of Japan reflects this influence, ingrained into the nation through the elevation of the samurai caste into a political or moral elite over a period of hundreds of years.

Warfare in Japan was originally the domain of aristocratic clans. These clans believed themselves to be descended from one of three sources: they thought they were direct descendants of deities, direct descendants of ancient emperors of Japan, or direct descendants of Chinese or Korean nobility. The imperial clan is one of the first category, those believed to be directly descended from deities. This particular clan is associated with the goddess of the sun, who was assigned precedence in the Shintō pantheon with the rise of this clan and its allies in ancient Japan. Their mythology is the basis of state Shintō, the imperial version of native Japanese religion.

The connections with Korea and China maintained by the powerful Japanese clans enabled them to develop the arms with which they asserted political dominance. In their mythology, the sword is one of the symbols of the imperial family of the sun goddess clan, and the process of sword making has traditionally been associated with Shintō. Sword fetishism, eventually to become a characteristic exaggeration of Bushidō, reflects an element of primitive Shintō in the psychology of the samurai.

Territorial conflicts continued even after the allies of the sun goddess clan established a national Japanese state on the Chinese model around 600 C.E. Genocidal warfare against the other peoples inhabiting those islands also continued. Frontier wars and clan competition among the Japanese themselves stimulated the development of a separate military caste, descended from the old aristocracy but with its own distinct history and heritage. This new caste also produced the stewards, marshals, and sheriffs engaged by upper-class landowners in the capital to manage and police their far-flung estates. Eventually the military men demanded more for their services, and the first centralized martial paragovernment was set up in 1185. This was the beginning of the Bakufu "Tent Government" of the Shogunate.

Three military regimes dominated Japanese society and politics from 1185 to 1868. Two more martial regimes have appeared since but have ruled in the name of the emperor rather than the Shōgun. The first two Shogunates patronized Zen Buddhism, breaking with the established Buddhist schools whose churches were all run by members of the old aristocracy. The third Shogunate patronized Confucianism and attempted to divide and repress Buddhism. The fourth martial regime openly suppressed Buddhism in the late nineteenth and early twentieth centuries, in the name of Shintō nationalism. The fifth martial regime forced Buddhist churches into an alliance with state Shintō during the second quarter of the twentieth century.

Zen Buddhist elements in the Japanese warrior code originally came from the time when Zen became fashionable among samurai clans through the encouragement of the Shōguns. Neo-Confucianism was also passed on to the warriors by early Zen Buddhists, but it was probably not until the establishment of Neo-Confucianism as state orthodoxy in the seventeenth century that this element came to predominate in the samurai codes of Bushidō.

All Japanese traditions were codified during the era of the last Shogunate, except for Bushidō, which was written in some way into house rules for clans and organizations, but never unified or finalized. There are Shintō, Buddhist, Taoist, Confucian, Legalist, and militarist elements to be found in various representations of Bushidō, but no generalizations as to their proportion in an abstract "Bushidō" may be made, except on the level where concrete facts are evident to common view in the light of history. This may reflect the inherently competitive nature of the art of war, the deliberate vagueness of the art of the advantage, in which anything might be set forward according to the convenience of the time.

This volume explores the relationship between Zen Buddhism and the samurai cult of Bushidō through the works of four distinguished authors, two Zen masters and two martial artists. The popular idea of Zen spirituality in the martial arts is examined critically with a

view to discerning the discontinuity as well as the continuity between these two facets of Japanese culture. The connection is considered from two points of view: Zen influence on the way of the
warrior, and the influence of militarism on the development of Japanese Zen.

The four authors whose works form the bones of this book represent several distinct types among those involved in Zen and the martial arts. Zen master Takuan elucidates the essence of Zen
mindfulness as it applies to the way of the warrior. The swordsman
Yagyū Munenori applies the ethics and psychology of Zen to martial
arts. Zen master Suzuki Shōsan demonstrates the spirit or warriorhood in the practice of Zen. Miyamoto Musashi the duelist represents
the warlike strategy of militarist using Zen techniques without Buddhist ethics.

In Takuan's work on the immutable mind, there is no express morality. Yagyū applies Zen to martial arts but subordinates martial arts
to the service of political morality. Shōsan uses the psychology of the
warrior in the art of Zen self-mastery; he is both technical and ethical, going further than Takuan and Yagyū in depth and extension.
Musashi is not as clear as the more spiritual Zennists; he may have
been trying to use the warrior's way to master himself, but it looks
like that way got the better of him. Musashi shows a warlike spirit
appearing to be ultimately devoted neither to Zen enlightenment nor
to social morality but only to the perfection of his art in itself, which
embodies the quest for victory as the supreme goal. It does not seem
odd that Musashi surpasses the others in the ruthlessness of his strategy and appears to fall short of the others in Buddhist understanding;
yet his dedication, discipline, and winning record still pass for admi-
rable things in themselves.

None of these types alone may be taken to represent a general picture of Japanese culture and psychology as they are manifested in
those areas influenced by Zen or militarism over the centuries. All of
them are present in various proportions, sometimes even within the
same individual. Interactive confusion and misunderstanding often
result from failure to distinguish the different aspects of Zen and mar-
tialism as they actually operate in various mixtures.

There is an inside (ura) and an outside (omote) to every form of
Japanese culture. Matters of "face" are therefore as important as
matters of substance in social, business, or political interactions.

What is outwardly made most visible of any form of Japanese culture, whether it be Zen, martial arts, or any other facet of that civilization, normally consists of the most commercialized and/or politicized versions, not necessarily the most refined or authentic. The obvious front is not the measure of what it is supposed to represent, even though the existence of the facades is an inescapable fact of life when dealing with Japanese culture as a political reality. As an aspect of strategic maneuvering, the commercialized and politicized outward forms of culture belong to the category of Japanese behavior deriving from the "art of the advantage" developed by martialists.

The substitution of overgeneralizations and clichés for authentic information and critical analysis is itself a common "art of war." Its use to pit the emotions of nations and cultures against one another is also an art of war, one that camouflages an underlying opposition of a different nature. It is the impersonal insight that marked original noncultural Zen Buddhism, and not the kind of superficial intercultural understanding that confuses the surface with the interior, that can distinguish this fundamental opposition between those who exploit ignorance and those in need of knowledge.

THE BOOK OF FIVE RINGS

Miyamoto Musashi

TRANSLATOR'S PREFACE

The Japanese word *shin-ken* means "real sword," but it is now more generally used in a metaphorical sense. In common parlance, to do something with a real sword means to do it with utmost earnestness. To have an attitude proper to a real sword means to be deadly serious. *Shin-ken shō-bu*, literally a contest with real swords, means something done in deadly earnest.

This molecule of linguistic anthropology hints at a very good reason why the Japanese are as persistent and skilled as they are at survival and adaptation. Through centuries of cultural training under the martial rule of the samurai, the Japanese are generally able to experience and address virtually anything as a life and death situation.

This book shows how they do it.

TRANSLATOR'S INTRODUCTION

The Book of Five Rings and *The Book of Family Traditions on the Art of War* are two of the most important texts on conflict and strategy emerging from the Japanese warrior culture. Originally written not only for men-at-arms, they are explicitly intended to symbolize processes of struggle and mastery in all concerns and walks of life.

The Book of Five Rings was written in 1643 by Miyamoto Musashi, undefeated dueler, masterless samurai, and independent teacher. *The Book of Family Traditions on the Art of War* was written in 1632 by Yagyū Munenori, victorious warrior, mentor of the Shogun, and head of the Secret Service.

Both authors were professional men-at-arms born into a long tradition of martial culture that had ultimately come to dominate the entire body of Japanese polity and society. Their writings are relevant not only to members of the ruling military caste, but also to leaders in other professions, as well as people in search of individual mastery in whatever their chosen path.

The Book of Five Rings and *The Book of Family Traditions on the Art of War* are both written in Japanese, rather than the literary Chinese customary in elite bureaucratic, religious, and intellectual circles in Japan at that time. The Japanese in which they are written, furthermore, is relatively uncomplicated and quite free of the subtle complexities of classical high court Japanese. Although the crudity of Musashi's syntax and morphology make for clumsy reading, nevertheless the basic simplicity and deliberate clarity of both works make them accessible to a wide and varied audience.

The rise and empowerment of the samurai class in Japan may be seen in the two terms used to refer to its members, *samurai* and *bushi*. The word *samurai* comes from the Japanese verb *saburau*, which means "to serve as an attendant." The word *samurai* was used by other social classes, while the warriors referred to themselves by the more dignified term *bushi*.

The original samurai were attendants of nobles. In time their functions expanded to the administration, policing, and defense of the vast estates of the nobles, who were mostly absentee landlords. Eventually the samurai demanded and won a greater share of the wealth and political power that the nobles had called their own. Ultimately the military paragovernment of the Shōguns, known as the Bakufu, or Tent Government, overshadowed the imperial organization and dominated the whole country.

Musashi and Yagyū lived in the founding era of the third Tent Government, which lasted from the beginning of the seventeenth century through the middle of the nineteenth century. While inheriting the martial traditions of its predecessors, this third Tent Government differed notably in certain respects.

The first Tent Government was established in eastern Japan near the end of the twelfth century and lasted for nearly one hundred and fifty years. The warriors of this time were descendants of noble houses, many of whom had honed their martial skills for generations in warfare against the Ainu people in eastern Japan. As the Tent Government was seated in Kamakura, a small town near modern Tōkyō, this period of Japanese history is commonly called the Kamakura era.

The second Tent Government supplanted the first in 1338. The warrior class had expanded and become more differentiated by this time, with lesser and thinner genealogical ties to the ancient aristocracy. The Shōguns of this period established their Tent Government in Kyōto, the old imperial capital, and tried to establish high culture among the new samurai elite. This period of Japanese history is commonly called the Ashikaga era, after the surname of the Shōguns, or the Muromachi era, after the name of the outlying district of Kyōto in which the Tent Government was located.

To understand Japanese history and culture, it is essential to realize that no government ever united the whole country until the Meiji Restoration of 1868. The imperial government had always ruled the whole land in theory, but never in fact. The imperial house had never really been more than a center of powerful factions, competing with other powerful factions. Even when everyone recognized the ritual and political status of the emperor in theory, direct imperial rule only reached a portion of the land.

As this is true of the imperial house, so is it also true of the military governments. The reign of the Shōguns was always complicated and mitigated by the very nature of the overall Japanese power structure. The rule of the Kamakura Tent Government was not absolute, that of the Muromachi Tent Government even less. Separatism, rivalry, and civil warfare marked the fifteenth and sixteenth centuries.

By this time, known as the era of the Warring States, the way of war was open to anyone who could obtain arms by any means. Lower-class samurai rose up to overthrow the upper-class samurai, and Japan was plunged into chaos. It was not until the latter part of the sixteenth century that a series of hegemons emerged with strategy and power sufficient to move dramatically toward unification. The third Tent Government was built on the achievements of those hegemons.

Within the context of traditional Japanese society, the founder of the third Shogunate was an upstart and a usurper. Aware of this, he set out to establish a most elaborate system of checks and controls to ensure the impossibility of such an event ever occurring again. Moving his capital again to eastern Japan, away from the heartland of the ancient aristocracy and imperial regime, the new Shōgun disarmed the peasants and disenfranchised the samurai class, removing all warriors from the land and settling them in castle towns. This period of Japanese history is commonly known as the Tokugawa era, after the surname of the Shōguns, or the Edo period, after the name of the new capital city, now called Tōkyō.

Tokugawa Japan was divided into more than two hundred baronies, which were classified according to their relationship to the Tokugawa clan. The barons were controlled by a number of methods, including regulation of marriage and successorship, movement of territories, and an elaborate hostage system. The baronies were obliged to minimize their contingents of warriors, resulting in a large number of unemployed samurai known as *rōnin*, or wanderers.

Many of the disenfranchised samurai became schoolteachers, physicians, or priests. Some continued to practice martial traditions, and to teach them to others. Some became hooligans and criminals, eventually to constitute one of the most serious social problems of the later Tokugawa period. Certain differences, both technical and philosophical, between *The Book of Five Rings* and *The Book of Family Traditions on the Art of War* stem from the fact that Miyamoto Musashi was a masterless samurai pursuing a career as a dueler and an independent teacher of martial arts, while Yagyū Munenori was a distinguished war veteran and a servant of the central military government.

The Book of Five Rings

More properly titled in English *The Book of Five Spheres*, Miyamoto Musashi's work is devoted to the art of war as a purely pragmatic enterprise. Musashi decries empty showmanship and commercialization in martial arts, focusing attention on the psychology and physics of lethal assault and decisive victory as the essence of warfare. His scientifically aggressive, thoroughly ruthless approach to military science, while not universal among Japanese martialists, represents a highly concentrated characterization of one particular type of samurai warrior.

Although a vast body of legend grew up around his dramatic exploits, little is known for certain about the life of Miyamoto Musashi. What he says of himself in *The Book of Five Rings* is the primary source of historical information. He killed a man for the first time when he was thirteen years old, for the last time when he was twenty-nine. At some point he apparently gave up using a real sword but continued to inflict mortal wounds on his adversaries until the end of his fighting career.

The last three decades of Musashi's life were spent refining and teaching his military science. It is said that he never combed his hair, never took a bath, never married, never made a home, and never fathered children. Although he also took up cultural arts, as indeed he recommends to everyone, Musashi himself basically pursued an ascetic warrior's path to the end.

Born into strife, raised in mortal combat, ultimately witness to a transition to peacetime polity on a scale unprecedented in the history of his nation, Miyamoto Musashi abandoned an ordinary life to exemplify and hand on two essential elements of ancient and martial and strategic traditions.

The first of these basic principles is keeping inwardly calm and clear even in the midst of violent chaos; the second is not forgetting about the possibility of disorder in times of order. As a warrior of two very different worlds, a world of war and a world of peace, Musashi was obliged to practice both of these fundamental aspects of the warrior's way in a most highly intensified manner, lending to his work a keenness and a ferocity that can hardly be surpassed.

The Book of Family Traditions on the Art of War

The life of Yagyū Munenori (1571–1646) contrasts sharply with that of Miyamoto Musashi, even though both men were professional warriors of the same age. Yagyū received training in martial arts from his father and became the teacher of Tokugawa Hidetada in 1601, when he was barely thirty years old. The Tokugawa Tent Government was established two years later, and Hidetada became the second Shōgun in 1605. Yagyū Munenori was now the official *shōgunke heihō shihan*, or Martial Arts Teacher to the Family of the Shōguns.

Yagyū subsequently distinguished himself in battle in the still unsettled early years of the new Tent Government. In one famous incident when the Shōgun was unexpectedly ambushed, Yagyū personally cut down seven of the attackers with his "killing sword." More and more of the barons and their brothers and sons were now seeking entry into the "New Shadow" school of Yagyū, now a famous warrior and master swordsman.

In spite of his distinguished military career, Yagyū writes of himself that he did not realize the deeper meanings of martial arts until he was already past fifty years old. Miyamoto Musashi, it will be noted, made a similar remark, even though he had been undefeated in his youthful fighting career. Like Musashi, Yagyū also wrote his book on martial arts late in life, after much reflection on his experiences.

The Book of Family Traditions on the Art of War was completed in 1632, the same year that Yagyū Munenori was appointed head of the Secret Service. Under the Tokugawa Tent Government, the role of the Secret Service was to oversee the direct vassals of the Tokugawa Family, police the castle at Edo, oversee the performance of lower-level government officers, watch over official ceremonies, attend the Shōgun, and participate in the high court. Yagyū's writing thus reflects a far more developed social and political consciousness than Musashi's.

The Book of Family Traditions on the Art of War consists of three main scrolls, entitled "The Killing Sword," "The Life-Giving Sword," and "No Sword." These are Zen Buddhist terms adapted to both wartime and peacetime principles of the samurai. The killing sword represents the use of force to quell disorder and eliminate violence. The life-giving sword represents the preparedness to perceive impending problems and forestall them. "No sword" represents the capacity to make full use of the resources of the environment.

Zen and Martial Art

Yagyū's work contains a comparatively large amount of material drawn from Zen Buddhist sources, invoking the similarity between Zen and martial arts on certain points. Yagyū himself makes it clear, however, that the correspondence between Zen and martial arts is imperfect and incomplete, and that he himself has not actually mastered Zen.

Ever since the samurai took power in Japan, centuries before Musashi and Yagyū were born, Buddhists had been trying to civilize and educate the warriors. This does not mean that the samurai caste in general was successfully imbued with Buddhist enlightenment, or even with a Buddhist spirit. One prominent reason for this was that the Buddhists were kept busy, not only trying to civilize the samurai, but also trying to clean up after them and their follies. Buddhism was burdened with the tasks of burying the dead, taking in and raising the many children orphaned by war or poverty or cast off as bastards, and sheltering abused and abandoned wives.

In the relationship between Zen and the samurai, therefore, the teacher should not be assessed by the level of the student. If martial arts were really considered the highest form of study in Japan, as has been suggested by some apologists, Zen masters would have been the students of the warriors, and not the other way around.

The prolonged domination of Japan by the martial caste was an anomaly in human affairs, as reflected by its discord with both native Japanese and greater East Asian sociopolitical ideals. Because of the way martial rule was established by power, it was fated to bend social and philosophical ideals to its own purposes, rather than submit itself completely to the judgment and guidance of the traditional religions and philosophies it professed to uphold.

The Book of Five Rings

Miyamoto Musashi

PREFACE

The science of martial arts called the Individual School of Two Skies is something that I have spent many years refining. Now, wishing to reveal it in a book for the first time, I have ascended Mount Iwato in Higo province of Kyūshū. Bowing to Heaven, paying respects to Kannon, I face the Buddha. I am Shinmen Musashi no Kami, Fujiwara no Genshin, a warrior born in the province of Harima, now sixty years old.

I have set my mind on the science of martial arts since my youth long ago. I was thirteen years old when I had my first duel. On that occasion I won over my opponent, a martial artist named Arima Kihei of the New School of Accuracy. At sixteen years of age I beat a powerful martial artist called Akiyama of Tajima province. When I was twenty-one, I went to the capital city and met martial artists from all over the country. Although I engaged in numerous duels, never did I fail to attain victory.

After that, I traveled from province to province, meeting martial artists of the various schools. Although I dueled more than sixty times, never once did I lose. That all took place between the time I was thirteen years old and the time I was twenty-nine.

When I had passed the age of thirty and reflected on my experiences, I realized that I had not been victorious because of consummate attainment of martial arts. Perhaps it was because I had an inherent skill for the science and had not deviated from natural principles. It may also have been due to shortcomings in the martial arts of other schools. In any case, I subsequently practiced day and night in order to attain an even deeper principle, and spontaneously came upon the science of martial arts. I was about fifty years old at that time.

Since then I have passed the time with no science into which to inquire. Trusting in the advantage of military science, as I turn it into the sciences of all arts and skills, I have no teacher in anything.

Now, in composing this book, I have not borrowed the old sayings of Buddhism or Confucianism, nor do I make use of old stories from military records or books on military science. With Heaven and Kannon for mirrors, I take up the brush and begin to write, at 4:00 A.M. on the night of the tenth day of the tenth month, 1643.

THE EARTH SCROLL

Martial arts are the warrior's way of life. Commanders in particular should practice these arts, and soldiers must also know this way of life. In the present day there are no warriors with certain knowledge of the way of martial arts.

First let us illustrate the idea of a way of life. Buddhism is a way of helping people, Confucianism is a way of reforming culture. For the physician, healing is a way of life; a poet teaches the art of poetry. Others pursue fortune-telling, archery, or various other arts and crafts. People practice the ways to which they are inclined, developing individual preferences. Few people are fond of the martial way of life.

First of all, the way of warriors means familiarity with both cultural and martial arts. Even if they are clumsy at this, individual warriors should strengthen their own martial arts as much as is practical in their circumstances.

People usually think that all warriors think about is being ready to die. As far as the way of death is concerned, it is not limited to warriors. Mendicants, women, farmers, and even those below them know their duty, are ashamed to neglect it, and resign themselves to death; there is no distinction in this respect. The martial way of life practiced by warriors is based on excelling others in anything and everything. Whether by victory in an individual duel or by winning a battle with several people, one thinks of serving the interests of one's employer, of serving one's own interests, of becoming well known and socially established. This is all possible by the power of martial arts.

Yet there will be people in the world who think that even if you learn martial arts, this will not prove useful when a real need arises. Regarding that concern, the true science of martial arts means practicing them in such a way that they will be useful at any time, and to teach them in such a way that they will be useful in all things.

On the Science of Martial Arts

In China and Japan, practitioners of this science have been referred to as masters of martial arts. Warriors should not fail to learn this science.

People who make a living as martial artists these days only deal with swordsmanship. The priests of the Kashima and Kantori shrines in Hitachi province have established such schools, claiming their teachings to have been transmitted from the gods, and travel around from province to province passing them on to people; but this is actually a recent phenomenon.

Among the arts and crafts spoken of since ancient times, the so-called "art of the advantage" has been included as a craft; so once we are talking about the art of the advantage, it cannot be limited to swordsmanship alone. Even swordsmanship itself can hardly be known by considering only how to win by the art of the sword alone; without question it is impossible to master military science thereby.

As I see society, people make the arts into commercial products; they think of themselves as commodities, and also make implements as items of commerce. Distinguishing the superficial and the substantial, I find this attitude has less reality than decoration.

The field of martial arts is particularly rife with flamboyant showmanship, with commercial popularization and profiteering on the part of both those who teach the science and those who study it. The result of this must be, as someone said, that "amateuristic martial arts are a source of serious wounds."

Generally speaking, there are four walks of life: the ways of the knight, the farmer, the artisan, and the merchant.

First is the way of the farmer. Farmers prepare all sorts of agricultural tools and spend the years constantly attending to the changes in the four seasons. This is the way of the farmer.

Second is the way of the merchant. Those who manufacture wine obtain the various implements required and make a living from the profit they gain according to quality. Whatever the business, merchants make a living from the profits they earn according to their particular status. This is the way of the merchant.

Third, in regard to the warrior knight, that path involves constructing all sorts of weapons and understanding the various properties of weapons. This is imperative for warriors; failure to master weaponry and comprehend the specific advantages of each weapon would seem to indicate a lack of cultivation in a member of a warrior house.

Fourth is the way of the artisan. In terms of the way of the carpenter, this involves skillful construction of all sorts of tools, knowing how to use each tool skillfully, drawing up plans correctly by means of the square and the ruler, making a living by diligent practice of the craft.

These are the four walks of life, of knights, farmers, artisans, and merchants. I will illustrate the science of martial arts by likening it to the way of the carpenter.

The carpenter is used as a metaphor in reference to the notion of a house. We speak of aristocratic houses, military houses, houses of the arts; we speak of a house collapsing or a house continuing; and we speak of such and such a tradition, style, or "house." Since we use the expression "house," therefore, I have employed the way of the master carpenter as a metaphor.

The word for carpenter is written with characters meaning "great skill" or "master plan." Since the science of martial arts involves great skill and master planning, I am writing about it in terms of comparison with carpentry.

If you want to learn the science of martial arts, meditate on this book; let the teacher be the needle, let the student be the thread, and practice unremittingly.

Likening the Science of Martial Arts to Carpentry

As the master carpenter is the overall organizer and director of the carpenters, it is the duty of the master carpenter to understand the regulations of the country, find out the regulations of the locality, and attend to the regulations of the master carpenter's own establishment.

The master carpenter, knowing the measurements and designs of all sorts of structures, employs people to build houses. In this respect, the master carpenter is the same as the master warrior.

When sorting out timber for building a house, that which is straight, free from knots, and of good appearance can be used for front pillars. That which has some knots but is straight and strong can be used for rear pillars. That which is somewhat weak yet has no knots and looks good is variously used for door sills, lintels, doors, and screens. That which is knotted and crooked but nevertheless strong is used thoughtfully in consideration of the strength of the various members of the house. Then the house will last a long time.

Even knotted, crooked, and weak timber can be made into scaffolding, and later used for firewood.

As the master carpenter directs the journeymen, he knows their various levels of skill and gives them appropriate tasks. Some are assigned to the flooring, some to the doors and screens, some to the sills, lintels, and ceilings, and so on. He has the unskilled set out floor joists, and gets those even less skilled to carve wedges. When the master carpenter exercises discernment in the assignment of jobs, the work progresses smoothly.

Efficiency and smooth progress, prudence in all matters, recognizing true courage, recognizing different levels of morale, instilling confidence, and realizing what can and cannot be reasonably expected—such are the matters on the mind of the master carpenter. The principle of martial arts is like this.

The Science of Martial Arts

Speaking in terms of carpentry, soldiers sharpen their own tools, make various useful implements, and keep them in their utility boxes. Receiving instructions from a master carpenter, they hew pillars and beams with adzes, shave floors and shelving with planes, even carve openwork and bas relief. Making sure the measurements are correct, they see to all the necessary tasks in an efficient manner; this is the rule for carpentry. When one has developed practical knowledge of all the skills of the craft, eventually one can become a master carpenter oneself.

An essential habit for carpenters is to have sharp tools and keep them whetted. It is up to the carpenter to use these tools masterfully, even making such things as miniature shrines, bookshelves, tables, lamp stands, cutting boards, and pot covers. Being a soldier is like this. This should be given careful reflection.

Necessary accomplishments of a carpenter are avoiding crookedness, getting joints to fit together, skillful planing, avoiding abrasion, and seeing that there is no subsequent warping.

If you want to learn this science, then take everything I write to heart and think it over carefully.

On the Composition of This Book in Five Scrolls

Distinguishing five courses, in order to explain their principles in individual sections, I have written this book in five scrolls, entitled Earth, Water, Fire, Wind, and Emptiness.

In the Earth Scroll is an outline of the science of martial arts, the analysis of my individual school. The true science cannot be attained just by mastery of swordsmanship alone. Knowing the small by way of the great, one goes from the shallow to the deep. Because a straight path levels the contour of the earth, I call the first one the Earth Scroll.

Second is the Water Scroll. Taking water as the basic point of reference, one makes the mind fluid. Water conforms to the shape of the vessel, square or round; it can be a drop, and it can be an ocean. Water has the color of a deep pool of aquamarine. Because of the purity of water, I write about my individual school in this scroll.

When you attain certain discernment of the principles of mastering swordsmanship, then, when you can defeat one opponent at will, this is tantamount to being able to defeat everyone in the world. The spirit of overcoming others is the same even if there are thousands or tens of thousands of opponents.

The military science of commanders is to construe the large scale from the small scale, like making a monumental icon from a miniature model. Such matters are impossible to write about in detail; to know myriad things by means of one thing is a principle of military science. I write about my individual school in this Water Scroll.

Third is the Fire Scroll. In this scroll I write about battle. Fire may be large or small, and has a sense of violence, so here I write about matters of battle. The way to do battle is the same whether it is a battle between one individual and another or a battle between one army and another. You should observe reflectively, with overall awareness of the large picture as well as precise attention to small details.

The large scale is easy to see; the small scale is hard to see. To be specific, it is impossible to reverse the direction of a large group of people all at once, while the small scale is hard to know because in the case of an individual there is just one will involved and changes can be made quickly. This should be given careful consideration.

Because the matters in this Fire Scroll are things that happen in a flash, in martial arts it is essential to practice daily to attain familiarity, treating them as ordinary affairs, so the mind remains unchanged. Therefore I write about contest in battle in this Fire Scroll.

Fourth is the Wind Scroll. The reason I call this scroll the Wind Scroll is that it is not about my individual school; this is where I write about the various schools of martial arts in the world. As far as using the word *wind* is concerned, we use this word to mean "style" or "manner" in speaking of such things as ancient style, contemporary style, and the manners of the various houses; so here I write definitively about the techniques of the various schools of martial arts in the world. This is "wind." Unless you really understand others, you can hardly attain your own self-understanding.

In the practice of every way of life and every kind of work, there is a state of mind called that of the deviant. Even if you strive diligently on your chosen path day after day, if your heart is not in accord with it, then even if you think you are on a good path, from the point of view of the straight and true, this is not a genuine path. If you do not pursue a genuine path to its consummation, then a little bit of crookedness in the mind will later turn into a major warp. Reflect on this.

It is no wonder that the world should consider the martial arts to consist solely of swordsmanship. As far as the principles and practices of my martial arts are concerned, this is a distinctly different matter. I write about other schools in this Wind Scroll in order to make the martial arts of the world known.

Fifth is the Emptiness Scroll. The reason this scroll is entitled Emptiness is that once we speak of "emptiness," we can no longer define the inner depths in terms of the surface entryway. Having attained a principle, one detaches from the principle; thus one has spontaneous independence in the science of martial arts and naturally attains marvels: discerning the rhythm when the time comes, one strikes spontaneously and naturally scores. This is all the way of emptiness. In the Emptiness Scroll I have written about spontaneous entry into the true Way.

On Naming This Individual School "Two Swords"

The point of talking about two swords is that it is the duty of all warriors, commanders and soldiers alike, to wear two swords. In olden times these were called *tachi* and *katana*, or the great sword and the sword; nowadays they are called *katana* and *wakizashi*, or the sword and the side arm. There is no need for a detailed discussion of the business of warriors wearing these two swords. In Japan, the way of warriors is to wear them at their sides whether they know anything about them or not. It is in order to convey the advantages of these two that I call my school Two Swords in One.

As for the spear, the halberd, and so on, they are considered extra accoutrements; they are among the tools of the warrior.

For beginners in my school, the real thing is to practice the science wielding both swords, the long sword in one hand and the short sword in the other. When your life is on the line, you want to make use of all your tools. No warrior should be willing to die with his swords at his side, without having made use of his tools. However, when you hold something with both hands, you cannot wield it freely both right and left; my purpose is to get you used to wielding the long sword with one hand.

With large weapons such as the spear and the halberd, there is no choice; but the long and short swords are both weapons that can be held in one hand.

The trouble with wielding a long sword with both hands is that it is no good on horseback, no good when running hurriedly, no good on marshy ground, muddy fields, stony plains, steep roads, or crowded places.

When you have a bow or a spear in your left hand, or whatever other weapon you are wielding, in any case you use the long sword with one hand; therefore, to wield the long sword with both hands is not the true way.

When it is impossible to strike a killing blow using just one hand, then use two hands to do it. It should not require effort. Two Swords is a way to learn to wield the long sword in one hand, whose purpose is first to accustom people to wielding the long sword in one hand.

The long sword seems heavy and unwieldy to everyone at first, but everything is like that when you first take it up: a bow is hard to draw, a halberd is hard to swing. In any case, when you become accustomed to each weapon, you become stronger at the bow, and you acquire the ability to wield the long sword. So when you attain the power of the way, it becomes easy to handle.

To swing the long sword with great velocity is not the right way, as will be made clear in the second section, the Water Scroll. The long sword is to be wielded in spacious places, the short sword in confined spaces; this is the basic idea of the way to begin with.

In my individual school, one can win with the long sword, and one can win with the short sword as well. For this reason, the precise size of the long sword is not fixed. The way of my school is the spirit of gaining victory by any means.

It is better to wield two swords than one long sword when you are battling a mob all by yourself; it is also advantageous when taking prisoners.

Matters such as this need not be written out in exhaustive detail; myriad things are to be inferred from each point. When you have mastered the practice of the science of martial arts, there will be nothing you do not see. This should be given careful and thorough reflection.

On Knowing the Principles of the Words Martial Arts

In this path, someone who has learned to wield the long sword is customarily called a martial artist in our society. In the profession of martial arts, one who can shoot a bow well is called an archer, while one who has learned to use a gun is called a gunner. One who has learned to use a spear is called a lancer, while one who has learned to use a halberd is called a halberdier.

If we followed this pattern, one who has learned the way of the sword would be called a longswordsman and a sidearmsman. Since the bow, the gun, the spear, and the halberd are all tools of warriors, all of them are avenues of martial arts. Nevertheless, it is logical to speak of martial arts in specific reference to the long sword. Because society and individuals are both ordered by way of the powers of the long sword, therefore the long sword is the origin of martial arts.

When you have attained the power of the long sword, you can singlehandedly prevail over ten men. When it is possible to overcome ten men singlehandedly, then it is possible to overcome a thousand men with a hundred, and to overcome ten thousand men with a thousand. Therefore, in the martial arts of my individual school, it is the same for one man as it is for ten thousand; all of the sciences of warriors, without exception, are called martial arts.

As far as paths are concerned, there are Confucians, Buddhists, tea connoisseurs, teachers of etiquette, dancers, and so on. These things do not exist in the way of warriors. But even if they are not your path, if you have wide knowledge of the ways, you encounter them in everything. In any case, as human beings, it is essential for each of us to cultivate and polish our individual path.

On Knowing the Advantages of Weapons in Martial Arts

In distinguishing the advantages of the tools of warriors, we find that whatever the weapon, there is a time and situation in which it is appropriate.

The side arm, or short sword, is mostly advantageous in confined places, or at close quarters, when you get right up close to an opponent. The long sword generally has appropriate uses in any situation. The halberd seems to be inferior to the spear on a battlefield. The spear is the vanguard, the halberd the rear guard. Given the same degree of training, one with a spear is a bit stronger.

Both the spear and the halberd depend on circumstances; neither is very useful in crowded situations. They are not even appropriate for taking prisoners; they should be reserved for use on the battlefield. They are essential weapons in pitched battle. If you nevertheless learn to use them indoors, focusing attention on petty details and thus losing the real way, they will hardly prove suitable.

The bow is also suitable on the battlefield, for making strategic charges and retreats; because it can be fired rapidly at a moment's notice from the ranks of the lancers and others, it is particularly good for battle in the open fields. It is inadequate, however, for sieging a castle, and for situations where the opponent is more than forty yards away.

In the present age, not only the bow but also the other arts have more flowers than fruit. Such skills are useless when there is a real need.

Inside castle walls, nothing compares to a gun. Even in an engagement in the open fields, there are many advantages to a gun before the battle has begun. Once the ranks have closed in battle, however, it is no longer adequate.

One virtue of the bow is that you can see the trail of the arrows you shoot, which is good. An inadequacy of the gun is that the path of the bullets cannot be seen. This should be given careful consideration.

As for horses, it is essential for them to have powerful stamina and not be temperamental.

Speaking in general terms of the tools of the warrior, one's horse should stride grandly, one's long and short swords should cut grandly, one's spear and halberd should penetrate grandly, and one's bow and gun should be strong and accurate.

You should not have any special fondness for a particular weapon, or anything else, for that matter. Too much is the same as not enough. Without imitating anyone else, you should have as much weaponry as suits you. To entertain likes and dislikes is bad for both commanders and soldiers. Pragmatic thinking is essential.

On Rhythm in Martial Arts

Rhythm is something that exists in everything, but the rhythms of martial arts in particular are difficult to master without practice.

Rhythm is manifested in the world in such things as dance and music, pipes and strings. These are all harmonious rhythms.

In the field of martial arts, there are rhythms and harmonies in archery, gunnery, and even horsemanship. In all arts and sciences, rhythm is not to be ignored.

There is even rhythm in being empty.

In the professional life of a warrior, there are rhythms of rising to office and rhythms of stepping down, rhythms of fulfillment and rhythms of disappointment.

In the field of commerce, there are rhythms of becoming rich and rhythms of losing one's fortune.

Harmony and disharmony in rhythm occur in every walk of life. It is imperative to distinguish carefully between the rhythms of flourishing and the rhythms of decline in every single thing.

The rhythms of the martial arts are varied. First know the right rhythms and understand the wrong rhythms, and discern the appropriate rhythms from among great and small and slow and fast rhythms. Know the rhythms of spatial relations, and know the rhythms of reversal. These matters are specialties of martial science. Unless you understand these rhythms of reversal, your martial artistry will not be reliable.

The way to win in a battle according to military science is to know the rhythms of the specific opponents, and use rhythms that your opponents do not expect, producing formless rhythms from rhythms of wisdom.

With the science of martial arts of my individual school outlined above, by diligent practice day and night the mind is naturally broadened; transmitting it to the world as both collective and individual military science, I write it down for the first time in these five scrolls entitled Earth, Water, Fire, Wind, and Emptiness.

For people who want to learn my military science, there are rules for learning the art:

1. Think of what is right and true.
2. Practice and cultivate the science.
3. Become acquainted with the arts.
4. Know the principles of the crafts.
5. Understand the harm and benefit in everything.
6. Learn to see everything accurately.
7. Become aware of what is not obvious.
8. Be careful even in small matters.
9. Do not do anything useless.

Generally speaking, the science of martial arts should be practiced with such principles in mind. In this particular science, you can hardly become a master of martial arts unless you can see the immediate in a broad context. Once you have learned this principle, you should not be defeated even in individual combat against twenty or thirty opponents.

First of all, keep martial arts on your mind, and work diligently in a straightforward manner; then you can win with your hands, and you can also defeat people by seeing with your eyes. Furthermore, when you refine your practice to the point where you attain freedom of the whole body, then you can overcome people by means of your body. And since your mind is trained in this science, you can also overcome people by means of mind. When you reach this point, how could you be defeated by others?

Also, large-scale military science is a matter of winning at keeping good people, winning at employing large numbers of people, winning at correctness of personal conduct, winning at governing nations, winning at taking care of the populace, winning at carrying out customary social observances. In whatever field of endeavor, knowledge of how to avoid losing out to others, how to help oneself, and how to enhance one's honor, is part of military science.

The Water Scroll

The heart of the individual Two Skies school of martial arts is based on water; putting the methods of the art of the advantage into practice, I therefore call this the Water Scroll, in which I write about the long sword system of this individual school.

It is by no means possible for me to write down this science precisely as I understand it in my heart. Yet, even if the words are not forthcoming, the principles should be self-evident. As for what is written down here, every single word should be given thought. If you think about it in broad outlines, you will get many things wrong.

As for the principles of martial arts, although there are places in which I have written of them in terms of a duel between two individuals, it is essential to understand in terms of a battle between two armies, seeing it on a large scale.

In this way of life in particular, if you misperceive the path even slightly, if you stray from the right way, you fall into evil states.

The science of martial arts is not just a matter of reading these writings. Taking what is written here personally, do not think you are reading or learning, and do not make up an imitation; taking the principles as if they were discovered from your own mind, identify with them constantly and work on them carefully.

State of Mind in Martial Arts

In the science of martial arts, the state of mind should remain the same as normal. In ordinary circumstances as well as when practicing martial arts, let there be no change at all—with the mind open and direct, neither tense nor lax, centering the mind so that there is no imbalance, calmly relax your mind, and savor this moment of ease thoroughly so that the relaxation does not stop its relaxation for even an instant.

Even when still, your mind is not still; even when hurried, your mind is not hurried. The mind is not dragged by the body, the body is not dragged by the mind. Pay attention to the mind, not the body. Let there be neither insufficiency nor excess in your mind. Even if superficially weakhearted, be inwardly stronghearted, and do not let others see into your mind. It is essential for those who are physically small to know what it is like to be large, and for those who are physically large to know what it is like to be small; whether you are physically large or small, it is essential to keep your mind free from subjective biases.

Let your inner mind be unclouded and open, placing your intellect on a broad plane. It is essential to polish the intellect and mind diligently. Once you have sharpened your intellect to the point where you can see whatever in the world is true or not, where you can tell whatever is good or bad, and when you are experienced in various fields and are incapable of being fooled at all by people of the world, then your mind will become imbued with the knowledge and wisdom of the art of war.

There is something special about knowledge of the art of war. It is imperative to master the principles of the art of war and learn to be unmoved in mind even in the heat of battle.

Physical Bearing in Martial Arts

As for physical appearance, your face should not be tilted downward, upward, or to the side. Your gaze should be steady. Do not wrinkle your forehead, but make a furrow between your eyebrows. Keep your eyes unmoving, and try not to blink. Narrow your eyes slightly. The idea is to keep a serene expression on your face, nose straight, chin slightly forward.

The back of the neck should be straight, with strength focused in the nape. Feeling the whole body from the shoulders down as one, lower the shoulders, keep the spine straight, and do not let the buttocks stick out. Concentrate power in the lower legs, from the knees down through the tips of the feet. Tense the abdomen so that the waist does not bend.

There is a teaching called "tightening the wedge," which means that the abdomen is braced by the scabbard of the short sword in such a manner that the belt does not loosen.

Generally speaking, it is essential to make your ordinary bearing the bearing you use in martial arts, and make the bearing you use in martial arts your ordinary bearing. This should be given careful consideration.

Focus of the Eyes in Martial Arts

The eyes are to be focused in such a way as to maximize the range and breadth of vision. Observation and perception are two separate things; the observing eye is stronger, the perceiving eye is weaker. A specialty of martial arts is to see that which is far away closely and to see that which is nearby from a distance.

In martial arts it is important to be aware of opponents' swords and yet not look at the opponents' swords at all. This takes work.

This matter of focusing the eyes is the same in both small- and large-scale military science.

It is essential to see to both sides without moving the eyeballs.

Things like this are hard to master all at once when you're in a hurry. Remember what is written here, constantly accustom yourself to this eye focus, and find out the state where your eye focus does not change no matter what happens.

Gripping the Long Sword

In wielding the long sword, the thumb and forefinger grip lightly, the middle finger grips neither tightly nor loosely, while the fourth and little fingers grip tightly. There should be no slackness in the hand.

The long sword should be taken up with the thought that it is something for killing opponents. Let there be no change in your grip even when slashing opponents; make your grip such that your hand does not flinch. When you strike an opponent's sword, block it, or pin it down, your thumb and forefinger alone should change somewhat; but in any case you should grip your sword with the thought of killing.

Your grip when cutting something to test your blade and your grip when slashing in combat should be no different, gripping the sword as you would to kill a man.

Generally speaking, fixation and binding are to be avoided, in both the sword and the hand. Fixation is the way to death, fluidity is the way to life. This is something that should be well understood.

On Footwork

In your footwork, you should tread strongly on your heels while allowing some leeway in your toes. Although your stride may be long or short, slow or fast, according to the situation, it is to be as normal. Flighty steps, unsteady steps, and stomping steps are to be avoided.

Among the important elements of this science is what is called complementary stepping; this is essential. Complementary stepping means that you do not move one foot alone. When you slash, when you pull back, and even when you parry, you step right-left-right-left, with complementary steps. Be very sure not to step with one foot alone. This is something that demands careful examination.

Five Kinds of Guard

The five kinds of guard are the upper position, middle position, lower position, right-hand guard, and left-hand guard. Although the guard may be divided into five kinds, all of them are for the purpose of killing people. There are no other kinds of guard besides these five.

Whatever guard you adopt, do not think of it as being on guard; think of it as part of the act of killing.

Whether you adopt a large or small guard depends on the situation; follow whatever is most advantageous.

The upper, middle, and lower positions are solid guards, while the two sides are fluid guards. The right and left guards are for places where there is no room overhead or to one side. Whether to adopt the right or left guard is decided according to the situation.

What is important in this path is to realize that the consummate guard is the middle position. The middle position is what the guard is all about. Consider it in terms of large-scale military science: the center is the seat of the general, while following the general are the other four guards. This should be examined carefully.

The Way of the Long Sword

To know the Way of the long sword means that even when you are wielding your sword with two fingers, you know just how to do it and can swing it easily.

When you try to swing the long sword fast, you deviate from the Way of the long sword, and so it is hard to swing. The idea is to swing the sword calmly, so that it is easy to do.

When you try to swing a long sword fast, the way you might when using a fan or a short sword, you deviate from the Way of the long sword, so it is hard to swing. That is called "short sword mincing" and is ineffective for killing a man with a long sword.

When you strike downward with the long sword, bring it back up in a convenient way. When you swing it sideways, bring it back sideways, returning it in a convenient way. Extending the elbow as far as possible and swinging powerfully is the Way of the long sword.

Procedures of Five Formal Techniques

FIRST TECHNIQUES

In the first technique, the guard is in the middle position, with the tip of the sword pointed at the opponent's face. When you close ranks with the opponent, and the opponent strikes with the long sword, counter by deflecting it to the right. When the opponent strikes again, you hit the point of his sword back up; your sword now having bounced downward, leave it as it is until the opponent strikes again, whereupon you strike the opponent's hands from below.

These five formal techniques can hardly be understood just by writing about them. The five formal techniques are to be practiced with sword in hand. By means of these five outlines of swordplay, you will know my science of swordplay, and the techniques employed by opponents will also be evident. This is the point of telling you that there are no more than five guards in the Two Sword method of swordsmanship. Training and practice are imperative.

SECOND TECHNIQUE

In the second technique of swordplay, the guard is in the upper position, and you strike the opponent at the very same time as the opponent tries to strike you. If your sword misses the opponent, leave it there for the moment, until the opponent strikes again, whereupon you strike from below, sweeping upward. The same principle applies when you strike once more.

Within this technique are various states of mind and various rhythms. If you practice the training of my individual school by means of what lies within this technique, you will gain through knowledge of the five ways of swordplay and will be able to win under any circumstances. It requires practice.

THIRD TECHNIQUE

In the guard of the third technique, the sword is held in the lower position; with a feeling of taking matters in hand, as the opponent strikes, you strike at his hands from below. As you strike at his hands, the opponent strikes again; as he tries to knock your sword down, bring it up in rhythm, then chop off his arms sideways after his has struck. The point is to strike an opponent down all at once from the lower position just as he strikes. The guard with the sword in the lower position is something that is met with both early on and later on in the course of carrying out this science; it should be practiced with sword in hand.

FOURTH TECHNIQUE

In the guard of the fourth technique, the sword is held horizontally to the left side, to hit the opponent's hands from below when he tries to strike. When the opponent tries to knock down your sword as it strikes upward from below, block the path of his sword just like that, with the idea of hitting his hands, and cut diagonally upward toward your shoulder. This is the way to handle a long sword. This is also the way to win by blocking the path of the opponent's sword if he tries to strike again. This should be considered carefully.

FIFTH TECHNIQUE

In the fifth procedure, the sword is held horizontally to your right side. When you note the location of the opponent's attack, you swing your sword from the lower side diagonally upward into the upper guard position, then slash directly from above. This is also essential for expertise in the use of the long sword. When you can wield a sword according to this technique, then you can wield a heavy long sword freely.

These five formal techniques are not to be written down in detail. To understand the use of the long sword in my school, and also generally comprehend rhythms and discern opponents' swordplay techniques, first use these five techniques to develop your skills constantly. Even when fighting with opponents, you perfect the use of the long sword, sensing the minds of opponents, using various rhythms, gaining victory in any way. This requires careful discernment.

On the Teaching of Having a Position Without a Position

Having a position without a position, or a guard without a guard, means that the long sword is not supposed to be kept in a fixed position. Nevertheless, since there are five ways of placing the sword, the guard positions must follow along. Where you hold your sword depends on your relationship to the opponent, depends on the place, and must conform to the situation; wherever you hold it, the idea is to hold it so that it will be easy to kill the opponent.

Sometimes the upper guard position is lowered a bit, so that it becomes the middle position, while the middle guard position may be elevated a bit, depending on the advantage thereof, so that it becomes the upper position. At times the lower guard position is also raised a bit, to become the middle position. The two side-guard positions may also be moved somewhat toward the center, depending on where you are standing vis-à-vis your opponent, resulting in either the middle or lower guard position.

In this way, the principle is to have a guard position without a position. First of all, when you take up the sword, in any case the idea is to kill an opponent. Even though you may catch, hit, or block an opponent's slashing sword, or tie it up or obstruct it, all of these moves are opportunities for cutting the opponent down. This must be understood. If you think of catching, think of hitting, think of blocking, think of tying up, or think of obstructing, you will thereby become unable to make the kill. It is crucial to think of everything as an opportunity to kill. This should be given careful consideration.

In large-scale military science, the arraying of troops is also a matter of positioning. Every instance thereof is an opportunity to win in war. Fixation is bad. This should be worked out thoroughly.

Striking Down an Opponent in a Single Beat

Among the rhythms used to strike an opponent, there is what is called a single beat. Finding a position where you can reach the opponent, realizing when the opponent has not yet determined what to do, you strike directly, as fast as possible, without moving your body or fixing your attention.

The stroke with which you strike an opponent before he has thought of whether to pull back, parry, or strike is called the single beat. Once you have learned this rhythm well, you should practice striking the intervening stroke quickly.

The Rhythm of the Second Spring

The rhythm of the second spring is when you are about to strike and the opponent quickly pulls back or parries; you feint a blow, and then strike the opponent as he relaxes after tensing. This is the stroke of the second spring.

It will be very difficult to accomplish this stroke just by reading this book. It is something that you understand all of a sudden when you have received instruction.

Striking Without Thought and Without Form

When your opponent is going to strike, and you are also going to strike, your body is on the offensive, and your mind is also on the offensive; your hands come spontaneously from space, striking with added speed and force. This is called striking without thought or form, and is the most important stroke. This stroke is encountered time and time again. It is something that needs to be learned well and refined in practice.

The Flowing Water Stroke

The flowing water stroke is used when you are going toe to toe with an opponent, when the opponent tries to pull away quickly, dodge quickly, or parry your sword quickly: becoming expansive in body and mind, you swing your sword from behind you in an utterly relaxed manner, as if there were some hesitation, and strike with a large and powerful stroke.

Once you have learned this stroke, it is certainly easy to strike. It is essential to discern the opponent's position.

The Chance Hit

When you launch an offensive and the opponent tries to stop it or parry it, you strike in his head, hands, and feet with one stroke. Striking wherever you can with one swoop of the long sword is called the chance hit. When you learn this stroke, it is one that is always useful. It is something that requires precise discernment in the course of dueling.

The Spark Hit

The spark hit is when your opponent's sword and your sword are locked together and you strike as strongly as possible without raising your sword at all. One must strike quickly, exerting strength with the legs, torso, and hands.

This blow is hard to strike without repeated practice. If you cultivate it to perfection, it has a powerful impact.

The Crimson Foliage Hit

The idea of the crimson foliage hit is to knock the opponent's sword down and take the sword over. When an opponent is brandishing a sword before you, intending to strike, hit, or catch, you strike the opponent's sword strongly, your striking mood that of "striking without thought and without form," or even "spark hitting." When you then follow up closely on that, striking with the sword tip downward (kissakisagari), your opponent's sword will inevitably fall.

If you cultivate this blow to perfection, it is easy to knock a sword down. It must be well practiced.

The Body Instead of the Sword

The body in this sense can also be called the body that takes the place of the sword. In general, when you take the offensive, your sword and your body are not launched simultaneously. Depending on your chances of striking the opponent, you first adopt an offensive posture with your body, and your sword strikes independently of your body.

Sometimes you may strike with your sword without your body stirring, but generally the body goes on the offensive first, followed up by the stroke of the sword. This requires careful observation and practice.

Striking and Hitting

By *striking* and *hitting*, I mean two different things. The sense of *striking* is that whatever stroke you employ, you make a deliberate and certain strike. Hitting means something like running into someone. Even if you hit an opponent so hard that he dies on the spot, this is a hit. A strike is when you consciously and deliberately strike the blow you intend to strike. This requires examination and reflection.

To hit an opponent on the hands or legs means to hit first, in order to make a powerful strike after hitting. To hit means something like "feel out." If you really learn to master this, it is something extraordinary. It takes work.

The Body of the Short-Armed Monkey

The posture of the short-armed monkey means not reaching out with your hand. The idea is that when you close in on an opponent, you get in there quickly, before the opponent strikes, without putting forth a hand at all.

When you intend to reach forth, your body invariably pulls back; so the idea is to move the whole body quickly to get inside the opponent's defense. It is easy to get in from arm's length. This should be investigated carefully.

The Sticky Body

The sticky body means getting inside and sticking fast to an opponent. When you get inside the opponent's defenses, you stick tight with your head, body, and legs. The average person gets his head and legs in quickly, but the body shrinks back. Sticking to an opponent means that you stick so close that there is no gap between your bodies. This should be investigated carefully.

Comparing Height

Comparing height means that when you close in on an opponent, under whatever circumstances, you extend your legs, waist, and neck, so that your body does not contract; closing in powerfully, you align your face with the opponent's, as if you are comparing height and proving to be the taller of the two. The essential point is to maximize your height and close in strongly. This requires careful work.

Gluing

When your opponent and you both strike forth, and your opponent catches your blow, the idea is to close in with your sword glued to the opponent's sword. Gluing means that the sword is hard to get away from; you should close in without too much force. Sticking to the opponent's sword as if glued, when you move in close it does not matter how quietly you move in.

There is gluing and there is leaning. Gluing is stronger than leaning. These things must be distinguished.

The Body Blow

The body blow is when you close in on an opponent's side and hit him with your body. Turning your face slightly to the side and thrusting your left shoulder forward, you hit him in the chest.

In making the hit, exert as much strength as possible with your body; in making the hit, the idea is to close in with a bound at the moment of peak tension.

Once you have learned to close in like this, you can knock an opponent several yards back. It is even possible to hit an opponent so hard that he dies.

This requires thorough training and practice.

Three Parries

When you attack an opponent, in order to parry the blow of the opponent's sword, making as if to stab him in the eyes, you dash his sword to your right with your sword, thus parrying it.

There is also what is called the stabbing parry. Making as if to stab the opponent in the right eye, with the idea of clipping off his neck, you parry the opponent's striking sword with a stabbing thrust.

Also, when an opponent strikes and you close in with a shorter sword, without paying so much attention to the parrying sword, you close in as if to hit your opponent in the face with your left hand.

These are the three parries. Making your left hand into a fist, you should think of it as if you were punching your opponent in the face. This is something that requires thorough training and practice.

Stabbing the Face

When you are even with an opponent, it is essential to keep thinking of stabbing him in the face with the tip of your sword in the intervals between the opponent's sword blows and your own sword blows. When you have the intention of stabbing your opponent in the face, he will try to get both his face and his body out of the way. When you can get your opponent to shrink away, there are various advantages of which you can avail yourself to win. You should work this out thoroughly.

In the midst of battle, as soon as an opponent tries to get out of the way, you have already won. Therefore it is imperative not to forget about the tactic of "stabbing the face." This should be cultivated in the course of practicing martial arts.

Stabbing the Heart

Stabbing the heart is used when fighting in a place where there is no room for slashing, either overhead or to the sides, so you stab the opponent. To make the opponent's sword miss you, the idea is to turn the ridge of your sword directly toward your opponent, drawing it back so that the tip of the sword does not go off kilter, and thrusting it into the opponent's chest.

This move is especially for use when you are tired out, or when your sword will not cut. It is imperative to be able to discern expertly.

The Cry

A cry and a shout are used whenever you launch an attack to overcome an opponent and the opponent also strikes back; coming up from below as if to stab the opponent, you strike a counterblow.

In any case, you strike with a cry and a shout in rapid succession. The idea is to thrust upward with a cry, then strike with a shout.

This move is one that can be used anytime in a duel. The way to cry and shout is to raise the tip of the sword with the sense of stabbing, then slashing all at once, immediately upon bringing it up. The rhythm must be practiced well and examined carefully.

The Slapping Parry

When you are exchanging blows with an opponent in a duel, you hit the opponent's sword with your own sword as he strikes; this is called the slapping parry. The idea of the slapping parry is not to hit particularly hard, nor to catch and block; responding to the opponent's striking sword, you hit the striking sword, then immediately strike the opponent.

It is essential to be the first to hit and the first to strike. If the rhythm of your parrying blow is right, no matter how powerfully an opponent strikes, as long as you have any intention at all of hitting, your sword tip will not fall. This must be learned by practice and carefully examined.

A Stand Against Many Opponents

A stand against many opponents is when an individual fights against a group. Drawing both long and short swords, you hold them out to the left and right, extending them horizontally. The idea is that even if opponents come at you from all four sides, you chase them into one place.

Discerning the order in which opponents attack, deal with those who press forward first; keeping an eye on the whole picture, determining the stands from which opponents launch their attacks, swinging both swords at the same time without mutual interference, it is wrong to wait. The idea is to immediately adopt the ready position with both swords out to the sides and, when an opponent comes forth, to cut in with a powerful attack, overpower him, then turn away to the next one to come forth and slash him down.

Intent on herding opponents into a line, when they seem to be doubling up, sweep right in powerfully, not allowing a moment's gap.

It will be hard to make headway if you only chase opponents around en masse. Then again, if you think about getting them one after another as they come forth, you will have a sense of waiting and so will also have a hard time making headway. The thing is to win by sensing the opponents' rhythms and knowing where they break down.

If you get a group of practitioners together from time to time and learn how to corner them, it is possible to take on one opponent, or ten, or even twenty opponents, with peace of mind. It requires thorough practice and examination.

Advantage in Dueling

Advantage in dueling means understanding how to win using the long sword according to the laws of martial arts. This cannot be written down in detail; one must realize how to win by practice. This is the use of the long sword that reveals the true science of martial arts; it is transmitted by word of mouth.

The Single Stroke

This means to gain victory with certainty by the accuracy of a single stroke. This cannot be comprehended without learning martial arts well. If you practice this well, you will master martial arts, and this will be a way to attain victory at will. Study carefully.

The State of Direct Penetration

The mind of direct penetration is something that is transmitted when one receives the true path of the school of Two Swords. It is essential to practice well, so as to train the body to this military science. This is transmitted orally.

Epilogue

The above is an overall account of the arts of swordsmanship in my individual school, which I have recorded in this scroll.

In military science, the way to learn how to take up the long sword and gain victory over others starts with using the five formal techniques to learn the five kinds of guard position, then learning how to wield a long sword and gain total freedom of movement, sharpening the mind to discern the rhythms of the path, and taking up the sword oneself. When you are able to maneuver your body and feet however you wish, you beat one person, you beat two people, and you come to know what is good and what is bad in martial arts.

Studying and practicing each item in this book, fighting with opponents, you gradually attain the principles of the science; keeping it in mind at all times, without any sense of hurry, learning its virtues whenever the opportunity arises, taking on any and all opponents in duels, learning the heart of the science, even though it is a path of a thousand miles, you walk one step at a time.

Thinking unhurriedly, understanding that it is the duty of warriors to practice this science, determine that today you will overcome your self of the day before, tomorrow you will win over those of lesser skill, and later you will win over those of greater skill. Practicing in accord with this book, you should determine not to let your mind get sidetracked.

No matter how many opponents you beat, as long as you do anything in contravention of training, it cannot be the true path. When this principle comes to mind, you should understand how to overcome even dozens of opponents all by yourself. Once you can do that, you should be able to grasp the principles of large-scale and individual military science by means of the power of knowledge of the art of the sword.

This is something that requires thorough examination, with a thousand days of practice for training and ten thousand days of practice for refinement.

The Fire Scroll

In the military science of the individual Two Sword school, combat is thought of as fire. Matters pertaining to victory and defeat in combat are thought of as a scroll of fire and so are written down herein.

To begin with, people of the world all think of the principles of advantage in martial arts in small terms. Some know how to take advantage of a flick of the wrist, using the tips of the fingers. Some know how to win using a fan, by a timely movement of the forearm. Then again, using a bamboo sword or something like that, they may just learn the minor advantage of speed, training their hands and feet in this way, concentrating on trying to take advantage of a little more speed.

As far as my military science is concerned, I have discerned the principles of living and dying through numerous duels in which I set my life on the line, learning the science of the sword, getting to know the strength and weakness of opponents' sword blows, comprehending the uses of the blade and ridge of the sword, and practicing how to kill opponents. In the course of doing this, little sissy things never even occurred to me. Especially when one is in full combat gear, one does not think of small things.

Furthermore, to fight even five or ten people singlehandedly in duels with your life on the line and find a sure way to beat them is what my military science is all about. So what is the difference between the logic of one person beating ten people and a thousand people beating ten thousand people? This is to be given careful consideration.

Nevertheless, it is impossible to collect a thousand or ten thousand people for everyday practice to learn this science. Even if you are exercising alone with a sword, assess the knowledge and tactics of all adversaries, know the strong and weak moves of adversaries, find out how to beat everyone by means of the knowledge and character of military science, and you will become a master of this path.

Who in the world can attain the direct penetration of my military science? Training and refining day and night with the determination to eventually consummate it, after having perfected it, one gains a unique freedom, spontaneously attains wonders, and is endowed with inconceivable powers of penetration. This is how cosmic law is carried out through martial arts.

The Physical Situation

In discerning the lay of the physical situation, there is what is known as positioning yourself with the sun at your back. This means that you take up your stance with the sun behind you. If the situation does not allow you to keep the sun at your back, then you should strive to keep the sun to your right.

This also applies indoors, where you should keep the light to your back, or to your right. It is desirable to be sure that there is nothing in the way behind you, and that there is plenty of room to your left, taking a stance in such a way as to cut off the space to your right and close in.

At night also, where you can see your opponents, take your stand with fires to your back and lights to your right, as indicated above.

In order to "look down on the enemy," understand that you should take your stand on the highest ground, even if it is only slightly elevated. Indoors, the seat of honor should be regarded as the high ground.

Anyway, when it comes to battle, the idea is to chase opponents to your left; it is essential to make sure that obstacles are to the rear of your opponents, then chase them into an obstacle any way you can.

When you get opponents to an obstacle, in order to prevent them from observing the situation, press your attack without letup so that they cannot look around. The same thing about not letting opponents observe the situation also applies indoors, when you are chasing them into doorsills, head jambs, doors, screens, verandas, pillars, or other obstacles.

In any case, the direction in which you chase opponents should be toward places where the footing is bad or there is obstruction on either side. Use whatever qualities of the setting you can, concentrating on taking advantage of the situation. This is something that calls for careful and thorough reflection and practice.

Three Preemptions

There are three kinds of preemption. One is when you preempt by attacking an opponent on your own initiative; this is called preemption from a state of suspension. Another is when you preempt an opponent making an attack on you; this is called preemption from a state of waiting. Yet another is when you and an opponent attack each other simultaneously; this is called preemption in a state of mutual confrontation.

These are the three ways of preemption. At the beginning of any battle, there are no other choices but these three initiatives. Since it is a matter of gaining victory quickly by preemption, therefore preemption is the foremost concern in martial arts.

There are many details involved in preemption, but they cannot be fully written down because it is a matter of putting priority on the pattern of the particular time, perceiving the intention of opponents, and using your knowledge of martial arts to win.

First there is preemption from a state of suspension. When you want to attack, you remain calm and quiet, then get the jump on your opponent by attacking suddenly and quickly. You can preempt by being outwardly powerful and swift while inwardly leaving reserves. You can also get the jump by steeling your mind to the utmost, accelerating your pace a bit, and making a violent attack the instant you get up close to the opponent. You can also win by letting your mind go free, determining to beat your opponent at the same thing from start to finish, gaining victory by thoroughgoing strength of heart. All of these are examples of preemption from a state of suspension.

Second is preemption from a state of waiting. When an opponent comes at you, you do not react but appear to be weak: then, when the opponent gets near, you spring away with a powerful leap, almost as if you were flying; then, when you see the opponent slack, you forcefully overcome him straightaway. This is one way of preemption. Also, when an opponent attacks and you aggressively meet the attack, the moment you sense a change in the rhythm of the opponent's attack, you can gain victory right then and there. This is the principle of preemption from a state of waiting.

Third is preemption in a state of mutual confrontation. In case an opponent attacks swiftly, you attack calmly yet powerfully; when the opponent gets close, tighten your bearing with absolute resolve, and when the opponent shows signs of slacking, overcome him with force immediately. Then again, when an opponent attacks calmly and quietly, accelerate your own attack slightly, with your body lightly buoyant; when the opponent gets close, clash once and then, adapting to his condition, overcome him forcefully. This is preemption in a state of mutual confrontation.

These moves are hard to write about in detail; they should be worked out along the general lines of the moves written down here. These three ways of preemption depend on the time and logic of the situation. Even though you are not to be always the one to attack, if it amounts to the same thing, you would rather take the initiative and put opponents on the defensive.

However it may be, the idea of preemption is gaining certain victory through the power of knowledge of martial arts. It must be cultivated and refined very thoroughly.

Holding Down the Pillow

Holding down the pillow means not letting someone raise his head. In martial arts, in the course of dueling, it is bad to be maneuvered around by others. It is desirable to maneuver opponents around freely, by whatever means you may.

Therefore opponents will be thinking along these lines, and you too have this intention, but it is impossible to succeed in this without comprehending what others are doing.

Martial arts include stopping an opponent's striking blows, arresting his thrusts, tearing away his grips. Holding down the pillow means that when you have attained my science in reality and are engaged with an opponent, whenever the opponent evinces any sign of intending to make a move, you perceive it before he acts. Stopping an opponent's attack at the initial outset, not letting him follow through, is the sense of "holding down the pillow."

For example, you inhibit an opponent's attack from the letter a, so to speak; you inhibit an opponent's leap from the letter l, and inhibit an opponent's cut from the letter c. These are all the same idea.

Whenever opponents try to attack you, let them go ahead and do anything that is useless, while preventing them from doing anything useful. This is essential to military science.

Here, if you consciously try to thwart opponents, you are already late. First, doing whatever you do scientifically, thwart the opponent's very first impulse to try something, thus foiling everything. To manipulate opponents in this way is mastery of the art of war, which comes from practice. The act of holding down the pillow requires thorough examination.

Crossing a Ford

When you cross a sea, there are places called straits. Also, places where you cross a sea even twelve or fifteen miles wide are called fords. In going through the human world as well, in the course of a lifetime there will be many points that could be called crossing a ford.

On the sea lanes, knowing where the fords are, knowing the state of the boat, knowing the weather, even without launching companion boats, you adapt to the state of the time, sometimes taking advantage of crosswinds, sometimes even getting favorable winds, knowing that even if the wind changes you can still reach port by oar, you take command of the ship and cross the ford.

With that attitude, in passing through the human world you should also have a sense of crossing a ford in an emergency.

In martial arts, in the midst of battle, it is also essential to "cross the ford." Sensing the state of opponents, aware of your own mastery, you cross the ford by means of the appropriate principles, just as a skilled captain goes over a sea-lane.

Having crossed over the ford, furthermore, there is peace of mind.

To "cross a ford," put the adversary in a weak position and get the jump yourself; then you will generally quickly prevail. Whether in large-scale military science or individual martial arts, the sense of crossing a ford is essential. It should be savored thoroughly.

Knowing the State of Affairs

In large-scale military science, knowing the state of affairs means discerning the flourishing and decline of opponents, discerning the intentions of adversary troops and perceiving their condition, clearly seeing the state of affairs, determining how to deploy your own troops so as to gain certain victory by the principles of military science, and doing battle with knowledge of what lies ahead.

Also, in individual martial arts, you determine opponents' traditions, observe the personal character of adversaries, find out people's strengths and weaknesses, maneuver in ways contrary to opponents' expectations, determine opponents' highs and lows, ascertain the rhythms in between, and make the first move; this is essential.

If your own power of insight is strong, the state of affairs of everything will be visible to you. Once you have attained complete independent mastery of martial arts, you will be able to figure out the minds of opponents and thus find many ways to win. This demands work.

Stomping a Sword

Stomping a sword is a move used only in martial arts. First of all, in large-scale military science, even with bows and guns, when opponents attack you with whatever they have, after they have shot their first volley and are renewing their barrage, it is hard for you to make your attack if you are cocking a bow or loading a gun. The idea is to attack quickly while the enemy is in the process of shooting.

The sense of this is that if you attack quickly, it is hard to use arrows against you, hard to shoot you with a gun. The idea is that whatever opponents attack with, you immediately sense the pattern and gain victory by stomping down anything the opponent does.

In the context of individual martial arts as well, if you strike in the wake of an opponent's striking sword, it will turn into a clashing, clanging volley of blows, and you will get nowhere. When an opponent lashes out with his sword, you overpower his assault by stomping the sword down with your foot, seeing to it that he cannot strike a second blow.

Stomping is not only done with the feet. You should also learn to "stomp" with your body, "stomp" with your mind, and of course "stomp" with a sword, in such a way as to prevent opponents from making a second move.

This means getting the jump on everything. It does not mean randomly hitting an opponent with the idea of settling the contest all at once. It means instantaneous and unyielding follow-up. This should be investigated thoroughly.

Knowing Disintegration

Disintegration is something that happens to everything. When a house crumbles, a person crumbles, or an adversary crumbles, they fall apart by getting out of rhythm with the times.

In large-scale military science, it is also essential to find the rhythm of opponents as they come apart and pursue them so as not to let openings slip by. If you miss the timing of vulnerable moments, there is the likelihood of counterattack.

In individual martial arts it also happens that an adversary will get out of rhythm in combat and start to fall apart. If you let such a chance get by you, the adversary will recover and thwart you. It is essential to follow up firmly on any loss of poise on the part of an opponent, to prevent him from recovering.

The follow-up calls for directness and power; it is a matter of lashing out violently in such a way that an opponent cannot recover. This lashing out must be carefully analyzed. If you do not let go, there is a sense of slovenliness. This is something that requires work.

Becoming the Opponent

Becoming the opponent means you should put yourself in an opponent's place and think from the opponent's point of view.

As I see the world, if a burglar holes up in a house, he is considered a powerful opponent. From his point of view, however, the whole world is against him; he is holed up in a helpless situation. The one who is holed up is a pheasant; the one who goes in there to fight it out is a hawk. This calls for careful reflection.

In large-scale military science as well, opponents are thought of as powerful and dealt with carefully. When you have good troops, know the principles of martial arts well, and sense the way to overcome an opponent, you need not worry.

You should also put yourself in the opponent's position in individual martial arts. When one meets a master of the science, someone who comprehends martial arts and is good at the science, one thinks one will lose. Consider this well.

Letting Go Four Hands

Letting go four hands is for when you and an opponent are in a dead-lock and no progress is being made in the fight. It means that when you think you are going to get into a deadlock, you stop that right away and seize victory by taking advantage of a different approach.

In large-scale military science as well, if there is total deadlock and no progress is being made, there will be a loss of personnel. It is essential to stop right away and seize victory by taking advantage of a tactic unsuspected by the enemy.

In individual martial arts also, if you think you are getting into a deadlock, then it is essential to immediately change your approach, ascertain the opponent's state, and determine how to win by means of a very different tactic.

Moving Shadows

Moving shadows is something you do when you cannot discern what an adversary is thinking.

In large-scale military science, when you cannot discern the enemy's state, you pretend to make a powerful attack to see what they will do. Having seen opponents' methods, it is easy to seize victory by taking advantage of different tactics specially adapted to each case.

In individual martial arts also, when an opponent is brandishing his sword behind him or to his side, when he is suddenly about to strike, he shows his intent in his sword. Once it shows perceptibly, you should immediately sense the advantage and know how to win with certainty. If you are inattentive, you will miss the rhythm. This should be examined thoroughly.

Arresting Shadows

Arresting shadows is something you do when adversaries' aggressive intentions toward you are perceptible.

In large-scale military science, this means to arrest the enemy's action at the point of the very impulse to act. If you demonstrate strongly to opponents how you control the advantage, they will change their minds, inhibited by this strength. You change your attitude too—to an empty mind, from which you take the initiative and seize victory.

In individual martial arts as well, you use an advantageous rhythm to arrest the powerful determination of the adversary's motivation; then you find the winning advantage in the moment of pause and now take the initiative. This must be worked out thoroughly.

Infection

There is infection in everything. Even sleepiness can be infectious, and yawning can be infectious. There is even the infection of a time.

In large-scale military science, when adversaries are excited and evidently are in a hurry to act, you behave as though you are completely unfazed, giving the appearance of being thoroughly relaxed and at ease. Do this, and adversaries themselves are influenced by this mood, becoming less enthusiastic.

When you think opponents have caught that mood, you empty your own mind and act quickly and firmly, thus to gain the winning advantage.

In individual martial arts as well, it is essential to be relaxed in body and mind, notice the moment an opponent slackens, and quickly take the initiative to win.

There is also something called "entrancing" that is similar to infection. One entrancing mood is boredom. Another is restlessness. Another is faintheartedness. This should be worked out thoroughly.

Upset

Upset happens in all sorts of things. One way it happens is through a feeling of being under acute pressure. Another is through a feeling of unreasonable strain. A third is through a feeling of surprise at the unexpected.

In large-scale military science, it is essential to cause upset. It is critical to attack resolutely where enemies are not expecting it; then, while their minds are unsettled, use this to your advantage to take the initiative and win.

In individual martial arts also, you appear relaxed at first, then suddenly charge powerfully; as the opponent's mind changes pitch, it is essential that you follow what he does, not letting him relax for a moment, perceiving the advantage of the moment and discerning right then and there how to win. This must be investigated diligently.

Threat

There is fright in everything. This means being frightened by the unexpected.

Even in large-scale military science, threatening an adversary is not something right before the eyes. You may threaten by sound, you may threaten by making the small seem large, and you may threaten by making an unexpected move from the side. These are situations in which fright occurs. If you can seize the moment of fright, you can take advantage of it to gain victory.

In individual martial arts also, you can threaten by means of your body, you can threaten by means of your sword, and you can threaten by means of your voice. What is essential is to suddenly make a move totally unexpected by the opponent, pick up on the advantage of fright, and seize victory right then and there. This must be worked out thoroughly.

Sticking Tight

Sticking tight means when you are fighting at close range, you and your adversary each exerting great force against the other, and you see that it is not going well, you then stick tight to your opponent; the essential point is to take advantage of opportunities to win even as you wrestle together.

Whether in large- or small-scale military science, when you and opponents have taken sides and are facing off and it is not clear who will prevail, right then and there you stick tight to the opponents, so that you cannot be separated, and in that process find the advantage, determine how to win, and seize victory powerfully; this is quintessential. This must be studied diligently.

Coming Up Against Corners

Coming up against corners means that when you push something that is strong, it hardly gives way immediately, just like that.

In large-scale military science, observe the opposing troops; where they have surged ahead, hit the corner of this strong front, and you should get the advantage.

As the corner collapses, everyone gets the feeling of collapse. Even as they are collapsing, it is essential to realize when each corner is ready to go and sense when to overcome it.

In individual martial arts too, when you inflict pain on part of his body each time an opponent makes an aggressive move, his body will weaken by degrees until he is ready to collapse and it is easy to beat him.

It is essential to study this carefully to discern where you can win.

Flustering

Flustering opponents means acting in such a way as to prevent them from having a steady mind.

In large-scale military science, this means that you assess adversaries' minds on the battlefield and use the power of your knowledge of the art of war to manipulate their attention, making them think confusing thoughts about what you are going to do. It means finding a rhythm that will fluster adversaries, accurately discerning where you can win.

In individual martial arts as well, you try various maneuvers according to the opportunity of the moment, making the opponent think you are now going to do this, now that, now something else, until you find the opponent starting to get flustered, and thus you win at will. This is the essence of battle; it should be studied very carefully.

Three Shouts

The three shouts are called the initial, middle, and final shout. The essential point is to call out in accord with the situation. Because a shout is forceful, we shout in emergencies like fires and squalls; the voice shows force and power.

In large-scale military science, at the beginning of battle the shouting should be as loud as possible, in the course of battle the shouting should be low-pitched and booming from the depths, while after victory the shouting should be loud and strong. These are the three shouts.

In individual martial arts, you feint and shout in order to stir the opponent, then lash out after your cry. You also shout after having struck an opponent down, with a cry signaling victory. These are called before and after shouts.

You never shout at the same time as you swing your sword. When you shout in the midst of battle, you use the sound to mount a rhythm, crying out in a low pitch.

Mixing

In the context of large-scale combat, mixing means that when two groups are facing off and your opponents are strong, you attack one of the opponents' flanks, as if to mix in with them; then, when you see the opponents crumble, you leave off and attack again where they are strong. In general, the idea is to attack in a winding zigzag.

This is also essential in the context of individual martial arts, when you face a group of adversaries singlehandedly. Each time you have finished one off or driven one off, again you attack a strong one, finding the opponents' rhythm, zigzagging left and right in a suitable rhythm, observing the condition of the adversary so as to attack effectively.

When you have found an enemy's range and are going to cut through, the principle of the advantage is to seize victory forcefully, without any reservations. This state of mind also applies to a situation when you are closing in on a powerful opponent in individual combat.

The sense of mixing is to plunge right in without any hesitation in your steps. This should be distinguished carefully.

Crushing

Crushing requires a crushing mood, as when you view an opponent as weak and become strong yourself, thus overwhelming your adversary.

In large-scale military science, this means you look down upon an enemy whose numbers are small, or even if there are many of them, when opponents are demoralized and weakening, you concentrate your force on crushing them, thus mowing them down.

If your crushing is weak, it can backfire. You have to carefully distinguish the state of mind in which you are fully in control as you crush.

In the context of individual martial arts too, when your opponent is not as skilled as you are, or when his rhythm is fouled up, or when he starts to back off, it is essential not to let him catch his breath. Mow him right down without even giving him time to blink his eyes. The most important thing is not to let him recover.

This should be studied very carefully.

Mountain and Sea Changing

"Mountain and sea" means that it is bad to do the same thing over and over again. You may have to repeat something once, but it should not be done a third time.

When you try something on an opponent, if it does not work the first time, you will not get any benefit out of rushing to do it again. Change your tactics abruptly, doing something completely different. If that still does not work, then try something else.

Thus the science of martial arts involves the presence of mind to act as the sea when the enemy is like a mountain, and act as a mountain when the enemy is like a sea. This requires careful reflection.

Knocking the Heart Out

When you fight with an adversary and appear to win by your skill in this science, your opponent may still have ideas and, while appearing to be beaten, still inwardly refuse to acknowledge defeat. Knocking the heart out is for such cases.

This means that you suddenly change your attitude to stop the enemy from entertaining any such ideas; so the main thing is to see that adversaries feel defeated from the bottom of their hearts.

You can knock the heart out of people with weapons or with your body or with your mind. It is not to be understood in just one way.

When your enemies have completely lost heart, you do not have to pay attention to them anymore. Otherwise, you remain mindful. As long as adversaries still have ambitions, they will hardly collapse.

In both large- and small-scale martial arts, knocking the heart out should be practiced thoroughly.

Becoming New

When fighting with enemies, if you get to feeling snarled up and are making no progress, you toss your mood away and think in your heart that you are starting everything anew. As you get the rhythm, you discern how to win. This is "becoming new."

Anytime you feel tension and friction building up between yourself and others, if you change your mind that very moment, you can prevail by the advantage of radical difference. This is "becoming new."

In large-scale military science, it is essential to understand becoming new. It is something that suddenly appears through the power in knowledge of martial arts. This must be well considered.

Small and Large

When you are fighting adversaries and get to feeling snarled up in petty maneuvers, remember this rule of military science: while in the midst of minutiae, suddenly you shift to a large perspective.

Changing to great or small is an intentional part of the science of the art of war. It is essential for warriors to seek this even in the ordinary consciousness of human life. This mentality is critical to military science, whether large or small scale.

This concern should be given careful consideration.

A Commander Knowing Soldiers

"A commander knowing soldiers" is a method always practiced in times of conflict after having reached the mastery to which one aspires. Having attained the power in the knowledge of the arts of war, you think of your adversaries as your own soldiers, understanding that you should do with them as you wish, intending to manipulate them freely. You are the commander, the opponents are the troops. This takes work.

Letting Go of the Hilt

"Letting go of the hilt" has various meanings. It has the meaning of winning without a sword, and it also has the meaning of failing to win with a sword. The various different senses cannot be written down but call for thorough training and practice.

Being Like a Rock Wall

"Being like a rock wall" is when a master of martial arts suddenly becomes like a rock wall, inaccessible to anything at all, immovable. This is transmitted by word of mouth.

Epilogue

What is written above consists entirely of things that constantly come to mind in the course of practicing the art of swordsmanship of my individual school. Because I am now writing these principles down for the first time, they are somewhat mixed up in terms of order, and it is hard to define them in detail. Nevertheless, they can be guidelines for people who are supposed to learn this science.

I have concentrated on martial arts since youth, training my hands and body to the mastery of swordsmanship, getting into all sorts of various states of mind. What I see on inquiry into other schools is that some are pretentious talkers, and some perform fancy maneuvers with their hands; even though they may look good to people, there is surely no true heart there at all.

Of course, it may seem as if people are training body and mind even when they are practicing such things, but they become sicknesses of the path, persistent and hard to get rid of; they are bases of the decay of the straight path of martial arts in the world, and of the abandonment of the Way.

For the art of swordsmanship to be a real science, such as to win victory in battle with adversaries, no change whatsoever is to be made in these principles. When you attain the power of knowledge of my military science and put it into practice in a straightforward manner, there can be no doubt of victory.

THE WIND SCROLL

Military science involves knowledge of the methods of other schools. Here in this Wind Scroll, I have written about the various other schools of martial arts. Unless you know the ways of other schools, you certainly cannot understand the way of my individual school.

What I see on inquiry into others' martial arts is that some schools use large long swords and concentrate on power in their moves. Some practice their science using a short long sword they call a "little long sword." There are also schools that contrive many moves with the long sword, calling the positions of the sword the formal techniques and transmitting the science as the inner teaching.

In this scroll I will clearly expose the fact that none of these are the real Way, thus to let it be known what is good and what bad, what true and what false. The principle of my individual school is something distinctly different. Other schools become theatrical, dressing up and showing off to make a living, commercializing martial arts; therefore it would seem that they are not the true Way.

Furthermore, martial art is conventionally viewed in a limited way, as if it consisted only of swordsmanship. Do you think you have realized how to attain victory just be learning to wield a long sword and training your body and hands? This is not a certain way in any case.

I have exposed each of the deficiencies of other schools in this book. The point is to examine carefully and savor thoroughly, to come to an understanding of the advantages of the individual school of Two Swords.

On Wielding Extra-Long Swords in Other Schools

There are some other schools that are fond of extra-long swords. From the point of view of my martial art, I see them as weak schools. The reason for this is that these other schools do not know about prevailing over others by any means necessary; considering the length of the sword its virtue, they must want their swords to be extra long so that they can beat opponents from a distance.

The conventional saying about winning by even an inch in reach is something that refers to people who know nothing about martial arts. Therefore, to try to win from a distance by an advantage in sword length without knowing the principles of martial arts is something that people do because of weakness of heart. That is why I consider this weak martial art.

At times when you are engaged with an opponent at close quarters, the longer your sword is, the harder it is to strike with it; you cannot swing the sword back and forth enough, and it becomes a burden. Then you are in a worse situation than someone wielding a small sidearm sword.

For those who prefer extra-long swords, they have their own reason, but it is logical for themselves alone; from the point of view of the real Way of the world, it is illogical. Will you necessarily lose if you use a shorter long sword and not an extra-long sword?

And suppose the physical situation is such that above, below, and/ or the sides are blocked; or suppose the social situation is one where only side arms are worn; to wish for an extra-long sword under these conditions is a bad attitude, because it is to doubt the science of martial arts.

Furthermore, there are people who lack the requisite physical strength.

Since ancient times it has been said that the great includes the small, so it is not a matter of indiscriminately disliking length; it is a matter of disliking the attitude of bias in favor of length.

In the context of large-scale military science, an extra-long sword is a large contingent, a shorter one is a small contingent. Is a battle between a small contingent and a large contingent impossible? There are many examples of a small contingent winning over a large contingent. Thus in my individual school there is an aversion to a narrow, biased attitude. This calls for careful examination.

Powerful Sword Blows in Other Schools

There should be no such thing as strong sword blows or weak sword blows. A swing of a sword made with the intention to swing powerfully is rough, and you can hardly win by roughness alone.

Furthermore, if you slash with unreasonable force when you are going to kill someone, intending to deal a powerful blow of the sword, you will not be successful.

Even when you are making a test cut on a dummy or something, it is wrong to try deliberately to slash powerfully.

When facing an enemy in mortal combat, nobody thinks of striking weakly or powerfully. When one only thinks of killing the other, there is no sense of strength, and of course no sense of weakness; one only thinks of the death of the enemy.

If you hit someone else's sword strongly using an extra-powerful swing, it will turn out badly because of excessive force. If you hit someone else's sword forcefully, your own sword will be delayed.

So there is no such thing as a particularly powerful sword blow. Even in large-scale military science, if you have a powerful contingent wishing to gain a forceful victory in battle, the fact is that your opponent also has powerful people and wants to fight forcefully. In that respect, both are the same. When it comes to winning victory in everything, it is impossible to prevail without reason.

In my school, no consideration is given to anything unreasonable; the heart of the matter is to use the power of the knowledge of martial arts to gain victory any way you can. This must be worked out thoroughly.

The Use of Shorter Long Swords in Other Schools

To think of winning by means of a shorter long sword alone is not the true Way. Since ancient times long and short swords have been distinguished in terminology.

Physically powerful people can wield even a large long sword with ease, so there is no point in unreasonable fondness for a shorter sword. The reason for this is that spears and halberds are also carried to make use of their length. The idea that you are going to use a shorter long sword to cut through, plunge in, and seize an opponent in the interval between swings of his sword is biased and therefore wrong.

Furthermore, when you watch out for gaps, everything else is neglected, and there comes to be a sense of entanglement, which is to be avoided. And if you try to use a short weapon to penetrate the enemy's defense and take over, that will not be of any use when in the midst of numerous opponents.

Even if you think that what you gain from a shorter weapon is the ability to cut through a crowd, leap freely, and whirl around, in each case you are in a defensive mode of swordplay and are thus in a distracted state of mind. This is not a reliable way to go.

You might just as well chase people around in a powerful and straightforward manner, making people jump out of the way, contriving to throw them into confusion, taking the route that aims solely at certain victory.

This logic also applies to large-scale military science. All else being equal, you might as well take a large contingent, attack the enemy all of a sudden, and destroy them at once. This attitude is the focus of military science.

What people of the world ordinarily study when they practice martial arts is to parry, deflect, get away, and get through safely; therefore their minds are drawn by this method and wind up being maneuvered and manipulated by others. Since the Way of martial arts is direct and straightforward, the intent to stalk and overcome people rightly is essential. This should be considered carefully.

Numerous Sword Strokes in Other Schools

When an excessive number of sword moves are taught, it must be to commercialize the art and impress beginners with knowledge of many moves with a sword. This attitude is to be avoided in military science.

The reason for this is that it is delusion to think that there are all sorts of ways of cutting people down. In the matter of cutting people down, there are no different ways in the world. Whether or not one is knowledgeable, and even if one is a woman or a child, there are not so many ways to strike and cut; if there are variants, they are no more than stabbing and slashing.

To begin with, since the point is killing, there is no reason for there to be a large number of ways to do it. Even so, depending on the situation, according to events, in cases where there is obstruction in the surroundings, such as above or to the sides, there have to be five positions so that there is a way to wield a sword without getting stuck.

To add anything else, things like cutting an opponent down with a twist of the hands, a twirl of the body, or a leap to a distance, are not the true way. To cut someone down, you cannot cut them down by twisting or twirling; these are useless things.

In my military science, it is essential that the physical aspect and the mental state both be simple and direct, gaining victory by causing opponents to strain distortedly and go off kilter, causing the hearts of adversaries to do the twisting and twirling. This should be examined carefully.

Positions of the Sword in Other Schools

It is wrong to concentrate solely on the guard position of the sword. Whenever there are guard positions in the world, it must be when there are no opponents.

The reasoning behind this is that to set up standard rules as customary standards or current rules is not feasible in the course of actually contesting for victory. The thing is to contrive to put the adversary at a disadvantage.

Whatever the point of reference, the adoption of a guard position has the sense of making use of immovability. To guard a castle, or to array a battle line in a defensive position, has the sense of being strong and unaffected even under attack; this is the normal meaning.

In the course of struggle for victory by military science, the thing is to concentrate on seizing the initiative and getting the jump on others in everything. The sense of a guard or defensive posture is that of awaiting the initiative. This should be worked out thoroughly.

In the course of struggle for victory by military science, you win by disrupting others' defenses, by making moves opponents do not expect, by confusing opponents, or irritating them, or scaring them, sensing the pattern of the rhythm when opponents get mixed up to seize victory. Thus there is an aversion to the defensive attitude involved in concern with guard positions. Therefore in my science there is what is called having a guard without a guard, meaning that one has a defense without being defensive.

In large-scale military science also, the main concern for a pitched battle is to learn how many troops the adversary has, note the lay of the battleground, know the state of your own troops, marshal their best qualities, rally them, and only then start to fight.

There is a totally different feeling in being attacked by others first than in attacking others yourself. The sense of being able to wield a

sword well enough to catch and parry an opponent's blows is tantamount to taking your spear and halberd and sticking them in the
ground as fence posts. When you are going to strike an adversary, in
contrast, you can even pull up a fence post and use it as you would a
spear or halberd. This is something that should be examined carefully.

The Focus of the Eyes in Other Schools

The focus of the eyes depends on the school: there are those who fix
their eyes on the opponent's sword, and there are also those who fix
their eyes on the opponent's hands; there are those who fix their eyes
on the opponent's face, and there are also those who fix their eyes on
the opponent's feet, and so on. When you try to fix your eyes on some
particular point, there is a sense of distraction, and this becomes what
is known as an affliction in martial arts.

People playing football may not keep their eyes on the ball, yet
they can still steal it away with a kick and dribble it around, because
when one is thoroughly practiced in something, it is not necessary to
look deliberately. In the arts of jugglers too, when they are practiced
in the techniques, they can balance a door on the nose and juggle
several swords at once, all without deliberately watching; since they
are involved in practice all the time, they see what is going on spontaneously.

In the context of the science of martial arts as well, when you
become familiar with each adversary, perceive the degree of seriousness of people's minds, and are able to practice the science effectively,
you can see even the distance and speed of a sword. Generally speaking, the focus of the eyes in martial arts is on the hearts and minds of
the people involved.

When it comes to large-scale military science, the eyes are also
focused on the state of the opposing troops.

Of two ways of perception, observing and seeing, the observing eye
is stronger, perceiving the heart and mind of the adversary, seeing
the state of the situation, focusing the eyes broadly, perceiving the
conditions for battle, perceiving the strength and weakness of the occasion, concentrating on seizing victory with precision.

Whether in large- or small-scale military science, there is no narrow focus of the vision. As I have already written, by finicky narrow-

ness of focus, you forget about bigger things and get confused, thus letting certain victory escape you. This principle demands careful reflection and thorough practice.

Footwork in Other Schools

There are various ways of quick-stepping, such as those known as the floating step, the leaping step, the springing step, the stomping step, the crow step, and so on. From the point of view of my martial art, all of these seem deficient.

The reason why I dislike the floating step is that one's steps are in any case likely to become unsteady in battle, so the proper course is to stride as surely as possible.

The reason I do not like the leaping step is that there is a sense of excitement in the leaping and a sense of fixation on leaping. Since there is no reason to leap over and over again, a leaping step is bad.

Also, the springing step is ineffective because there is a sense of bounding. The stomping step is a passive stance and is especially objectionable.

Other than these, there are also various quick-steps such as the crow step.

Since you may engage opponents in marshes or swamps, or in mountains and rivers, or on rocky plains, or on narrow roads, depending on the place, there are situations in which it is impossible to leap and spring or to quick-step.

In my martial art, there is no change in footwork; it is just like walking along a road as usual. Following the rhythm of the opponent, finding the right physical position in conditions of both hurry and calm, the stride should be orderly, without slack or excess.

In large-scale military science as well, footwork is critical. The reason for this is that if you attack indiscriminately without knowing the intentions of your adversary, you will miss the rhythm and find it hard to win. Also, if you are striding calmly and do not notice when opponents are demoralized and crumbling, you will let victory elude you and will be unable to effect a quick settlement of the contest.

It is essential to perceive discouragement and crumbling, then overwhelm adversaries by not letting them relax for even a moment. This requires thorough training and practice.

The Use of Speed in Other Schools

In martial arts, speed is not the true Way. As far as speed is concerned, the question of fast or slow in anything derives from failure to harmonize with the rhythm.

When you master an art or science, your performance does not appear to be fast. For example, there are professional courier runners who travel a route of about fifteen miles; but even so, they do not run fast from morning to night. As for those who lack the training, even if they seem to run all day, they do not reach the goal.

In the art of the dance, if a poor singer accompanies the song of a skilled singer, there is a sense of lag, which results in haste. Also, when "Old Pine" is played on the drums, it is a quiet piece, but in this case too, someone who is unskilled will tend to fall behind or get ahead. And while "High Dunes" has a rapid tempo, it is wrong to perform it too fast.

As the saying goes, the fast one stumbles and fails to get there on time. Of course, being too slow and too late is also bad.

The performance of an expert seems relaxed but does not leave any gaps. The actions of trained people do not seem rushed. The principle of the Way can be known from these illustrations.

Speed is particularly bad in the context of the science of martial arts. The reasons for this are as follows. Here too, depending on the place, say for example in a bog, it is impossible to move and run fast. With a long sword, there is no such thing as killing with greater speed; unlike a fan or short sword, if you try to cut quickly, you will not be able to cut at all. This calls for careful discernment.

In large-scale military science as well, the feeling of speed and hurry is bad. With the attitude of "holding down the pillow," there is no being slow.

Furthermore, when people speed rashly, it is essential for you to be the reverse, becoming calm and quiet, not being drawn in by them. The way to work on this state of mind requires training and practice.

The Esoteric and Exoteric in Other Schools

In the context of matters of martial arts, what is to be called exoteric, what is to be called esoteric? Depending on the art, there are esoteric transmissions of the ultimate realization that are passed on as inner oral traditions, but when it comes to the principle of dueling with opponents, it is not a matter of fighting exoterically and killing esoterically.

My way of teaching martial arts is to have beginners learn and practice those of the techniques that are easily mastered, first teaching them the principles that they will readily understand. As for those things that their minds have a hard time reaching, I observe the understanding of each individual, subsequently teaching them deeper principles gradually, step by step. Even so, since I generally make them learn such things as have actual relevance to addressing these matters, there is no such thing as a distinction between the esoteric and the exoteric.

So it is in the world, when you go into the depths of the mountains, if you want to go farther, you will again come out of the mountains. In any art or science, there is that for which secrecy or reserve is appropriate, and that which may well be spoken of openly. But when it comes to the principles of war, what is to be hidden, what is to be revealed?

Accordingly, in transmitting my science, I do not care for written pledges or articles of penalties. Observing the intellectual power of students, teaching them a straight path, having them abandon the bad aspects of the "five ways" or "six ways" of martial arts, so that they naturally enter into the real science of warriors, causing their minds to be free from doubt—this is the way I teach martial arts. Thorough training and practice are necessary.

Epilogue

In the preceding nine articles on the martial arts of other schools, where I have written their outlines in this Wind Scroll, although it is imperative to write clearly about each school, from the initiation to the inner lore, I do not make a point of writing the names of which particular secret of which particular school I am referring to.

The reason for this is that the views of each school, and the logic of each path, are realized differently according to the individual person, depending on the mentality; so even in the same school there are some slight differences of understanding. Thus for the sake of posterity I have not recorded the particular schools to which I refer.

Having divided the general run of other schools into nine categories, when we look from the point of view of the right way for the world, from the point of view of straightforward human reason, things such as preferences for extra-long or extra-short swords, preferences for force or yielding, concern with crudeness and fineness, are all biased paths; so even if I do not reveal them as the initiatory or inner lore of other schools, everybody should know about them.

In my individual school, there is no such thing as a distinction between initiatory and inner lore about the long sword. There is no such thing as the ultimate guard. It is only a matter of understanding its effective qualities in your heart and mind; this is what is essential to martial art.

THE SCROLL OF EMPTINESS

In writing about the science of martial arts of the individual school of Two Swords in the Scroll of Emptiness, the meaning of emptiness is that the realm where nothing exists, or cannot be known, is seen as empty.

Of course, emptiness does not exist. Knowing of nonexistence while knowing of existence is emptiness.

Wrongly viewed among people of the world, not understanding anything is itself considered emptiness. This is not real emptiness; it is all delusion.

In the context of this science of martial arts as well, in carrying out the way as a warrior, not knowing the laws of warriors is not emptiness; being confused, one may call a state of helplessness emptiness, but this is not real emptiness.

Warriors learn military science accurately and go on to practice the techniques of martial arts diligently. The way that is practiced by warriors is not obscure in the least. Without any confusion in mind, without slacking off at any time, polishing the mind and attention, sharpening the eye that observes and the eye that sees, one should know real emptiness as the state where there is no obscurity and the clouds of confusion have cleared away.

As long as they do not know the real Way, whether in Buddhism or in worldly matters, everybody may think their path is sure and is a good thing, but from the point of view of the straight way of mind, seen in juxtaposition with overall social standards, they turn away from the true Way by the personal biases in their minds and the individual warps in their vision.

Knowing that mentality, taking straightforwardness as basic, taking the real mind as the Way, practicing martial arts in the broadest sense, thinking correctly, clearly, and comprehensively, taking emptiness as the Way, you see the Way as emptiness.

In emptiness there is good but no evil. Wisdom exists, logic exists, the Way exists, mind is empty.

12 May 1645

Notes

275   *Two Skies* is one name for Musashi's school of martial arts, which he referred to as the individual school of Two Skies or Two Swords.

275   *Kannon* is one of the most popular of Buddhist icons, representing the activity of universal compassion. Kannon happened to be the icon of the temple where Musashi went into retreat; there is no indication that he had any particular devotion to Kannon.

278   *The Kashima and Kantori shrines* in eastern Japan were dedicated to war. The Kashima Shrine propitiates the god Takemikazuchi-no-mi-koto, worshiped as a god of war since ancient times. The cult of this shrine was important in the early Japanese conquest of the largest of the islands in antiquity. The Kashima New School of Accuracy, a school of martial arts associated with this shrine, was said to have been founded in the time of the prehistorical sixteenth emperor, Nintoku Tennō, who built Mozunomimihara-no-naka-no-misasagi, the largest mound tomb in the world. The Kashima New School of Accuracy is attributed to an ancient descendant of the god Kuninatsu-o-o-kashima-no-mikoto. The Ka(n)tori Shrine propitiates the god Futsunushi-no-kami. This shrine is reputed to have been established in the time of Jimmu Tennō, the first emperor of Japan, whose name Jimmu means Divine Warrior. A school of martial arts called the Katori Shinto School, or the Katori School of the Divine Sword (the two names are homonyms), was founded as recently as 1940.

292   *Five Kinds of Guard.* The word for "guard," *kamae*, comes from the verb *kamaeru*, which means to build, set up, adopt a (usually defensive) stance, posture, or attitude. In social parlance, when someone *kamaeru*, that means the person becomes defensive in attitude. The related verb *kamau* means to take trouble over someone or something, to make a fuss.

312   *Infection.* The great pianist Josef Hofmann taught that a performer should convey excitement to an audience by means of the performer's memory of excitement, not by actually becoming excited oneself. This is a sublime example of the principle of infection.

312   *The infection of a time.* The mentality or mood of a time or an era dominates more effectively by infection than it could by overt persuasion or coercion, because the source and nature of the infection are not obvious.

327   *Five ways and six ways of martial arts.* Here Musashi refers to stylistic embellishment for its own sake, in contrast to the fundamental practicalities of the art of war.

The Book of Family Traditions
on the Art of War

Yagyū Munenori

The Killing Sword

Preface

There is an old saying, "Weapons are instruments of ill omen, despised by the Way of Heaven. To use them only when unavoidable is the Way of Heaven." The reason weapons are instruments of ill omen is that the Way of Heaven is the Way that gives life to beings, so something used for killing is truly an instrument of ill omen. Thus the saying has it that what contradicts the Way of Heaven is despised.

Nevertheless, it also says that to use arms when unavoidable is also the Way of Heaven. What does this mean? Although flowers blossom and greenery increases in the spring breeze, when the autumn frost comes, leaves always drop and trees wither. This is the judgment of nature.

This is because there is logic in striking down something when it is completed. People may take advantage of events to do evil, but when that evil is complete, it is attacked. That is why it is said that using weapons is also the Way of Heaven.

It may happen that myriad people suffer because of the evil of one man. In such a case, myriad people are saved by killing one man. Would this not be a true example of "the sword that kills is the sword that gives life"?

There is a science to the use of arms. If you try to kill someone without knowing the science, you will probably get killed yourself.

On careful reflection, in matters of martial arts, the martial art involved in one-on-one sword dueling has but one winner and one loser. This is extremely small martial art, and what is gained or lost by winning or losing is trifling.

When the whole land wins with one individual's victory, and the whole land loses with one individual's loss, this is martial art on a large scale. The one individual is the commander, the whole land is the military forces. The forces are the hands and feet of the commander. To work the forces well is to get the hands and feet of the commander to work well. If the forces do not work, that means the hands and feet of the commander do not work.

Just as one faces off with two swords, operating the great function of the great potential, using one's hands and feet skillfully so as to gain victory, in the same way the martial art of the commander, properly speaking, is to successfully employ all forces and skillfully create strategies so as to win in war.

Furthermore, while it is a matter of course to go out on the field of combat to determine victory and defeat when two battle formations are pitched against each other, one who is a commander pitches two battle formations in his chest, mentally leading a great army into battle; this is the art of war in the mind.

Not forgetting about disturbance when times are peaceful is an art of war. Seeing the situation of states, knowing when there will be disruption, and healing disturbance before it happens, is also the art of war.

When a country is pacified, the consideration given to the selection of officials and the security of the nation is also a martial art. When officials pursue personal interest and thus oppress the common people, this above all is the beginning of the end for a nation. To observe the situation carefully, planning in such a way as to avoid letting the state perish through the self-seeking of officials, is like watching an opponent in a duel to see his move before he makes it. Should one not observe with utmost attention? This is what makes martial art a matter of such great potential.

Also, surrounding rulers, there are treacherous people who pretend to be righteous when in the presence of superiors yet have a glare in their eyes when they look at subordinates. Unless these people are bribed, they present the good as bad, so the innocent suffer and the guilty gloat. To see the potential for this happening is even more urgent than to notice a concealed scheme.

The country is the ruler's country, the people are the ruler's people. Those who serve the ruler personally are subjects of the ruler just as are those who serve at a remove. How far apart is their distance? They are like hands and feet in the service of the ruler. Are the feet any different from the hands just because they are farther away? Since they both feel pain and itch the same, which can be called nearer, which farther away?

Therefore people will resent even an honest ruler if those close to the ruler bleed those far away and cause the innocent to suffer.

There are only a few people close to a ruler, perhaps five or ten. The majority of people are remote from rulers. When many people resent their ruler, they will express their feelings. Now, when those close to the ruler have all along been after their own interests, and not acting in consideration of the ruler, and therefore serve in such a way that the people resent the ruler, when the time comes, those close to the ruler will be the first to set upon him.

This is the doing of those close to the ruler, not the personal fault of the ruler. It is desirable that the potential for such situations be clearly perceived and that those distant from the rulership not be excluded from its benefits.

Also, in social and professional relationships, since you are acting as you see situations develop, the attitude is the same as that of the warrior, even when there is no discord. The mindfulness to observe the dynamic of situations even in a group is an art of war.

If you do not see the dynamic of a situation, you may remain too long in company where you should not be and get into trouble for no reason. When people say things without seeing others' states of mind, thus getting into arguments, even forfeiting their lives as a result, this is all a matter of the difference between seeing or not seeing the dynamic of a situation and the states of the people involved.

Even to furnish a room so that everything is in the right place is to see the dynamic of a situation. Thus it involves something of the mindfulness of the warrior's art.

Indeed, although the phenomena may differ, the principle is the same. Therefore it can be applied accurately to the affairs of state.

It is bias to think that the art of war is just for killing people. It is not to kill people, it is to kill evil. It is a strategy to give life to many people by killing the evil of one person.

What is written in these three scrolls is a book that does not go outside of the house. Nevertheless, that does not mean the Way is secret. Secrecy is for the sake of conveying knowledge. If knowledge is not conveyed, that is tantamount to there being no book. Let my descendants think on this well.

The Great Learning

It is said that *The Great Learning* is the gate of elementary learning. Whenever you go to a house, first you go in through the gate. Therefore the gate is a sign that you have reached the house. Going through this gate, you enter the house and meet the host.

Learning is the gate to attainment of the Way. Therefore learning is the gate, not the house. When you see the gate, do not think it is the house. You have to go through the gate to get to the house, which is inside, behind it.

Since learning is a gate, when you read books do not think this is the Way. This misconception has made many people remain ignorant of the Way no matter how much they study or how many words they know. Even if you can read as fluently as a commentary of an ancient, if you are unaware of the principles, you cannot make the Way your own.

Nevertheless, even though this is so, it is also hard to reach the Way without learning. It is also hard to say that someone understands the Way simply by virtue of being learned and articulate. There are some people who naturally conform to the Way without learning how.

The Great Learning speaks of consummating knowledge and perfecting things. Consummating knowledge means knowing the principles of everything that people in the world know. Perfecting things means that when you know the principle of everything thoroughly, then you know everything and can do everything. When there is nothing more you know, there is nothing you can do either. When you do not know the principle, nothing at all comes to fruition.

In all things, uncertainty exists because of not knowing. Things stick in your mind because of being in doubt. When the principle is clarified, nothing sticks in your mind. This is called consummating knowledge and perfecting things. Since there is no longer anything sticking in your mind, all your tasks become easy to do.

For this reason, the practice of all the arts is for the purpose of clearing away what is on your mind. In the beginning, you do not know anything, so paradoxically you do not have any questions on your mind. Then, when you get into studies, there is something on your mind and you are obstructed by that. This makes everything difficult to do.

When what you have studied leaves your mind entirely, and practice also disappears, then, when you perform whatever art you are engaged in, you accomplish the techniques easily without being inhibited by concern over what you have learned, and yet without deviating from what you have learned. This is spontaneously conforming to learning without being consciously aware of doing so. The science of the art of war can be understood through this.

To learn all the sword strokes, the physical postures, and the focus of the eyes, to thoroughly learn all there is to learn and practice it, is the spirit of consummating knowledge. Then, when you have succeeded in learning, when everything you have learned disappears from your conscious mind and you become innocent, this is the spirit of perfecting things.

When you have built up achievement in cultivation of learning and practice, even as your hands, feet, and body act, this does not hang on your mind. You are detached from your learning yet do not deviate from your learning. Whatever you do, your action is free.

At this time, you do not even know where your own mind is; neither the celestial devil nor outsiders can spy into your heart. The learning is for the purpose of reaching this state. Once you have learned this successfully, learning disappears.

This is the ultimate sense and the progressive transcendentalism of all the Zen arts. Forgetting learning, relinquishing mind, harmonizing without any self-conscious knowledge thereof, is the ultimate consummation of the Way.

This stage is a matter of entering from learning into no learning.

Mood and Will

The mind with a specific inward attitude and an intensive concentration of thought is called will. Will being within, what emanates outwardly is called mood.

To give an illustration, the will is like the master of a house, while the mood is like a servant. The will is within, employing the mood.

If the mood rushes out too much, you will stumble. You should have your will restrain your mood, so that it does not hurry.

In the context of martial arts, lowering the center of gravity can be called will. Facing off to kill or be killed can be called the mood. Lower your center of gravity securely, and do not let your mood become hurried and aggressive. It is essential to control your mood by means of your will, calming down so that your will is not drawn by your mood.

Appearance and Intention

Appearance and intention are fundamental to the art of war. Appearance and intention mean the strategic use of ploys, the use of falsehood to gain what is real.

Appearance and intention inevitably ensnare people when artfully used, even if people sense that there is an ulterior intention behind the overt appearance. When you set up your ploys and opponents fall for them, then you win by letting them act on your ruse.

As for those who do not fall for a ploy, when you see they will not fall into one trap, you have another one set. Then, even if opponents have not fallen for your original ploy, in effect they actually have.

In Buddhism this is called expedient means. Even though the real truth is hidden inside while strategy is employed outwardly, when you are finally led into the real truth, the pretenses now all become real truth.

In the spirit religion, there is what is called the mystery of the spirits. The mystery is kept secret in order to foster religious faith. When people have faith, they and others benefit from it.

In the warrior's way, this is called strategy. Although strategy is falsehood, when the falsehood is used in order to win without hurting people, the falsehood finally becomes true. This is an example of what is called achieving harmonious order by means of its contrary.

Beating the Grass to Scare the Snakes

There is something in Zen called "beating the grass to scare the snakes." To startle or surprise people a little is a device, like hitting at snakes in the grass to scare them.

To do something unexpected as a ploy to startle an opponent is also an appearance concealing an ulterior intention, an art of war.

When an opponent is startled and the feeling of opposition is distracted, the opponent will experience a gap in reaction time.

Even simple, ordinary gestures like raising your hand are used to distract an opponent's attention.

Throwing down your sword is also an art of war. If you have attained mastery of swordlessness, you will never be without a sword. The opponent's sword is your sword. This is acting at the vanguard of the moment.

The Vanguard of the Moment

The vanguard of the moment is before the opponent has begun to make a move. This first impulse of movement is the energy, feeling, or mood, held back in the chest. The dynamic of the movement is energy, feeling, and mood. To accurately see an opponents' energy, feeling, and mood, and to act accordingly in their presence, is called the vanguard of the moment.

This effective action is a specialty of Zen, where it is referred to as the Zen dynamic.

The energy, feeling, or mood hidden within and not revealed is called the potential of the moment. It is like a hinge, which is inside the door. To see the invisible workings hidden inside, and to act upon that, is called the art of war at the vanguard of the moment.

Aggressive and Passive Modes

The aggressive mode is when you attack intently, slashing with extreme ferocity the instant you face off, aggressively seeking to get in the first blow.

The feeling of aggression is the same whether it is in the mind of the opponent or in your own mind.

The passive mode is when you do not attack precipitously but wait for the opponent to make the first move. Being extremely careful should be understood as a passive mode.

The aggressive and passive modes refer to the distinction between attacking and waiting.

Logical Principles of Aggressive and Passive Attitudes of Body and Sword

Looming over your opponent with your body in an aggressive attitude and your sword in a passive attitude, you draw out a first move from your opponent by means of your body, feet, or hands, you gain victory by inducing your opponent to take the initiative. Thus, your body and feet are in the aggressive mode, while your sword is in the passive mode. The purpose of putting your body and feet in the aggressive mode is to get your opponent to make the first move.

Mental and Physical Aggressive and Passive Modes

The mind should be in the passive mode, the body in the aggressive mode. The reason for this is that if the mind is in the aggressive mode, you will rush, and that is wrong. Therefore you control the mind and keep it impassive while using physical aggressiveness to get the opponent to make the first move, and thus you gain victory. If the mind is aggressive, you will lose by trying to kill your opponent right away.

In another sense, it can be understood that the mind is to be in the aggressive mode and the body in the passive mode. The point of this is to cause your mind to work intently, putting the mind in an aggressive mode while keeping your sword passive, getting your adversary to make the first move.

The "body" can be understood to mean the hands that hold the sword. Thus it is said that the mind is aggressive while the body is passive.

Although there are two meanings, ultimately the sense is the same. In any case, you win by inducing your opponent to take the initiative.

Things to Learn When You Face an Aggressive Opponent

There are three points on which to focus the eyes: (1) the Two Stars (the opponent's two hands gripping his sword); (2) Peak and Valley (the bending and extension of the opponent's arms); and (3) when engaged, the Distant Mountains (the shoulders and chest). The details of these points of eye focus are to be transmitted orally.

The next two items have to do with the sword and the posture of the body: (1) the rhythm of the distance and (2) the position of the body and the sandalwood state of mind.

The next five items are in the body and in the sword; they are impossible to explain in writing, and each one must be learned by dueling: (1) making the fist into a shield; (2) making the body unified; (3) taking an opponent's fist on your shoulder; (4) the sense of extending the rear leg; and (5) adopting the same stance and guard as the opponent, whatever it may be.

Anyway, the proper state of mind in all five items is to prepare yourself carefully before facing off with an opponent, not allowing yourself to be inattentive; it is essential to make sure that you do not get shook up once the duel begins. If you face off suddenly, without mental preparation, the moves you have learned will not be forthcoming.

Things Learned for Facing Off in a Contest of Adversaries

As for the significance of these three items—the Two Stars, Peak and Valley, and the Distant Mountains—when an opponent is firmly entrenched in a passive, waiting mode, you should not take your eyes off the places described in these three expressions.

These points of focus, however, are used for both aggressive and passive modes. These points of focus are essential. When wading in slashing, you focus your eyes on the Peak. When exchanging blows, you focus your eyes on the Distant Mountains. As for the Two Stars, you should always keep an eye on them.

The Mental Postures of Three Ways of Feinting

The three ways of feinting are three ways of seeing: sticking, pinning, and studied assault. When you cannot tell what opponents might do, you should use these three feints to feel them out.

The thing is to find out adversaries' intentions. When opponents are secured in a passive or waiting mode, you cast these three kinds of impression for the three ways of seeing, implementing strategic maneuvers with covert intentions, inducing adversaries to tip their hands, and thus using this to enable you to gain victory.

Addressing and Adapting to Changes of Mind

The sense of this is that when you deliberately convey various changes of mind to passive opponents, their changes of mind become evident. You win by adapting to those changes of mind.

Double Looks

When you try various ploys on passive opponents to see what they will do, you see without looking, seeing without appearing to see, constantly attentive, not placing your eyes on one single place, you shift your eyes around, seeing in quick glances.

There is a line of a poem that says, "Watching in stolen glances, the dragonfly evades the shrike." Seeing a shrike in a stolen glance, a dragonfly takes to flight. Quickly but surely seeing the actions of opponents in stolen glances, you should work with constant attention.

In *Nōh* drama, there is something called the double look. This means to look and see, then shift the eyes to the side. This means not fixing the gaze.

Hit and Be Hit At: The Sense of Winning by Letting Yourself be Hit At

It is easy to kill someone with a slash of a sword. It is hard to be impossible for others to cut down.

Even if someone lashes out at you with the intention of cutting you down, carefully note the margin of safety where you are out of reach, and calmly let yourself be hit at by the enemy. Even if an adversary lashes out thinking he will score a blow, as long as there is that margin, he will not manage to strike you.

A stroke of the sword that does not hit its target is the sword stroke of death; you reach over it to strike the winning blow. Your adversary's initiative having missed its mark, you turn the tables around and get the jump on your adversary.

Once a sword fight has started, the thing is not to let your opponent raise his hands. Once the fight has started, if you get involved in thinking about what to do, you will be cut down by your opponent with the very next sword blow.

Here you will lose if you are inattentive. You get hit by your opponent when your mind dallies on the blow you have just struck, making naught of your initiative. When you strike a blow, do not let your mind dally on it, not concerning yourself with whether or not it is a telling blow; you should strike again and again, over and over, even four and five times. The thing is not to let the opponent even raise his head.

As for victory, it is determined by a single blow of the sword.

Three Rhythms

One rhythm is a simultaneous strike. Another is to close in and strike when the adversary's sword is raised. The third is to cross over and strike when the adversary's sword is lowered.

Matching rhythm is bad, incongruous rhythm is good. If your rhythm matches, that makes it easier for an adversary to use his sword. If your rhythm is incongruous, the adversary's sword is rendered useless.

You should strike in such a way as to make it difficult for opponents to use their swords. Whether closing in or crossing over, you should strike unrhythmically. In general and in particular, a rhythm that can be tapped into is bad.

A Small Rhythm to a Large Rhythm, a Large Rhythm to a Small Rhythm

When an adversary wields his sword in a large rhythm, you should use yours with a small rhythm. If your adversary uses a small rhythm, you should use a large rhythm. Here too the idea is to use your sword in such a way that the rhythm is incongruous with that of your opponent. If he gets into your rhythm, the adversary's sword becomes easy to employ.

For example, since an expert song goes over the intervals without lapsing into a fixed pattern, a mediocre drummer cannot drum to it. Just as if you put a mediocre drummer in with an expert singer, or a mediocre singer with an expert drummer, making it hard to sing and drum, to contrive in such a way to make it impossible for opponents to strike is called "a small rhythm to a large rhythm, a large rhythm to a small rhythm."

Even if a mediocre singer tries to handle a grandiose rhythm fluently, or an expert drummer tries to tap a little rhythm lightly, it will not work. Also, if an expert singer sings lightly, a mediocre drummer will fall behind and be unable to keep time.

An expert bird hunter shows the bird his pole, shaking it to make it jiggle, smoothly using that as a means to spear the prey. The bird, mesmerized by the rhythm of the jiggling pole, flaps its wings trying to take off but is unable to take off and thus gets speared.

It is imperative to act in a rhythm different from that of adversaries. If your rhythm is incongruous, you can wade right in without your own defenses being crossed. Such a state of mind should also be savored as an object of reflective study.

Noting the Tempo

Neither song nor dance can be performed without knowing the tempo. There must also be a sense of tempo in martial arts. To see with certainty how an adversary's sword is working, how he is handling it, and to discern what is in his mind, must be the same state of mind as that of one who has mastered the tempos of song and dance. When you know your opponent's moves and manners well, you can make your own maneuvers freely.

Techniques I

1. Accompanying a blow of the sword
2. Three inches on either side, opposing or supporting
3. Sneaking in quickly
4. Focusing the eyes on the elbows in the upper position
5. Circling swords; keeping an eye on both right and left
6. Reckoning the three-foot margin

The above six items are learned by working with a teacher and must be taught by word of mouth. They are not completely revealed in writing.

When you use such techniques to launch various preliminary blows and project appearances with covert intentions, and yet your adversary remains unruffled and refuses to make a move, remaining secure in a passive waiting mode, when you then sneak into the range of the sword, slipping right up to your adversary, he can no longer hold back and shifts into the aggressive mode; then you induce the adversary to take the initiative, whereupon you let him hit out at you, and thus strike him down.

In any case, if the opponent does not lash out, you cannot win. Even if an opponent lashes out at you, if you have properly learned how to gauge the margin of safety where you are out of reach, you will not get struck all of a sudden. Having practiced this step thoroughly, you can fearlessly slip right up to an adversary, get him to lash out, and then turn the tables on him to win. This is the sense of being a step ahead of the one who takes the initiative.

Techniques II

1. The major opus, including the initial assault; this must be transmitted by word of mouth.
2. Sustained attention, used in both aggressive and passive modes; this must be transmitted by word of mouth.
3. The one-cubit margin of a small sword.
4. The existence of both aggressive and passive modes when attacking should be understood as the body being in the aggressive mode while the sword is passive.

Each of the above items are learned by working with a teacher and must be passed on by word of mouth. It is impossible to express them well in writing.

Hearing the Sound of Wind and Water

This science is in any case all about how to win by getting your opponent to take the initiative, using tactical ploys as your basis, launching various preliminary blows, and shifting strategically.

Before facing off, you should consider your adversary to be in the aggressive mode, and should not be inattentive. Mental preparation is essential. If you do not think of your adversary as in the aggressive mode, the techniques you have been learning all along will be of no avail once you are attacked with great vehemence the very instant the duel starts.

Once you have faced off, it is essential to put your mind, body, and feet in the aggressive mode, while putting your hands in the waiting mode. You should be sure to pay attention to what is there. This is what is meant by the saying "Take what is there in hand." If you do not observe with utmost calm, the sword techniques you have learned will not be useful.

As for the matter of "hearing the sound of wind and water," this means being calm and quiet above while keeping an aggressive mood underneath. Wind has no sound; it produces sound when it hits things. Thus wind is silent when it blows up above. When it makes contact with things like trees and bamboo below, the sound it produces is noisy and frantic.

Water also has no sound when it is falling from above; it makes a frantic sound down below when it comes down and hits things.

Using these images as illustrations, the point is to be calm and quiet above, while sustaining an aggressive mood underneath. These are images of being extremely serene, unruffled, and calm on the surface, while inwardly being aggressively watchful.

It is bad when the body, hands, and feet are hurried. The aggressive and passive modes should be paired, one inward and one outward; it is bad to settle into just one mode. It is imperative to reflect on the sense of yin and yang alternating. Movement is yang, stillness is yin. Yin and yang interchange, inside and outside. When yang moves inwardly, outwardly be still, in the yin mode; when you are inwardly yin, movement appears outwardly.

In this kind of martial art as well, inwardly you activate your mental energy, constantly attentive, while outwardly you remain unruffled and calm. This is yang moving within, while yin is quiet without. This is in accord with the pattern of nature.

Furthermore, when outwardly intensely aggressive, if you are calm within while aggressive without, so that your inner mind is not captured by the outside, then you will not be outwardly wild. If you move both inwardly and outwardly at once, you become wild. The aggressive and passive modes, movement and stillness, should be made to alternate inside and outside.

Keeping the inner mind attentive, like a duck swimming on the water, calm above while paddling below, when this practice builds up, the inner mind and the outside both melt, so that inside and outside become one, without the slightest obstruction. To reach this state is the supreme attainment.

Sickness

It is sickness to be obsessed with winning, it is sickness to be obsessed with using martial arts, and it is sickness to be obsessed with putting forth all one has learned. It is sickness to be obsessed with offense, and it is also sickness to be obsessed with defense. It is also sickness to be obsessed with getting rid of sickness. To fix the mind obsessively on anything is considered sickness. Since all of these various sicknesses are in the mind, the thing is to tune the mind by getting rid of such afflictions.

The Sense of Elementary and Advanced Levels of Removal of Sickness

The elementary level of removing sickness is when you get into thought to be free from thought and get into attachment to be free from attachment.

The meaning of this is that the wish to get rid of sickness is thought; to wish to get rid of the sicknesses in your mind is to be "in the midst of thought."

Also, even though we use the term *sickness*, this means obsessive thought. To think of getting rid of sickness is also thought. Therefore you use thought to get rid of thought. When you get rid of thoughts, you are free from thought, so this is called getting into thought to be free from thought.

When you take thought to get rid of the sickness that remains in thought, after that the thought of removal and the thoughts to be removed both disappear. This is what is known as using a wedge to extract a wedge.

When you cannot get a wedge out, if you drive another one in so as to ease the tightness, the first wedge comes out. Once the stuck wedge comes out, the wedge driven in afterward does not remain. When sickness is gone, the thought of getting rid of sickness no longer remains; so this is called getting into thought to be free from thought.

To think of getting rid of sickness is to be attached to sickness, but if you use that attachment to get rid of sickness, the attachment will not remain; so this is called getting into attachment to be free from attachment.

In the advanced level, getting rid of sickness means having no thought whatsoever of getting rid of sickness. To think of riddance is itself sickness. To let sickness be, while living in the midst of sickness, is to be rid of sickness.

Thinking of getting rid of sickness happens because sickness is still in the mind. Therefore sickness does not leave at all, and whatever you do and think is done with attachment; so there can be no higher value in it.

How is this to be understood? The two levels, elementary and advanced, have been set up for this function. You cultivate the state of mind of the elementary level, and when this cultivation builds up, attachment leaves on its own, without your intending to get rid of it.

Sickness means attachment. Attachment is despised in Buddhism. Mendicants who are free from attachment can mix in with the ordinary world without being affected or influenced; whatever they do is done freely and independently, stopping where it naturally should.

Masters of the arts cannot be called adepts as long as they have not left behind attachment to their various skills. Dust and dirt adhere to an unpolished gem, but a perfectly polished gem will not be dirtied even if it falls into mud. Polishing the gem of your mind by spiritual cultivation so that it is impervious to stain, leaving sickness alone and giving up concern, do as you will.

The Normal Mind

A monk asked an ancient worthy, "What is the Way?" The ancient worthy replied, "The normal mind is the Way."

This story contains a principle that applies to all the arts. Asked what the Way is, the ancient worthy replied that the normal mind is the Way. This is truly the ultimate. This is the state where the sicknesses of mind are all gone and one has become normal in mind, free from sickness even while in the midst of the sickness.

To apply this to worldly matters, suppose you are shooting with a bow and you think you are shooting while you are shooting; then the aim of your bow will be inconsistent and unsteady. When you wield a sword, if you are conscious of wielding a sword, your offense will be unstable. When you are writing, if you are conscious of writing, your pen will be unsteady. Even when you play the harp, if you are conscious of playing, the tune will be off.

When an archer forgets consciousness of shooting and shoots in a normal frame of mind, as if unoccupied, the bow will be steady. When using a sword or riding a horse as well, you do not "wield a sword" or "ride a horse." And you do not "write," you do not "play music."

When you do everything in the normal state of mind, as it is when totally unoccupied, then everything goes smoothly and easily.

Whatever you do as your Way, if you are obsessed with it, or think that this alone is of importance to you, then it is not the Way. It is when you have nothing in your chest that you are on the Way. Whatever you do, if you do it with nothing in your chest, it works out easily.

This is like the way everything reflects clearly in a mirror precisely because of the formless clarity of the mirror's reflectiveness. The heart of those on the Way is like a mirror, empty and clear, being mindless and yet not failing to accomplish anything.

This is the "normal mind." Someone who does everything with this normal mind is called an adept.

Whatever you do, if you keep the idea of doing it before you and do it with singleminded concentration, you will be uncoordinated. You will do it well once, and then, when you think that is fine, you will do it badly. Or you may do it well twice, then do it badly again. If you are glad you did it well twice and badly only once, then you will do it badly again. There is no consistency at all, because of doing it with the thought of doing it well.

When the effects of exercise build up unawares and practice accumulates, thoughts of wishing to quickly develop skill disappear quietly, and whatever you do, you spontaneously become free from conscious thoughts. At this time, you do not even know yourself; when your body, feet, and hands act without your doing anything in your mind, you make no misses, ten times out of ten.

Even then, if it gets on your mind, you will miss. When you are not consciously mindful, you will succeed every time. Not being consciously mindful does not, however, mean total mindlessness; it just means a normal mind.

Like a Wooden Man Facing Flowers and Birds

This is a saying of Layman Pang: "Like a wooden man facing flowers and birds." Although his eyes are on the flowers and birds, his mind does not stir at the flowers and birds.

Because a wooden man has no mind, it is not moved; this is perfectly logical. But how does a person with a mind become like a wooden man?

The wooden man is a metaphor, an illustration. As a human being with a mind, one cannot be exactly like a wooden manikin. As a human being, one cannot be like bamboo and wood. Even though you do see flowers, you do not see them by reproducing the consciousness of seeing the flowers.

The point of the saying is just to see innocently with the normal mind. When you shoot, you do not shoot by reproducing the consciousness of shooting. In other words, you shoot with the normal mind.

The normal mind is called unminding. If you change the normal mind and instead reproduce another consciousness, your form will also change, so you will stir both internally and externally. If you do everything with a stirring mind, nothing will be as it should.

Even if it is only a matter of speaking a word, people will praise it if and only if your manner of saying it is unstirring and unshakable. What they call the unstirring mind of the Buddhas seems truly sublime.

The Free Mind

Master Zhongfeng said, "Embody the free-minded mind." There are elementary and advanced levels of applying this saying.

When you let the mind go, it stops where it has gone; therefore the first level of practice is to get it to come back each time, so that the mind does not stay anywhere. When you strike a blow of the sword and your mind lingers where you struck, this teaching has you get it to return to you.

At the advanced level, the message is to let your mind be free to go wherever it will. You release your mind after having made it such that it will not stop and linger anywhere even if it is set free.

To embody the free-minded mind means that as long as you use the mind that releases the mind to rope the mind and keep dragging it back, you are not free and independent. The mind that does not stop and linger anywhere even when it is set free is called the free-minded mind.

When you embody this free-minded mind, you can act independently. You are not independent as long as you are holding on to a halter. Even dogs and cats should be raised unleashed. Cats and dogs cannot be raised properly if they are tied up all the time.

People who read Confucian books dwell on the word *seriousness* as if it were the ultimate, spending their whole lives on seriousness, thus making their minds like leashed cats.

In Buddhism as well, seriousness does in fact exist. Scripture speaks of being singleminded and undistracted. This would correspond to seriousness. It means to place the mind on one thing and not scatter it elsewhere.

There are, of course, passages that say, "We seriously declare of the Buddha . . . ," and we speak of singlemindedly and seriously paying respects when we face a Buddha image in what we call reverent obeisance. These usages all have meanings congruous with that of seriousness.

However, these are in any case expedient means for quelling distraction of mind. A well-governed mind does not use expedients to pacify it.

When we chant "Great Sage, Immovable One," with our posture correct and our hands joined in a gesture of reverence, in our minds we visualize the image of the Immovable One. At this time, our three modes of action, physical, verbal, and mental, are equal, and we are singleminded and undistracted. This is called "equality of the three mysteries." In other words, this has the same import as seriousness.

Seriousness corresponds to a quality of the basic mind, yet it is a state of mind that lasts only so long as it is practiced. When we let go of our reverential gesture and stop chanting Buddha names, the image of Buddha in our minds also disappears. What then remains is the former distracted mind. This is not a thoroughly pacified mind.

People who have successfully managed to pacify their minds once do not purify their physical, verbal, and mental actions; they are unstained even as they mingle with the dust of the world. Even if they are active all day, they are unmoved, just as the moon reflected in the water does not move even though thousands and tens of thousands of waves roll one after another. This is the state of people who have consummated Buddhism; I have recorded it here under the instruction of a teacher of that doctrine.

The Life-Giving Sword

Perceiving Abilities and Intentions

"There may be a hundred stances and sword positions, but you win with just one." The ultimate point of this is perceiving abilities and intentions.

Even if a hundred or a thousand manners of swordplay are taught and learned, including all sorts of positions of the body and the sword, the perception of abilities and intentions alone is to be considered the eye.

Even if your opponent knows a hundred stances and you know a hundred stances, the ultimate point is solely in the perception of abilities and intentions.

Because this is transmitted secretly, it is not written in the real way, but in homophonic code words.

The Rhythm of Existence and Nonexistence and the Existence of Both the Existent and the Nonexistent

These expressions refer to the custom of using the terms *existence* and *nonexistence* in reference to abilities and intentions. When evident, they are existent, when concealed, they are nonexistent. These hiding and revealing "existence and nonexistence" refer to perceptions of abilities and intentions. They are in the hand that grips the sword.

There are analyses of existence and nonexistence in Buddhism; here we use the terms analogously. Ordinary people see the existent, but not the nonexistent. In perception of abilities and intentions, we see both the existent and the nonexistent.

The fact is that existence and nonexistence are both there. When there is existence, you strike the existent; when there is nonexistence, you strike the nonexistent. Also, you strike the nonexistent without waiting for its existence, and strike the existent without waiting for its nonexistence. Therefore it is said that both existence and nonexistence are there.

In a commentary on the classic of Lao-tzu, there is something called "always existent, always nonexistent." Existence is always there, and nonexistence is always there as well. When concealed, existence becomes nonexistence; when revealed, nonexistence becomes existence.

For example, when a duck is floating on top of the water, it is "present," and when it dives under the water, it is "absent." So even when we think something exists, once it is concealed it is nonexistent. And even if we think something is nonexistent, when it is revealed it exists. Therefore existence and nonexistence just mean concealment and manifestation, of what is essentially the same thing. Thus existence and nonexistence are both always there.

In Buddhism, they speak of fundamental nonexistence and fundamental existence. When people die, the existent is concealed. When people are born, the nonexistent is manifested. The reality is the same thing.

There is existence and nonexistence in the hand that grips the sword. This is transmitted secretly. This is called perception of ability and intention. When you have hidden your hand, what you have there is concealed. When you turn your palm face up, what is not there is revealed.

Even so, without personal transmission, these words are hard to understand.

When there is existence, you should see this existence and strike it. When there is nonexistence, you should see this nonexistence and strike it. That is why we say that both existence and nonexistence exist.

The thing called existence is nonexistent. The thing called nonexistence exists. Existence and nonexistence are not two.

If you misperceive the existence and nonexistence of abilities and intentions, even if you use a hundred techniques to the fullest, you will not attain victory. Every sort of martial arts is consummated in this one step.

The Moon in the Water and Its Reflection

There is a certain distance between an adversary and yourself at which you will not get hit by the adversary's sword. You employ martial arts from outside this space.

To get close to an opponent by striding into this space or slipping into it is called "the moon in the water," being likened to the moon sending its reflection into a body of water.

One should engage an opponent only after having set up a theoretical "moon in the water" field in one's mind before even facing off. The measurement of the spacing has to be transmitted by word of mouth.

The Quiescent Sword

The quiescent sword is a most extremely important matter. There is in oneself a way to wear it as a quiet sword; in reference to oneself, the character for *sword* (*ken*) in "quiescent sword" is written and understood as "sword." Whether it is positioned to the right or the left, as long as the sword has not left the state of quiescence, there is meaning in the use of the character for *sword.*

Then again, in reference to adversaries, the character *ken* for "sword" should be written and understood as the word *ken* for "see." Since you are to see the position of quiescent swords clearly in order to wade in slashing, the seeing is essential. Thus there is meaning in the character *ken* for "seeing."

Explanation of the Characters Used for "Quiescent"

[The two characters used for "quiescent" in the expression "quiescent sword" literally mean "spirit" and "wonder."] The spirit is within, the wonder manifests outwardly; this is called an inscrutable marvel. For example, because there is the spirit of tree within a tree, therefore its flowers blossom fragrantly, it turns green, its branches and leaves flourish; this is called the marvel.

Even though you may break wood down, you do not see anything you may call the spirit of tree; yet if there were no spirit, the flowers and foliage would not come out. This is also true of the human spirit; even though you cannot open up the body to see something you may call the spirit, it is by virtue of the existence of the spirit within that you perform various actions.

When you stabilize the spirit in situations where swords are quiescent, thereby all sorts of marvels appear in the hands and feet, causing flowers to bloom in battle.

The spirit is the master of the mind. The spirit resides within, employing the mind outside. This mind, furthermore, employs psychic energy. Employing psychic energy in external activities for the sake of the spirit, if this mind lingers in one place, its function is deficient. Therefore it is essential to make sure that the mind is not fixated on one point.

For example, when the master of a house, staying at home, sends a servant out on an errand, if the servant stays where he goes and does not return, he will be missing for further service. In the same way, if your mind lingers on things and does not return to its original state, your ability in martial arts will slip.

For this reason, the matter of not fixating the mind on one point applies to everything, not only martial arts.

There are two understandings, spirit and mind.

Stride

Your stride should not be too quick or too slow. Steps should be taken in an unruffled, casual manner.

It is bad to go too far or not far enough; take the mean. When you go too quickly, it means you are scared and flustered. When you go too slowly, it means you are timid and frightened.

The desired state is one in which you are not upset at all.

Usually people will blink when something brushes by right in front of their eyes. This is normal, and the fact that you blink your eyes does not mean that you are upset. Also, if something is swung at your eyes two or three more times to startle you, if you did not blink your eyes at all, that would actually mean you were upset.

To deliberately hold back spontaneous blinking indicates a much more disturbed mind than does blinking.

The immovable or imperturbable mind is normal. If something comes at your eyes, you blink. This is the state of not being upset. The essential point is just not losing the normal state of mind. To try not to move is to have moved. To move is an immovable principle.

It is good to take steps in a normal manner, and in a normal frame of mind. This is the stage where neither your appearance nor your mind is upset.

The First Principle:
The mental attitude in a face-off is as when facing a spear. What to do when you have no sword.

"The first principle" is a code word in martial arts. In the context of the art of war in general, it means to be independent in every possible way.

The important thing is what happens when you are hard pressed. "The first principle" means you keep that clearly in mind, pay close attention, and make sure you do not get caught in a pinch, unprepared.

The concentrated attention exerted in a face-to-face confrontation with swords when an opponent's stab nearly reaches you, or when a spear is thrust into the cubit margin of safety, is called the first principle.

This is the concentrated attention exerted at such times as when you are being attacked with your back to a wall. It should be understood as a most critical and most difficult situation.

When you have no sword, the one-cubit margin of safety is quite impossible to maintain if you fix your eyes on one spot, let your mind linger on one place, and fail to keep up sustained watchfulness.

To keep things like this in mind is called the first principle, something that is kept secret.

The One-Foot Margin on Both Sides
When both swords are the same size, attention is to be concentrated in the same way as when having no sword.

The weapons on both sides are one foot away from the body. With a margin of one foot, you can slip and parry. It is dangerous to get within this space.

"This is Ultimate"/The First Sword

"This is the ultimate" is a manner of referring to what is supremely consummate. "The first sword" does not literally refer to a sword.

"The first sword" is a code word for seeing incipient movement on the part of opponents. The expression "the critical first sword" means that seeing what opponents are trying to do is the first sword in the ultimate sense.

Understanding the perception of impulses and incipient actions of adversaries as the first sword, understand the weapon that strikes according to what they do as the second sword.

With this as fundamental, you use it in various ways. Perceiving abilities and intentions, the moon in the water, the quiescent sword, and sicknesses make four; with the working of hands and feet, all together they make five. These are learned as "five observations, one seeing."

To perceive abilities and intentions is called "one seeing." The other four are held in mind, so they are called observations. Perceiving with the eyes is called seeing, perceiving with the mind is called observation. This means contemplation in the mind.

The reason we do not call this four observations and one seeing, instead speaking of five observations, is that we use five observations as an inclusive term, of which one, perceiving abilities and intentions, is called "one seeing."

Perceiving abilities and intentions; the moon in the water; the quiescent sword; sickness; body, hands, and feet: these are five items. Four of these are observed in the mind, while the perception of abilities and intentions is seen with the eyes and is called "one seeing."

Analysis of the Moon in the Water; the Quiescent Sword; Sickness; Body, Hands, and Feet

The moon in the water is a matter of the choice of the physical setting of a duel. The quiescent sword is a matter of the choice of your own location. Body, hands, and feet refer to watching what opponents do, and to your own movements. Getting rid of sickness is for the purpose of perceiving abilities and intentions. Therefore the primary thing is to perceive the existence or nonexistence of abilities and intentions. The other four are generalities.

Getting rid of sickness is for the purpose of seeing abilities and intentions. As long as you are not rid of sickness, you will be distracted by it and fail to see. When you fail to see, you lose.

Sickness means sickness of mind. Sickness of mind is when the mind tarries here and there. One should make sure not to let the mind linger on the point where one has struck a blow of the sword. This is a matter of relinquishing the mind without abandoning it.

Moves

If an adversary is positioned such that the tip of his sword is facing you, strike as he raises it. When you intend to strike an opponent, let him hit at you. As long as your adversary lashes out at you, you have as good as struck him.

The Margin of Safety

Take up a position at the margin of safety; after that, concentrate on your state of mind.

When you try to take up a position, if your adversary has already taken up a position, make that yours.

As long as the spacing does not change, even if your opponent approaches five feet, or you approach five feet, the distance between you and your opponent remains the same.

If others have taken up positions, it is best to let them take those positions for the time being. It is bad to get too wrapped up in jockeying for position. Keep your body buoyant.

Maneuvering

Footwork and disposition of the body should be such as not to miss the location of the quiescent sword. This determination should be remembered all along, from even before facing off.

Seeing the Quiescent Sword: Distinction of Three Levels

Seeing with the mind is considered basic. It is because of seeing from the mind that the eyes also perceive. Therefore seeing with the eyes is subordinate to seeing with the mind. Next after that is to see with your body, feet, and hands.

Seeing with your body, feet, and hands means that you do not let your body, feet, and hands miss the quiescent sword of an adversary.

Seeing with the mind is for the purpose of seeing with the eyes.
Seeing with the eyes means aiming your feet and hands at the location of an adversary's quiescent sword.

"The Mind Is Like the Moon in Water, the Body Is Like an Image in a Mirror."

The sense in which these expressions are applied to martial arts is as
follows.

Water reflects an image of the moon, a mirror reflects an image of
a person's body. The reflection of things in the human mind is like
the reflection of the moon in the water, reflecting instantaneously.

The location of the quiescent sword is likened to water, your mind
is likened to the moon. The mind should be reflected in the location
of the quiescent sword. Where the mind goes, the body goes; the body
follows the mind.

A mirror is also likened to the quiescent sword, in which case
these expressions are used to mean moving your body to the locus of
the quiescent sword like a reflection. The principle is not letting your
hands and feet miss the location of the quiescent sword.

The reflecting of the moon in the water is an instantaneous phenomenon. Even though it is way out in space, the moon casts its
reflection in water the very instant the clouds disappear. The reflection does not descend gradually from the sky; it is cast at once, before
you can even blink an eye. This is a simile for the way things reflect
in people's minds as immediately as the moon reflects in a body of
water.

There is a passage of Buddhist scripture that says the mind is as
instantaneous as the moon reflected in water or an image cast in a
mirror. The point of this is not that the moon reflected in water appears to be there but is not. It simply refers to casting an instant
reflection from far away in the sky. A form being reflected in a mirror,
which immediately reflects whatever is before it, is also a simile for
immediacy.

This is the way the human mind reflects in things. The mind may
travel even as far as China in the blink of an eye. Just as you think
you are dozing off, your dreams travel to your native village far away.
The Buddha explained this kind of reflection of the mind as being like
the moon in water or images in a mirror.

These expressions also apply similarly to "the moon in the water" in martial arts. You should transfer your mind to the appropriate locus like the moon reflecting in a body of water. Where the mind goes, the body goes; so as soon as a face-off begins, you should shift your body to the appropriate spot like an image reflecting in a mirror. If you do not send your mind there beforehand in preparation, your body will not go.

In reference to the locus, it is "the moon in the water." In terms of the person, it is "the quiescent sword." In either case, the sense of shifting the body, feet, and hands is the same.

Hasty Attack

A hasty attack is an exceptionally bad thing. The thing is to press aggressively only after having properly prepared yourself mentally and having observed the situation thoroughly once the face-off has begun. It is essential not to get flustered.

Bringing Back the Mind

The sense of this expression is that when you strike a blow of the sword, if you think to yourself that you have scored, then the mind thinking you have scored stops and stays right there. Since your mind does not come back from the blow you have scored, you become careless and get hit by the adversary's "second sword." Your initiative turns out to be for naught, and you lose by getting hit with a counterblow.

When you strike a blow, do not keep your mind on where you hit; after striking, bring your mind back to observe your adversary's condition. Once he is struck, an opponent's mood changes; when one gets hit, one becomes resentful and angry. When angered, an adversary becomes vehement; if you are inattentive, you will get hit.

Think of an adversary who has been hit as a raging wild boar. When you are conscious of having struck a blow, you let your mind tarry and are thus inattentive. You should be aware that an opponent's energy will emerge when he is hit. Also, an adversary will be careful of a place where he has already been hit, so if you try to strike again in the same way, you will miss. When you miss, your opponent will counter and hit you.

Bringing back the mind means bringing your mind back to your body, not letting it tarry at the point where you have struck. The thing is to bring your mind back to observe your opponent's condition.

On the other hand, to repeatedly strike when you have struck a focused blow, slashing again and again without bringing your mind back, not letting your opponent so much as turn his head, this too is a supremely effective state of mind. This is what is meant by the expression "not a hairsbreadth's gap." The idea is to keep slashing without the slightest interval between one stroke and the next.

In a Zen dialogue, which is referred to as a religious battlefield, an answer is given to a question without the slightest gap. If you delay, you will be overtaken by your opponent. Then it is clear who will win and who will lose.

This is what is meant by leaving no gap, not even so much as could admit a single strand of hair. It refers to rapidity of the sword in repeated strokes.

The Sense of Total Removal, the Sense of the Void, the Sense of Presenting the Mind

Total removal means completely removing all sickness. Sickness here means sickness of mind. The thing is to get rid of all the sickness in the mind in one fell swoop.

The varieties of sickness are indicated elsewhere in this book. The general meaning of sickness is the lingering or tarrying of the mind. In Buddhism this is called clinging, and it is severely rejected. If the mind clings to one spot and lingers there, you will miss what you should see, and suffer unexpected defeat.

The expression "total removal" refers to the idea that one should get rid of all these sicknesses in one fell swoop. The sense is that one should totally remove all sicknesses and not fail to perceive "the only one."

Now then, "the only one" refers to the void. "The void" is a code word, which has to be taught secretly. It refers to the mind of an adversary. Mind is shapeless and immaterial; that is why it is "void." To see "the void, the only one" means to see the minds of adversaries.

Buddhism is a matter of realizing the emptiness of mind. Although there are people who preach that mind is empty, it is said that there are few who realize it.

As for "presenting the mind," the mind of an adversary is presented in the hands that grip the sword. The thing is to strike the adversary's grip before he even makes a move.

"Complete removal" is for the purpose of seeing that moment of imminent movement. The point is to get rid of all sicknesses at once, and not fail to see "the void."

The mind of an adversary is in his hands; it is presented in his hands. To hit them while they are still is called hitting the void. The void does not move, has no form, no motion. To hit the void means swiftly striking before movement.

Voidness is the eye of Buddhism. There is a distinction between false voidness and real voidness. False voidness is a simile for nothingness. Real voidness is genuine emptiness, which is the emptiness of mind. Although the mind is like empty space insofar as it is formless, the one mind is the master of the body, so the performance of all actions is in the mind.

The movement and working of the mind is the doing of the mind. When the mind is inactive, it is void; when the void is active, it is mind. The void goes into motion, becoming mind and working in the hands and feet. Since you are to hit the adversary's hands holding the sword quickly, before they move, it is said that you should "hit the void."

Even though we speak of "presenting the mind," the mind is invisible to the eye. It is called void because of being invisible, and it is also called void when it is not moving. Although the mind is presented in the hands gripping a sword, it is invisible to the eye. The point is to strike when the mind is presented in the hands but has not yet moved.

If you suppose that this mind-void is nothing because it is invisible, yet when the mind-void moves, it does all sorts of things. Gripping with the hands, treading with the feet, all possible marvels are products of the action of this void, this mind.

It is hard to understand this mind by reading books; this is a path hard to reach by listening to sermons. People who write and people who preach just write and preach based on traditional religious writings and lectures; those who have realized the mind at heart are rare.

Since all human actions, even marvels, are doings of the mind, this mind is also in the universe. We call this the mind of the universe. When this mind moves, there is thunder and lightning, wind and rain;

it does things like create unseasonable cloud formations and cause hail to rain in midsummer, producing ill effects on humanity.

Thus, in the context of the universe, the void is the master of the universe; and in the context of the human body, it is the master of the human body. When dancing, it is the master of dance; when acting, it is the master of drama. When shooting, it is the master of the gun and bow; when riding, it is the master of the horse. If there is a personal warp in the master, one cannot ride a horse or hit the mark with a bow or a gun.

When the mind has found its proper place and position in the body and is settled where it ought to be, one is free in all paths. It is important to find this mind and understand it.

People all think they have perceived and opened up their own minds and are able to employ their own minds usefully, but very few people have actually found this mind for sure. The signs that they have not attained realization will be evident in their persons, visible to all who have the perception to see.

When people are awakened, everything they do, all their physical actions, will be direct. If they are not upright, they can hardly be called enlightened people. The direct, upright mind is called the original mind, or the mind of the Way. The warped, polluted mind is called the false or errant mind, or the human mentality.

People who have actually realized their own original mind, and whose actions accord with that original mind, are a fascinating phenomenon. I do not speak such words from my own understanding. Although I speak like this, it is hard for me to be direct and straightforward in mind, and to behave in a manner consistent with a direct mind; nevertheless, I write of it because it is the Way.

Even so, in martial arts, technique cannot be perfected as long as your mind is not straight and your body, hands, and feet are not in accord. Although our everyday behavior is not in accord with the Way, in the path of martial arts this attainment of the Way is imperative.

Even though your actions are not apart from this mind, and you accord with this mind in a particular art, it does not work when you try to apply it elsewhere. One who knows everything and can do everything is called an adept. Those who master one art or one craft are called masters of their particular way, but this is not to be called adepthood.

True and False Mind

There is a poem that says,

It is the mind
that is the mind
confusing the mind.
Do not leave the mind,
O mind,
to the mind.

The mind in the first line refers to the false mind, which is bad because it is false and which confuses the original mind. The mind in the second line refers to the false mind. The mind in the third line refers to the original mind, which the false mind confuses. The mind in the fourth line refers to the original mind. The mind in the fifth line refers to the original mind. The mind in the sixth line refers to the false mind.

This poem expresses the true and the false. There are two minds, the original mind and the false mind. If you find the original mind and act in accord, all things are straightforward. When this original mind is warped and polluted by the obscurity of the false mind covering it up, all actions are therefore warped and polluted.

The original mind and the false mind are not two distinct entities. The original mind is the "original countenance," which is there before our parents give birth to us; having no form, it has no origination and no extinction. It is the physical body that is borne by our parents; since the mind is formless and immaterial, we cannot say our parents have given birth to it. It is inherently there in the body when people are born.

Zen is understood to be a teaching that communicates this mind. There is also imitation Zen. A lot of people say similar things that are not really the right path, so people who are supposedly Zennists are not all the same.

When we speak of the false mind, this refers to the energy of the blood, which is personal and subjective. Blood energy is the action of blood; when blood rises, the color of the face changes and one becomes angry.

Also, when people despise what we love, we become angry and

resentful. But if others similarly despise what we despise, we enjoy this and twist wrong into right.

When people are given valuables, they receive them with delight; they break into smiles, and blood energy produces a glow in their faces. Then they take what is wrong to be right.

These are all states of mind that come from the energy in the blood in the body, from this physical body, when dealing with temporal situations. These states of mind are referred to as the false mind.

When this false mind is aroused, the original mind is concealed, becoming a false mind, so nothing but bad things emerge. Therefore enlightened people are honorable because they reduce the false mind by means of the original mind. In unenlightened people, the original mind is hidden, while the false mind is powerful; therefore they act wrongly and get a sullied reputation.

Although the poem quoted above is nothing special, it expresses the distinction between the false and true quite well. Whatever the false mind does is wrong. If this wrong mind emerges, you will lose at martial arts; you will miss the mark with bow and gun, and will not even be able to ride a horse. If you performed in a drama or a dance in this state, it would also be unpleasant to watch and listen. Mistakes will also show up in what you say. Everything will be off. If you accord with the original mind, however, everything you do will be good.

People contrive falsehoods, yet claim they are not false. That is the false mind acting, so its falsehood is immediately evident. If the heart is truthful, people who listen eventually realize it, without any need for explanations or rationalizations. The original mind needs no rationalizations or excuses.

The false mind is sickness of mind; getting rid of this false mind is called getting rid of sickness. Rid of this sickness, the mind is healthy. This sound mind is called the original mind. If you accord with the original mind, you will excel in martial arts. This principle is relevant to everything, without exception.

No Sword

Being "swordless" does not necessarily mean you have to take your opponent's sword. It also does not mean making a show of sword-snatching for your reputation. It is the swordless art of not getting killed when you have no sword. The basic intention is nothing like deliberately setting out to snatch a sword.

It is not a matter of insistently trying to wrest away what is being deliberately kept from your grasp. Not grasping attempts to avoid having it taken away is also "swordlessness." Someone who is intent upon not having his sword taken away forgets what he is opposed to and just tries to avoid having his sword taken away. Therefore he will be unable to kill anyone. Not being killed oneself is considered victory.

The principle is not to make an art of taking people's swords. It is learning to avoid being cut down by others when you have no sword yourself.

Swordlessness is not the art of taking another's sword. It is for the purpose of using all implements freely. When you are unarmed, if you can even take away another's sword and make it your own, then what will not be useful in your hands? Even if you only have a folding fan, you can still prevail over someone with a sword. This is the aim of swordlessness.

Suppose you are walking along with a bamboo cane, and someone draws a long sword and attacks you. You win if you take his sword away, even though you respond with only a cane; or if you do not take the sword away, you win if you thwart him so he cannot cut you down. This attitude should be regarded as the basic idea of swordlessness.

Swordlessness is not for the purpose of taking swords, nor for killing people. When an enemy insistently tries to kill you, that is when you should take his sword. The taking itself is not the original inten-

tion to start with. It is for the purpose of attaining an effective understanding of the margin of safety. This means gauging the distance
between you and an enemy at which his sword will not hit you.

If you know the distance at which you are out of range, you are not
fearful of an opponent's striking sword. When your body is exposed
to attack, then you actively think about this exposure. When you
have no sword, as long as you are out of range of another's sword, you
cannot take it away. You have to be within striking range to take a
sword; you have to expose yourself to being killed in order to take a
sword away.

Swordlessness is the attitude whereby you let others have the
swords, while you engage them using your hands as your instruments. So, since swords are longer than hands, you have to get close
to an adversary, within killing range, in order to be successful at this.

It is necessary to distinguish the interplay of your opponent's
sword and your hands. Then your adversary's sword overshoots your
body, while you get underneath the hilt of the sword, aiming to arrest
the sword. When the time comes, do not freeze into a fixed pattern.
In any event, you cannot take away an opponent's sword unless you
get right up close to him.

Swordlessness is the foremost secret of this school. Physical posture, positioning of the sword, taking a stand, distance, movement,
contrivance, striking, attacking, appearance and intention—all come
from the attitude of swordlessness, so this is the essential eye.

Great Potential and Great Function

Everything has body and function. For example, a bow is a body,
while drawing, shooting, and hitting the mark are functions of a bow.
A lamp is a body, light is its function. Water is a body, moisture is a
function of water. An apricot tree is a body, fragrance and color are
functions. A sword is a body, cutting and stabbing are functions.

Therefore, potential is the body, while the existence of various
capabilities, manifesting outwardly from the potential, is called function. Because an apricot tree has a body, flowers blossom from the
body, giving off color and scent. In the same way, function resides
within potential and works outside; sticking, attacking, appearance
and intention, aggressive and passive modes, the casting of various

impressions, and so on, manifest external action because there is potential at the ready within. These are called function.

Great is a word of praise. When we say "Great Spirit," "Great Incarnation," and "Great Saint," the word *great* is an expression of praise. Great function appears because of great potential. When Zen monks are able to use their bodies freely and independently, harmonizing with truth and communing with truth whatever they say and do, this is called "great spiritual power" or "great function of great potential."

Spiritual powers and miraculous manifestation are not wonders produced by ghosts or spirits from outer space; these terms refer to working freely and independently whatever you do. All the many sword positions, appearances concealing intentions, deceptions, use of implements, leaping up and leaping down, grabbing a blade, kicking someone down, all sorts of actions, are called great function when you attain independence, beyond what you have learned. Unless you always have the potential within, the great function will not appear.

Even when you are sitting indoors, first look up, then look left and right, to see if there is anything that might happen to fall from above. When you are seated by a door or a panel, take note of whether it might not fall over. If you happen to be in attendance near nobles of high rank, be aware of whether something unexpected might happen. Even when you are going in and out of a door, do not neglect attention to the going out and going in, always keeping aware.

All of these are examples of potential. When marvels come forth immediately at naturally appropriate times because the potential is always there within, this is called great function.

When the potential is unripe, however, the function does not manifest. In all paths, when concentration builds up and exercise is repeated, potential matures and great function emerges. When potential freezes, stiffens up, and remains inflexible, it is not functional. When it matures, it expands throughout the body, so that great function emerges through the hands and feet, eyes and ears.

When you meet people with this great potential and great function, martial arts using only what you have learned will not even enable you to raise a hand. Glared at once by the eyes of someone with the great potential, you will be so captivated by the look that you will forget to draw your sword, just standing there doing nothing.

If you delay for even the time it takes to blink an eye, you will have lost already. When a cat glares at it, a mouse falls down from the ceiling; captivated by the look in the cat's eyes, the mouse forgets even to run, and falls. Encountering someone with the great potential is like a mouse running into a cat.

There is a Zen saying that goes, "When the great function appears, it does not keep to guidelines." This means that people with the great potential and great function are not at all constrained by learning or rules. In all fields of endeavor, there are things to learn and there are rules. People who have attained supreme mastery are beyond them; they act freely and independently. To act independently, outside of rules, is called personifying great potential and great function.

Potential means to be thinking attentively of everything. Therefore, when that intently thought potential becomes stiff and frozen and hard, then you are entangled by potential and thus are not free. This is because potential is immature, unripe. If you build up effective exercise, potential will mature, expanding throughout the body, working freely and independently. This is called the great function.

Potential is mental energy. It is called potential according to the situation. Mind is the inside, mental energy is the entrance. Since the mind is the master of the whole body, it should be understood as that which resides within. Mental energy is at the door, working outside for its master, the mind.

The division of the mind into good and bad comes from potential, as it goes out from states of potential to good and to bad. Mental energy that is kept watchfully at the door is called potential. When people open a door and go outside, whether they do good, do evil, or even work marvels is due to the ideas in their minds before opening the door.

Thus this potential is something very important. If this potential is working, it emerges outside and the great function manifests. In any case, if you understand it as mental energy, you will not be off. It is called differently according to where it is.

Even so, just because we speak of the inside and the entrance, there are no fixed definitions of inside and entrance somewhere in the body. We speak of inside and entrance by way of metaphor. For example, when people speak, the beginning of their speech could be called the entrance, while the end could be called the inside; in the words themselves there are no specific locations of inside and entrance.

Mind and Objects

A verse of Saint Manora says, "Mind turns along with myriad situations; its turning point is truly recondite."

This verse refers to a Zen secret. I cite it here because this idea is quintessential in martial arts. People who do not study Zen will find it quite hard to comprehend.

In the context of martial arts, "myriad conditions" means all the actions of adversaries; the mind turns with each and every action. For example, when an opponent raises his sword, your mind turns to the sword. If he whirls to the right, your mind turns to the right; if he whirls to the left, your mind turns to the left. This is called "turning along with myriad situations."

"The turning point is truly recondite." This is the eye of martial arts. When the mind does not leave any traces in any particular place, but turns to what lies ahead, with the past dying out like the wake of a boat, not lingering at all, this should be understood as the turning point being truly recondite.

To be recondite is to be subtle and imperceptible; this means the mind not lingering on any particular point. If your mind stops and stays somewhere, you will be defeated in martial arts. If you linger where you turn, you will be crushed.

Since the mind has no form or shape, it is basically invisible; but when it clings and lingers, the mind is visible as such in that condition. It is like raw silk: dye it red and it becomes red, dye it violet and it becomes violet. The human mind also manifests visibly when it is attracted and fixated by things. If you are attracted to boys, eventually people will notice. When the thought is within, the impression appears outwardly.

When you are watching an opponent's moves carefully, if you let your mind linger there, you will lose at martial arts. The verse cited above is quoted to illustrate this point. I omit the last two lines of the verse. For Zen study, it is necessary to know the whole verse; in martial arts, the first two are enough.

Martial Arts and Buddhism

There are many things in martial arts that accord with Buddhism and correspond to Zen. In particular, there is repudiation of attachment and avoidance of lingering on anything. This is the most urgent point. Not lingering is considered quintessential.

A courtesan wrote this poem in response to one by the Buddhist priest Saigyō:

> If you ask as a leaver of home,
> I simply think you should
> not let your mind linger
> on a temporary dwelling

In martial arts we should deeply savor the last lines, and see if we are not like this. No matter what kind of secret transmission you obtain and what move you employ, if your mind lingers on that move, you will have lost in martial arts. It is essential to practice an attitude of not dwelling on anything, be it the actions of an opponent, your own skills, or slashing and stabbing.

Yes and No

Master Longji said to a group, "The pillar of affirmation does not see the pillar. The pillar of denial does not see the pillar. Having gotten rid of affirmation and denial altogether, attain understanding within affirmation and denial."

This story is to be applied to all arts. A certain teacher told it to me, and I thought of its application to martial arts, so I record it here.

As for the pillar of affirmation and the pillar of denial, this means that judgments of right and wrong, good and bad, stand firmly in the heart, affirmation and denial being like pillars standing. Insofar as keeping in mind something that is right will become onerous all of a sudden, it will be even more onerous if it is something wrong. Therefore the saying has it that you do not see the pillar. This means that you should not look at the pillars of affirmation and denial, right and wrong.

These judgments of good and bad are sicknesses of the mind. As long as these sicknesses do not leave the mind, whatever you do is not good. Therefore the saying goes that we should attain understanding within affirmation and denial after having gotten rid of affirmation and denial. This means that after having detached from affirmation and denial, you should then mix in with affirmation and denial, rising from the midst of affirmation and denial to the supreme state.

The eye detached from affirmation and denial is truly hard to attain, even if you have understood Buddhism.

Truth and Untruth

"Even truth is to be relinquished, to say nothing of untruth." In this passage, "truth" means really true teaching. Even really true teaching should not be kept in the mind once you have become completely enlightened. Thus "even truth is to be relinquished."

After you have realized true teaching, if you keep it in your chest, it pollutes your heart; how much more so does untruth! Since even truth is to be relinquished, to say nothing of untruth, this should not be kept in your heart. That is what this passage says.

Having seen all true principles, do not keep any of them in your chest. Let go of them cleanly, making your heart empty and open, and do what you do in an ordinary and unconcerned state of mind. You can hardly be called a maestro of martial arts unless you reach this stage.

I speak of martial arts because military science is my family business, but this principle is not limited to martial arts; all arts and sciences, and all walks of life, are like this. When you employ martial arts, unless you get rid of the idea of martial arts, it is a sickness. When you shoot, unless you get rid of the idea of shooting, it is a sickness of archery.

If you just duel and shoot with a normal mind, you should have no trouble with the bow and you should be able to wield the sword freely. The normal mind, not upset by anything, is good for everything. If you lose the normal mind, your voice will quiver whatever you try to say. If you lose the normal mind, your hand will quiver if you try to write something in front of others.

The normal mind keeps nothing in the heart, but lightly relinquishes the past, so that the heart is empty and therefore is the normal mind. People who read Confucian books, failing to understand this principle of emptying the mind, only concern themselves with "seriousness." Seriousness is not the ultimate realization; it is training in the first couple of steps.

Notes

335 *Weapons are instruments of ill omen.* This is a paraphrase of the Taoist classic *Tao Te Ching*, chapter 31. Yagyū's opening remarks follow Taoist theories; see *The Book of Leadership and Strategy* and *Wentzu*, listed in the Bibliography.

337 *A strategy to give life to many people by killing the evil of one person.* Most wars do the opposite, sacrificing many people for the sake of a few. Buddhist theory on killing as an act of mercy is found in the great *Mahāparinirvāna-sūtra*, elucidated by the Tiantai master Huisi in these terms: "If enlightening beings practice mundane tolerance and thus do not stop evil people, allowing them to increase an evil and destroy true teaching, then these enlightening beings are actually devils, not enlightening beings."

338 *The Great Learning.* This is an ancient Chinese treatise (*Da Xue*, Japanese *Daigaku*), one of the Four Books of Neo-Confucianism, on which orthodox education in Japan under martial rule was founded. The Four Books are the *Analects* of Confucius, the works of Mencius, *Balance in the Center*, and *The Great Learning*. *The Great Learning* is the easiest of these books and generally was the first to be memorized and studied in primary school.

339 *Entering from learning into no learning.* In Buddhist terms, "no learning" represents the state of a graduate of the phrase of self-liberation, who has nothing more to learn for personal salvation.

339 *Mood and will.* "Mood" here should be understood in a wider than usual sense, to embrace the whole range of meaning of state of mind and disposition of psychic energy. The original term (*ki*) is untranslatable in itself, assuming as it does many meanings and nuances according to usage, especially in compound terms. In the context of martial arts, it should be noted that the Japanese word *ki* does not in fact coincide in meaning with the Chinese word *qi*, in spite of the facts that they are originally the same word and some of the psychological aspects of the handling of *ki/qi* are indeed similar.

340 *Appearance and intention.* See *Japanese Art of War* for further discussion of these terms.

342 *The sandalwood state of mind.* This refers to striking twice at once with the same alignment.

350 *The normal mind.* This does not refer to conventional normalcy, which is nothing but conformity to inculcated expectations, but normalcy in the Zen sense, which is the mind in its pristine state, not warped by environmental influences.

351 *Like a wooden man.* Layman Pang was a famous lay Buddhist of eighth-century China. He studied with the greatest Chan masters of the time and was himself highly regarded as an adept. His wife, daughter, and son were also enlightened Chan Buddhists.

352 *The free mind.* Master Zhongfeng Mingben was one of the distinguished Chan Buddhist masters of thirteenth-century China.

353 *Three mysteries.* A Shingon Buddhist term referring to the actions of body, speech, and mind.

354 *The rhythm of existence and nonexistence.* See *Tao Te Ching*, chapter 1.

356 *The quiescent sword.* This refers to a state of potential, the hidden or dormant resources or possibilities of an individual, group, or situation.

366 *Original countenance.* A Zen term for the pristine mind untrammeled by acquired habits of thought.

366 *The energy of the blood.* Rendered literally here for the purpose of Yagyū's argument, *kekki* refers to so-called animal spirits or hot blood, vigor, ardor, vehemence, impetuosity, animal courage, blind daring, etc.

368 The "No Sword" scroll goes to an even higher level. The art of "swordlessness" is the way to achieve security even when unarmed, how to accomplish tasks even when you have no resources.

372 *Saint Manora* is reckoned as the twenty-second patriarch of Zen Buddhism in India. The last two lines of the verse cited run, "When you recognize nature and accord with its flow, there is no more elation, and no more sorrow." The great Japanese psychiatrist Morita Masatake often quoted this verse. Yagyū's deliberate omission of the last lines demonstrates the lack of complete coincidence between Zen and martial arts.

373 *Saigyō* was a very famous Japanese poet of the twelfth century. Born in 1118, Saigyō was originally a soldier but abandoned the world at the age of twenty-three to become a Buddhist priest. He spent much of his life traveling and passed away in 1190. The poem cited by Yagyū

is part of an extremely well-known incident in the travels of the great poet-monk, which took place one evening when he sought lodging for the night. One of the morals of the story, aside from the obvious message about impermanence and nonattachment, is that a courtesan may understand Buddhism as well as or better than a distinguished priest. Being able to see objectively without dwelling on preconceived expectations is also an art of war.

373 *Longji* was a distinguished Chinese Chan (Zen) master of the Xuansha school in the late classical era of Chan. He lived from 869 to 928.

374 *Truth and untruth.* The passage cited illustrates one of the hallmarks of Mahayana Buddhism. It is from a very popular scripture known in Japanese as the *Kongo-kyō*, or *Diamond Sutra*. This scripture was a favorite of lay people in China and of Zen Buddhists in Japan, where it was ritually recited as part of a common Zen liturgy.

Bibliography

As Miyamoto Musashi emphasizes in his guidelines for students, martial artists in the Japanese warrior traditions were admonished to develop rounded mentalities and broad perceptions by studying cultural arts along with military science. The following books represent essential elements of East Asian martial and cultural traditions.

The Art of War. Translated by Thomas Cleary. Boston: Shambhala Publications, 1988. The most eminent Chinese classic of strategy, also studied by Japanese warriors.

The Book of Leadership and Strategy. Translated and edited by Thomas Cleary. Boston: Shambhala Publications, 1992. This book is a compendium of classical Taoist teachings, spiritual and cultural as well as political and martial. Yagyū Munenori's Zen teacher Takuan was also a student of Taoism, which is generally considered to have been an ancient congener of Zen Buddhism.

The Essential Confucius. Translated and presented by Thomas Cleary. San Francisco: Harper San Francisco, 1992. The sayings of Confucius were regularly memorized in Japanese primary schools for centuries. Acquaintance with Confucius is absolutely indispensable for understanding the traditional fabric of East Asian societies.

The Japanese Art of War, by Thomas Cleary; within this volume. An analysis of the influences of martial rule on Japanese culture, including a discussion of the relationship between the ways of the warriors and Zen Buddhism.

Mastering the Art of War. Translated and edited by Thomas Cleary. Boston: Shambhala Publications, 1989. Illustrative elucidations of the principles of the classic *Art of War*, including moral and social teachings paralleling the work of Yagyū Munenori, and war stories demonstrating tactics paralleling the work of Miyamoto Musashi.

Wen-tzu. Translated by Thomas Cleary. Boston: Shambhala Publications, 1991. Attributed to Lao-tzu, the *Wen-tzu* is one of the great classics of ancient Taoism, presenting teachings on the arts of strategy within the broader social and psychological context.

Zen Essence. Translated and edited by Thomas Cleary. Boston: Shambhala Publications, 1989. Fundamental Zen teachings and techniques presented by distinguished masters in easy conversational and discursive styles. The basic level of Zen mainly represented in this book is that primary freedom emphasized in martial arts by Yagyū Munenori.

Zen Lessons. Translated by Thomas Cleary. Boston: Shambhala Publications, 1989. Precious documents from distinguished Zen master describing and illustrating the social and psychological aspects of Zen Buddhism, both genuine and imitative.

WAYS OF WARRIORS
CODES OF KINGS

*Lessons in Leadership
from the Chinese Classics*

INTRODUCTION

For more than two thousand years, ever since Greece and Rome began importing silk from China, there has been a stream of transmission in arts and sciences East to West. Sometimes sinking underground in deserts of political isolation and warfare, sometimes springing to life in oases of new hybrid civilizations, over the centuries this stream of knowledge produced many technical innovations in material culture—in medicine, metallurgy, ceramics, papermaking, textiles, agriculture, pyrotechnics, printing, transport, mathematics, astronomy.

Many seminal forms of social and political science are also found in the works of the ancients—theocracy, bureaucracy, hierarchy, monarchy, plutarchy, oligarchy, feudalism, imperialism, militarism, despotism, fascism, legalism, anarchism, socialism, paternalism, individualism, conformism—these conceptions and more were all articulated by Chinese political philosophers of olden times. Even revolutionary and democratic ideas are to be found in Chinese lore of more than two thousand years ago, as are more subtle spiritual conceptions of state, society, and individuality.

Ideas tend to travel with trade, as with diplomacy and warfare, often taking on new forms as they are transformed by new environments and applied to new situations, expressed in different languages, and adapted by diverse peoples. It is not always possible to track cultural drift, especially in the shifting sands of global events, but it is clear that for all the variety of world civilizations, we share intersecting histories and have common interests.

Among the spheres of Chinese culture that have attracted the attention of other peoples near and far, past and present, the sciences of statecraft and warfare have been particularly prominent. Many of the Asian nations, including Korea, Japan, Tibet, Vietnam, and various Mongolian, Turkic, and Tungusic nations of north and central Asia, rose to peaks of political power employing Chinese methods of organization and operation.

These techniques were probably brought west from China long ago by the Huns, who were longtime major trading partners, territorial rivals, and both enemies and allies of the Chinese. The eastern Huns eventually joined the Chinese empire, and the western Huns headed west, where, centuries later, under the infamous Attila, they briefly terrorized Europe before settling down.

Marco Polo undoubtedly also brought some knowledge of these matters back to Italy after his travels in China in the fourteenth century. The resemblances of many of the ideas of sixteenth-century Machiavelli to Chinese political and military strategists' may derive from information gathered by Marco Polo, or later by Jesuit missionaries. This knowledge was also obtained by the princes of Muscovy, who laid the foundations of the Russian empire in the fourteenth and fifteenth centuries. The Russians learned these principles from their erstwhile Mongol-Tatar masters, the Golden Horde. This was the western branch of the great Mongolian empire, which had taken over the rulership of China in the thirteenth century.

In the latter eighteenth century, a French Jesuit scholar made an early literary attempt to introduce Chinese strategic lore in Western Europe. Interest in Eastern mysticism was peaking in France at that time, and the French cleric's treatment of Chinese tactical literature emphasized the humanistic elements of the material. Deriving from the Taoist background, this aspect of classical Chinese strategic lore was an intriguing surprise to Western observers.

During the nineteenth century, Europe and America were more concerned with exploiting China materially than studying Chinese civilization, yet there were secular thinkers of the West who developed a sympathetic and even admiring interest in the Confucian idea of a state governed by learned philosophers and poets. This aspect of Chinese culture seemed consonant with familiar classical ideals of Greek philosophers and was also close to the Celtic tradition once dominant in Europe and ardently admired by many scholars of the late nineteenth century. Not seeming to require specific religious belief, Confucianism presented Western secularists with an interesting contrast to the religious sectarianism infesting European politics.

The emergence of modern Japan as an international military and economic power, heralded by the defeat of imperial China and Russia at war in 1895 and 1905, renewed Western interest in traditional Chinese strategic literature. Japan was one of the principal heirs of Chinese culture, and its meteoric rise to power in modern times strengthened Western interest in the effects of certain social values and organizational techniques transmitted through the heritage of Chinese philosophies, including the peculiar combination of Confucian idealism and tactical pragmatism.

Widespread Western interest in Chinese culture today is due in part to recent historical events and contemporary political and demographic conditions, but it is also a natural continuation of a complex trend of centuries' standing. The East-West polarization of the last five hundred years has not inhibited either trade or cultural exchange, even if it has created acrimony and violence.

It is the spells of interruption and ignorance, however prolonged, that ought to be regarded as anomalous, rather than contact and interchange. Acrimony and violence may be more dramatic and exciting than humane interest and understanding, but the passage of time has shown that when the dust clears in the aftermath of conflict on the stage of history, no matter who wins or loses, former enemies always learn to learn more about each other.

The rise of modern China on the international scene has stimulated increased interest in Chinese civilization, particularly in the strategic and tactical lore so prized in the fields of statecraft, diplomacy, military affairs, and commerce. The problems of balancing partnership and rivalry in an inherently competitive international theater are among the foremost concerns of world leaders in business and politics as we enter the twenty-first century.

While misunderstandings may naturally arise concerning different ways of seeing and doing things, nevertheless, as nations and peoples continue to take constructive interest in one anothers' cultures and philosophies of life, the foundation for mutual understanding and conflict resolution will continue to develop. With the growth of the world population, the power of modern technology, and the proliferation of deadly weaponry, these conceptual facilities for mediation and cooperation become ever more critical to the survival and prosperity of human society.

This book contains an anthology of selections translated from several famous works of classical Chinese strategic lore. Some of the ideas are easily applied to current conditions, some of them are more like warnings. All are about human potential, for better and for worse. There are many organizational concepts in this lore that are equally applicable within different political and social contexts, while there are others that essentially illustrate drastic and dubious measures taken by tyrants.

Through observation of the whole range of human possibilities, for good and for bad, moral and practical acumen can be developed. Through cultivation of moral and practical acumen, powers of independent decision and choice can be attained. The excitable observer will pass judgment first and then make knowledge conform to judgment; the prudent observer will first learn to know and then judge according to knowledge.

Whether it is in the domain of statecraft, or military action, or commerce, or social, familial, and interpersonal relations, empathic understanding of human nature and behavior is crucial to successful and satisfying interaction. In classical literature designed to help us attain human understanding in all of its aspects, here and there we may see reflections of ourselves or others as we are and act. We may also see how effective we or others could become if we tried, or what ill could become of us all if we were too careless to avoid it. Thus we can find that there are important and useful things for us to learn along the whole spectrum of human possibilities, pieces of insight that can help us on our way.

Lessons from the Chinese Classics

Harmony First

When there is disharmony in a nation, it cannot launch an army. When there is disharmony in an army, it cannot set forth a battlefront. When there is disharmony in a battlefront, it cannot proceed into combat. When there is disharmony in combat, victory cannot be assured.

Therefore when rulers who have the Way are going to mobilize their people, they first establish harmony before major undertakings.

Wu Qi's Art of War

Four Corners

The Way is for returning to fundamentals and going back to beginnings. Duty is for doing business and achieving success. Strategy is for avoiding harm and gaining advantages. Contracts are for protecting business and preserving achievements.

If their actions do not conform to the Way and their undertakings do not accord with duty, those in important positions of high rank will inevitably get into trouble.

Therefore sages guide people with the Way, manage them with duty, show them how to behave with decorum, and treat them with humaneness. If you cultivate these four virtues, you thrive, while if you neglect them you decline.

Wu Qi's Art of War

Government

Whether governing a nation or an army, it is imperative to teach people decorum, inspire them with duty, and cause them to have a sense of shame.

Wu Qi's Art of War

Winning and Losing

When people have a sense of shame, in great countries that is sufficient for combat, in small countries it is sufficient for defense.

However, it is easier to win by fighting than it is to win by defense.

Therefore it is said that of the warring states in the land, those who win five victories will be a disaster, those who win four victories will be exhausted; those who win three victories will be hegemons, those who win two victories will be kings; the one who wins one victory will be emperor.

So those who win the world by numerous victories are rare; those who perish thereby are many.

Wu Qi's Art of War

OCCASIONS FOR WARFARE

There are five occasions for warfare. First is fighting for honor. Second is fighting for profit. Third is accumulated antipathy. Fourth is internal disorder. Fifth is on account of famine.

They also have five names. The first is called a war of duty. The second is called a war of strength. The third is called a war of hardness. The fourth is called a war of violence. The fifth is called a war of rebellion.

Stopping violence and remedying chaos is called duty. Relying on the masses to attack is called strength. Mobilizing an army on account of rage is called hardness. Seeking profit by eliminating disorder is called violence. Initiating action and mobilizing the masses when the country is chaotic and the people are exhausted is called rebellion.

There is a tactic for each of these five. Duty must be overcome by courtesy. Strength must be overcome by modesty. Hardness must be overcome by talking. Violence must be overcome by deception. Rebellion must be overcome by strategy.

Wu Qi's Art of War

GOOD MANAGEMENT

If the leader can put worthy people in higher positions while keeping unworthy people in subordinate positions, then the battlefront is stable.

If the people are secure in their fields and houses and familiar with the local officials, then defense is secure.

When the people all approve of their own leadership and disapprove of the neighboring country, then war is already won.

Wu Qi's Art of War

When to Avoid Conflict

Avoid conflict with opponents when

1. their land is vast and their population is large;
2. their rulers care for the ruled, resulting in general welfare;
3. their rewards are reliable and punishments judicious, always timely;
4. they are ranked according to achievement on the battle line, with responsibilities entrusted to the worthy and tasks to the able;
5. their armed forces are massive and their weaponry is advanced;
6. they have help from neighbors all around and assistance from large countries.

If you do not match up to an enemy in these respects, avoid them unhesitatingly.

Wu Qi's Art of War

When Attack is Feasible

It is imperative to examine the enemy's emptiness and fullness and aim for their vulnerabilities.

When enemies have newly arrived from afar, while their columns are still unsettled, they can be attacked.

When they have just eaten and have not yet made preparations, they can be attacked.

When they are running, they can be attacked.

When they are tired out, they can be attacked.

When they have not yet gotten an advantageous location, they can be attacked.

When they miss opportunities and things are not going smoothly for them, they can be attacked.

When they are stretched out endlessly on a long journey, they can be attacked.

When they are crossing water and have reached halfway, they can be attacked.

When they are in defiles or narrow roads, they can be attacked.

When their signals are confused, they can be attacked.

When their battle lines keep shifting, they can be attacked.

When their commanders alienate the officers and soldiers, they can be attacked.

When their hearts are afraid, they can be attacked.

Wu Qi's Art of War

VICTORY IS MADE BY ORDER

If rules and orders are unclear, rewards and penalties are unsure, and the troops do not stop and go on signal, even if you have a million of them, what is the use?

Order means having decorum when at rest; having dignity when on the move; being unopposable in advance, unpursuable in retreat, orderly in forward and reverse movements; responding to signals left and right: even if cut off they form battle lines, even if scattered they form columns. Whether in safety or danger, the troops can be joined but not divided, can be deployed but not exhausted. Wherever you hurl them, none in the world can stand up to them.

Wu Qi's Art of War

LIFE AND DEATH

A battlefield is a place where corpses are made. If you are sure you'll die, then you'll survive; if you have your heart set on getting out alive, then you'll die.

Good commanders are as if they were sitting in a leaking boat or lying under a burning roof: when they can baffle the planning of the intelligent and present no target for the rage of the brave, then they can take on opponents.

Wu Qi's Art of War

EDUCATION AND TRAINING

People always die for their inability and suffer defeat for their lack of training. Therefore education and discipline are priorities of the arts of war.

Wu Qi's Art of War

GENERALSHIP

One who has mastered both culture and warfare can be the commander of an army; one who can be both hard and soft can direct the military. Usually when people talk about military leaders, they consider their bravery, but bravery is only one fraction of military leadership. The fact is that brave men will readily clash; if they readily clash without knowing whether it will be advantageous, they are not yet competent.

So there are five things military leaders treat carefully: (1) order, (2) preparedness, (3) resoluteness, (4) discipline, (5) simplicity.

1. Order means governing many as effectively as governing few.
2. Preparedness means being as if you'll see your enemies the moment you step out your door.
3. Resoluteness means not thinking of living when facing the enemy.
4. Discipline means being as if only beginning to fight even when you have won.
5. Simplicity means that rules and orders are minimal and not overcomplicated.

To accept a mission without refusing, not considering returning until the opponent is broken—these are the manners of commanders. Therefore on the day an army goes out, there is death with glory rather than life with disgrace.

Wu Qi's Art of War

ASSESSING OPPONENTS

It is essential in any war to figure out the other side's commander first, examining his abilities, employing strategy according to conditions. Then you will succeed without laboring.

If the commander is stupid and trusting, he can be deceived and seduced.

If he is greedy and shameless, he can be bribed and bought.

If he is mercurial and lacks strategy, he can be tired out.

If the upper classes are rich and arrogant while the lower classes are poor and resentful, they can be alienated and divided.

If they are hesitant in their movements and their troops have nothing to rely on, they can be stampeded.

If the officers disrespect their commander and want to go home, then block the highways and leave narrow roads open, where they can be ambushed.

Wu Qi's Art of War

MANAGEMENT, NOT MAGIC

King Wei of Liang asked Master Wei Liao, "Is it true that the Yellow Emperor punished and rewarded in such a way as to win all the time?"

Master Wei Liao said, "Attacking with punishment and maintaining with reward is not a matter of astrology, divination, or geomancy. The Yellow Emperor only attended to human management.

"Why? Suppose there is a city that cannot be taken by siege from east or west and cannot be taken by siege from north or south—could no one take advantage of it at an opportune moment? The reason it cannot be taken, however, is that the walls are high, the moats are deep, it is fully armed, it has abundant supplies of goods and grains, and the great men are of one mind. If the walls were low, the moats were shallow, and the defense were weak, then it would be taken. Seen in this way, astrology, divination, and geomancy are not as good as human management.

"According to *Celestial Agencies*, 'A battle formation with its back to water is a ground that is cut off; a battle formation facing a hill is a lost army.' Yet when King Wu attacked Emperor Zhou of the Shang dynasty, he set out his battle formation with its back to the Ji River, facing the mountain slopes; striking Zhou's 100,000 troops with 22,500 men, he destroyed the Shang dynasty. Was Zhou not in accord with the principles of battle formation given in *Celestial Agencies!*

"When Zixin, lord general of Chu, was at war with the men of Qi, a comet appeared with its tail pointed toward Qi. The direction of a comet's tail is supposed to indicate victory, suggesting that Qi should not be attacked. Lord Zixin said, 'What does a comet know! When people fight with brooms, the one who uses the broom backward wins.' The next day he engaged the men of Qi in battle and routed them.

"The Yellow Emperor said, 'Before spirits and before ghosts, first consult your own intelligence.' This refers to natural faculties, and is just a matter of human management.

"*Military Configuration* says, 'Ban soothsayers, and do not let them divine the fortunes of warfare for officials.' "

Master Wei Liao

ORDER

In any army, order must be established first; then the soldiers will not be unruly. When the soldiers are not unruly, discipline is clear. When you have a hundred troops all fighting according to directions, they can bring down columns and disrupt battlefronts; when you have a thousand troops all fighting, they can overthrow armies and kill their guards. When ten thousand troops align their blades, no one in the world can fight them.

Master Wei Liao

ORGANIZATION

It is said, "Appoint the intelligent, employ the capable, and business will show a profit before long; make rules clear and directions precise, and business will be auspicious without divination; honor achievement and support hard work, and prosperity will be attained without prayer."

It is also said, "The timing of the heavens is not as good as the advantage of the earth; the advantage of the earth is not as good as harmony among people." What sages value is human management.

Master Wei Liao

RECRUITING TALENT

If people say they have a way to overcome opponents, don't accept them on word alone—be sure to test their ability to fight. Have them take over someone else's land and govern some other people; make sure to bring in those who prove to be talented. If you cannot bring in talented people yet want to take over the world, you'll be overthrowing your own forces and killing your own commanders. This way, even if you win at war your country will grow weaker and weaker, and the more land you win the poorer your country will be. This lies within corruption of the internal organization of the nation.

Master Wei Liao

THE CONSCIOUSNESS OF SOCIETY

Social order makes the people unselfish. If the people are unselfish, the whole land is one family and there is no plowing or spinning for private personal purposes; they share cold and hunger in common. Therefore a household with ten sons has no more to eat, while a household with but one son has no less to eat. How could there be brawling and drunkenness to ruin good folk?

When the people are inconsiderate of one another, then greed arises, and problems of contention occur. When a leader becomes unruly, then the people have their own private stores of goods and their own caches of money; once people violate prohibitions, they are arrested and punished. Where are the qualifications to lead people?

Good governments organize their systems so as to get the people to be unselfish. If the common people do not presume to be selfish, then none will do wrong. Return to fundamentals, focus on principles, set forth on a unified course; then greed will leave, contention will stop, prisons will be empty. The fields will be full and cereals abundant, giving security to the people and consideration to those afar; then there will be no difficulties with the world outside and no violence or chaos within. This is the epitome of order.

Master Wei Liao

FUNDAMENTALS

Assess the relative fertility or barrenness of the soil to establish towns and build cities. Have the cities fit the land, let the land fit the population, let the population fit the produce. When these three fit each other, it is possible to keep secure within, and possible to win at war outside.

Land is the means of supporting the population, walled cities are the means of defending the land, warfare is the means of defending cities. Therefore if you see to the tilling, the populace will not hunger; if you see to defense, the land won't be imperiled; if you see to warfare, cities won't be surrounded.

Master Wei Liao

INFLUENCE WITHOUT AGGRESSION

Making clear what is forbidden and what is allowed, what will work and what will not, attract disenfranchised people and utilize unused land. If the land is extensive and put to use, the country grows rich; if the people are numerous and orderly, then the nation will be peaceful. A wealthy and peaceful nation can influence the global order without aggression.

Master Wei Liao

BASIC TASKS

We coordinate our directives and clarify our penalties and rewards, so that no one gets to eat without producing and no one attains rank without fighting, causing the people to compete enthusiastically in agriculture and warfare, so none in the world can oppose us.

These things were the basic tasks of ancient kings; among these basic tasks, warfare is most urgent. Therefore ancient kings focused on the military in five regards: if supplies are not abundant, then operations cannot be carried out; if rewards are not generous, then the people will not be encouraged; if warriors are not specially selected, the troops will not be strong; if equipment is not on hand, power will not be full; if penalties and rewards are not appropriate, the troops will not be wary. Those who see to these five things can maintain their holdings while at rest and can obtain what they want when they go into action.

When you are on the defense and go on the offense, your defense must be secure, your battle lines must be firm, your attacks must be all-out, and your combat must be coordinated.

Master Wei Liao

INSCRUTABILITY

When you master warfare, you are as though hidden in the earth, as if far out in space, emerging from nothing.

Master Wei Liao

WHEN TO ACT

A military operation should not be initiated in a state of excitement. If you see victory, then you mobilize; if not, you desist.

Master Wei Liao

LEADERSHIP

A commander is not ruled by heaven above, not ruled by earth below, and not ruled by other people. He is mellow and cannot be needled into anger; he is pure and cannot be bribed. If you let the crazy, blind, and deaf lead others, there's trouble!

Master Wei Liao

PREPARATION

When the trouble is within a hundred miles, you do not mobilize a day's force. If the trouble is within a thousand miles, you do not mobilize a month's force. When the trouble is global, you do not mobilize a year's force.

Master Wei Liao

PRUDENCE

If a bandit is swinging a sword in the middle of town, everyone will run away. I don't think that means one man is brave while everyone else is a bunch of cowards. Why? Because there's a difference between life and death.

Master Wei Liao

DIPLOMATIC DEBILITATION

The reason the nation is troubled is that valuable resources are spent on diplomatic presents, beloved children are sent out as diplomatic hostages, and territory is diplomatically ceded, in order to get reinforcements from all over. In name they may number a hundred thousand, but in reality they are not more than several tens of thousands. When those troops arrive, they all tell their commanders that there is no reason for them to be the first to fight. In reality, they are not able to fight.

Master Wei Liao

THE HIDDEN KEY

We put the world's goods to our own use, we organize the world's organizations for our organization.

Master Wei Liao

WINNING WARS

Wars might be won by strategy, by threat, or by force. When you cultivate military training and size up enemies so well as to cause them to lose their spirits so their armies dissolve, and though fully prepared you do not need to act, that is winning by strategy.

When you maintain precise order, make rewards and penalties clear, prepare equipment and supplies, and induce a fighting spirit in the people, that is winning by threat.

When you destory armies and kill their commanders, storm ramparts and unleash catapults, expelling populations and taking their territories, returning only after succeeding, that is winning by force.

Master Wei Liao

SPIRIT

What enables commanders to go to war is the people; what enables the people to go to war is spirit. When they are full of spirit, they fight; when their spirit is taken away, they run.

There are five ways to dispirit enemies before setting upon them and clashing. First is the issue of strategy. Second is the issue of mobilization. Third is the issue of crossing borders. Fourth is the issue of fortification and defense. Fifth is the issue of formation and offense.

These five things should be put into action after first sizing up enemies so as to dispirit them by striking their gaps. Those who are skilled at warfare are able to dispirit others without being dispirited by others. Dispiriting is a mental mechanism.

Master Wei Liao

ORDERS

Orders are for unifying a multitude. If the multitude does not clearly understand, then there will be repeated changes; when there are repeated changes, even if orders are issued the multitude will not trust them.

Therefore the rule for giving others is that they are not changed on account of minor errors and not reissued on account of minor questions. Thus when the leadership issues unhesitating orders, then the group listens with undivided attention; when it acts without hesitation, the group has no divided will.

Master Wei Liao

TRUST

Those who led the people in ancient times could never have gotten their power without winning their trust; they could never have gotten them to fight to the death without getting their power.

Therefore a nation must have principles of courtesy, faithfulness, and friendliness; then it can exchange hunger for sufficiency. A nation must have customs of respect, kindness, and modesty; then it can exchange death for life.

Those who led the people in ancient times put courtesy and faithfulness before rank and salary, modesty before discipline, and friendliness before regulation.

Master Wei Liao

INSPIRATION BY EXAMPLE

Those who make war must inspire their troops by their own example, like the mind employing the limbs. If they are not inspired, soldiers will not die for the cause; if the soldiers will not die for the cause, the army will not fight.

On a toilsome campaign, commanders must not put themselves first. In the heat they should not spread canopies, in the cold they should not double their clothing. On precipitous paths, they should dismount and walk; they should drink only after the troops' wells have been made, eat only after the soldiers' food has been cooked, and pitch camp only after the soldiers' camp is set. They must share the same hardship and ease; that way, even if the campaign goes on for a long time, the troops will not wane away and wear out.

Master Wei Liao

GROUP INTEGRITY

A military force is firm when calm, victorious when united. Those whose power is divided are weak, those who are suspicious fall out: therefore they are not robust in their movements, and they let their enemies escape their grip.

The commanders, officers, and soldiers are like a body in their actions: when they have doubts and suspicions in their minds, then even if plans are determined, they are not acted on; and when action is decided on, there is no control. There are divergent opinions, empty talk, commanders without dignity and soldiers without discipline, guaranteed to fail if they launch a seige. This is called an unhealthy army, incompetent to fight.

Master Wei Liao

THE HEART

The leader is the heart, the followers are the limbs and joints. If the heart acts truthfully, the limbs and joints will be strong; if the heart acts suspiciously, the limbs will rebel.

If the leadership is not disciplined of heart, the soldiery is not active of limb; even if they win a victory, it is a lucky win, not the strategy of the attack.

Master Wei Liao

AFFECTION AND RESPECT

You cannot employ people you cannot please; you cannot mobilize people you cannot impress by sternness. Where there is affection, underlings obey; where there is respect, leadership is established. Because of affection, there is no division; because of respect, there is no offense. Therefore leadership is a matter of affection and respect.

Master Wei Liao

Overflowing and Leaking

A kingdom enriches its commoners, a hegemony enriches its gentry; a barely surviving nation enriches its grandees, a moribund nation enriches its treasury. That is called overflowing on top while leaking at the bottom—nothing will help when calamity comes.

Master Wei Liao

Respect and Disrespect, Victory and Defeat

When your people respect you, they disrespect your enemies; if they respect your enemies, they disrespect you. The one who is disrespected loses, while the one whose dignity is established wins. If the commanders are capable, the officers respect the commanders; when the officers respect the commanders, the common people respect the officers; when the common people respect the officers, their enemies respect those people. Therefore to know the course of victory and defeat, it is necessary to first know the workings of respect and disrespect.

Master Wei Liao

Trust and Efficiency

If you are not sure of winning a battle, don't talk of fighting. If you are not sure to take the object of a siege, don't talk of attack. Otherwise, even if penalties and awards are announced, that cannot win trust.

Trust must be there before you can make plans; events must be foreseen before they happen. So a group that has gathered does not disperse without doing anything, an army that has gone forth does not come back without doing anything: they stalk enemies as one would look for a lost child, and strike enemies as one would save a drowning man.

Master Wei Liao

Psychological Weaknesses

Those imprisoned in narrow straits haven't the heart to fight; those who spoil for fights are deficient in spirit; those who are belligerent have no victorious army.

Master Wei Liao

FIGHTING

Whenever you fight for justice, the initiative should come from yourself.

You should engage in hostilities in private competition only when it cannot be helped.

When trouble arises from antagonism, you should not make the first move but wait and see what happens first. Therefore when there is a dispute, you should wait watchfully; while there is peace, you should prepare yourself.

Master Wei Liao

WINNING

Some military operations win victory at court, some win victory in the field, some win victory in the market. If you fight unsuccessfully but are lucky enough not to get beat, this is a partial victory by unexpectedly getting at an opponent's fears. Partial victory means it is not complete; one whose victory is incomplete is not known for strategy.

Master Wei Liao

DEFENSE

When on the defense, if you fight back without being able to advance beyond your own walls or retreat into your strongholds, that is not good. If you have all the warriors, armor, and weaponry concentrated inside your walls and then take in the storage depots and dismantle the houses of the people and bring them into the city, that will inflame the invaders' spirit while dampening the defenders' spirit. If the enemy attacks, it will cause a lot of casualties. Nevertheless, the commanders of the age do not know this.

Master Wei Liao

DEFINITIONS

Dignity is a matter of not changing. Generosity is a matter of timing. Cleverness is a matter of responding to events. Combat is a matter of mastering spirit. Attack is a matter of unexpectedness. Defense is a matter of external array. Impeccability is a matter of measure and calculation. Stamina is a matter of preparation. Prudence is a matter of wariness of the small. Wisdom is a matter of management of the great. Getting rid of pests is a matter of decisiveness. Winning followers is a matter of being humble to others.

Regret is in trusting the dubious. Evil is in massacre. Bias is in selfishness. Misfortune is in hating to hear one's own faults. Excess is in exhausting the wealth of the people. Unclarity is in admitting interlopers. Insubstantiality is in acting out too easily. Narrowmindedness is in alienating the intelligent. Calamity is in profiteering. Injury is in familiarity with petty people. Ruin is in not having any defense. Peril is in having no order.

Master Wei Liao

ETHICS OF WARFARE

In general, a military force is not to attack an inoffensive city and does not kill innocent people. To kill people's fathers and brothers, to profit from people's money and goods, and to enslave people's sons and daughters are all robbery.

Therefore the military is to execute the violent and unruly and to stop injustice. Where a military force attacks, the farmers do not leave their work in the fields, the merchants do not leave their shops, the officials do not leave their offices: since the target of the military is only the top man, the soldiers do not have to bloody their blades for everyone to be won over.

Master Wei Liao

PRIORITIES

A large country emphasizes farming and fighting; a middling country emphasizes relief and defense; a small country emphasizes business and livelihood. With farming and fighting, they don't seek external power; with relief and defense, they don't seek external help; with business and livelihood, they don't seek external resources.

Master Wei Liao

BUSINESS

Those who can neither fight nor defend should be assigned to business; business is a means of providing for warfare and defense. Even if a large country does not have reinforcements equivalent to a middling country, it will invariably have a market equivalent to a small country.

Master Wei Liao

PUNISHMENT AND REWARD

Penalties and rewards are means of showing martial prowess. If the armed forces can all be made to shudder at the execution of one man, kill him; if ten thousand people can be gladened by awarding one man a prize, then give him a prize. The most impressive executions are of important people; the most impressive rewards are those given to lesser people.

When those who deserve to be executed are invariably executed even if they are high-ranking, important people, that means punishment reaches all the way upward; if awards are given even to cowherds and horse grooms, that means rewards flow downward. To be able to penalize the highest echelons and reward the lowest ranks is the martial prowess of a military commander; that is the reason leaders of men take commanders seriously.

Master Wei Liao

THE BURDEN OF LEADERSHIP

It is the military commanders who give the call to arms, deciding to fight when they face difficulty, engaging in combat with armies. If their call to arms is right, they are rewarded for their achievement and become famous; if their call is not right, then they themselves die and the country is ruined. The question of survival and ruin, security and peril, is the reason for the call to arms—how can military leadership not be considered a serious matter?

Master Wei Liao

INCOMPETENCE

An ancient said, "They attack without war chariots, defend without barbed wire." This refers to incompetent armies. When there is nothing to be seen or heard, it is because the country has no commercial organization. Commercial organization means management of goods.

Buying cheap and selling dear constricts the people of the middle and lower classes. When the people look hungry and their horses are emaciated, what does this mean? The market has produce but its regulation is unsupervised. Any who run vast political systems without regulating commerce would not be considered able to do battle.

Master Wei Liao

PERILS OF POWER

A military commander is not controlled by heaven above, not controlled by earth below, not controlled by people in between. That is why armaments are instruments of ill omen, fighting is a vice, a general is an officer of death, and these are employed only when unavoidable. There is no heaven above, no earth below, no ruler behind, no adversary in front: an army that is as one man is like a wolf, like a tiger, like wind, like rain, like thunder, like lightning; when it rumbles ominously, the whole world is frightened.

Master Wei Liao

COHESION AND CONSISTENCY

Winning armies are like water. Water is extremely soft, but where it touches, even hills will be eroded by it, for no other reason than that it is cohesive by nature and its pressure is constantly applied.

Master Wei Liao

MANNERS OF WARRIORS

When Wu Qi warred with Qin, he didn't have bordered fields leveled for bunkers, he just used brushwood for cover against frost and dew. Why? Because he did not elevate himself over others. When you are asking people to die, you don't demand their reverence; when you are using people's strength, you don't complain of their manners.

Therefore in ancient times warriors in armor didn't bow, to show people that no one could put them to a lot of bother. I have never heard of a case, past or present, where anyone could bother people and hope to ask them to die and use all their strength.

Master Wei Liao

COMMAND

The day a general gets his orders, he forgets his home; when an army camps in the field, the troops forget their families; when the signal drum is sounded, they forget themselves.

When Wu Qi was overseeing a battle, an attendant presented a sword. Wu Qi said, "A general's only job is to give directions. Solving doubts in the face of trouble, conducting the troops and directing their blades—that is the work of a general. Wielding an individual sword is not the business of a general."

Master Wei Liao

ORDER

When Wu Qi was warring with Qin, before the armies clashed, one man who could not contain his boldness went out and took two enemy heads. When he came back, Wu Qi was going to execute him on the spot. The military inspector admonished him, "This is a talented soldier—he should not be executed." Wu Qi said, "He may be a talented soldier all right, but that was not my order." And he executed him.

Master Wei Liao

SUBJECTIVITY AND EGOISM

Military leadership is a directorate, in charge of myriads of people, so it is not to be affected by the subjective whims of one individual. If you are not an egomaniac, all sorts of people can come to you and you can organize them; all sorts of people can come to you and you can direct them.

Master Wei Liao

GETTING INFORMATION

If you carefully examine the circumstances, expressions, emotions, and states of mind of prisoners, then you can find out the truth about them without beating it out of them. If you flog people's backs, brand people's sides, and thumbscrew people's fingers, even among soldiers of national distinction there would be those who would make false confessions because they could not bear the torture.

Master Wei Liao

BRIBERY

There's a contemporary saying, "For a thousand pieces of gold, you won't be executed; for a hundred pieces of gold, you won't be imprisoned." Try to listen to my words and follow my methods: then even the smartest wits will not be able to speak a false word, and even if they had ten thousand pieces of gold they couldn't spend a bit in bribes.

Master Wei Liao

SOCIAL AND POLITICAL ORDER

Officials in charge of affairs are basic to social order. Organization means division of labor, which is part of social order. High ranks and large salaries must be fitting; that is the substance of hierarchy. Favoring the good, punishing the bad, and making census methods correct are tools for taking account of the populace. Equalizing land distribution and regulating taxes are standards of taking and giving. Regulating artisans and providing tools and equipment is the achievement of master craftsmen. Drawing boundaries and building barricades is for eliminating the suspicious and stopping the excessive and the obscene.

Master Wei Liao

THE PRISON POPULATION

Now those who are incarcerated number in the dozens in small jails, in the hundreds in middle-sized prisons, and in the thousands in large penitentiaries. Ten people are occupied in the custody of a hundred people, a hundred people are occupied in the custody of a thousand people, a thousand people are occupied in the custody of ten thousand people. Those who are in their custody are their relatives and brothers, their relatives by marriage, their acquaintances and friends.

So the farmers are taken away from their work in the fields, the merchants are taken away from their shops, the officials are taken away from their offices. Thus the law-abiding people involved are all in a state of incarceration. According to the laws of warfare, the mobilization of a force of a hundred thousand costs a thousand pieces of gold a day. Now there are a hundred thousand law-abiding citizens involved in the prison system; if the government cannot reduce this, I consider that dangerous.

Master Wei Liao

RULERSHIP AND ADMINISTRATION

Maintaining the law, investigating and judging, are duties of administrators; promulgating laws and examining their effects are operations of rulers. Clarifying charges and unifying standards are strategies of administrators and rulers.

Clear rewards and strict punishments are methods of stopping treachery. Examining what to encourage and what to prohibit, keeping to one path, are essentials for government. Effective communication between lower and upper echelons is all-hearing attentiveness.

Knowing what the country has and has not, use the surplus. Knowing others' weaknesses is the essence of strength; knowing others' movements determines stillness. Offices are divided into the civil and the military; these are the two methods of rulership.

Master Wei Liao

ECONOMIC FUNDAMENTALISM

What is there to governing people? They must have food to eat and clothes to wear. So it is a matter of having grain to fill their stomachs and cloth to cover their bodies.

When husbands plow and wives spin, and the peasants do nothing else, then there are surpluses. The men do not engage in painting or sculpture, the women do not embroider fancy sashes. Wooden vessels leak, metal vessels smell; sages cooked in earthenware and ate from earthenware: so if earthen vessels are used there will be no waste.

Master Wei Liao

LAPSE

Now metal and wood vessels naturally do not themselves feel cold, yet people put brocaded coverings over them; horses and oxen naturally eat grasses and drink water, yet they are given beans and millet.

This government has lost its basis; regulations should be established. If the men go out into the fields in the spring and summer and the women make cloth in the fall and winter, then the peasants will not suffer hardship. Now their clothes are inadequate to cover their bodies, dregs and bran won't fill their stomachs; order has been lost.

In ancient times, there were no questions of relative fertility of land or relative diligence of the people. What did the ancients have that people today have lost? If the fields are not completely plowed and the looms are stopped every day, what can be done about cold and hunger? What was practiced in ancient government has lapsed in modern government.

Master Wei Liao

EMPERORS

There are four qualifications for being an emperor: genius, generosity, order, and inviolability.

Master Wei Liao

KINGS OF YORE

According to legends of kings of yore, they commissioned the upright, dismissed the dishonest, gave security to the genial and harmonious, and passed judgments without delay.

Master Wei Liao

TOTAL DEDICATION

Total dedication is a matter of spiritual clarity. Military strategy is a matter of attaining the Way. When what is there is made to seem as if it were not, and what is not there is made to seem as if it were, how can this be trusted?

Master Wei Liao

QUALITIES OF GOVERNMENTS

Consultants today say, "A hundred-league ocean cannot provide even one man with enough to drink, whereas a three-foot spring can quench the thirst of three armies." It seems to me that greediness is born of immoderation, perversity is born of unruliness.

The finest government is by spiritual influence; the next adapts to actualities; the lowest is a matter of not depriving the people of their time and not diminishing the people's possessions. Prohibitions are established by force, awards are established by culture.

Master Wei Liao

STRATEGY AND FORCE

According to the laws of warfare, a thousand men can succeed by strategy, ten thousand men can succeed by force. When you apply strategy to others first, enemies will not clash with you; when you apply force to others first, enemies will not confront you. Therefore in warfare it is important to be first: if you win at this, you will win over others; if you do not win at this, you will not win over others.

Master Wei Liao

AGGRESSIVENESS

Those who know the Way must first take into account the failure of not knowing where to stop; they reject the idea that aggressive action will necessarily have success.

If you seek battle at the drop of a hat, your opponent will then be still, calculating; if you go ahead, your opponent has secured victory.

Therefore the art of warfare dictates that if you follow enemies in pursuit, attacking them on sight, and their leaders do not seem willing to put up a fight, you are losing to their strategy.

Those who have been outmaneuvered are dispirited; those who are intimidated are vulnerable. When people disappear from the losing side, it is because their army did not have the Way.

When you can proceed deliberately without doubt, then you go ahead. When you can outmaneuver an enemy without fail, then you do it. When you can see clearly and remain out of reach, then you overawe others. This is the consummation of military science.

Master Wei Liao

SUPREMACY WITHOUT COMBAT

If soldiers' talk is indiscreet, they are not serious; if they are bellicose and aggressive without reason, they are bound to crumble. If they attack in bursts and blitzes, their cohorts will be confused. It is necessary to secure dangerous conditions and get rid of problems, resolving them wisely.

Elevate your soldiers' pride in their nation, increase their sense of the importance of their mission, and sharpen their sense of responsibility. Then enemy nations can be subdued without combat.

Master Wei Liao

SEVERE PENALTIES

Military commanders of more than a thousand people who lose in battle, who surrender when on the defensive, who don't stand their ground but desert their troops, are condemned as thieves of the nation. They are executed, their families are destroyed, their birth records are discarded, their ancestral tombs are dug up, their bones are exposed in public, and their sons and daughters are made state slaves.

Those in command of more than a hundred people who lose in battle, surrender when on the defensive, or abandon their ground and desert their troops are condemned as thieves of the army. They are put to death, their families are destroyed, and their children are enslaved.

If the people are caused to be wary of severe punishments at home, they will think lightly of enemies abroad. Therefore kings of yore clarified regulations at the outset and punished severely and sternly afterward. When punishment is severe, there is internal wariness, and the inwardly wary are outwardly firm.

Master Wei Liao

MUTUAL SURETY SYSTEM

In the organization of the military, five people are a team; the members of the team are surety for each other. Ten people are a squad; the members of the squad are surety for each other. Fifty people make a band; the members of the band are surety for each other. One hundred people make a group; the members of the group are surety for each other.

If a team has members who violate orders or break rules, the others are exempted from punishment if they report it; if they know but don't report it, the whole team is punished. If a squad has members who violate orders or break rules, the others are exempt from punishment if they report it; if they know but do not report it, the whole squad is punished.

If a band has members who violate orders or break rules, the others are exempted from punishment if they report it; if they know but don't report it, the whole band is punished. If a group has members who violate orders or break rules, the others are exempted from punishment if they report it; if they know but don't report it, the whole group is punished.

The officers, from squad leaders to major generals, are all surety for each other: if any violate orders or break rules, those who report it escape punishment, whereas those who know but do not report it are subject to the same punishment.

When the teams and squads are linked and the upper and lower echelons are connected, there is no treachery that is not found out, no wrongdoing that is not reported. Fathers cannot favor their own sons, elder brothers cannot favor their younger brothers. Especially when countrymen lodge together and eat together, how can there be any violation of orders or personal favoritism?

Master Wei Liao

EXTREME TEAMWORK

The rule for binding teams is as follows: Five people make a team, with the same insignia, assigned to a commanding officer. If they lose part of their team but take out a team, these are weighed against each other. If they take out a team without loss, there is an award. If they lose part of their team without taking out a team, they are executed and their families are killed.

If a squad or group chief is lost but a chief is taken out, these are weighed against each other. If a chief is taken out without loss, then there is a reward. If a chief is lost without taking out a chief, the responsible ones are executed and their families are killed, unless they go back into battle and take the head of an enemy chief, which will absolve them.

If a commander is lost in taking out an enemy commander, these are weighed against each other. If an enemy commander is taken out with no losses, there is a reward. If a commander is lost while failing to take out an enemy commander, the responsible ones are charged with desertion.

Master Wei Liao

WARTIME DISCIPLINE

The rule for punishment in wartime is as follows: A squad leader can punish ten people, a group chief can punish a squad leader, a commander of a thousand can punish a chief of a hundred, a commander of ten thousand can punish a commander of a thousand. The generals of the left and right can punish a commander of ten thousand, and a generalissimo can punish anyone.

Master Wei Liao

TIMELINESS

Make decisions as soon as possible, before your enemies do. If your plans are not determined first and your concerns are not quickly resolved, then your maneuvers are uncertain; when hesitation arises, you'll lose out. Therefore an orthodox military operation values preemption, while a surprise military operation values follow-up. Whether to preempt or follow up is a matter of which will overcome the enemy.

Master Wei Liao

THREE HANDICAPS IN WAR

Military commanders of the world who do not know the art of war and who act on their own, taking bold initiatives, are all losers. They do not question questionable things in their operations, they doubt what is certain in their campaigns, they do not slow down and speed up when they need to. These three are handicaps in war.

Master Wei Liao

SENDING THE PEOPLE TO WAR

There is a way to get the people to leave their country to decide issues of life and death, teaching them so that they would go to their death without hesitation. Make sure the defenders are firm, the fighters are combative, interlopers don't act, and liars don't speak. Let orders be carried out without changes, let the troops move without speculation.

Master Wei Liao

TWELVE WAYS OF WINNING VICTORY

There are twelve ways of winning victory, by which it is possible to annex and expand territory and unify a system so that it overpowers everyone:

1. Collective punishment—members of surety teams share mutual responsibility for crimes
2. Area restriction—travel is prohibited so as to net outside interlopers
3. Orderly linking of armored vehicles and infantry
4. Building border fortifications, defended by warriors who will stay at their posts even to their deaths
5. Formation of divisions—left and right watch out for each other, vanguard and rear guard depend on each other, with a wall of armored vehicles for security, to attack and to defend
6. Distinction of signals, so that as the forward lines strive to advance, they are distinguished from the backup such that there is not a disorderly rush in a struggle to be first
7. Insignia to show the order of the lines, so the first and the last are not confused
8. Complete organization, meaning intricate coordination, with everyone having a part
9. Cymbals and drums—effective at arousing and instilling power
10. Arraying armored vehicles—a solid front line, with blinders on the horses
11. Warriors willing to die—talented and strong warriors to man the battle chariots, going back and forth and every which way, coming out with surprise maneuvers to overcome enemies
12. Strong soldiers who man the banners and keep the battalions together, not moving without orders

When these twelve things are taught and established, those who violate the order are not to be pardoned. Then if the army is weak it can be strengthened; a ruler from a lower class can be ennobled; deteriorated order can be revived; disenfranchised people can be attracted; large masses of people can be governed; and large expanses of territory can be maintained. The whole world will be awed, even without aggressive action.

Master Wei Liao

THE ART OF THE ATTACK

When you attack a country, you must take advantage of its changes. Observe its economy to see its deficits; observe its corruption to see its problems. When those above are perverse and those below are alienated, this is a basis for attacking it.

Master Wei Liao

TARGETING PRIORITIES

Where the land is large but the cities small, first take the land; where the cities are large and the land is restricted, first attack the cities. Where the territory is extensive but the population small, cut off the passes; where the territory is small but the population large, build massive earth rings against them.

Master Wei Liao

CAUSING THE PEOPLE TO THRIVE

Do not nullify their gains, do not take their time; govern them liberally, facilitate their work, and help them with their problems: then you can command the world.

Master Wei Liao

MORALITY OF WARFARE

Weapons are instruments of ill omen; contention is a vice. Things must have a basis, so kings strike the violent and unruly, based on humaneness and justice.

Warring states try to establish their prestige, resist adversaries, and plot against each other, so they cannot do without armaments.

Master Wei Liao

MARTIAL AND CULTURAL FUNCTIONS

Military prowess forms the beams of the army, culture forms the pillars. Military prowess is outside, culture is inside. Those who can discern these know who will win and lose. Culture is the means of seeing what is beneficial and what is harmful, what is safe and what is dangerous; military prowess is the means of attacking strong enemies and empowering offense and defense.

Master Wei Liao

CONSCRIPT ARMIES

Those whose soldiers fear their commanders more than their enemies will win, while those whose soldiers fear their enemies more than their commanders will lose.

If soldiers show up for duty even a day late, their parents, wives, and children are all equally guilty. If soldiers go absent without official leave to return to their homes for even a day, their parents, wives, and children are equally guilty if they do not arrest them and report them.

Master Wei Liao

UNITY

Unity leads to victory, disunity leads to defeat.

Master Wei Liao

CALMNESS

The calm are orderly; a mad rush leads to chaos.

Master Wei Liao

DESERTION

Soldiers who desert their commanders, and officers who desert their troops, are all to be executed. If an officer in front deserts his troops, an officer in back will be rewarded if he can cut him down and take over command of his troops. Those who do not achieve anything in the army are to be posted at the borders for three years.

Master Wei Liao

ENFORCING PERFORMANCE

When all three armies engage in a major battle, if the top general dies and the commanders of at least five hundred men cannot resist the enemy to the death, they are executed. The top general's right and left guards at the front are all executed. As for the other soldiers, those who served well in combat are only demoted one grade, while those who did not are posted to the frontier for three years.

Master Wei Liao

THREE EXCELLENCES

If regulations stop absence without official leave and prevent desertion, this is one excellence in an army. If the teams and squads are linked together and the soldiers and officers assist each other in battle, this is a second excellence in an army. If the commanders effectively establish their authority and the soldiers are disciplined and orderly, signals and orders are clear and trustworthy, and offense and defense are both competent, this is a third excellence in an army.

Master Wei Liao

MOTIVATION

I have heard that those skilled at employing armies in ancient times could get half their soldiers to fight to the death; the next best could get three out of ten to fight to the death; the least could get one out of ten to fight to the death. Those who could get half their soldiers to fight to the death can threaten a whole continent; those who can get three out of ten to fight to the death can overpower sundry lords. As for those who can get one out of ten to fight to the death, their orders are carried out by both officers and soldiers.

Master Wei Liao

COMMON CAUSE

The methods of leadership are to strive to capture the hearts of valiant heroes, reward achievement, and convey intentions to the masses. Therefore anything that is liked in common with the masses can be accomplished, and anything that is disliked in common with the masses can be demolished. Governing the nation and making the home secure are matters of winning people; ruining the nation and destroying the family are due to losing people. All living creatures want to get their will.

Three Strategies

SOFT AND HARD

Military Indicators says, "The soft can overcome the hard, the weak can overcome the strong. Softness is benign, hardness is malignant. The weak are helped by others, the strong are attacked by enemies. There is a place to feign softness, a place to exercise hardness, a place to employ weakness, and a place to apply strength: include all four, and use whichever is best according to the circumstances."

Military Indicators says, "If it can be soft and can be hard, that country will flourish more and more. If it can be weak and can be strong, that country will thrive more and more. If it is only soft or only weak, that country will deteriorate; if it is only hard or only strong, that country will perish."

Three Strategies

THE SUBTLE

It is said, "Everyone craves power, but few can keep the subtle." If you can keep the subtle, you can safeguard your life. Sages maintain this, acting in response to the triggers of events. When they roll it out, it extends throughout the continent; when they roll it up, it does not even fill a cup. They house it without a house, protect it without walls; they hide it in their hearts, and opponents submit to them.

Three Strategies

ADAPTATION

Change according to adversaries, not taking the initiative but following up on their moves.

Three Strategies

COORDINATION

The way to manage a country is particularly a matter of the elite and the commoners. When you can trust the elite like your own heart and employ the commoners like your four limbs, then no strategy will fail. Wherever you go you will be like limbs and body following each other, bones and joints helping each other; spontaneously following the course of nature, that skill is impeccable.

Three Strategies

CASE BY CASE

Essential to military and civil government is to observe the mentalities of the people in order to distribute the jobs.

The imperiled are to be given security, the fearful are to be humored. Deserters are to be won back, the falsely accused are to be absolved, those with complaints are to be given a hearing.

The lowly are to be elevated, the powerful are to be restrained, the hostile are to be eliminated. The greedy are enriched, the ambitious are employed.

The frightened are sheltered, the crafty are befriended. Slanderers are silenced, critics are tested. Rebels are rejected, the violent are broken down. The self-satisfied are criticized, the submissive are welcomed. The conquered are settled, those who surrender are freed.

Fastnesses taken are held, defiles taken are blocked, inaccessible places taken are garrisoned, cities taken are partitioned, land taken is divided, goods taken are distributed.

Three Strategies

MILITARY METHODS

Enemy movements are watched, preparations are made when enemies approach: when enemies are at ease, they are avoided; when enemies are overbearing, they are waited out; when enemies are violent, they are placated. When enemies are obstreperous, they are treated with justice; when enemies are friendly, they are made allies.

Break them down as they rise up, smash them when there is an opportunity; release statements to mislead them, catch them by dragnet.

Acquire without possessing, dwell without staying, siege without prolonging, stand without taking. The one who does it is yourself, while the ones who take possession are the officers; who knows where the profit is? They become the lords, while you become the emperor, having the cities secure themselves and having the officers make their own exactions.

Three Strategies

RESPECT AND REMUNERATION

The key to employing an army is to respect order and pay well. If you respect order, intelligent people will come; pay well, and dutiful warriors will readily risk death. So pay the intelligent ungrudgingly and reward achievement promptly; then the lower echelons will pull together and enemy nations will weaken.

The way to employ people is to honor them with ranks and provide for them financially; then knights will come on their own. Treat them with courtesy, inspire them with justice, and the knights will risk death for you.

Three Strategies

FOLLOWING ORDERS

Military Indicators says, "The means by which commanders exert authority is by issuing orders. The means by which a battle is won completely is by order in the army. The reason officers will readily fight is that they are following orders. Therefore commanders do not rescind orders, and rewards and penalties are sure as heaven and earth; then they can command others. When officers and soldiers follow orders, then they can cross the borders.

Three Strategies

GOING STALE

It is the general who leads the army and maintains its form; it is the troops who seize victory and overcome enemies. Therefore an undisciplined general cannot be employed to superintend an army, and unruly troops cannot be employed to attack others. Otherwise they will not succeed in taking the cities they seize or in conquering the towns they surround. Unsuccessful at both, the soldiers will tire, so the general will be isolated and the troops rebellious—then they will be unsure at defense and will flee in combat. This is called a stale army.

When an army goes stale, the general's authority is ineffective; when the general has no authority, then the officers and soldiers slight the rules. When the officers and soldiers slight the rules, the team organization is lost. When team organization is lost, then officers and soldiers run away. When soldiers run away, enemies take advantage. When enemies take advantage, then the army will perish.

Three Strategies

ORGANIZATION AND AUTHORITY

Military Indicators says, "The army has reward on the outside, punishment on the inside. When rewards and punishments are clear, then the authority of the commander is effective. When offices are filled by the right people, then the soldiers obey. When those to whom authority is delegated are intelligent, then enemy nations tremble."

Three Strategies

EFFECTS OF ATTITUDE

Military Indicators says, "Wherever the intelligent go, there are no opponents before them. Therefore officers should be humble, not arrogant; commanders should be cheerful, not anxious; planning should be deeply hidden, not suspicious. If officers are arrogant, their subordinates will not obey them. If commanders are anxious, then those on the inside and outside will not trust each other. If planning is suspected, enemy nations will be aroused."

Three Strategies

THE CHARACTER OF A COMMANDER

Military Indicators says, "A commander is pure, calm, fair, orderly, receptive to advice, listens to complaints, recruits people, samples opinions, knows the customs of nations, can depict the landscape and show the dangers and difficulties, and is able to control the direction of the army. Therefore it is said, 'Commanders should listen to the wisdom of the humane and intelligent, the thoughts of sages and illuminates, the words of peasants, the statements of officials, the things that have to do with flourishing and decline.' "

Three Strategies

ADVICE AND PLANNING

If commanders take their advisers seriously, their plans will be followed. If commanders refuse advice, then valiant heroes will drift away. If plans are not followed, planners will rebel. If good and bad are treated equally, then meritorious administrators will be discouraged.

When the commander is autocratic, subordinates lay all blame on him; when he takes all the credit for himself, his subordinates accomplish little. If he believes slanderers, the troops will become alienated at heart. If he is greedy for money, then conniving cannot be stopped.

Three Strategies

CONFIDENTIALITY, UNITY, AND ALACRITY

Military Indicators says, "The plans of the commander should be confidential; the officers and men should be unified; attacks on enemies should be swift." When the plans of the commander are confidential, then traitors cannot get ideas. When the officers and men are unified, then the army is psychologically cohesive. When attacks on enemies are swift, then they will not have time to prepare against them. If an army has these three things, its plans will not be thwarted.

Three Strategies

LEAKS, GAPS, AND BRIBES

If the commander's plans leak out, then the army will have no power. If outsiders can see inside, then calamity cannot be stopped. When bribe money enters camp, then the dishonest collect. If commanders have these three things, the army is sure to lose.

Three Strategies

FLAWS IN COMMANDERS

If commanders are thoughtless, planners will leave. If commanders lack bravery, officers will be afraid. If commanders move arbitarily, their armies will not be calm. If commanders take out their anger on others, the whole army will be fearful.

Three Strategies

Psychological and Material Inducements

Military Indicators says, "Where there is tasty bait, there will be hooked fish; where there are serious rewards, there will be men willing to risk their lives. Therefore courtesy is what soldiers take to, rewards are what soldiers risk death for. Invite them to what they resort to, show them what to risk death for, and those who are sought will come. Therefore if you treat them courteously but afterward regret it, soldiers will not stay. If you reward them but afterward regret it, soldiers will not serve. If you do not slack off courtesy and rewards, then soldiers will eagerly risk their lives."

Three Strategies

Knowing the Enemy

Military Indicators says, "Essential to military operations is prior examination of the condition of the enemy. See their stores, calculate their food supplies, figure out their strengths and weaknesses, examine their climate and terrain, search out their voids and gaps."

Three Strategies

Benefits and Popularity

Military Indicators says, "A country that is going to launch a military operation must first grant many benefits; a country that is going to lay a siege must first cherish its people. What enables few to overcome many is appreciation of benefits; what enables the weaker to overcome the stronger is popularity. Therefore good commanders treat the soldiers no different from the way they treat themselves. Thus, if you can command the three armies as if they were of one mind, your victory can be total."

Three Strategies

Oppression

Military Indicators says, "When superiors act cruelly, subordinates are peremptory and harsh. When taxes and levies are heavy and numerous, punishments are unlimited, and the people prey on each other, that is called a lost nation."

Three Strategies

CORRUPTION

Military Indicators says, "When officials cluster in cliques, each promoting their friends, nominating crooks for appointments, suppressing and thwarting the good and the intelligent, turning their backs on the public for the sake of their own private interests, slandering their colleagues, this is called a source of disorder."

Three Strategies

POWERFUL CLANS

Military Indicators says, "When powerful clans gather crafty villains, they become distinguished without having any official rank, making everyone tremble at their power. Like entangling vines, they get others indebted to them by selective favors; usurping the authority of those in office, they violate and abuse the common people. The country is in an uproar, but the government ministers conceal it and do not report it. This is called a root of disorder."

Three Strategies

DAMAGE AND HARM

Military Indicators says, "When there are disproportionately many officials in comparison with the size of the populace, or the noble and the base are on a par, or the strong victimize the weak, or no one follows controls, this affects the leadership, and the nation suffers consequent damage."

Military Indicators says, "When the good are recognized as good but are not promoted, the evil are recognized as evil but are not dismissed, the wise are obscured while the corrupt are in office, the nation suffers harm from that."

Three Strategies

SUBTLE STRATEGY

Military Indicators says, "Use intelligence, use bravery, use greed, use folly. Intellectuals like to establish their merit, the brave like to carry out their ambitions, the greedy seek profit, the foolish are unfazed by the risk of death. To use them according to their true conditions is the subtle strategy of warfare."

Three Strategies

THE EVOLUTION OF GOVERNMENT

The Three August Ones made no speeches, but their influence circulated everywhere, so the world had nowhere to attribute the merit.

As for the emperors, they emulated heaven and followed the laws of the earth; they made speeches and gave orders, so the world became very peaceful. The leaders and administrators deferred the merit to each other, so while their influence prevailed everywhere, the common people did not know why it was so. Therefore they employed administrators effectively without the need for ceremonies or prizes, getting along fine without impediment.

As for the kings, they governed people by means of the Way, conquering their hearts and winning their minds, establishing regulations to guard against corruption. Local leaders from all over convened, and tribute to the kings was kept up. Though they had military preparations, they had no warfare. The rulers were not suspicious of the administrators, and the administrators were not suspicious of the rulers. The country was stable, the ruler secure, the administrators retired when proper. They too could get along fine, without obstruction.

As for the hegemons, they governed men by means of strategy, mustered men by means of confidence, and employed men by means of awards. When confidence deteriorated, the men drifted away; when awards were lacking, the men would not obey orders.

Three Strategies

INTEGRITY AND DIGNITY

Leaders must have integrity, for if they lack integrity their administrators will defy them. Leaders must have dignity, for if they lack dignity they will lose their authority.

Three Strategies

FASCISM

Military Configurations says, "Do not let orators extol the virtues of adversaries, lest they confuse the masses. Do not put philanthropists in charge of finances, because they will give away a lot and win the adherence of the lower classes."

Three Strategies

CONSCIENCE

Military Configurations says, "You cannot employ righteous people just by money. Righteous men will not risk death for the inhumane, wise people will not devise strategies for ignorant rulers."

Three Strategies

SUBTERFUGE AND SECRECY

When sage kings rule the world, they observe flourishing and decline, assess gain and loss, and legislate accordingly. Therefore local lords have one army, regional overlords have three armies, and the emperor has six armies.

When society is chaotic, rebellion arises, government benefits dry up, and factions form and attack each other. If their merits are similar and their powers comparable, so they cannot overthrow each other, that is the time to capture the hearts and minds of heroic stalwarts, share the likes and dislikes of the masses, and then after that apply tactical adaptations.

So without strategy there is no way to settle confusion and doubt; if not for subterfuge and surprise there is no way to defeat treachery and stop enemies; without secret planning there is no way to achieve success.

Three Strategies

THE STRATEGY OF HEGEMONS

Once an army has been assembled, it cannot be dispersed abruptly; once authority has been granted, it cannot be transferred abruptly. Demobilizing an army is a life-and-death situation—weaken them with positions, undermine them with land grants: this is called the strategy of hegemons.

Three Strategies

THREE LEVELS OF STRATEGY

Sages emulate heaven, the wise emulate earth, the knowledgeable emulate ancients. Therefore three levels of strategy were devised for deteriorating societies.

Higher strategy establishes honors and awards, distinguishes frauds from stalwarts, clarifies the causes of victory and defeat, success and failure.

Intermediate strategy differentiates qualities and behaviors and analyzes strategic adaptations.

Lower strategy sets forth normative virtues, examines safety and danger, and clarifies the error of thwarting the wise.

So if leaders have a profound understanding of higher strategy, they are able to appoint the wise and capture enemies.

If they have a profound understanding of intermediate strategy, they can command generals and rule the troops.

If they have a profound understanding of lower strategy, they can understand the sources of flourishing and decline, and comprehend the principles of governing a nation.

If administrators have a deep understanding of intermediate strategy, they can complete their work and preserve themselves.

Three Strategies

BENEVOLENCE

Those who can help the world when in danger can thus establish peace in the world. Those who can eliminate the world's anxieties can thus experience the world's pleasures. Those who can save the world from calamity can thus obtain the blessings of the world.

So if your benevolence extends to the people, then wise men will take to you; if your benevolence reaches all creatures, then sages will take to you. If wise men take to you, your country will be strong; if sages take to you, the whole world will be united.

Seek wise men by integrity, bring sages by the Way. When wise men leave, then a country weakens; when sages leave, a country loses social cohesion. Weakness borders on peril; lack of social cohesion is a foresign of ruin.

Three Strategies

Mastery of Body and Mind

Government by the intelligent masters people physically; government by sages masters people mentally. By mastery of the body, it is possible to plan beginnings; by mastery of the mind, it is possible to guarantee ends.

Mastering the body is done by ritual, mastering the mind is done by enjoyment. Enjoyment does not mean music: it means people enjoy their homes, it means people enjoy their families, it means people enjoy their jobs, it means people enjoy their cities, it means people enjoy their social order, it means people enjoy their virtues.

Three Strategies

Teaching Others

Those who try to teach others while ignoring themselves are opposed. Those who teach others after having rectified themselves are obeyed. Opposition beckons disorder, obedience is key to order.

Three Strategies

Planning, Relaxation, and Security

If you leave aside the near at hand and plan for the remote, you will toil without success; if you leave aside the remote and plan for the near at hand, you will be at ease and yet will succeed.

A relaxed government has many loyal administrators; a burdensome government has many resentful people. Therefore it is said that those who strive to expand territory become destitute, while those who strive to expand benevolence become strong.

Those who can keep what they have are secure, while those who crave what others have are destroyed. The afflictions caused by destructive policies are felt for generations. Artificially create excessive regulation, and even if it works it will eventually fail.

Three Strategies

Values

The Way, virtue, humaneness, justice, courtesy—these five are one body. The Way is for people to tread, virtue is for people to attain, humaneness attracts people, justice is what is right for people, courtesy is what people embody; it will not do to lack even one of these.

Rising early and retiring late is a form of courtesy; striking down brigands and wreaking vengeance on enemies is the decisiveness of justice; feeling pity is an expression of humaneness; self-mastery and winning others are routes of virtue; and causing people to be equal, not out of place, is the influence of the Way.

Three Strategies

DIRECTIVES, ORDERS, AND POLICIES

What comes from the ruler to the administrators is called a directive; in written form it is called an order; in action it is called a policy. If a directive is mistaken, the order is ineffective. If the order is ineffective, the policy is not right. If the policy is not right, the Way does not go through. If the Way does not go through, then corrupt administrators prevail. If corrupt administrators prevail, then the prestige and authority of the ruler are injured.

Three Strategies

NEAR AND FAR

Welcome the wise from a thousand miles away, and the road is far; bring on the dishonest, and the road is near. In this sense enlightened rulers leave the near aside and take the far; then they can complete their work and elevate people, while subordinates put forth all their effort.

Three Strategies

GOOD AND BAD

Ignore one good, and all good deteriorates; reward one evil, and myriad evils come. When the good is fostered and the bad is punished, then the country is secure and all good arrives.

Three Strategies

UNCERTAINTY AND CONFUSION

When the masses are uncertain, there is no stabilizing the nation; when the masses are confused, there is no governing the populace.

When uncertainties are settled and confusion removed, then the country can be secure.

Three Strategies

EQUALITY BY PURITY

When one order is opposed, a hundred orders are neglected. When one evil is perpetrated, a hundred evils accumulate. So when good is done to docile people and ill is visited upon vicious people, then order prevails without resentment. If you govern bitter people with bitterness, that is called violating nature. If you govern hostile people with hostility, calamity will be inevitable. Govern the people so as to make them equal, effecting equality by purity, and the people will find their places and the world will be at peace.

Three Strategies

PURE PEOPLE

When the rebellious are honored and the greedy are rich, even a sage king could not bring about order. When the rebellious are punished and the greedy are restrained, then order prevails and myriad evils vanish.

Pure people cannot be won by ranks and salaries; just people cannot be threatened by intimidation or imprisonment. Therefore when enlightened rulers seek wise people, they must attract them by considering their motivations. To attract pure people, cultivate your courtesy. To attract just people, cultivate the Way. Then people can be attracted and honor can be preserved.

Three Strategies

SAGACIOUS GENTLEMEN

Sagacious gentlemen understand the sources of flourishing and decline, comprehend the beginnings of success and failure, understand the triggers of order and chaos, and know the timing of actions. Even if they are in straits, they will not occupy the throne of a moribund nation, and even if they are poor, they will not live off a stipend from a disorderly nation. Those who anonymously embrace the Way go into action when the time comes.

Three Strategies

INSIDERS AND OUTSIDERS

When wise ministers are on the inside, corrupt ministers are kept out. When corrupt ministers are on the inside, then wise ministers die out. When inside and outside lose their proper places, calamity and disorder go on for generations.

Three Strategies

PRETENDERS AND PROXIES

When high-ranking administrators pretend to rulership, the treacherous gather. When ministers are as respected as rulers, then hierarchy is obscured. When rulers are in the position of ministers, the hierarchy loses its order.

Three Strategies

PROMOTING THE WISE

For those who injure the wise, troubles continue for three generations. Those who obscure the wise personally suffer harm from that. Those who envy the wise are not completely reputable. For those who promote the wise, blessings extend to their descendants. Therefore if rulers are intent on promoting the wise, they will get a good reputation.

Three Strategies

COHESION

If you harm a hundred in profiting one individual, the people will leave; if you harm ten thousand to profit one individual, the country will lose cohesion. If you profit a hundred by getting rid of one individual, people will appreciate the favor. If you profit ten thousand by getting rid of one individual, social order will not be disrupted.

Three Strategies

THE WAY OF ANCIENT SAGES

King Wen asked Taigong, "May I hear where the Way of ancient sages stops and where it starts?"

Taigong said, "To be indolent when seeing good to be done, to be hesitant when the time arrives, to abide what is known to be wrong—these are where the Way stops.

"To be soft and calm, respectful and serious, strong yet flexible, tolerant yet firm—these four are where the Way starts. So when your sense of justice overcomes desire, you flourish; when desire overcomes your sense of justice, you perish. When seriousness overcomes indolence, that is auspicious; when indolence overcomes seriousness, that is destructive."

Six Strategies

WEALTH AND WELFARE

Rulers must pursue wealth, because without wealth they have no way to practice benevolence; if they are not generous, they have no way to unite clansmen. Those who alienate clansmen come to harm; those who lose the masses come to ruin. Do not lend others sharp instruments; if you lend others sharp instruments you will be harmed by others and not live out your life.

Six Strategies

BENEVOLENCE AND DUTY

King Wen asked, "What are benevolence and duty?"

Taigong said, "Respect the masses, unify your clansmen. If you respect the masses, they will be harmonious; if you unify your clansmen, they will be joyful. These are the outlines of benevolence and duty.

"Don't let anyone take away your dignity. Use your insight, follow normalcy. Those who are obedient should be employed rewardingly; those who are disruptive should be stopped powerfully. Honor these without doubt, and the whole land will peacefully submit."

Six Strategies

DEMAND AND SUPPLY

When the land is orderly, humane sages hide; when the land is chaotic, humane sages rise.

Six Strategies

LEADERSHIP AND QUALITY OF LIFE

King Wen asked Taigong, "The world is complex. Now waxing, now waning, now orderly, now chaotic—why is it like this? Is it because of differences in the quality of leadership? Is it a natural result of changes in the times?"

Taigong said, "If the leadership is unworthy, a nation is perilous and its people unruly. If the leadership is wise, a nation is peaceful and its people are orderly. Calamity and fortune depend on the leadership, not on the times."

Six Strategies

DEMEANOR

Be calm and serene, gentle and moderate. Be generous, not contentious; be openhearted and even-minded. Treat people correctly.

Six Strategies

ARBITRARY APPROVAL

Do not give arbitrary approval, yet do not refuse out of mere contrariness. Arbitrary approval means loss of discipline, while refusal means shutting off.

Six Strategies

BASES OF DEMOCRACY

Look with the eyes of the whole land, and there is nothing you will not see. Listen with the ears of the whole land, and there is nothing you will not hear. Think with the minds of the whole land, and there will be nothing you do not know.

Six Strategies

SIX ELEMENTS OF DEFENSE

There are six elements of defense: (1) humanity, (2) duty, (3) loyalty, (4) trustworthiness, (5) courage, (6) strategy.

There are ways to choose people for these six elements of defense.

1. Enrich them and see if they refrain from misconduct. (This proves humanity.)
2. Ennoble them and see if they refrain from hauteur. (This proves duty.)
3. Give them responsibilities and see if they refrain from autocratic behavior. (This proves loyalty.)
4. Employ them and see if they refrain from deceit. (This proves trustworthiness.)
5. Endanger them and see if they are unafraid. (This proves courage.)
6. Burden them and see if they are unflagging. (This proves strategy.)

Six Strategies

How to Preserve Territory

Do not alienate relatives.
Do not neglect the masses.
Treat associates well.
Keep the four quarters under control.
Do not lend national authority to another.
Do not take from the have-nots to give more to the haves.
Do not neglect fundamentals to deal with trivia.

Six Strategies

Six Parasites

1. Officials who build huge mansions and estates and pass their time in entertainment
2. Workers who don't work but go around getting into others' business, disrupting social order
3. Officials who form cliques that obscure the good and the wise and thwart the enlightened
4. Ambitious officers who independently communicate with leaders of other groups, without deference to their own leaders
5. Executives who disregard rank, look down on teamwork, and are unwilling to go to trouble for employers

6. Strong factions who overpower the weak and resourceless

Six Strategies

SEVEN HARMFUL THINGS

1. Those who are lacking in intelligent tactical strategy but are pugnacious and combative out of ambition for reward and titles should not be made into commanders.
2. Self-contradicting opportunists and pretenders who obscure the good and elevate the bad should not be made into planners.
3. Those who put on the appearance of austerity and desirelessness in order to get something should not be approached.
4. Those who pretend to be eccentric intellectuals, putting on airs and looking upon the world with aloof contempt, should not be favored.
5. The dishonest and unscrupulous who seek office and entitlement by flattery and unfair means, who display bravery out of greed for emolument, who act opportunistically without consideration of the big picture, who persuade leaders with tall tales and empty talk, should not be employed.
6. Compromising primary production by needless luxury should be prohibited.
7. Use of supposed occult arts and superstitious practices to bewilder decent people should be stopped.

Six Strategies

DUTIES

People who do not do their best are not my people.

Warriors who are not truthful and trustworthy are not my warriors.

Ministers who do not admonish faithfully are not my ministers.

Officials who do not care for the people with fairness and integrity are not my officials.

Administrators who cannot enrich the country, strengthen the military, harmonize the negative and the positive, stabilize the national government, keep all the ministers honest, define titles and realities, clarify rewards and punishments, and bring happiness to the common people are not my administrators.

Six Strategies

The Way of the Dragon

The way of rulership is like the head of a dragon, dwelling on high and gazing afar, looking deeply and listening closely. It shows its form but hides its feelings. As high as the sky, it cannot be comprehended; as deep as the abyss, it cannot be fathomed.

Six Strategies

Anger

If you do not get angry when it is appropriate to be angered, treacherous ministers will act. If you do not execute those who should be executed, major rebellions will break out. If the power of the military cannot be mobilized, enemy nations are strong.

Six Strategies

False Reputation

King Wen asked Taigong, "If the leadership tries to promote the worthy but cannot get effective results, why is that?"

Taigong said, "Promoting the worthy without letting them work— that is, to have the reputation of promoting the worthy but in reality not using them."

King Wen asked, "Where is the fault?"

Taigong said, "It is in the leadership's going on the basis of vulgar popularity or social recommendation and not finding really worthy people."

King Wen asked, "How is this?"

Taigong said, "If the leadership considers popular approval to be worthy and unpopularity to be unworthy, then those with many partisans get ahead, while those with few partisans fall behind. If so, then crooks will be everywhere, obscuring the worthy; loyal administrators will be executed for no crime, while treacherous bureaucrats will assume rank by means of false reputations. Thus social disorder increases, so the nation cannot avoid peril and perdition."

Six Strategies

Appointing the Worthy

King Wen asked Taigong, "How are the worthy appointed?"

Taigong said, "Military commanders and civilian administrators each have their own separate jobs, so people are nominated individually for specific offices. Examine the reality of the office in respect to its title, choose people with the appropriate talents, taking their abilities into consideration, making the realities fit the titles."

Six Strategies

AWARDS AND PUNISHMENTS

King Wen asked, "Awards are for encouragement, punishments are for admonition. I want to reward one in such a way as to encourage a hundred, and punish one in such a way as to admonish everyone—how can I do that?"

Taigong said, "Rewards should be reliable, penalties should be inevitable. When rewards are reliable and penalties are inevitable within the range of seeing and hearing, then those out of range of seeing and hearing will be unknowingly affected."

Six Strategies

THE WAY OF WARFARE

King Wen asked Taigong, "What is the way of warfare?"

Taigong said, "Nothing in the way of warfare is more important than unity. Unity means the ability to come and go independently. The Yellow Emperor said, 'Unity is approaching the Way, drawing near to the uncanny. Its use is in opportunity, its manifestation is in formation and momentum; its fulfillment is a matter of leadership.' Therefore sage kings called weapons instruments of ill omen, to be used only when unavoidable."

Six Strategies

SWIFT RESPONSE

King Wu asked Taigong, "If enemies find out our true conditions and know our plans, what should we do about it?"

Taigong said, "The art of military victory is to intimately examine enemies' workings and quickly take advantage of them, and quickly attack where they do not expect it."

Six Strategies

Reciprocity

The world opens up to those who profit the world; the world closes down to those who harm the world. The world is not one individual's world, it is the world's world.

Those who would take the world are like chasing wild animals, with everyone wanting a share of the meat. Those who cross over a river in the same boat share the same advantage if they make it across, and they share the same harm if they fail: therefore everyone has a reason to facilitate the crossing, and none will stop it.

Those who do not take from the people are those who take the people; those who do not take from the nation are those who take the nation; those who did not take from the world are those who take the world.

The people help those who do not take from the people; a nation helps those who do not take from the nation; the world helps those who do not take from the world.

Six Strategies

Subtleties of Strategy

The Way is a matter of invisibility, business is a matter of confidentiality, victory is a matter of inscrutability. This is very subtle.

Six Strategies

Symptoms of Sickness

When many voices confuse each other, disorder goes on and on, and sexual debauchery is unlimited, these are signs of a moribund nation. If we see weeds and reeds choking the valleys in the countryside, if we see the crooked prevailing over the honest among the populace, if we see cruelty and viciousness in officials, if the legal system is corrupt and the leadership is not aware of it, that is the time when a nation is perishing.

Six Strategies

Efficiency

Where government works effectively, no one is aware of its influence; when the time is the present, no one is aware of its movement.

Six Strategies

PEOPLE

People are like flowing water: obstruct them and they stagnate, open channels for them and they move, calm them and they become purified.

Six Strategies

NONVIOLENT ATTACK

King Wen asked Taigong, "What are the methods of nonviolent attack?"

Taigong said, "There are twelve elements of nonviolent attack:

1. "Go along with what enemies like, to get them to indulge their will. They will get conceited, there will surely be misconduct—if you can make use of this, you will be able to get rid of them.

2. "Get close to those they love, in order to divide their influence. When a people is divided in mind, their loyalty inevitably deteriorates. When there are no loyal ministers at court, the nation is surely in peril.

3. "Secretly bribe their associates to get information in great depth. Where information leaks out from insiders, that country is going to have problems.

4. "Encourage them in debauchery and hedonism, to extend their desires. Ply them with pearls and jade, delight them with beautiful women. Speak to them humbly and listen fawningly, following their directions and agreeing, until they would no longer fight with you; then the scene is set for treachery.

5. "Honor their loyal ministers but without giving them much. Keep their ambassadors but without listening to their business; have them replaced quickly, sending them off with something true to gain friendship and trust, so that the rulers will ally with you. If you can honor them, their country can be plotted against.

6. "Buy off insiders at court and alienate those in the field: when talented ministers serve the interests of other countries and enemy nations invade, rare is the state that does not perish.

7. "To control their minds, bribe them richly while buying the loyalty and affection of their associates, secretly showing them advantages, inducing them to slight their work, thus building up deficiencies.

8. "Bribe them with valuables, using this to conspire with them in planning strategies that will profit them. If you profit them, they will trust you; this is called rapprochement. When rapprochement builds up, you can exploit them. When the state is subject to external influence, its land will be much reduced.

9. "Honor them with praise and do not criticize their persons. Appear to regard them as very powerful, and go along with them, assuring them of your sincerity. Flatter and glorify them so they put on airs, and their country will become dishonest.

10. "Humble yourself to them so they are sure you are sincere, in order to win their hearts; do things as they wish, as if you were family. Once you have won them over, subtly take them in; when the time comes, it will be as if heaven had destroyed them.

11. "Cloister them strategically. All human subjects value wealth and status and hate death and disaster. Present prospects of high rank while stealthily handing out valuables to buy off their stalwarts. Build up abundant surpluses within while outwardly seeming poor. Covertly bring in knowledgeable people and have them formulate strategies; bring in brave warriors and elevate their spirits; satisfy them with riches and rank, and their numbers will continue to increase. Once you have cohorts, that means you can cloister others; if they have states but are cloistered, how can they maintain their states?

12. "Cultivate their unruly ministers to mislead them, provide them with beautiful women and licentious music to befuddle them, send them hounds and horses for recreation, seduce them by always conceding great power to them, and watch for the chance to plot against them with the rest of the world."

Six Strategies

GOVERNING THE WORLD

When your mettle covers the world, then you can embrace the world; when your faithfulness covers the world, then you can bind the world to a compact. When your humaneness covers the world, then you can take the world to heart. When your generosity covers the world, then you can preserve the world. When your conduct of affairs is not hesitant or doubtful, then celestial movements cannot alter it, changes in the times cannot shift it. When these six elements are all present, then you can govern the world.

Six Strategies

FAIR TRADE

The world opens up to those who benefit the world, and the world closes down on those who harm the world. The world rewards those who put the world first, and the world destroys those who kill the world. The world communicates with those who understand the world; the world opposes those who frustrate the world. The world relies on those who give security to the world; the world annihilates those who endanger the world.

Six Strategies

PLAYING HARDBALL

How to attack the strong, cause disaffection within an enemy camp, and cause their following to dissolve:

Use them, be careful of your strategy, and use money.

To attack the strong, it is necessary to strengthen them even more, until they get overextended: those who are too strong must break, those who are overextended must have gaps. Attack strength by means of strength, cause disaffection by means of affection, dissolve a group by means of the group.

In general, the way of strategy values comprehensiveness and secrecy. Propose things to them, tease them with prospects of gain, and contentiousness is sure to arise. If you want to alienate their familiars, use their loved ones and favorites: offer them what they desire, show them how they can profit, and use this to estrange them, so they cannot get their will. In the glee of their greed for gain, residual doubts about you will cease.

In general, the way to attack is to first make sure to block off their information; then attack their power, destroy their major cities, and get rid of things that harm their people. Debauch them with sex, bait them with favors, fatten them with feasts, entertain them with music. Once you have alienated their familiars, you can surely distance them from their people. Without letting them know your strategy, take them in by being supportive. When no one is aware of your intentions, then you can succeed.

Six Strategies

DOMESTICATING PEOPLE

There must be no stinting in generosity to the people. People are like oxen and horses: if you feed them repeatedly, they will follow you with affection.

Six Strategies

CAPACITIES OF COMMANDERS

Commanders should have five capacities: courage, intelligence, benevolence, trustworthiness, loyalty.

The courageous cannot be violated.

The intelligent cannot be thrown into confusion.

The benevolent are humanistic.

The trustworthy do not deceive people.

The loyal have no duplicity.

Six Strategies

EXCESSES IN COMMANDERS

There are ten excesses in the ways of commanders:

1. There are those who are so bold they slight death.
2. There are those who rush so much their minds are speedy.
3. There are those who are so greedy they are inclined to profiteering.
4. There are those who are so kindly they cannot bear to let people get hurt.

5. There are those who are so intelligent they are timid.

6. There are those who are so trusting they like to trust others.

7. There are those who are so puritanical they don't care for other people.

8. There are those who are so intelligent they are psychologically easygoing.

9. There are those who are so strong they act on their own initiative.

10. There are those who are so soft they like to delegate authority to others.

Those who are so bold they slight death can be induced to expose themselves to violence.

Those who rush so much their minds are speedy can be waited out.

Those who are so greedy they are inclined to profiteering can be bribed.

Those who are so kindly they cannot bear to let people get hurt can be put to a lot of trouble.

Those who are so intelligent they are timid can be squeezed.

Those who are so trusting they like to trust others can be fooled.

Those who are so puritanical they don't care for other people can be degraded.

Those who are so intelligent they are psychologically easygoing are vulnerable to sudden assault.

Those who are so strong they act on their own initiative are vulnerable to preoccupation.

Those who are so soft they like to delegate authority to others can be deceived.

Six Strategies

WARFARE

Warfare is a major affair for a nation, leading to survival or destruction, and its direction is up to the general. The general is a helper of a nation, so it is imperative to be particular when appointing a general. So it is said that both sides don't win at war; neither do both lose: if a military force goes beyond the borders, if it hasn't overthrown an enemy state, there will be a general with a broken army.

Six Strategies

APPEARANCE AND REALITY

Outward appearances may not correspond to inner realities in fifteen ways:

1. There are those who are smart but are unworthy.
2. There are those who are nice but are thieving.
3. There are those who put on an appearance of respect while being contemptuous at heart.
4. There are those who are outwardly modest but inwardly insincere.
5. There are those who are energetic and spirited but without real sense.
6. There are those who are very serious yet are insincere.
7. There are those who like strategizing but lack decisiveness.
8. There are those who seem bold but lack ability.
9. There are those who seem honest but are unreliable.
10. There are those who seem unstable but are actually loyal and solid.
11. There are those who use subterfuge and agitation but get effective results.
12. There are those who are outwardly courageous but inwardly cowardly.
13. There are those who are very proper and mannerly but actually slight people.
14. There are those who are stern and severe yet calm and guileless.
15. There are those who seem void of forcefulness and physically inferior yet when they go forth never fail to reach their objective and never fail to succeed.

What the whole world looks down upon is valued by sages. What ordinary people do not know, you cannot even begin to see unless you are very clear and lucid.

These distinctions are known by means of eight tests:

1. Question people verbally to observe their expression.
2. Cross-examine them thoroughly to observe their versatility.
3. Spy on them to see whether they are truthful.
4. Question them in revealing ways to observe their integrity.

5. Put them in charge of funds to see if they're honest.
6. Test them with sex to see if they're chaste.
7. Warn them of trouble to see if they're brave.
8. Intoxicate them with alcohol to see how they behave.

If you do all these things, the worthy and unworthy will be distinct.

Six Strategies

PENALTIES AND PRIZES

A commander establishes his authority by executing people of high status and establishes his intelligence by rewarding people of low status; he makes prohibitions and orders effective by thoroughness.

Therefore if there is one man whose execution would make the armed forces all tremble, he executes him; if there is one man whose reward would make myriad men happy, he rewards him. Executions are most effective when big people are executed; rewards are most effective when little people are rewarded.

When even high-ranking, important ministers in office can be executed, then penalties reach all the way to the top echelons. When even oxherds, horse grooms, and stable workers can be rewarded, then awards reach all the way to the lower echelons. When penalties reach all the way up and prizes reach all the way down, the commander's authority is effective.

If the armed forces do not listen when one man is executed, if myriad people do not pay attention when one man is executed, if the masses are not afraid when one man is executed, then even if he executes many men the commander is not taken seriously.

When the armed forces are not happy when one man is enfeoffed, when myriad people are not delighted when one man is rewarded, this means that rewards are ineffective; the rewards are valuing the incapable. Under these conditions, the armies will not work for the commander; this is how to lose the people.

Six Strategies

TOP TALENT

Those who are skilled at eliminating troubles manage them before they arise; those who are skilled at overcoming enemies prevail in formlessness. The highest warfare does not involve combat; therefore those who fight for victory on fronts of naked blades are not good commanders; those who set up defenses after already having lost are not top sages. Those whose wisdom is average are not leaders of nations; those whose skills are average are not artisans of nations.

Six Strategies

CERTAINTY AND SECRECY

No concern is greater than certain victory. No function is greater than inscrutable silence. No action is greater than the unexpected. No strategy is greater than the unknown.

Six Strategies

HALVING THE WORK

Sure winners battle only after seeing weakness in an enemy; this halves the work and doubles the effect.

Six Strategies

ADVANTAGE AND TIMING

Those who are skilled in warfare sit tight, unruffled: when they see victory, they rise; if not, they desist. Therefore it is said, "Don't be afraid, don't be hesitant."

Nothing is more damaging to military operations than hesitation; nothing is more harmful to armed forces than doubt. The skilled do not miss the opportunity when they see an advantage; when the right time comes, they do not doubt.

If you lose the advantage and miss the right timing, you will have trouble. Therefore the wise pursue advantage and timing relentlessly; the skillful do not hesitate once they have made a decision.

Six Strategies

FORESIGHT

How does one know whether an army is strong or weak, and foresee the signs of victory and defeat before entering into combat?

Of the signs of victory and defeat, the psychological ones show first. Enlightened commanders observe them; the proof is in the people. Carefully watch enemies' comings and goings, observe their movements and their repose, see what the officers and soldiers are saying, if their talk is pessimistic or optimistic.

Six Strategies

SIGNS OF STRENGTH AND WEAKNESS

When the armed forces are happy, the officers and soldiers respect the rules and honor the directives of their commander, finding mutual joy in smashing enemies, inspiring each other with bravery and ferocity, honoring each other for awesome martial prowess; these are signs of strength.

If the armed forces repeatedly fret, the officers and soldiers are unkempt, they scare each other with talk about the enemy, they talk about unfavorable possibilities, they snoop and gossip no end, myriad mouths confusing each other, with no fear of rules or orders and no respect for the commander, these are signs of weakness.

Six Strategies

HUMANITY AND JUSTICE

In ancient times, humaneness was considered basic and government by justice was considered standard. When the standard did not achieve its aim, then strategy was formulated. Strategy emerges in conflict; it does not come from mediators. Therefore, if killing some individuals secures peace for the people, then killing them is acceptable; if attacking a state would be food for its populace, then attacking it is acceptable. If it is possible to stop war by waging war, then even warfare is acceptable.

The Warrior Code of the Charioteers

LOVE AND AWE

The humane are beloved, the just are appreciated, the wise are relied upon, the brave are emulated, the trustworthy are trusted. To gain the love of one's own people is means of defense; to win the awe of others is means of waging war.

The Warrior Code of the Charioteers

CARING FOR BOTH SIDES

The way of war is to avoid violating the season and distressing the people, thus caring for one's own populace; to avoid attacking when there is confusion and taking advantage of misfortune, caring for the populace of the adversary; and to avoid mobilizing the military in winter or summer, so as to care for the population on both sides.

The Warrior Code of the Charioteers

MILITARISM AND DEFENSE

Even if a state is big, if it is militaristic it will perish. But even if the world is at peace, if it forgets about war it is in peril.

The Warrior Code of the Charioteers

PREPAREDNESS

Once the land is pacified, the emperor relaxes yet still practices hunting in spring and autumn, while the local leaders organize troops in spring and train militias in autumn. By this means they do not forget about warfare.

The Warrior Code of the Charioteers

ETHICS OF ANCIENT WARRIORS

In ancient times, warriors did not chase fleeing soldiers more than a hundred paces and did not pursue a retreating army more than three marches; thus they showed their chivalry.

They did not overtax the incapable and were merciful to the wounded and sick; thus they showed their humaneness.

They let battalions form before attacking them; thus they showed their fairness.

They fought for principle, not for profit; thus they showed their justice.

They granted amnesty to those who surrendered; thus they showed their courage.

They knew how things begin and how they turn out; thus they showed their intelligence.

These six virtues were taught together at appropriate times as a means of uniting the people. This is the policy of time immemorial.

The Warrior Code of the Charioteers

GOVERNMENT BY ENLIGHTENED VIRTUE

The government of ancient kings followed the laws of nature, built upon the advantages of earth, and assigned the virtuous among the people to offices; they kept things in order by accurate definition, set up states and divided duties, paying salaries according to rank. Local leaders were gladly sympathetic, while foreign powers paid tribute. Punishments disappeared and war ceased. This is government by enlightened virtue.

The Warrior Code of the Charioteers

THE GOVERNMENT OF WISE KINGS

Next best to government by enlightened virtue is the government of wise kings, who established ritual, music, and law, then created penalties and mobilized soldiery to attack the unjust.

Going on fact-finding tours, examining regional ways, they assembled local leaders and considered their differences. If any had forfeited their mandate, disturbing normalcy, rejecting morality, opposing nature, and threatening a meritorious leader, wise kings would announce it to all the local chieftains, making the crime clearly known, declaring it even to God on high, and to the Sun, Moon, stars, and planets.

Praying to the spirits of the earth and seas, mountains and local shrines, they appealed to their ancestors. Only after that would the prime ministers draft troops from the local chieftains.

The Warrior Code of the Charioteers

COMMANDS TO THE TROOPS OF AN INVADING ARMY

"When you enter the territory of an offender, let there be no desecration of sacred shrines, no hunting in the fields, no destruction of infrastructure, no burning residential areas, no deforestation, no confiscation of domestic animals, grains, or machinery. When you see the old and the young, escort them to safety and do not let them get hurt; and even if you meet able-bodied men, do not attack them if they do not engage you in confrontation. If you wound opponents, give them medical treatment and send them home."

When the offender has been executed, the central and local authorities restructure the state, nominating good people to establish enlightened leadership, restoring social order.

The Warrior Code of the Cavaliers

CENTRAL AND LOCAL AUTHORITY (1)

Central authority has six ways of governing local leaders: (1) circumscribing the territories of local leaders, (2) equalizing local leaders by government policy, (3) winning the goodwill of local leaders by courtesy and trustworthiness, (4) pleasing local leaders by employing the talented, (5) using strategies to bind local leaders, and (6) using armaments to overpower local leaders. Sharing their troubles as well as their gains to unite local leaders, harmonize local leaders through closeness with the small and service to the great.

The Warrior Code of the Cavaliers

CENTRAL AND LOCAL AUTHORITY (2)

There are nine reasons for central authorities to assemble local leaders and issue interdictions.

1. Those who take advantage of the weak and violate the rights of minorities are to have their territories reduced.
2. Those who persecute the good and harm the populace are to be struck down.
3. Those who are cruel in their own domains and contemptuous of others are to be imprisoned.
4. Those whose fields are overgrown and populace scattered are to have their territory cut down.
5. Those who take advantage of fastnesses to be rebellious are to be invaded.
6. Those who kill their parents are to be corrected.
7. Those who depose or assassinate their rulers are to be eliminated.

8. Those who disobey orders and are contemptuous of the government are to be terminated.

9. Those who are unruly abroad and at home, behaving like animals, are to be exterminated.

The Warrior Code of the Cavaliers

DUTIES

The duty of emperors is to derive laws purely from nature and consider the examples of past sages.

The duty of ordinary people is to serve their parents and be correct in respect to their leaders and elders.

The Warrior Code of the Cavaliers

EDUCATION AND TRAINING

Even if there are enlightened leaders, if the people are not first educated and trained they cannot be employed.

Ancient education and training established a hierarchical order with distinct ranks, so that virtue and duty did not overstep each other, generalists and specialists did not obscure each other, daring and force did not encroach upon each other's domains. Thus power was united and minds were in harmony.

The Warrior Code of the Cavaliers

CIVIL AND MILITARY ORGANIZATION

In ancient times, the form of a nation was not incorporated into militias, and military forms were not incorporated into the state. Therefore virtue and duty did not overstep each other.

The Warrior Code of the Cavaliers

UNAFFECTED PEOPLE

Ancient leaders esteemed people who were not conceited; unaffected people were administrators of leadership. Since they were unaffected, they had no ambitions; and having no ambitions, they were not contentious. The true facts about conditions in a nation could be heard from them, and appropriate information about military affairs could be heard from them. Therefore generalists and specialists did not obscure each other.

The Warrior Code of the Cavaliers

EMPLOYMENT

Once you have educated and trained your people, then you may carefully select them for employment. When everything is as orderly as possible, all posts are filled. When education and training are as efficient as possible, the interests and initiatives of the people are wholesome. When customs are established, the body of the populace is normalized. This is what the influence of education can attain.

The Warrior Code of the Cavaliers

SECURITY AND VICTORY

The ancients did not pursue the fleeing far and did not chase down those in retreat. Because they did not go far, they were hard to lure; because they did not give chase, they were hard to entrap. They achieved security by courtesy and victory by humaneness. After they had won, their training could be reused; that is why cultured people esteem it.

The Warrior Code of the Cavaliers

STERNNESS AND STRICTNESS

If the military is too stern, the people will be discouraged; if it is not strict enough, the people will not be victorious.

When the leadership works the people improperly, drafting peasants without regard to age and drafting artisans without regard to skills, and the officials in charge are contemptuous, this is called being too stern. Be too stern, and the people will be discouraged.

When the leadership does not honor the worthy but trusts deceivers and villains, does not honor the Way but trusts the bold and powerful, does not value those who follow orders but values those who disobey, does not value good conduct but values violence, and debases itself to officials, this is called insufficient strictness. If there is insufficient strictness, the people will not be victorious.

The Warrior Code of the Cavaliers

RELAXATION

Military operations should be relaxed in the main. When relaxed, the strength of the people is full; even if they cross swords, the foot soldiers do not run, the chariots do not bolt; they do not break ranks to chase fleeing enemies and so do not lose order. The stability of a military operation is in not losing order, not using up the strength of man or beast, and not violating instructions in matters of pacing.

The Warrior Code of the Cavaliers

STATECRAFT AND MILITARY AFFAIRS

In ancient times, statecraft was not involved in military affairs, and militarism did not penetrate states. When militarism penetrates states, the virtues of the people wither away; when statecraft is involved in military affairs, the virtues of the people weaken.

Therefore in matters of state, discourse is cultured and speech is warm. At court, one is respectful and humble; one refines itself and treats others accordingly. One does not go anywhere unless invited, does not speak unless asked; and one retires more readily than one steps forward.

In the military, one stands proudly and defiantly, versatile and effective in action. Warriors do not bow, war chariots do not go on parade in ceremonies. On the ramparts there are no manners; in emergencies there is no seniority.

Therefore, etiquette is to law as outside to inside; culture is to warriorhood as left is to right.

The Warrior Code of the Cavaliers

VIRTUES AND SKILLS

In ancient times, wise kings brought people's virtues to light and made full use of people's skills, so there were no neglected virtues and no negligent people. There was no reason to create rewards and no reason to apply penalties.

The Warrior Code of the Cavaliers

DETERIORATION OF CHARISMA

King Shun (r. 2255–2207 B.C.E.) neither rewarded nor punished, yet his people were willingly useful; this is the epitome of charisma. The

Xia dynasty (2205–1766 B.C.E.) rewarded and did not punish; this is the epitome of education. The Yin dynasty (1766–1122 B.C.E.) punished and did not reward; this is the epitome of authoritarianism. The Zhou dynasty (1122–256 B.C.E.) relies on both reward and punishment; its charisma has deteriorated.

The Warrior Code of the Charioteers

IMMEDIATE FEEDBACK

Rewards are handed out immediately, so that the people may quickly gain the benefit of doing good. Punishments are executed on the spot, so that the people may quickly see the harm in doing wrong. The greatest good is not rewarded, so people do not become conceited about being good, either in the higher or lower echelons.

The Warrior Code of the Charioteers

HUMILITY

When the upper chelons are not conceited about being good, then they do not become haughty and overbearing; when the lower echelons are not conceited about being good, then they are classless. When upper and lower echelons are thus not conceited about being good, this is the epitome of deference.

The Warrior Code of the Charioteers

FAILURE AND FAULT

Great failure is not punished, so that people in the upper and lower echelons attribute the fault to themselves. When the upper echelons attribute faults to themselves, they will repent of their errors; when the lower echelons attribute fault to themselves, they will avoid wrongdoing. When the upper and lower echelons share the negative in this way, that is the epitome of deference.

The Warrior Code of the Charioteers

HARMONY

In ancient times, fighting troops were not drafted for three years, seeing the toil of the people. Those in higher positions and those in lower positions were responsive to each other. Under these conditions, there was the epitome of harmony. When the aim was attained, they sang songs of triumph to show joy. Putting down arms and constructing spiritual monuments in response to the work of the people, they showed when to rest.

The Warrior Code of the Charioteers

PREPARATIONS

Whenever there is warfare, define ranks and positions, publish rewards and punishments, round up mercenaries, promulgate orders, inquire into public opinion, seek out the skilled, think analogically and find out about things, remove doubt and get rid of suspicion, nurture strength and look for skill, and go by the movement of hearts and minds.

When you are going to war, consolidate the masses, ascertain where advantage lies, govern the disorderly, cause the stalled to advance, get everyone to follow what is right and develop a sense of shame, streamline rules, and minimize punishments. Crack down on minor offenses, because if minor offenses prevail, major offenses will follow.

The Warrior Code of the Cavaliers

FIVE CONSIDERATIONS

Obey nature, amass goods, gladden the masses, take advantage of the lay of the land, and outfit the soldiers: these are called the five considerations.

To obey nature, act according to the season. To amass goods, plunder the enemy. To gladden the masses, be diligent. To take advantage of the lay of the land, guard narrow passes. To outfit the soldiers, provide bows and arrows for surrounding, spears and lances for defense, and pikes and halberds for standby.

Generally speaking, these five kinds of weapons have five appropriate uses. The longer-ranged are used to surround the shorter-ranged, the shorter-ranged are used to help out the longer-ranged. When they are used alternately in battle, then you can last a long time; when they are all used, then you are strong. When you use weaponry appropriate to what you see opponents using, this is called matching them.

The Warrior Code of the Cavaliers

STRATEGIC MEASUREMENTS

War is a national crisis; it is necessary to examine the grounds of death and life, and the ways to survival and extinction. Thus you measure militias in terms of five parameters, comparing them in terms of strategic measurements to find out the real situation. First is guidance. Second is climate. Third is ground. Fourth is leadership. Fifth is order.

Guidance is what induces popular accord with the rulership, so the people are willing to follow it to death and follow it in life, without opposition.

Climate refers to darkness and light, cold and heat, the structure of the seasons.

Grounds may be high or low, near or far, treacherous or easy, broad or narrow, deadly or viable.

Leadership is a matter of knowledge, trustworthiness, humaneness, valor, and strictness.

Order involves organizational structure, chain of command, and logistics.

All leaders have heard of these five things; those who know them prevail over those who do not. That is why we make comparisons in terms of strategic measurements, to find out the real situation. Which civil leadership has guidance? Which military leadership has ability? Whose climate and grounds are advantageous? Whose order is enforced? Whose forces are stronger? Whose officers and soldiers are better trained? Whose rewards and punishments are clearer?

Sun Tzu's Art of War

SUBTERFUGE

One can assess advantages through listening, then take up an appropriate posture or make an appropriate disposition to bolster one's exterior.

To take up a posture or a disposition means to manipulate strategy according to advantage. Warfare is a path of subterfuge. That is why you make a show of incompetence when you are actually competent, make a show of ineffectiveness when you are in fact effective. When nearby you appear to be distant, and when distant you appear to be nearby.

Seducing opponents by prospects of gain, take them over by means of confusion. Even when you are solid, still be on the defensive; even when you are strong, be evasive. Use anger to make them upset, use humility to make them arrogant. Tire them while taking it easy, cause division among them while acting friendly. Attack where they are unprepared, emerge when they least expect it.

This means that the victories of warriors cannot be told of beforehand.

Sun Tzu's Art of War

CONTINGENCY PLANNING

Those who figure out how to win before doing battle have the majority of advantageous plans, while those whose schemes prove to be failures even before battle have the fewer advantageous plans. Those with many such plans win, those with few such plans lose; there is no need to even mention those with no such plans. When I view a situation in this way, it becomes evident who will win and who will lose.

Sun Tzu's Art of War

EFFICIENCY

In actual combat, what is important to win; go on too long, and you blunt your troops and snap your edge. Besiege a citadel, and your strength is depleted; keep an army in the field too long, and the resources of the nation will be insufficient. When you blunt your troops, snap your edge, deplete your strength, and exhaust resources, then rivals will arise to take advantage of your predicament. Then it will be impossible to effect a good ending, even with knowledge.

Therefore in military affairs we may hear of being clumsy but swift, while we never see the skillful prolonging in action. This is because a nation never benefits from prolonging a military action.

Sun Tzu's Art of War

BALANCE

Those who are not completely aware of drawbacks of military action cannot be completely aware of advantages in military action.

Sun Tzu's Art of War

ECONOMIC CONSEQUENCES OF WARFARE

The reason that nations are impoverished by their armies is that those who send their armies far away ship goods far away, and when goods are shipped far away, the farmers grow poor. Those who are near the army sell dear, and because of high prices money runs out. When the money runs out, there is increased pressure to appropriate things for military use, exhausing the heartland, draining the households.

Sun Tzu's Art of War

KEEPING INTACT

The general rule for military operations is that keeping a nation intact is best, while destroying a nation is next; keeping a militia intact is best, destroying a militia is next. Keeping a battalion intact is best, destroying a battalion is next. Keeping a company intact is best, destroying a company is next. Keeping a squad intact is best, destroying a squad is next.

Sun Tzu's Art of War

FOILING OPPONENTS

One hundred percent victory in battle is not the finest skill; foiling others' military operations without even fighting is the finest skill.

Sun Tzu's Art of War

FOUR LEVELS OF ATTACK

A superior military operation attacks planning, the next best attacks alliances; the next attacks armed forces, the lowest attacks cities.

Sun Tzu's Art of War

PLANNING ATTACK

When a military leader cannot contain anger and has his men swarm the citadel, this kills a third of his soldiers; and with the citadel still not taken, this is a fiasco of a siege. Therefore, one who uses the military skillfully foils the military operations of others without fighting, takes others' citadels without attacking, and crushes others' states without taking a long time, making sure to remain intact to contend with the world, so that his forces are not blunted and the advantage can be complete. This is the rule for planning attack.

Sun Tzu's Art of War

FIRMNESS AND STUBBORNNESS

Thus what would be firmness in the face of a small opponent will get you captured by a large opponent.

Sun Tzu's Art of War

KNOWING WINNERS

There are five ways to know winners. Those who know when to fight and when not to fight are winners. Those who know the uses of large and small groups are winners. Those whose upper and lower echelons have the same desires are winners. Those who await the unprepared with preparedness are winners. Those whose military leaders are capable and not dominated by the civilian leaders are winners. These five items are ways to know winners.

So it is said that if you know others and know yourself, you will not be imperiled in a hundred battles. If you do not know others but do know yourself, you will win some and lose some. If you do not know others and do not know yourself, you will be imperiled in every battle.

Sun Tzu's Art of War

INVINCIBILITY AND VULNERABILITY

The ancients who were skilled in combat first became invincible, and in that condition awaited vulnerability on the part of enemies. Invincibility is up to you yourself; vulnerability depends on the opponent. Therefore those who are skilled in combat can become invincible but cannot make opponents vulnerable to certain defeat. This is why it is said that victory can be discerned but cannot be made.

Invincibility is a matter of defense, vulnerability is a matter of offense. When you defend, it is because you are outgunned; when you attack, it is because the opponent is no match.

Those skilled at defense hide in the deepest depths of the earth; those skilled at offense maneuver in the highest heights of the sky. Thus they can preserve themselves and make victory complete.

Sun Tzu's Art of War

INCONSPICUOUS SUCCESS

Those considered good warriors in ancient times were those who won when it was easy to win. Thus the victories of good warriors have nothing extraordinary about them: they are not famed for brilliance, not accorded merit for bravado. Thus their victories in battle are not in doubt. They are not in doubt because the measures they take are sure to win, since they are overcoming those who have already lost.

Sun Tzu's Art of War

VICTORY AND DEFEAT

Therefore those who are skilled in combat take a stand on an invincible ground without losing sight of opponents' vulnerabilities. Thus a victorious militia wins before ever seeking to do battle, while a defeated militia seeks victory after it has already gotten into a fight.

When those who employ military forces will put the Way into practice and keep its laws, they can thereby judge the outcome. The laws are as follows: first is measure, second is capacity, third is order, fourth is efficacy, fifth is victory. The ground gives rise to measures, measures produce capacity. Capacity gives rise to order, order produces efficacy. Efficacy gives rise to victory.

Thus a victorious militia is like a weight balanced against another weight that is five hundred times less, while a defeated militia is like a weight balanced against another weight that is five hundred times more. Those who get the people to fight from a winning position are as though opening up dammed waters into a mile-deep canyon; this is a matter of the formation of force.

Sun Tzu's Art of War

ORGANIZATION AND OPERATION

What normally makes managing a large group similar to managing a small group is a system of order. What makes fighting a large group similar to fighting a small group is the use of emblems and signals. What enables military forces to take on enemies without defeat is the implementation of surprise tactics as well as conventional strategies. What makes a military intervention as effective as a stone thrown onto eggs is discernment of openings and solidity.

Sun Tzu's Art of War

SURPRISE TACTICS

Usually battle is engaged in a conventional manner but is won by surprise tactics. So those who are good at surprise maneuvers are endless as sky and earth, inexhaustible as the great rivers, finishing, then starting again, as epitomized by the sun and moon, dying and then being born again, as epitomized by the four seasons.

Sun Tzu's Art of War

MOMENTUM

The fact that the velocity of rushing water can reach the point where it can sweep away boulders is due to momentum; the fact that the strike of a bird of prey can attain a crushing force is due to timing and control. Thus those skilled at combat make sure their momentum is closely channeled and their timing closely controlled. Their momentum is like drawing a catapult, their timing and control are like pulling the trigger. In the midst of confusion they fight wildly without being thrown into disarray; in the midst of chaos their formations are versatile, so they cannot be defeated.

Sun Tzu's Art of War

PARADOX AND LOGIC

Rebellion arises from orderliness, cowardice arises from bravado, weakness arises from strength. Whether there is order or unruliness depends on the operative logic of the order. Bravery and cowardice depend on the configurations and momentum of power. Strength and weakness depend on formation.

Sun Tzu's Art of War

Maneuvering Others

Those who are good at maneuvering enemies mold them into specific formations, to which the enemies may be sure to conform. Give opponents an opportunity they are sure to take, maneuvering them in this way, then wait in ambush for them.

Sun Tzu's Art of War

Disposition of Force

For these reasons, those who are skilled in combat look to disposition of force and momentum; they do not put the onus on individual people. That is why they can choose people yet put their trust in momentum.

To rely on momentum is to get people to go into battle like rolling logs and rocks. By nature, logs and rocks remain still on even ground and roll when the ground is steep; they remain stationary when square, they roll when round.

The momentum of people who are good at combat is like rolling round rocks down a high mountain, because of the disposition of force.

Sun Tzu's Art of War

Taking a Stand

Generally speaking, those who have taken up their position on a battlefield first and await the enemy there are fresh, while those who take up their position on a battlefield last and thus rush into combat are wearied. Therefore skilled warriors bring others to them and do not go to others.

Sun Tzu's Art of War

Seducing Enemies

What effectively induces enemies to come of their own accord is the prospect of gain; what effectively prevents enemies from coming is the threat of harm. So to effectively tire a rested enemy, starve a well-fed one, or stir up a calm one is a matter of going where the enemy is sure to give chase.

Sun Tzu's Art of War

SUCCESSFUL ATTACK AND DEFENSE

Those who always take what they besiege do so by attacking where there is no defense. Those whose defense always stands firm defend where attack is certain.

Therefore a good attack is one against which an enemy does not know where to defend, while a good defense is one against which an enemy does not know where to attack. Be subtle, subtle even to the point of formlessness; be mysterious, mysterious even to the point of soundlessness; thus you can control the enemy's fate.

Sun Tzu's Art of War

ADVANCE AND RETREAT

To advance unstoppably, strike at openings. To retreat elusively, move too fast to be caught up with. Thus, when you want to fight, the way to make an enemy have no choice but to fight with you, even though he is secure behind high ramparts and deep moats, is to attack where the enemy is sure to go to the rescue. When you don't want to fight, to make an enemy unable to fight with you even if you are only defending a line drawn in the ground, divert his aim.

Sun Tzu's Art of War

CONCENTRATION AND DIVISION

If you induce others to adopt a form while you remain formless, then you will be concentrated while the enemy will be divided. When you are concentrated and thus united, whereas the enemy is divided into ten, that means you are attacking with ten times his strength, so you are a large contingent while the enemy is in small groups. If you can attack small groups with a larger contingent, then you will have fewer to fight against at a time.

Sun Tzu's Art of War

DISABLING DEFENSES

Your battleground should be unknown, because if it is unknown, then the enemy will have to post many defensive positions, and when the enemy has to man many defensive positions, then you will have fewer people to fight against at a time.

Thus when they are manned in front, they are undermanned in the rear; when they are manned in the rear, they are undermanned in front. When manned at the left, they are undermanned to the right; when manned at the right, they are undermanned to the left.

When they are manned everywhere, they are undermanned everywhere. Those who are undermanned are those who are on the defensive against others; those who have plenty of personnel are those who cause others to be on the defensive against them.

Sun Tzu's Art of War

EXAMINING ENEMIES

When you plot against others to discern winning and losing strategies, you work on them to discern their patterns of action. You induce them to adopt specific formations to discern deadly and viable grounds, you skirmish with them to discern where they are sufficient and where they are lacking.

Sun Tzu's Art of War

FORM

When you plan victory for the masses based on formation, the masses cannot discern it; everyone knows the form of your victory, but no one knows the form by which you achieved victory. This is why a victory in battle is not repeated; adaptive formation is of endless scope.

The formation of a militia is symbolized by water. Water travels away from higher places toward lower places; military victory is a matter of avoiding the solid and striking at openings. The course of water is determined by earth; the way to military victory depends on the opponent.

Thus a militia has no permanently fixed configuration, no constant form. Those who are able to seize victory by adapting to opponents are called experts.

No element is always dominant, no season is always present. Some days are shorter, some are longer; the moon wanes away and then reappears.

Sun Tzu's Art of War

FORMLESSNESS

The consummate formation of a militia is to reach formlessness. Where there is no specific form, even deeply placed agents cannot spy it out; even the canny strategist cannot scheme against it.

Sun Tzu's Art of War

INTELLIGENCE NEEDS

Those who do not know the plans of competitors cannot enter capably into preliminary negotiations; those who do not know the lay of the land cannot maneuver a militia; those who do not use local guides cannot gain the advantages of the terrain.

Sun Tzu's Art of War

SPIRIT AND HEART

The armed forces may have their spirits taken away, while the generals may have their heart taken away.

In this connection, in the morning spirits are keen, in the afternoon spirits fade, in the evening spirits wane away.

Good warriors avoid keen spirits, instead striking enemies when their spirits are fading and waning. This is the mastery of mood.

To face confusion with composure and face clamor with calm is the mastery of heart.

Sun Tzu's Art of War

STRENGTH AND ADAPTATION

To stay close to home to face those who come from far away, to face the weary in a condition of ease, to face the hungry with full stomachs, is the mastery of strength. Not to stand in the way of an orderly march, and not to attack an impeccable battle line, is the mastery of adaptation.

Sun Tzu's Art of War

RULES FOR MILITARY OPERATIONS

Rules for military operations:

Don't face high ground.
Don't get backed up against a hill.

Don't pursue a feigned retreat.
Don't attack fresh troops.
Don't chase after decoys.
Don't try to stop an army on the way home.
Leave a way out for a surrounded army.
Don't press a desperate enemy.

Sun Tzu's Art of War

Sources

Thunder in the Sky: Secrets on the Acquisition and Exercise of Power, translated by Thomas Cleary. Boston: Shambhala Publications, 1993. Copyright © 1993 by Thomas Cleary.

The Japanese Art of War: Understanding the Culture of Strategy, by Thomas Cleary. Boston: Shambhala Publications, 1991. Copyright © 1991 by Thomas Cleary.

The Book of Five Rings, by Miyamoto Musashi, translated by Thomas Cleary. Boston: Shambhala Publications, 1993. Copyright © 1993 by Thomas Cleary.

Ways of Warriors, Codes of Kings: Lessons in Leadership from the Chinese Classics, translated by Thomas Cleary. Boston: Shambhala Publications, 1999. Copyright © 1999 by Thomas Cleary.

The Collected Translations of Thomas Cleary

THE TAOIST CLASSICS

VOLUME ONE

Tao Te Ching
Chuang-tzu
Wen-tzu
The Book of Leadership and Strategy
Sex, Health, and Long Life

VOLUME TWO

Understanding Reality
The Inner Teachings of Taoism
The Book of Balance and Harmony
Practical Taoism

VOLUME THREE

Vitality, Energy, Spirit
The Secret of the Golden Flower
Immortal Sisters
Awakening to the Tao

VOLUME FOUR

The Taoist I Ching
I Ching Mandalas

CLASSICS OF STRATEGY AND COUNSEL

VOLUME ONE

The Art of War
Mastering the Art of War
The Lost Art of War
The Silver Sparrow Art of War

VOLUME TWO

Thunder in the Sky
The Japanese Art of War
The Book of Five Rings
Ways of Warriors, Codes of Kings

VOLUME THREE

The Art of Wealth
Living a Good Life
The Human Element
Back to Beginnings